T0329795

UNEQUAL CITIES

UNEQUAL CITIES

OVERCOMING ANTI-URBAN BIAS TO REDUCE INEQUALITY IN THE UNITED STATES

RICHARD McGAHEY

Columbia University Press
New York

Columbia University Press
Publishers Since 1893
New York Chichester, West Sussex
cup.columbia.edu

Library of Congress Cataloging-in-Publication Data
Names: McGahey, Richard, author.
Title: Unequal cities : overcoming anti-urban bias to reduce inequality in the
United States / Richard McGahey.
Description: New York : Columbia University Press, 2022. |
Includes bibliographical references and index.
Identifiers: LCCN 2022014886 | ISBN 9780231173346 (hardback) |
ISBN 9780231557733 (ebook)
Subjects: LCSH: Urban economics—United States. | Income distribution—
United States. | Equality—United States.
Classification: LCC HT321 .M35 2022 | DDC 330.9173/2—dc23/eng/20220401
LC record available at https://lccn.loc.gov/2022014886

Cover design: Noah Arlow
Cover images: Shutterstock

CONTENTS

UNEQUAL CITIES

1

CITIES, THE ECONOMY, AND INEQUALITY

Pedestrians in New York City walking along Park Avenue between East 56th and 57th Streets can look up—and up and up—at an implausibly narrow and tall apartment building rising 129 feet higher than the Empire State Building. The soaring height isn't the most notable thing about this "super slender"[1] tower. Rather, it is that the building's eighty-eight floors contain only 104 living units—very, very expensive units. In September 2021, an 8,000-square-foot apartment listed for $135 million. (Separate apartments for maids and staff on lower floors can cost over $3.5 million.) It is a home for the super-rich who choose to live (at least part of the time) in New York. Soaring above city streets, 432 Park symbolizes two things about American cities. First, its apartments are the homes of wealth and prosperity. In 2020, the nation's ten largest metropolitan areas (or metros) were projected to account for 34.4 percent of America's gross domestic product (GDP). And after the Great Recession that began in late 2007, job growth slowed or declined everywhere but cities.[2]

The COVID-19 recession hit cities hard, but it also underscored the second major aspect of America's cities: inequality. *Fortune* magazine dubbed 432 Park as "the house that inequality built." Its architect, Rafael Viñoly, saw a polarized city, saying, "There are only two markets, ultraluxury and subsidized housing."[3] Even in economically growing cities, over a third of jobs are low wage and more at risk.[4] During the COVID-19 recession, employment in high-wage jobs recovered by October 2020, while lower-wage jobs remained 19.2 percent below prepandemic levels, down 27 percent in Boston and 34.7 percent in Chicago. But even with these lagging job recoveries, cities and metropolitan areas will drive future prosperity.

URBAN ECONOMIES IN POLITICALLY FRAGMENTED REGIONS

Cities' central economic role was lifted up in Harvard economist Edward Glaeser's 2011 best-selling book, *Triumph of the City*. Glaeser claimed humans are an "urban species" and "urban density provides the clearest path from poverty to prosperity."[5]

Why are cities central to economic prosperity? Although economists agree cities are key to a nation's growth, it isn't a universally recognized view. If you search the internet for the "key to American prosperity," you'll find claims for agriculture, "intact" families, developing women's workforce potential, Christianity, fracking, stable Federal Reserve interest rate decisions, and many other factors.

Glaeser's case for cities rests on data. In 2020, U.S. metropolitan areas produced 89 percent of real GDP. The New York metro region's economic output was larger than that of Canada, Russia, or the state of Texas. Los Angeles' regional GDP was greater than that of the state of Pennsylvania. In 2018, the combined output of America's top ten metros exceeded the total output of thirty-eight states.[6] On innovation, between 2000 and 2015, "59 percent of US patents were awarded . . . in metro areas with only 36 percent of the population."[7]

America's polarization and recent electoral results reflect the economic divide between urban and rural areas. In both the 2016 and 2020 presidential elections, counties won by Democrats produced a significant majority of America's jobs and economic output. The counties won by Democratic presidential candidate Joe Biden produced 71 percent of GDP in 2020, while Republican presidential candidate Donald Trump won in counties producing 29 percent of GDP.[8]

Although the urban-rural economic gap is important, it can obscure inequality within America's urban areas. Too often, analysts use the terms *cities* and *metropolitan areas* interchangeably, using data on metropolitan regions to make conclusions about cities. But they are not the same thing. Metropolitan areas—regional economies with a core city surrounded by many separately governed, smaller cities and suburbs—do produce economic prosperity. But cities at the center of these metros have inherited poverty, outdated infrastructure, inadequate schools and housing, and reduced tax capacity. This disjunction between the overall regional economy and its fragmented governance is central to understanding inequality. And even the most prosperous cities have a great deal of internal poverty and inequality.

The nation's economic divisions also can't be understood through a simple urban-rural dichotomy. Metropolitan areas with faster economic and growth also have high inequality. Many urban workers have more in common economically with people in declining rural areas than they do with the urban super-rich or suburban residents in separately governed towns who resist housing expansion, school integration, and revenue sharing. Aligning economics and policy must recognize the essential economic role of cities. But for shared and sustainable prosperity, we also need to address historic, structural, racial, and political barriers to greater equality that too often are neglected by market-oriented economics.

Focusing on strong metropolitan economies can distract us from the often-troubled cities at their cores. Failing to distinguish between cities and metros obscures political, economic, and racial disparities and makes new policies imprecise and ineffective. In the nineteenth century, states solidified their power over cities, controlling cities' annexation and financial powers, thus limiting their growth and removing their fiscal autonomy. States' victory in this power struggle is a major factor in the creation of today's metropolitan structures.

Although core cities are essential for regional economies, they are hemmed in geographically by politically independent and often hostile suburban jurisdictions. Many of those suburbs have higher incomes and wealth; restrictive zoning and housing policies; less racial and ethnic diversity; better schools; and fewer social problems such as crime, poverty, and rampant inequality.[9]

America's urban regions are fragmented with mismatched and often racially divided political and economic boundaries. Cities drive regional (and national) economic growth, but suburbs disproportionately reap the benefits. Economies are regional, but the political organization (and much policy) is fractured among independent and sometimes hostile governments. City politics deals with the negative externalities, while taxing capability and better schools and housing are concentrated in the suburbs. In short, America's metropolitan political footprint does not match its economic footprint, fostering inequality and racial division.[10]

Many economists agree that American public policy is deeply unfair to cities. Glaeser has decried an "anti-urban bias" pervading federal transportation, housing, and education policies.[11] The National League of Cities regularly criticizes federal policies for constraining "the ability of local elected officials to fulfill their duties."[12] If the economic benefits from cities cited by economists—innovation, growth, progress—are central to regional and national prosperity, why are American metropolitan areas so economically and socially unbalanced? Why are wealthy suburbs that depend economically on cities not paying their fair share for dealing with urban problems?

Glaeser and other economists aren't excessively troubled by inequality concentrating in cities. Indeed, in their view, inequality can be a healthy sign: "Cities aren't full of poor people because cities make people poor, but because cities *attract* poor people with the prospect of improving their lot in life." Inequality will recede with improved education, which in turn will improve economic outcomes. Inequality can also be good if caused by market forces rewarding education and technological innovation.[13]

Economists are right about cities being economic growth engines. But they are wrong to underplay structural factors that generate and reproduce inequality and poverty and thus hold back full prosperity. As a result, market-oriented economists' policy advice tends to be one-sided, and their prescriptions don't produce equitable outcomes and optimal economic growth.

Four factors cause the benefits of economic growth to be distributed unequally: (1) economic changes that favor businesses and increase inequality; (2) a long-standing federal bias against cities; (3) control of and hostility toward cities by state governments; and (4) structural racism interwoven with employment, education, housing, and political power. Cities' true economic promise can't be fully realized unless these factors are integrated into analysis and policy recommendations.

ECONOMICS, CITIES, AND GROWTH

Economists believe cities spur growth through four intertwined factors:

1. Cities **attract people**. Glaeser says that cities "are the absence of physical space between people and companies. They are proximity, denseness, closeness."[14] That proximity puts customers, workers, and entrepreneurs near each other, making it easier to produce goods and services and to gauge demand and appropriate prices.

2. Cities **foster innovation.** The density of customers, workers, and businesses and the diverse backgrounds of people who come to the city help competitive entrepreneurs create new goods and services. Not all new ideas succeed, but the winners feed economic growth. Cities generate economic innovation by linking private sector investments and nonprofit educational and research institutions. Proximity and communication connect new ideas to capital investment and skilled workers.

3. Cities **specialize.** Persistent urban innovation deepens the skills of the workforce and encourages other firms to provide services: trade and logistics, finance and legal support, communications, and distribution. Firms and workers also become more specialized, adding more value to goods and services, and creating new ones in the process. As cities specialize, they can trade with other cities and regions to their mutual advantage. And more specialized employment—what economists call thick labor markets—in turn can attract more investment and business.

4. Cities **educate** and **invest**. Success for these networks requires public investment, both in infrastructure for transportation, communication, and data and in an educated and healthy population and workforce. To attract mobile capital and workers, cities also need amenities such as low crime rates, arts and culture, a healthy environment, and a good overall quality of life.

These four factors—people and population density, innovation, specialization, and public investment and education—form a virtuous circle where population grows (both through births and through in-migration, especially of educated people) and investment capital is developed and attracted. New firms and specializations develop, while cities invest in the public goods necessary to keep growth moving forward. Networks of specialized cities can develop within a nation, mutually reinforcing each other's growth, which can lead in turn to national prosperity.

PEOPLE, POPULATION, AND DENSITY

People concentrated in cities—population density—is the essence of a city, and it is critical for economic growth. In standard macroeconomic theory, national economies grow in two basic ways: population growth and productivity increases. Cities provide both, but population density is a basic, core feature of cities.

Many studies have validated the link between population growth and economic growth. Glaeser, Scheinkman, and Shleifer found that between 1960 and 1990, "income and population growth move together," a finding typical of much economic research.[15] For economists, the basic link is straightforward—more people mean, at a minimum, more buyers and sellers of goods and services, more workers, and more investment opportunities.

It isn't just large numbers of households, firms, and workers that give cities their economic advantage. Concentrating workers, capital, technology, supplies, and customers also helps achieve economies of scale—basically, the more an economy supplies something, the cheaper it is to produce each additional unit. Urban density of customers and suppliers can also lower transportation costs and downtime for workers and facilities.[16]

But dense, crowded cities also create problems—what economists call negative externalities, a cost in a market transaction not fully priced into the transaction. (There are positive externalities as well.) Classic negative externalities are air pollution and traffic jams from cars and trucks, which are not paid for by car and truck users, or nightclub noise that keeps clubbers happy but nearby residents awake. And, of course, contagious diseases can spread more easily in crowded environments, from cholera to influenza, to COVID-19.

Balancing positive and negative externalities is what Fujita and Thisse call the "fundamental tradeoff" of urban economics.[17] Coal-fired power plants produce electricity, purchased by consumers. But customers don't pay for the full harm caused by air pollution. Density and proximity can produce more externalities—pandemic diseases are a negative, but better and more sophisticated health care along with scientific research are positives.

For economists, cities mostly produce more positive than negative externalities. Cities also benefit from economies of scale—as size increases, it becomes cheaper and more efficient to increase output. Cities support bigger factories, offices, and stores. There are more customers nearby, allowing savings on goods transportation and quicker discovery of what consumers want or can afford. Underscoring importance of scale economies for overcoming the negative effects of cities, Quigley writes, "Without scale economies, there is no [economic] role for cities at all."[18]

Other positive effects of size and density include concentrating key inputs to production, especially labor. A large and growing supply of workers gives firms more options for hiring or reconfiguring work processes and also reduces the time it takes workers to find jobs. More economic output attracts more workers and entrepreneurs. This virtuous cycle can continue, at least until it is slowed by negative externalities like crime, public health crises, overly expensive land and housing prices, or costly and congested transportation—or by other competing locations undercutting the city's advantages.

The beneficial effects of density go beyond scale economies. Average labor productivity also correlates with density and urbanization, with Ciccone and Hall finding that "a doubling of employment density in a county results in a 6-percent increase of average labor productivity."[19] Increasing numbers of workers, especially those with greater skills and higher education, help fuel these productivity increases.

Many urban economists attribute these effects to higher urban workforce education and skills, although it is hard to untangle how these effects are transmitted.[20] There are at least three ways that this process works: first, workers with more education move to larger and growing cities; second, dense concentrations of workers allow faster learning of skills; and third, managers and business owners find faster ways to innovate through more efficient forms of technology and work organization. All three effects can reinforce each other in the virtuous growth cycle.

Glaeser and Resseger argue the "quality" of a given population matters more than population size in increasing productivity. Productivity rises with population in cities with more highly educated workforces, with size accounting for up to 45 percent of the variation in per-worker productivity for cities with high education rates. In contrast, agglomeration effects on productivity in metropolitan areas with the lowest education rates are "weak or non-existent."[21]

Lobo, Stolarick, and Florida confirm this from data on 363 U.S. metropolitan economies. They found that, while low population growth was linked to low productivity growth, high productivity wasn't automatically linked to high population growth. They assert that "high productivity growth can be accompanied by relatively low population growth" in an urban area.[22] Cities with highly educated workforces can generate productivity gains even without sharp population growth.

INNOVATION

Of course, economists know that population and density alone aren't sufficient for optimal growth—just packing more people into ever-tighter space doesn't lead to prosperity. Instead, dense urban populations are vital for a central growth driver—innovation. As cities add people, and particularly as the population becomes more diverse and more educated, they benefit from effects not necessarily intended from individuals' own narrower economic pursuits.

The increasing scale and differentiation arising from denser and more diverse populations results in the positive externality of spillovers—ideas, innovations, and value not intended by the original parties to the transaction and available to others in the city. Spillovers facilitate development of new ideas, products, and services in cities. Although innovation has a strong national policy dimension, with policy advocacy around international trade, intellectual property and patents, and venture capital investment,[23] cities are seen by many as the place where innovations arise and come to market.[24]

Population density and agglomeration create opportunities for innovation, but they don't guarantee it. Innovation in cities results from doing something new but often with existing resources, frequently linking formerly separate economic processes. The automobile industry could be born in Detroit because of two older industries—Great Lakes shipping, including marine engine design and repair, and wagon and carriage building for animal-drawn transportation carrying agricultural products. Innovators in Detroit began putting engines into auto bodies, producing what was called a horseless carriage and giving rise to the modern automobile industry.

Innovation in cities isn't confined to market economic activity; it can also be seen in how cities foster breakthroughs in art and culture. In New Orleans, American brass and marching band music intersected with the musical styles, traditions, and creativity brought to the city by former slaves and Afro-Caribbean percussion and rhythms, giving rise to jazz, one of America's major contributions to world culture. In Paris, cubism arose when French painter Georges Braque shared his experiments using flattened, multidimensional visual forms with Spanish artist Pablo Picasso, who was experimenting with forms drawn from African masks and sculpture. More recently, in the Bronx, African American traditions of verbal jousting and spontaneous poetry were mixed with technological innovations and Jamaican dub music to create hip-hop.

To an economist, urban artistic innovation looks remarkably similar to economic innovation. Both emerge in an environment dense with diverse ideas and influences that are combined in new ways by experimenters who in turn foster more innovation. Out of that churning, some innovations find a market and new growth results.

By now, the importance of innovation spillovers isn't a mystery, and many cities work to foster them. Cities are home to universities and scientific research centers, to art and cultural institutions, and increasingly to programs that consciously attempt to generate innovation. Cities are appointing chief innovation officers, sometimes to work only on city functions but increasingly also to engage with private sector development.[25] And in an echo of earlier "enterprise zone" programs, cities are concentrating tax credits, infrastructure development, and financial and other supports in designated "innovation districts."[26]

In the past few decades, a virtual subindustry has grown up around finding ways that cities can attract and hold scientists, artists, and young educated professionals—what Richard Florida famously labeled the "creative class."[27] Florida defined this group broadly, stating in 2013 that "about 40 million Americans" were members, which would have made them a quarter of the entire U.S. labor force. He found that city rankings on his four-part "Creativity Index" were correlated with economic growth and that cities should attract creative class workers through urban amenities, good public services, distinctive urban environments, and tolerance of racial diversity and sexual orientation.[28]

Many economists view Florida's work as largely restating the positive impact of highly educated workers on a city's economy. Ann Markusen argued that the very broad occupational categories in Florida's definition (covering not only artists but occupations such as insurance claims adjusters and funeral directors) meant the analysis mostly reflected "high human capital as measured by educational attainment."[29] Hoyman and Faricy found no significant relationship between the creative class variables, economic growth, or in-migration of young professionals, concluding that human capital measures "account for most income and job growth differences across cities in different regions."[30] Glaeser said that Florida's analysis implied "a difference between the human capital theory of city growth and the 'creative capital' theory of city growth" but didn't find any analytic significance for several of Florida's measures. He noted Florida's agreement with the general proposition that highly educated workforces were better for economic and income growth.[31]

The debate over Florida's work highlights a cornerstone of market-oriented urban economic analysis—its focus on individual workers, their skills and education, and their mobility as the drivers for economic activity.[32] The field's canonical models focus on individual choices for work and residence as core factors to analyze and explain, downplaying the role of firms, institutions, discrimination, and relative power between workers and business.[33] As will be discussed in chapter 7, this focus on individuals gives economics a sharply focused but also a one-sided and partial understanding of urban realities.

SPECIALIZATION

Although disputes exist over the relevant pathway to innovation and economic growth, many economic analysts see cities as the locus of innovation, and innovation as central to leveraging population density for economic growth. As innovation proceeds, it intersects with another force for economic growth—specialization through an ever-increasing division of labor; development of skills among researchers and work-ers; and growth of supporting firms and institutions in finance, trade, and distribution.

Ever since Adam Smith's *The Wealth of Nations*, economists have focused on the productive power of the division of labor. After giving a meticulous description of how a simple factory produced pins and how the division of labor radically improved productivity, Smith made a leap of genius by applying the idea to an entire economy and society. Smith saw the division of labor as essential for societies to achieve widespread prosperity: "It is the great multiplication of the productions of all the dif-ferent arts, in consequence of the division of labour, which occasions, in a well-governed society, that universal opulence which extends itself to the lowest ranks of the people."[34]

As cities specialize in particular industries and trades, they can fos-ter increasing innovation both in their core industries and through new economic growth driven by innovation. Entrepreneurs take ideas and processes from one sector and create something new, as automobile innovators did in Detroit. Seeing new ideas put into practice can in turn encourage other innovators and attract investors, both in the main line of business and in related enterprises.

In the late nineteenth century, economist Alfred Marshall articulated why industries specialize and locate together, emphasizing what today we would call spillovers in worker skills, inventions, managerial techniques, and communication of ideas and innovation. His analysis still rings true:

> When an industry has thus chosen a locality for itself, it is likely to stay there long . . . The mysteries of the trade become no mysteries; but are as it were in the air . . . Good work is rightly appreciated, inventions and improvement in machinery, in processes and the general organization of the business have their merits promptly discussed: if one man starts a new idea it is taken up by others and combined with suggestions of their own; and thus it becomes the source of further new ideas.[35]

Specializing firms and industries generate new economic demands, and cities can foster new businesses and services in response. Successful cities change over time, building new sectors and growth that either coexist with or eventually displace older industries. New York City began around one of the world's great natural harbors, and its growing trade connected agriculture and fur trading to overseas markets. Its initial dependence on the harbor fostered shipbuilding and repair and also warehousing, goods shipment, and finance and insurance. As the city's population grew, food and clothing production developed along with more specialized finance and business services. Most manufacturing eventually left New York but financial and business services grew and thrived, with these sectors becoming the new wealth generators.

Specialization can have downsides. Cities may become dependent on one industry, and shifts in technology or other factors can erode their advantage. Cities relying on core industries can become complacent about their competitive position, thinking they will always prosper based on their current leadership. Some analysts suggest that cities sometimes stifle innovation and new industries by adopting taxation, land use, education, and labor policies favoring their dominant industry. In this view, Detroit's decline and collapse was caused by the city, firms, workers, and politicians becoming too dependent on the auto industry and refusing to invest in or foster new businesses.

Economic analysis is indeterminate on the relative benefits of industrial specialization and concentration. A 1992 study concluded knowledge spillovers between diverse industries spurred employment growth, but overconcentration in specific industries hurt growth: "at the city-industry level, specialization hurts, competition helps, and city diversity helps employment growth."[36] Later research presented more nuanced findings, arguing that, at least for manufacturing, there were advantages both to specialization and to diversity at different stages of growth.[37]

The nuanced view that specialization has both advantages and disadvantages has gained ground. Highly specialized localities provide proximity among related producers, but they have "less innovation and more exposure to risk as the fortunes of specific sectors and technologies rise or fall."[38] Although innovation fosters specialization, specialization and concentration can crowd out future innovation if economic diversity is stifled, especially in new sectors.

The innovation question is closely tied to why and where economic activity is concentrated. In 2018, "the top six largest US metro areas (NY, LA, Chicago, Dallas, DC, and San Francisco)" accounted for 24.7 percent of total U.S. output, and "those six metro areas combined as a separate country would have been the third-largest national economy in the world."[39] Urban economics still debates the issue: why is there such geographic concentration—why don't competitive forces even things out more, especially spreading jobs and people to lower-cost places?[40]

A simplified economic framing posits first- and second-nature geographies, the former relying more on characteristics like ports and trade routes, natural resources, or temperate weather, while the latter are driven by forces generated and reinforced over time by skills and labor market spillovers, accessibility to capital markets, and supportive government policies. Given the continuing urbanization of the global economy, the empirical evidence suggests that positive externalities for cities outweigh the negatives. And as natural factors decline in importance, the forces from positive spillovers and the resulting positive spiral continues to favor large urban concentrations.[41]

INVESTMENT IN PUBLIC GOODS AND SERVICES

Although urban density is essential for positive innovation and growth of specialized industries, cities also generate many negative externalities that can harm growth. Urban density, crowding, and specialization can have damaging spillovers, highlighting problems that markets don't solve on their own. And innovation requires a variety of infrastructures paid for by public investment.

An example is the case of an educated workforce. Although urban economists see skilled workforces as essential for productive growth in cities, firms often don't invest in worker skills and have even less interest in providing general education to their workforces. An educated worker can move to another firm, and a company's investment in skills can be lost.

Instead firms often work to reduce labor costs by opposing unionization and labor regulation. Their shared interests also can turn into collusion, with the potentially broad benefits of innovation captured by monopolies. (Adam Smith claimed, "People of the same trade seldom meet together, even for merriment and diversion, but the conversation ends in a conspiracy against the public, or in some contrivance to raise prices."[42]) And firms benefitting from urban density don't voluntarily take responsibility for the negative externalities of public health, substandard housing, crime, lack of high-quality education, or pollution.

Economists (sometimes grudgingly) recognize markets don't solve these negative externalities. Thus, the fourth core condition for successful urban economies is investment in public goods, especially those addressing market failures. Public goods are elements necessary for prosperity that market transactions don't provide, while negative externalities can be reduced though taxation and regulation.

But theoretical and policy economics features a wide and vigorous debate about the nature and depth of appropriate public goods. Economists generally agree on the need for public provision of basic services such as police and fire protection, some amount of universal public education for young people, maintenance of transportation infrastructure, legal systems to enforce contracts and resolve disputes fairly and efficiently, managing air and water pollution along with other public health problems (such as pandemics), and a tax and regulatory system to pay for and manage social and economic life and conflict.

Some economists argue for essentially limiting the public role to those functions. They think governments cannot operate efficiently and will take on activities better left to private firms or households. Market-oriented economists also see taxation and regulation as hindering and stifling innovation and effort, causing labor and capital to leave cities for more favorable environments. Glaeser agrees that "pure laissez-faire is rarely an option in urban economics" but argues that "economists remain more skeptical of many forms of government intervention than representatives of many other disciplines" because of "doubts about the competence and benevolence of government."[43]

Others call for a more expansive public sector, especially as the economy and society grow more complex and power tilts to particular sectors, especially businesses. As June Sekera points out, even the term "public goods" shows the dominance of market-based thinking in economics, viewing necessary public services as caused by "market failure."[44] While market-oriented economists fear an incompetent or power-seeking government will inhibit economic growth, it is also possible for governments to underinvest in necessary public services.

In some cases, inadequate investment in public services is found in recognized public goods like education, transportation, and research.

In other cases, advocates argue for adding new public benefits, like campaigns for universal prekindergarten education, paid sick days or family leave, or higher minimum wages and other labor benefits. Although "public goods" may sound like a fixed analytic category, defined technically by degrees of exclusivity and rivalry, public goods and services change over time through political battles over the appropriate public sector role.[45]

For example, late nineteenth-century industrialism in American cities resulted in crowded, dangerous workplaces. In New York City, garment workers were crammed into dense, poorly lit, and unventilated lofts. Many business leaders and political elites saw such conditions as a private contract issue between workers and owners. In 1909, magistrate Willard Olmsted told garment workers striking for safety regulations that they were striking "against God and nature." Some of them worked at the Triangle Shirtwaist Company, where two years later a fire swept through the factory, killing 146 people died, some trapped by locked exit doors and others leaping to their death to escape the flames. The political response finally led to union-advocated workplace health and safety regulations, in essence a new public good.[46]

Making health and safety protections into a public good is a dramatic but hardly unique case. What we consider to be public goods is contested and changes over time. Increased wealth, political advocacy, changing economic and social needs, voting, and court decisions all affect what we supply as public goods and services.

U.S. CITIES: ECONOMIC GROWTH AND HIGH INEQUALITY

It might seem that, because political and business leaders recognize cities' economic importance, they would work to strengthen it. In recent years, politicians and scholars have joined economists focusing on the economic prosperity driven by American cities and urban regions. A U.S. Conference of Mayors report claimed that "as cities and their metro areas go, so goes the nation."[47] Presidential candidate Barack Obama said in 2008, "[C]ities and metropolitan regions are key drivers of prosperity in the global economy."[48] And in 2012, the CEO of Gallup claimed, "Whether the country makes a historic comeback or slowly goes broke, it will do so one city at a time."[49] To some, cities seemed to be replacing nations as the key units of economic activity: "In a world that increasingly appears ungovernable, cities—not (nation)states—are the islands of governance on which the future world order will be built."[50]

Our economic prosperity depends on healthy cities. Cities and metros led the economic recovery after the Great Recession. Through 2016, the fifty-one metros in the United States with over 1 million in population, just over half of the total U.S. population, accounted for 87 percent of total job growth in the recovery from the Great Recession, in contrast to smaller metros that never fully recovered and the employment in non-metropolitan areas that remained below its 2007 peak in 2017.[51]

The recession resulting from COVID-19 measures hit the entire econ-omy hard, including cities and metropolitan areas. Although the pandem-ic's effects played out in complex ways, job losses in metropolitan areas were worse in cities with lots of tourism, leisure, and hospitality (such as Las Vegas and Honolulu). The same was true for metros with larger per-centages of jobs in health and education, and in manufacturing. Recovery has been slower in some larger cities, but much of their troubled job picture could have been predicted before the pandemic. As one study put it, metro areas with faster recoveries "were those that were growing most vigorously before the pandemic."[52]

But as New York's 432 Park Avenue skyscraper and other luxury devel-opments dramatically illustrate, American cities not only foster economic growth but also inequality, in both wage income and wealth. Between 1979 and 2019, the Economic Policy Institute reports wages for the top 1 per-cent rose by 160.3 percent, and by 345.2 percent for the top one-tenth of 1 percent; the bottom 90 percent had annual wages grow by 26 percent.[53] And wealth is far more unequally distributed than income. In 2019, the top 1 percent of American households owned 33.1 percent of total wealth, compared to 27 percent for the bottom 90 percent and only 2 percent for the lowest 50 percent of households

The top 5 percent of households in the United States gained the most in real income since the 1980s. The Occupy Wall Street movement focused on the gap between the bottom 99 percent and the wealthiest 1 percent, but the top 1 percent is itself unequal. The top one-tenth of 1 percent of

American households—one in 1,000—in 2012 owned 22 percent of total U.S. wealth—triple their 7 percent share in 1979. The top one-tenth of 1 percent own approximately the same share of American wealth as the bottom 90 percent. By 2015, the top one-tenth of 1 percent had 5 percent of total income.[54]

These patterns persisted through the pandemic. Although the share of total net worth held by the top 1 percent fell in the first months of the pandemic (because of a short, steep decline in financial markets), their share rebounded quickly and then grew. By the third quarter of 2021, the top 1 percent held 32.1 percent of the total net worth in the economy as a result of large increases in the stock market and in housing prices.[55] The pandemic actually increased the total amount—and in turn the relative percentage—of wealth held by the very richest.[56]

Inequality has been worse in rural areas historically, but urban areas are converging with them, not because rural areas are improving but "because inequality is getting worse in urban areas."[57] City inequality takes different forms. In wealthier cities like San Francisco; Seattle; or Washington DC, significant numbers of high-income households stretches the inequality ratio from the top, while in others like Detroit, Miami, or Cleveland, the growth of very poor households widens the gap from the bottom. But in either way, income inequality in American cities has been high and increasing. Many U.S. cities have inequality on a par with developing countries; in 2019, Atlanta, Miami, New York, Boston, and Los Angeles had inequality scores on par or worse than countries including Brazil, Angola, and Costa Rica.

A growing body of literature argues inequality constrains economic growth through multiple pathways.[58] These pathways include less investment in city infrastructure, schools, and health care and more spending on private goods leading to less upward mobility and growth. Inequality spurs unsustainable household debt because borrowers use credit to make up for stagnant wages.[59] Nobel Laureate Joseph Stiglitz emphasizes how inequality slows growth through decreased consumer spending; reduced education investment; fewer new business start-ups; and lowering tax revenues, which starve public investments in infrastructure, health, and education and contribute to boom-and-bust economic cycles.[60]

Because the wealthy can influence the tax codes and regulatory provisions in their favor, subpar investment and spending persist while inequality grows. Political scientists Martin Gillens and Benjamin Page analyzed 1,779 U.S. government policy outcomes and concluded that economic elites and organized interests consistently beat majority opinions.[61] For example, raising the federal minimum wage is enormously popular—polls have consistently shown around 70 percent support for an increase—but as of 2022, it had not been raised nationally for thirteen years.

Persistent and growing urban inequality and problems exacerbated by the pandemic have tempered the optimism of urban advocates and analysts like Richard Florida and Edward Glaeser. Florida had championed urban growth patterns driven by what he called the creative class in his earlier work, but he came to worry those patterns were generating "winner-take-all urbanism." He wrote in 2017 that "the very same clustering force that generates economic and social progress also divides us" and called for major public investments and pro-urban policies.[62] In a 2021 book coauthored with health economist David Cutler, Glaser remains pro-city, although he notes that "COVID-19 teaches us that our globally connected world has made pandemic not only possible but probable." His policy recommendations remain consistent with his long-standing skepticism about government's competence.[63]

INEQUALITY DAMPENS ECONOMIC GROWTH

The pandemic accelerated prior trends in inequality. But why does economic growth coexist with rising inequality? Conventional economists argue that inequality is initially a consequence of growth, innovation, and economic transition that will fall as economies grow. Old industries and jobs decline as competition introduces new technologies, goods, and services, and broader prosperity will eventually increase equality. Urban economists share this logic with international development economics, where inequality is viewed as a necessary but temporary moment in developing country economic growth that will recede as national prosperity grows.

This view is reflected in the well-known Kuznets curve, the basis for economist Simon Kuznets's 1971 Nobel Prize. It predicts inequality at first growing when workers displaced from an increasingly productive agriculture sector flood the relatively less productive manufacturing and service sectors. This less productive and excess labor supply holds down wages until the economy develops enough so workers in the new sector earn higher incomes, eventually shrinking inequality.[64] Inequality in wages and wealth reflected beneficial economic transitions and underlying differences in productivity and skills.

Glaeser applies a Kuznets-style convergence logic to cities, arguing that as cities become better places to live by controlling disease, building infrastructure, and—most important—growing and diversifying economically, they at first attract more poor people, driving up inequality and poverty. But over time, cities allow the poor to prosper through economic growth supported by public health, education, safety, and infrastructure. He says that "areas should be judged not by their poverty but by their track record in helping poorer people to move up."[65] So this line of economic thinking expects and tolerates inequality and poverty because it is temporary and will lead to eventual upward mobility.

But recent analysis of large data sets finds evidence for a different pattern—equality may in fact foster upward mobility. Economist Raj Chetty and colleagues studied intergenerational economic mobility (the life chances of children born in the bottom 20 percent of the income distribution ending up in the top 20 percent) of over 40 million children and their parents between 1996 and 2012. They found upward mobility varied by almost three times between the lowest ranking city (Charlotte, North Carolina, at 4.4 percent) and the highest (San Jose, California, at 12.9 percent). The probability of upward mobility was lowest where residential segregation, income equality, school quality, social networks and capital, and family structure were low and weak. They concluded that intergenerational mobility could be improved with "place-based policies" rather than time-based policies that work the problem out through human capital investments in individuals.[66]

Market-oriented economists see inequality as rooted primarily in differences in education, linked to neighborhood segregation by income, which fosters unequal educational quality. Subpar education in turn holds back labor market performance and upward mobility over generations. But individual choice remains as the behavioral root of persistent income segregation: "parents choose the neighborhood where to raise their children and invest in their children's education." Princeton economist Leah Boustan has qualified this standard choice model by highlighting the impact of racial segregation and so-called white flight as a response to Black in-migration from the South, although the ultimate pathway for unequal outcomes continues to flow through individual education. So market-oriented economists see the fundamental explanation for racial inequality as an individual story about education and human capital, even though it may be shaped over time by segregated neighborhoods and schools.[67]

Other evidence also suggests that greater equality can spur economic growth. In 2014, the Organization for Economic Cooperation and Development (OECD) found income inequality in advanced economies reduces medium-term economic growth. Inequality over the past twenty-five years is associated with an average loss of 8.5 percent of GDP in the OECD, and a 6 to 7 percent loss in the United States.[68] International Monetary Fund (IMF) researchers concur, finding inequality deters growth, while moderate income redistribution and reduced inequality are associated with "higher and more durable growth." And a paper for the World Bank concluded higher income inequality between 1970 and 2010 led to lower GDP per capita in rich countries as a result of lower overall investment and human capital.[69] The bond rating agency Standard and Poor's concluded in 2014 that "income inequality in the US is dampening GDP growth," while a 2014 research review summarized that "inequality is associated with lower long-term growth" in the United States.[70]

THE COVID-19 PANDEMIC ACCELERATED URBAN INEQUALITY

COVID-19 accelerated inequality while increasing economic pressures on cities. The pandemic hit cities hard, emptying office buildings and disproportionately harming minority and immigrant service workers. Population declines led some to speculate about the end of cities, or at least megacities like New York, Los Angeles, and Houston. But urban population growth in the United States had been slowing before the pandemic for several years, with near-zero or negative growth in many cities over 1 million population, such as New York, Los Angeles, Chicago, and San Jose, primarily because of slowing immigration and a tight housing supply.

The rapid and almost total closing of downtown offices early in the pandemic caused unemployment in office-based work, which in turn hurt jobs in the restaurants, bars, hotels, janitorial and security services, and other services supported by that sector. This in turn fueled speculation that much work was moving permanently from offices to homes, with dire consequences for cities. Localized upward blips in suburban housing markets also fed a journalistic trend of speculative reporting about permanent city decline.[71] But economists and other analysts noted cities had survived far worse pandemics. And by August 2020, the nation's highest per capita case and death rates were occurring in rural areas.

COVID-19 accelerated preexisting racial and ethnic gaps in unemployment, wealth, and wages. Latinos and Blacks live in households with less savings and higher income volatility, making them vulnerable to economic shocks. Because Black and Latino workers were disproportionately working in essential jobs (including health care and food sales and delivery), they suffered sustained exposure to the virus, made worse by inadequate protective equipment, unsafe working practices, and a lack of workplace safety standards against infectious disease.[72] Black and Latino city residents contracted COVID-19 much more than did Whites, even after controlling for housing, transportation, and other variables. Lack of adequate health care prior to the pandemic and living in more unhealthy neighborhoods accelerated existing disparities in health and wealth.

By late 2020, economists were describing a K-shaped recovery, with higher-income workers recovering virtually all of their jobs and enjoying skyrocketing financial market returns while lower-income nonwhite and female workers struggled. Economist Valerie Wilson documented the pandemic's impact on these groups, testifying to Congress that "the disparate racial impact of COVID-19 should come as no surprise given the ongoing legacy of racism that continues to produce unequal outcomes in nearly every aspect of life in the United States."[73]

The rapidity and depth of the COVID-19 recession hurt cities in other ways. State and local budgets suffered when income, property, and sales taxes declined, while health and education expenses rose. States cut spending, imposed furloughs and layoffs, and reduced aid to cities. And although the Federal Reserve established emergency borrowing through a new Municipal Lending Facility to stabilize private municipal debt markets, it didn't seek to relieve cities' budget pressures directly.[74]

Federal COVID-19 pandemic relief failed cities (and the rest of the nation) at every level. States and cities were forced to bid against each other and the federal government for protective equipment, increasing their costs. The Trump administration failed to provide accurate public health information or advocate steps to slow the virus's spread. Schools closed, hospitals were stretched to the limit, and people were frightened and sick.

CONCLUSION

Inequality hampers growth. And because cities and metros make up most of the economy and drive innovation and growth, urban inequality keeps the entire nation from reaching its full potential. It also keeps people from moving out of poverty to the middle class and beyond.

This inequality persists not only within cities but also in metropolitan areas. American metropolitan areas benefit from the gains produced by urban economies, but those gains go disproportionately to the wealthy, both in cities and in the suburbs that surround them. A key argument of this book is that misalignment between urban economies and fragmented political structures pens cities in a ring of politically separate suburban jurisdictions that don't share revenues, housing, education, and other amenities. These unequal resources put core cities behind and increase both regional inequality and inequality within the core city.

We have a paradox. If cities and urban areas are the incubators of innovation, productivity, and economic growth, why do policies neglect and harm them? We might expect public policy to foster urban economic development aggressively to generate increased prosperity and upward mobility. But rather than supporting cities or even being neutral toward them, American federal and state policy has a long history that continues today of disfavoring cities.

This chapter agrees with market-oriented economists that cities are the engines of economic growth, although that growth heightens inequality. But four factors, downplayed by many urban economists, cause the benefits of economic growth to be distributed unequally: (1) economic change that favors businesses and increasing inequality; (2) a long-standing federal bias against cities; (3) hostility toward cities by state governments; and (4) structural racism interwoven with employment, education, housing, and political power. Cities' full economic promise cannot be realized unless these factors are integrated into analysis and policy recommendations.

Our public policy should stop working against cities. Unfortunately, American anti-urban views date back to the nation's founding and are built into our political structure. Cities are underrepresented in the U.S. Senate and state legislatures, and fiscal policy tilts away from cities through government subsidies to suburbs, who obtain metropolitan economic benefits without paying their fair share of housing, education, infrastructure, and other necessary public goods. This structure is deeply intertwined with America's federal system that advantages states and rural areas over cities, and with structural racism that shapes urban economies, housing, education, and other key factors in economic prosperity.

The next two chapters review America's long-standing anti-city bias. I then examine three cities—New York, Detroit, and Los Angeles—that tried on their own to address inequality and economic growth, with at best mixed results. Understanding this history, and also the limits to conventional urban economic analysis, allows us to outline an agenda for political and policy reform that leads to greater equality while preserving and even strengthening cities' role at the heart of our economy.

2

AMERICA'S HOSTILITY TOWARD CITIES

"Pestilential to the Morals, the Health, and the Liberties of Man"

Economists share a broad consensus that healthy cities and metropolitan regions are essential to American economic prosperity. As we saw in chapter 1, cities are the centers of metropolitan regional economies, and metro economies in turn dominate the American economy. But our fragmented metropolitan regions, divided along economic and racial lines, produce too much inequality and limit our prosperity. The problem has deep roots reaching back to America's founding, with effects felt to this day. We need to understand the nation's fundamental anti-urban bias before we can craft policies to address inequality, racial justice, and sustainable economic growth both in cities and the nation.

AMERICA'S FEDERAL AND STATE ANTI-URBANISM

Historians confirm the mismatch between the reality that cities create wealth and America's anti-urban structure and ideology. Historian Richard Hofstadter wrote that America "was born in the country but moved to the city." The pervasive myth of the "happy yeoman" farmer influenced American ideology and politics long after the country was mostly urbanized, and even farmers themselves were not self-sufficient "yeomen" but commercial producers of cash crops for urban markets.[1]

In 2007, historian Paul Boller cited a continuing "suspicion and dread" of cities reaching back to the nation's founding.[2] American policies from the nation's beginnings up until today are stacked against cities and inhibit their success.

Consider Thomas Jefferson, the nation's third president and principal author of the Declaration of Independence. American politicians of all stripes quote him. Ronald Reagan once said, "Americans . . . would do well to pluck a flower from Thomas Jefferson's life, and wear it in our soul forever,"[3] while Barack Obama, visiting Jefferson's Monticello home in 2014, said, "Thomas Jefferson represents what's best in America."[4]

So it is jarring to hear this revered Founding Father's views on urban life. Arguing for an agriculture-based society, Jefferson's 1781 *Notes on the State of Virginia* said "those who labor in the earth are the chosen people of God, if ever he had a chosen people" while "the mobs of great cities add just so much to the support of pure government, as sores do to the strength of the human body."[5] In 1800, the year before his first presidential term, Jefferson wrote to Benjamin Rush that "I view great cities as pestilential to the morals, the health, and the liberties of man."[6]

We might dismiss these comments as typical for an eighteenth-century agrarian slaveholder, even one as sophisticated as Jefferson. But in reviewing American policy toward cities since the nation's founding, we see a persistent anti-urban pattern. While accepted as necessary for commerce, cities were not (and still often are not) viewed as the home of the real America. Although urban political movements were central to the rebellion, the British controlled the cities once the Revolutionary War began. As historian Benjamin Carp notes, "Political activity in the cities helped lead the colonists to independence, but in the process, the cities rendered themselves obsolete."[7]

After the nation's independence, cities were seen as hard to govern, given to strident and sometimes violent mass politics, and necessary for trade but requiring careful management and control. President George Washington wrote in 1791 that "the tumultuous populace of large cities are ever to be dreaded. Their indiscriminate violence prostrates for the time all public authority, and its consequences are sometimes extensive and terrible."[8]

America began as a rural nation, so its early anti-urban tilt isn't surprising. In the 1800 census, America's urban areas (any place over 2,500 people) totaled 6.1 percent of the nation's 5.3 million people, while almost 18 percent of the population was enslaved, concentrated in the rural South.[9] New York was the largest city, at 60,515.[10] Contrast this with England, where almost 34 percent of the population was counted as urban in its 1801 census, with over 1 million in greater London.[11]

The new United States' economy was dominated by agriculture, with a few commercial centers in New York, Boston, Philadelphia, and Charleston. The nation's politics was heavily influenced by large landowners, especially southern slaveowners. Slaves were a substantial share of the rural Southern population, but slaves were also held in urban areas and northern states by mercantile elites. Port cities exported agricultural goods and imported manufactured ones. Ports spurred demand for warehousing; ship building and repair; and professional services in insurance, financing, and the legal work needed for trade. Disorderly urban politics made political elites nervous, especially within living memory of the Paris-centered French Revolution, with its destruction of social order and political terror.

Besides cultural prejudice, early American cities were less powerful because of a key feature of American government, one that persists to this day—the power of state governments. American states were much stronger than regional governments in other democracies. Unlike Paris or London, where national politics, finance and economics, and arts and culture were centered in the same urban national capital, the United States even physically built the separate political capital of Washington, DC, away from its centers of economic power and cultural activity.

The U.S. Constitution adopted a decentralized structure built on compromises among formerly independent colonies to limit federal authority. The Constitution's Tenth Amendment reads: "The powers not delegated to the United States by the Constitution, nor prohibited by it to the States, are reserved to the States respectively, or to the people." States retained many powers relative to the federal government, including creation and control of their cities. Eighteenth-century England had strong central authority that confirmed cities with letters patent directly from the monarch without an intermediating layer of regional government.

In many states, cities got short shrift. Major colonial cities such as New York, Philadelphia, Boston, and Charleston were the first state capitals after the Revolution, but as populations spread out into the hinterland, state capitals were pressured to move. As new territories became states, many relocated their capitals from eastern territorial borders to more central locations.[12] Further weakening cities, state legislatures (which increasingly controlled cities legally) were malapportioned in favor of rural interests. Although some states invested in public works such as roads and canals, which assisted urban economies by linking agricultural production to city markets and ports, state governments often fought to keep large cities from dominating political life.[13]

Cities were not favored as the new American nation developed its political rules and institutions. Cities didn't have a common history of national economic, safety, and public health regulation or financial support. Agrarian economic interests and political views in the United States undergirded the federal structure, entrenching anti-urban forces in both houses of Congress. Anti-city bias was strengthened further by the Constitution's notorious "three-fifths compromise." Counting slaves as equal to three-fifths of a person for purposes of determining state representation in the House of Representatives and the Electoral College favored rural slaveholding interests that controlled southern states. And the Senate's equal representation to states regardless of their size gave further power to smaller, more rural, and slaveholding states.

Despite these political disadvantages, cities thrived and accrued power and prominence. Between 1820 and 1860, the urban population grew ten times while the national population only tripled, putting America's urban population just under 20 percent of the total national population at the start of the Civil War.[14] In the next seventy years, the urban population steadily increased until, by 1920, the majority of Americans, 51.4 percent, lived in urban areas.

Early constraints on city growth were not just political but also technological and spatial. Transportation was especially important. Urban historians characterize early American cities as "walking cities"—the great majority of the inhabitants walked everywhere (wealthier people rode on horseback or in carriages), making the city both compact and less economically differentiated within its boundaries. Housing intermingled with commercial space, with the wealthiest living near the city center or near their places of employment.

Business owners and merchants had to be near enough to their factories, shops, and warehouses to walk or ride there on a regular basis.

City outskirts often had higher poverty and disorder: they were further away from work and commerce and thus less desirable. Absent very sharp increases in housing density, something wealthy urban residents didn't want, cities did not grow spatially very much.[15]

These constraints were eroded by changing transportation technology, allowing affluent housing to be located further away from workplaces, leading eventually to suburbanization of urban areas.[16] Transport changes altered the city's physical order. "The introduction of the steam ferry, the omnibus, the commuter railroad, the horsecar, the elevated railroad, and the cable car gave additional impetus to an exodus that would turn cities 'inside out' and inaugurate a new pattern of suburban affluence and center despair."[17]

Whether it was the wealthy moving up Fifth Avenue in Manhattan; the growth of Brooklyn Heights across the East River from Manhattan (the river could be crossed by steam ferries); or the development of Boston suburbs like Somerville, Brookline, and Newton along horsecar and steam train lines, affluent residents no longer had to live in the city center. Detached houses with yards became more desired, and many wealthier residents now began to live near the city's edge rather than in the center, in homes with higher property values.

CITIES LOSE CONTROL

At first, population movements didn't present cities with major problems. To keep affluent residents (their tax base) and political control, cities simply annexed areas on their borders. Indeed, annexation was the major source of urban growth. Between 1850 and 1890, New York City doubled in size, from twenty-two to forty-four square miles. Boston made a much bigger jump, from five square miles in 1850 to thirty-four in 1890. But this was nothing compared to Chicago, which went from ten to 159 square miles, adding 125 square miles in 1889 alone, or Philadelphia, with its staggering 1854 growth from two to 128 square miles when it was consolidated with the surrounding county.

Historian Kenneth Jackson said that if annexation had continued logically, "Boston would probably encompass the entire area circumscribed by Route 128, New York City would reach to White Plains in West-chester County, and at least to the Suffolk County line on Long Island, and Chicago would stretch half the distance to Milwaukee."[18] And the American pattern of poor cities hemmed in by affluent suburbs might be less common than we see today. Although such geographically large cities may seem unusual, limits to city size and government control are dictated as much by political decisions as they are by spatial necessities. Greater London in the United Kingdom, governed at the highest level by one body and one mayor, is over 600 square miles, compared to New York City's 305 square miles.

But cities' annexing power was increasingly resisted by adjacent towns. In 1873, Boston suffered a historic defeat when the wealthy commuter sub-urb of Brookline rejected annexation, even though Boston had annexed Roxbury, Dorchester, Charleston, Brighton, and West Roxbury in the preceding five years. The rapid growth of Boston's immigrant population, driven by the Irish potato famine, resulted in deteriorating housing and neighborhoods. Brookline's wealthy and middle-class Protestant elites feared being sucked into the larger city, and 70 percent of the Brookline electorate voted against the proposal.[19]

Jackson calls Brookline's rejection "the first really significant defeat for the consolidation movement" and it inspired wealthy suburbs to reject annexation elsewhere.[20] Increasingly powerful affluent suburbs, often allied with rural interests, had state legislatures require majority approval from towns for annexation. Suburban voters feared losing their independence to urban machine politics. Their homogenous, wealthy, and white populations wanted to stay separate from increasing numbers of poor European immigrants and later from the 20 million whites and 8 million Blacks who came to Northern cities during the "Southern Diaspora" between 1916 and 1970.[21]

New York City's 1894 annexation of Brooklyn and other areas proved to be the high-water mark for America's older cities. Economic elites, advocates of public investment in civic infrastructure (especially municipal water systems), and landowners and home builders wanted a larger and more integrated city. Brooklynites feared dominance by Manhattan political machines but lost their battle. Queens, Staten Island, the Bronx, and parts of Westchester County all approved annexation with large majorities, but Brooklyn itself only approved annexation by 227 votes out of over

129,000 cast. Battles in the state legislature delayed actual consolidation until January 1, 1898, with the state coupling final approval with a prohibition on future annexations by New York City.[22]

The state legislature's control over Brooklyn's annexation underscores state government control over city growth, size, and powers. States ultimately won their power struggle with cities in the post–Civil War period. Again, this power for states was relatively unique to the United States. Parliament approved the size and scope of London's municipal powers, while governing and controlling Paris was a central preoccupation of French kings, emperors, and republics.

In contrast, the federal government had virtually nothing to say about annexations and expansions by New York City or cities in other states. States came to control cities, as they still do today, and they limited autonomous action by cities, including annexation. This helped create our modern metropolitan form—a poor central city ringed by wealthier suburbs that resist regional taxation, more public transportation, and integrated housing and schools.

Legal conflicts between states and cities continued after the Civil War in battles over municipal and state finance. Most American law governing relative power between cities and states now relies on Dillon's Rule, named after a nineteenth-century Iowa jurist, Judge John C. Dillon. In 1868, he ruled, "Municipal corporations (cities) owe their origin to, and derive their powers and rights wholly from, the legislature. It breathes into them the breath of life, without which they cannot exist. As it creates, so may it destroy. If it may destroy, it may abridge and control."[23]

As one legal scholar notes, Dillon's Rule means that "any doubts about the validity of the local initiatives are to be resolved *against* exercise of the (local) power." Under Dillon's Rule, cities could not freely annex other municipalities, or even unincorporated areas, without express state permission.[24]

Dillon himself was especially concerned with overspending by cities and aimed to limit their independent borrowing. (This city-state fiscal tension played out in twentieth-century fiscal crises in New York and Detroit, described in future chapters.) Municipalities in the late nineteenth century issued bonds for many reasons, including private railroad construction and municipal water systems. Sometimes these projects would fail and the bonds would default, angering investors and shaking financial markets, sometimes with profound economic impacts. The Panic of 1873, leading to the worst economic depression until the 1930s, was driven by defaults in railroad bonds, and "by the end of 1874, fully one-fourth of all US railroad companies had defaulted on their bonds."[25]

This economic disruption resulted in demands for more orderly finance markets. Dillon's aim, argues law professor Joan Williams, was creating a new legal ideology to calm bondholders and stabilize financial markets by sharply limiting cities' economic power. Dillion aimed to limit city tax-based financing and independent city financial actions, and to give bondholders and investors rights to repayment. Over time, the doctrine also became central in preventing cities from regulating private businesses.[26]

Dillon's Rule triumphed over alternative theories of municipal independence. Thomas Cooley, a justice of the Michigan Supreme Court, legal scholar, and first chair of the Interstate Commerce Commission (ICC), favored cities over states. Cooley saw state legislatures corrupted by powerful economic interests and hoped to empower local voters and urban elites to check state corruption. Cooley was no modern liberal. Williams describes him as a "Jacksonian" who feared state corruption and wanted cities to be a countervailing force slowing or blocking corrupt state interference and control.[27]

Dillon's Rule and state control over cities became the norm in American governance. Paradoxically, the political realignment shaped by Dillon's Rule meant that as cities became more densely populated, more economically powerful, and increasingly diverse, they lost political power relative to their surrounding towns and suburbs and to rural-dominated state governments.

INDUSTRIALIZATION AND IMMIGRATION

Cities were changing after the Civil War, transformed by the great wave of industrialization and immigrant labor in garment, food production, and then steel and other industries, and starting to specialize. For example, Chicago grew rapidly based on its proximity to agricultural and commodity markets and east-west transportation, especially the expanding network of railroads. From shipping raw commodities, Chicago increasingly produced higher value-added goods, led by meatpacking and agricultural products. The city also began producing agricultural machinery like the famous McCormick reaper. And its growing transportation hub fostered mail-order retailing and associated goods production by firms such as Montgomery Ward and Sears, Roebuck to service small rural towns. These growing firms strengthened the warehousing and logistics sector, along with increasing goods production and the legal and financial firms serving the complex, growing economy.[28]

Chicago's sharp increase in manufacturing and economic complexity was mirrored throughout urban America. Pittsburgh became a center of steel production (the population quadruped in forty years), and New York's garment industry grew explosively. Driven by the motor vehicle industry, Detroit's population grew over 240 percent between 1900 and 1920. Between 1880 and 1900—just twenty years—American manufacturing employment grew by over 4 million workers, a rate of over 107 percent.[29]

This rapid growth reflected the core economic strengths of cities—innovation, agglomeration, specialization, and economies of scale. In the early 1900s, over 270 American firms made some type of automobile or powered vehicles, with Detroit the location of 125 of them. Detroit was becoming the automotive innovation hub, with engineering, design, advanced production, innovative and increasingly specialized supplier firms, and skilled labor. But the increasing scale of production drove up entry costs, with large firms buying smaller ones. By the 1930s, the automobile industry was America's largest economic sector, with 80 percent of the output coming from the "big three"—Ford, Chrysler, and General Motors.[30]

Other cities also prospered from specialization, and the virtuous economic cycle—innovation, agglomeration, growth, production at scale, further specialization and innovation, and increased production at scale—continued. Chicago grew in food production and processing, agricultural machinery, and the mail-order retail business. Pittsburgh used its location on rivers and proximity to coal mining to lead in steel production. And New York not only developed the garment industry but also continued growing as the nation's leading financial center, providing banking, insurance, and legal services to fuel the rapidly growing economy.

Cities themselves grew through innovations. Higher buildings were enabled technically by Elisha Otis's modern safety elevator[31] and by steel-framed skyscrapers, which could go higher and higher as the frame, rather than the exterior walls, supported the building's weight. Ever-taller buildings allowed firms and owners to extract more value from the limited supply of land in urban cores as cities built up, not just out. Skyscraper design, sometimes attributed to romantic visions of architects, was economically driven as developers strove to maximize profits from buildings and land. Historian Carol Willis, in her pathbreaking book *Form Follows Finance*, emphasized that "the linkage between profit and program is fundamental to commercial architecture," noting architect Cass Gilbert's definition of a skyscraper as "a machine that makes the land pay."[32]

Another critical urban innovation was public health and sanitation. Cities attract travelers, who can bring epidemic diseases into places with inadequate sanitation and crowded living conditions, especially in poor neighborhoods. Smallpox, cholera, and other plagues were persistent urban dangers. Yellow fever killed 10 percent of Philadelphia's population in 1793; Alexander Hamilton was quarantined there, and Jefferson hoped the epidemic would produce "some good" as it would "discourage the growth of great cities in our nation."[33] Cholera spread from India through trade routes into Europe in the 1830s, and it hit New York in 1832, killing 1.2 percent of the city's population. Successive cholera outbreaks occurred in 1849, 1854, 1866, and 1892.

Low-paid, foreign-born workers transformed cities, with vibrant, diverse cultures and religions, while poverty led to overcrowded, substandard tenement housing. From New York's Little Italy and European Jewish Lower East Side (first a German neighborhood, Kleinduetschland or "Little Germany"), to Detroit's Poletown, the Irish-dominated neighborhood of South Boston ("Southie"), Chicago's "Polonia," and Pittsburgh's Slavic and Hungarian neighborhoods, European immigration permanently changed cities and the nation.

While public health had improved, the nation and cities were still vulnerable to epidemics. Typhoid, a form of salmonella, could spread rapidly, with a fatality rate of 10 percent; it and other diseases plagued cities. The 1918–1919 influenza pandemic killed 50 million people globally and 600,000 in the United States. Cities varied widely in their responses and death rates, which researchers attribute to varying "levels of health and poverty" associated with low literacy rates, high prepandemic infant mortality, prior exposure to diseases like tuberculosis, and poor air quality caused by coal-fired power plants and home heating.

But influenza's high death rates had little sustained impact on the economy and urbanization. "Most of the evidence indicates that the economic effects of the 1918 influenza pandemic were short-term," with sharper impacts on face-to-face work "in the service and entertainment industries."[34] Advances in science, garbage collection, sanitation, and clean water systems eventually brought most city diseases under control.[35]

Industrialization and immigration accelerated the rifts between cities and suburbs. Industrial work was crowded, hot, and polluting. Many low-paid workers and their families crammed into substandard tenement housing near meatpacking, garment, and steel factories, further driving wealthier families out of urban areas. And ethnic and political differences between cities and suburbs intensified the lack of regional cooperation and governance.

Unlike previous urban native-born populations, new urban workers came from two principal sources—European immigration and the internal Great Migration of Blacks and also poor southern whites. Between 1880 and 1920, over 20 million immigrants came to the United States, around 85 percent of them European. The foreign-born rose to 14 percent of the population, with many new immigrants giving birth to children after arrival. European immigrants' nationalities changed sharply during this period. In 1880, over 95 percent of European immigrants were from northern or western Europe, principally Ireland and Germany. But by 1920, 48 percent of European foreign-born people were from southern or eastern Europe, with Italians, Poles, and Russians making up the three largest groups.[36]

The new immigrants went to cities, and they worked in the rapidly growing manufacturing sector and in jobs serving the growing urban population during the massive sectoral shift from agriculture to manufacturing and related services between 1880 and 1920. In those forty years, agricultural employment fell from 48 percent to 25 percent of the working population, and manufacturing's share rose from 14 percent to 25 percent, an equal share with agriculture. Adding trade and service jobs, many related to urban manufacturing, meant that by 1920 most Americans lived in cities, not in rural areas.[37]

But city populations were distinct. In 1880, 61.4 percent of the foreign-born lived in urban areas compared to 36 percent of the total U.S. population. In 1920, 75.4 percent of the foreign-born lived in urban areas compared to 51.4 percent of the total population. In cities, immigrants and their children began to outnumber native residents. In 1900, about three-quarters of the populations of many large cities, including New York, Chicago, Boston, Cleveland, San Francisco, Buffalo, Milwaukee, and Detroit, were composed of immigrant households.[38]

Immigrants fueled economic growth, but the politics of the immigrant wave reinforced suburban isolation from central cities. Urban political machines helped new immigrants adapt by helping them find jobs, business contracts, and social services in exchange for political support. Peter Drier, John Mollenkopf, and Todd Swanstrom describe growing urban machines vying with and even replacing "business elites as the primary force in city politics." Elite and rural interests fought back by "promoting various 'reform' proposals to undermine the power of machines," from civil service reforms to limiting voting and city autonomy relative to state government.[39] These battles over urban political power were another major source of the conflict that Dillon's Rule resolved in favor of state governments.

The second great demographic wave economically and politically reshaping cities was the Great Migration, the movement of millions of poor Blacks, and many poor whites, from the mostly rural South to the industrial North and Midwest. The Great Migration was sparked by increasingly harsh Jim Crow laws, the ongoing debt peonage of rural sharecropping that economically imprisoned many Blacks, and outright racist violence, along with the rapidly growing demand for industrial labor in the North with the onset of World War I.[40] Whites actually moved in greater numbers, drawn by industrial jobs and the decline of agriculture, moving to the same industrial cities but also dispersing more widely across the country.

By 1920, the Black population grew by 148 percent in Chicago, 307 percent in Cleveland, and 611 percent in Detroit.[41] Some urban slums that had been populated by European immigrants now became crowded with Black migrants. Racial segregation within cities sharpened and, as large numbers of Blacks moved in, whites moved to other neighborhoods.[42] In New York City, Harlem went from just over 10 percent Black in 1910 to around 70 percent Black in 1930.[43]

The influx of Black residents affected cities in many ways, including outright explosions of racist violence. Anti-Black riots broke out in East St. Louis (1917), Chicago (1919), and other cities, and were part of a larger pattern of violence directed against Blacks in both the North and the South. Michael Jones-Correa sees urban anti-Black violence as part of a larger "ushering in an era of racial containment," which also drew on hostility to foreign immigrants. Blacks were confined not only to cities but also increasingly to specific neighborhoods through racially restrictive housing policies and violence from police and vigilante groups.[44]

Cities were the epicenter of America's structural economic transformation from agriculture to manufacturing, and that economic change was linked to massive population shifts, both foreign immigration and internal migration from the South. Both groups went to growing jobs in cities, helping to fuel the increasing expansion of large-scale industrialization. These population and economic shifts changed city and state politics with segregated neighborhoods and increasing conflict often tied to anti-immigrant, racial, and anti-urban sentiments.

SETTING THE STAGE FOR POSTWAR SUBURBAN GROWTH

The explosive growth of cities and the attendant problems of disease, crime, and overcrowding caught the attention of social reformers. From the early settlement houses on New York's Lower East Side to Jane Addams' founding of Hull House in Chicago, to myriad charitable efforts undertaken by churches and philanthropists and self-help movements and by emerging labor unions, cities struggled with these massive economic, population, and social shifts. These civil society groups helped stimulate the Progressive movement, which included the development of social work as a profession. Activist reformers sought to professionalize and manage government and nonprofit services more efficiently and also to assimilate Europeans and rural Southern Blacks and weaken the power of urban political machines.[45]

The growth of urban problems strengthened the suburban impulse. Historian Steven Conn documents urban experts advocating for "decentralization" and new "garden cities" surrounding the crowded and challenging core. Decentralizers like Lewis Mumford, and some founders of the Regional Planning Association of America (RPAA), "shared a hostility to the modern large-scale metropolis . . . and they believed in the need to decentralize industry and population in order to make cities more livable."[46] Regional planning aimed to contain city problems and deconcentrate housing and industry rather than to strengthen the city at the region's core. Conn quotes Mumford from a 1925 *Survey* magazine symposium on regional planning: "The hope of the city lies outside itself. Focus your attention on cities—in which more than half of us live—and the future is dismal."[47]

Although increasingly surrounded by sometimes hostile suburbs, urban populations continued growing. Improvements in public health, especially in water and sanitation, made cities more attractive places to live and invest. Sanitary water systems may have lowered mortality by around 13 percent and produced up to a three-quarters reduction in infant mortality.[48] Continuing growth of manufacturing jobs and unionization, disproportionately located in metropolitan areas, supported rising wages and household incomes.[49]

While core cities grew, suburbs (starting from a smaller base) grew faster. Between 1910 and 1940, central cities increased their national population share from 21.2 percent to 32.5 percent, while the newer suburbs more than doubled, from 7.1 percent to 15.3 percent of the population. Central cities were adding a higher total number of people, but suburban growth rates were much faster—almost double the growth rate of cities.[50]

Suburban growth was facilitated by transportation in the form of streetcars and rail lines, and increasingly through automobiles connecting more distant suburbs to central cities. Innovations in housing construction, especially the wooden balloon-frame method, made single-family home building much cheaper, as did cheap suburban land. And real estate developers used permissive zoning, land use, and incorporation laws to bring many new, small suburban jurisdictions into existence. State legislatures now largely controlled the formation and legal status of cities, often working with real estate interests for suburbanization at the expense of city growth.

Suburban towns often adopted economic and racially exclusionary policies, especially in housing. Zoning and other exclusionary tactics were developed to keep out lower-income and undesired racial and ethnic groups. In his pathbreaking book *The Color of Law*, Richard Rothstein notes that, in Brookline, Massachusetts, which resisted annexation by Boston, "as early as the nineteenth century, deeds . . . forbade resale of property to 'any negro or native of Ireland.'" Berkeley, California, pioneered racially restrictive private deed controls and used those to design some of the first public zoning, aimed in part to allow Berkeley "to prevent 'a negro dance hall' from locating on a 'prominent corner.'"[51]

The Great Depression interrupted movement to cities and the suburbs. Between 1880 and 1930, the urban share of the U.S. population grew by at least 5 percent every decade. But between 1930 and 1940, it slowed to only 1 percent—displaced rural dwellers did not always crowd directly into cities, but they moved elsewhere.

Franklin Delano Roosevelt's (FDR) New Deal pumped a good deal of money into cities through infrastructure projects ranging from the Boulder Dam to New York City's Triborough Bridge, public housing in cities from New York to Pittsburgh to Charleston, employment programs such as the Works Progress Administration (WPA), and support for cooperative or private low-cost housing construction. But New Deal spending was not aimed at cities in particular. Billions were spent in rural areas on farm supports, efforts to stabilize rural populations, and the Civilian Conservation Corps (CCC). Although there was a significant amount of urban spending, much of the New Deal focused on agricultural and rural problems and programs such as the CCC and Tennessee Valley Authority (TVA).[52]

There was some interest in using the New Deal for more comprehensive regional planning, but in practice this was only significant in rural areas with programs such as the TVA. Rexford Tugwell, a central member of FDR's so-called Brain Trust, headed a new Resettlement Administration (RSA) that focused on helping dispossessed farmers but also explored building federally owned satellite cities around major cities, reflecting the decentralizing spirit of the RPAA. But only three such towns were built, and they were sold to private developers in 1949.[53]

During the Great Depression, home prices collapsed by 50 percent or more. Borrowers whose mortgages came due could not refinance due to job and income losses. Small lenders, mostly local savings and loan associations, ended up with devalued properties which they then tried to sell, further depressing home prices. As a result, many of these small financial institutions collapsed, feeding a severe financial crisis affecting the entire banking sector.[54]

Depression-era housing finance programs, including the Home Owners Loan Corporation (HOLC), Federal Housing Administration (FHA), and others, were part of FDR's efforts to stabilize the U.S. banking system. They helped borrowers stretch out mortgages to fifteen- and eventually thirty-year terms to reduce defaults, panics, and bank runs.[55] Americans saved in savings and loans and building societies, so stretching out debt reduced the immediate financial threat to home mortgage portfolios, in turn lowering defaults and bank failures to reduce the pressure on the banking system.

According to Richard K. Green and Susan M. Wachter, the typical mortgage term before the 1930s was ten years or less, with full payment due at the end of the mortgage period (the so-called balloon mortgage) unless the borrower could refinance. Loan-to-value ratios hovered around 50 percent, meaning borrowers needed substantial liquid assets. This meant homeownership was concentrated among higher-income households. Most working people rented. And there were no effective national lending and underwriting practices or standards for construction, so most mortgage loans were held directly by small local financial institutions, with mainly limited local capital pools available for housing investment.[56]

Relief to the banking system was one of HOLC's central purposes, although the Depression pulled down the national homeownership rate between 1930 and 1940 by 4.2 percent.[57] But creating longer-term mortgages with federal oversight and consistent lending standards turned out to be important prerequisites for the postwar housing boom.[58]

HOLC made mortgage loans easier, allowing refinancing when balloon payments came due and private refinancing wasn't available. In 1933, home foreclosures were averaging 1,000 per day, and HOLC restructured over 1 million mortgages in just two years.[59] Lengthening these short-term balloon mortgages steadied the balance sheets of small housing lenders, slowing their failure rate and helping the overall financial system survive.

To carry out this massive refinancing effort across America's diverse housing markets, HOLC developed standardized appraisal methodologies that also contained anti-urban and racially discriminatory practices.[60]

Bonds couldn't finance mortgages for housing holding more than four families, tilting against urban multifamily housing and rentals. HOLC primarily offered short-term financing for restructuring existing mortgages; insurance for new loans was offered by the FHA. Because most existing homeowners were white, there was almost no impact on new homeownership for Blacks and other nonwhites.

But the most pervasive and significant racial impacts came from national home appraisal standards. To create national capital markets and funding for housing, the government needed consistent national standards for housing valuation. HOLC developed color-coded maps, partly as a way of training new government workers in the complex business of home appraisal. There were four categories, with codes ranging from A (best) to D (worst). Each code was assigned a color for mapping, and the worst category—D—was red. So HOLC literally drew "red lines" around certain neighborhoods on city maps, giving birth to the discriminatory practice we now know as redlining.[61]

HOLC was legitimately worried about standards for the quality and useful life of the housing it financed, but its system (spread nationally through its underwriting manuals and training sessions) was biased against older and multifamily housing in denser neighborhoods and by race and ethnicity. Although Black neighborhoods scored the worst, white ethnic and Jewish neighborhoods also were marked down. "The 1939 HOLC map of Newark, New Jersey did not designate a single neighborhood in that city of more than four hundred thousand as worthy of an 'A' rating" including high-income, prosperous Jewish neighborhoods like Weequahic.[62]

HOLC also included explicit racial criteria, especially for reselling of foreclosed properties.[63] Although some scholars attribute the FHA's racially discriminatory practices to HOLC's mapping, more recent scholarship shows the FHA "crafted and implemented its own redlining methodology" before HOLC did. But "staff at both agencies clearly espoused views that were discriminatory, pro segregation, and amount to what is today called redlining." The full impact of these discriminatory housing practices on America's housing markets wouldn't be seen until after World War II.[64]

The Great Depression ended when production ramped up for World War II, and cities received a major boost from war production, especially in the South and West. Mobile, New Orleans, Los Angeles, San Diego, and Seattle all grew rapidly as war production sites, and Los Angeles was the nation's fastest growing metropolitan area during the war. Major industries transformed and grew for war production, while the personnel enlisted for the armed forces created labor openings. Some of these were famously filled by women, immortalized in the image of Rosie the Riveter. But a significant share of the war's industrial labor force came from Black men, many already living in cities and more drawn in from the rural South. Blacks also were drawn out of the South by military service, with around 1 million serving during World War II. Often stationed out of the South or overseas, many Black veterans did not return to the South after the war but went to cities instead.

CONCLUSION

By the end of World War II, the economic stage was set for two seemingly contradictory trends: rapid metropolitan economic growth and prosperity, especially in newly forming suburbs, along with increasing segregation, poverty, and social dislocation in the core cities ringed by those suburbs. The economy underwent substantial structural shifts in the type and location of employment. State governments remained in control of metropolitan governance and favored suburbs and rural areas over cities, and states also administered and controlled education, economic development, and social welfare programs. And federal policy frameworks such as HOLC and FHA had been established, often including explicit racial criteria.

Although these conditions may seem largely the outcome of market economic forces, they were fostered by public policy. The rise of single-family housing in often segregated suburbs was interlinked with the growth of automobile transportation, facilitated by public investments in highways. Growing regional economies found their geographies composed of literally hundreds of local governments, with little coordination or cooperation among them. And tax and social welfare policy disadvantaged core cities further, making political change and formation of coalitions very challenging.

Consumer demand drove suburban growth, but the growth was shaped and subsidized by policies favoring suburbs and the automobile industry that hurt cities. The combination of better construction technology, higher incomes, more consumer durables like stoves and washing machines, car manufacturing, and domestic economic growth were linked by increased road building at the expense of mass transit; subsidies for single-family housing construction that excluded multifamily apartment buildings; and outright racial discrimination in a variety of forms, especially eligibility for mortgages and housing support and exclusionary zoning.

Mostly white suburbs grew, their rapidly increasing property values paying for small, locally controlled school districts because of the American reliance on property taxes to pay for education. In contrast, cities began stagnating with inadequate tax bases for the education and social services needed by their increasingly nonwhite residents. This policy framework channeled the economy's demand for housing and consumer durables disproportionately into suburban single-family houses, which worked to the detriment of cities because they were unable to annex the new suburbs. Thus, as the nation prospered, it simultaneously reinforced the social, economic, and racial isolation of American cities.

The next chapter describes how that urban isolation played out from the 1950s onward, with cities eventually left largely on their own to address inequality and poverty while still being central to innovation, productivity, and growth. A combination of structural economic change, anti-urban federal policy, state governments restricting cities and facilitating suburban growth, and structural racism fed this process. The history helps clarify the paradox of metropolitan-led economic growth and prosperity occurring simultaneously with impoverished, racially segregated, and isolated central cities.

3

ISOLATING AMERICA'S CITIES

From the Economic "Golden Age" to "Two Societies—
One Black, One White"

Aﬀter World War II, the economy shifted to domestic production
and consumption. The boom in housing construction and associated demand for consumer durables and automobiles spurred
significant investments in roads and transportation infrastructure. The
United States dominated the world economy, and commentators spoke of
an emerging American Century and a golden age in the economy.[1]

This growing prosperity was centered on America's cities—or, more
precisely, its metropolitan areas, especially the explosion of suburbs surrounding cities. Fueled by the increasing number of jobs along with favorable tax policies and new forms of finance and consumer credit ranging
from home mortgages to installment purchasing to credit cards suburbs
filled with single-family houses. The suburban share of the population
doubled in twenty years—from 15.3 percent in 1940 to 30.9 percent in 1960.
And by the 2000 census, a majority of all Americans lived in suburbs.

Yet during this golden age, America's older central cities persistently
declined, fueled in part by wealthier households moving to suburbs and
by explicit public policies favoring cars over public transit, and suburban housing over cities. Many central cities stopped growing and suffered
actual population declines. Policies were explicitly based on race, with
many tilted against Black inclusion and equality.

Thus, the golden age of macroeconomic and suburban prosperity
was simultaneously racially and economically biased. Cities dealt with

the negative externalities of economic activity such as crime, poverty, pollution, substandard education, and inadequate housing, while white suburbs reaped the economic benefits that cities create. Explosive urban racial conflict in the late 1960s revealed a nation divided by residential segregation and political isolation. And as economic and average household income growth slowed in the 1970s and beyond, support for equity and inclusion weakened. Cities increasingly were left on their own.

To understand what cities can do now to combat inequality, we have to understand how they became so unequal relative to the suburbs. Changes in industrial structure, anti-city state and federal policies, and pervasive structural racism were the major forces driving this inequality, even as America's economic growth came increasingly from metropolitan regions.

FROM THE WAR ECONOMY TO POSTWAR SUBURBANIZATION

As World War II ended, American cities were thriving. The war spurred production ranging from raw materials to finished goods across industrial sectors—coal and iron ore; military rations, clothing, and shoes; cars and trucks; ships and aircraft; and advanced electronics such as radar and nascent computers. In 1945, military expenditures were 45 percent of U.S. gross domestic product (GDP), with most of that production concentrated either in existing industrial urban areas or in new, emerging cities in the South and West.[2] West Coast cities benefitted from massive investments in shipbuilding and aircraft production and the associated industries that fed them. Meanwhile, traditional industrial cities also prospered: Pittsburgh in steel, Detroit in autos and trucks, Chicago in aircraft components, and shipbuilding all along the East Coast.

These economic changes propelled what one scholar has called the "the greatest sequence of human relocation in American history. At least 57 percent of the population changed residence during the war years, 21 percent of them migrating across county or state lines."[3] Driven by industrialized war production, the war made Americans much more urbanized, especially in the South and West. The urban share of the nation's population grew by less than 1 percent between 1930 and 1940, but it grew by 7.5 percent between 1940 and 1950. In the South, the urban population grew by 11.9 percent in the decade after 1940.[4]

The employment and composition of the workforce also changed. Manufacturing employment grew sharply for war production. And the workforce changed demographically because many working-age men entered military service and women and Blacks entered the civilian labor force in higher numbers. Married women's overall labor force participation increased from 15.6 percent in 1940 to 21.7 percent in 1944. Some women entered manufacturing and were celebrated as the famous Rosie the Riveters, although scholars now think "the war had far less direct influence on female labor supply than was believed."[5]

Although experts feared economic troubles when war spending dropped off, the sharp eight-month recession in 1945 didn't do lasting damage. Annual growth in real GDP averaged over 4.4 percent, and average annual real per capita income grew at 2.25 percent between 1950 and 1970. Driven by a complementary growth of productivity and capital stock, the changeover to consumer goods production, and American dominance of the global economy, real wages grew steadily for a large part of the labor force, while domestic consumption and division of labor fueled continuing growth.[6]

Much of America's growth came from an expanding service economy. Although many think postwar growth was led by expanding manufacturing, that sector peaked as a share of the domestic economy in 1953, with 28.1 percent of U.S. value added produced in manufacturing. Manufacturing continued growing in absolute terms but only as part of overall growth. In fact, it declined steadily as a share of value added—25.4 percent in 1960, 20.5 percent in 1980, down to 12.2 percent in 2010. Services, on the other hand, grew—the combination of finance, business services, education and health care was 20.4 percent of value added in 1960, equaling manufacturing's share in 1970 and reaching 39.6 percent of the U.S. total in 2010.

The same sectoral shifts are evident in employment. Although total U.S. manufacturing employment peaked in absolute terms in 1979, its highest share of total employment occurred much earlier—32 percent of all jobs in 1953. And even at that peak share of manufacturing employment, there were more jobs in the service sector as, in fact, there have always been throughout U.S. history.[7]

The growing economy demanded new managerial and service labor that was fed by a rapid rise in higher education, especially among return-ing (mostly male) veterans making use of the G.I. Bill of Rights (more formally known as the Servicemen's Readjustment Act of 1944). As with other postwar programs, Blacks were excluded from much of the G.I. Bill, in part because state governments administered much of it, includ-ing higher education. In the Jim Crow South, that meant segregation and exclusion of Black veterans from flagship state universities, which had more faculty members, better libraries, and better networks for employ-ment after graduation.[8]

Several factors fueled the rise of suburbs: expansive federal policy for cheap and widespread availability of mortgages, states favoring new sub-urbs over existing cities, cheap cars and expanding roads for them, new homebuilding techniques and real estate business models, and polices locating manufacturing and economic cities outside cities. War produc-tion attracted large numbers of rural residents to older industrial cities. When production shifted to domestic consumption, suburbs swelled with homeowning families who bought consumer durables and cars. (The federal government had prohibited commercial automobile production between February 1942 and October 1945.)

As described in chapter 2, the federal Home Owners Loan Corporation (HOLC) had created national lending standards to manage loan risk on their refinancing, which were shown on detailed neighborhood maps of major cities. Neighborhoods with the greatest default risk were category "D," outlined in red, giving birth to the term "redlining," which was used to distinguish entire neighborhoods on the basis of both economic and racial data.

The growing Federal Housing Administration (FHA) insured new mortgages, fostering a major increase in private lending. And the FHA's underwriting standards included explicit racial criteria. FHA's 1936 underwriters' manual stated "incompatible social and racial groups" should lower a neighborhood's rating because "a change in social or racial occupancy generally leads to instability and a reduction in val-ues." FHA recommended that housing contracts include covenants forbidding resale to Blacks, telling underwriters that racial "deed restrictions" would be even more effective in preserving house values than restrictive zoning.[9]

Incorporating racially discriminatory standards while liberalizing mortgage standards helped ensure that postwar suburbanization would be combined with metropolitan racial segregation. The U.S. government provided a further housing boost through veterans' programs, while states and private real estate developers leveraged public policy to build suburbs surrounding older central cities. These new suburbs would boost economic growth, but incorporating racialized standards also meant that they would be segregated.

Between 1940 and 1960, household homeownership jumped from 43.6 percent to 61.9 percent. One study attributed 40 percent of the increase to easier mortgage terms and government financing assistance, including the G.I. Bill. Designed to reintegrate military veterans to civilian life, the G.I. Bill funded job training and higher education, hospitals and rehabilitation services, unemployment compensation, and homeownership assistance. The Veterans Administration (VA) issued loans with no down payment, with 50 percent of the mortgage guaranteed to the lender. The program became more generous until 1950, when it guaranteed 60 percent of a thirty-year loan.

FHA and VA financing, along with resources released from war production, allowed the private housing sector to take off. In 1946, new non-farm private housing starts more than doubled over 1945, and between 1946 and 1958, annual new starts averaged more than 3.4 times the level in 1945. This was a major change in investment flows. Private residential fixed investment went from 14 percent of all private investment in 1945 to 24 percent in 1946, and 34 percent by 1950; it never fell below a 29 percent share, more than double the share in 1945, until 1966.[10] As H. V. Savitch notes, "people discovered it was as cheap to buy as to rent shelter and quickly took advantage of the benefits." And as capital and demand flowed to single-family housing, it moved away from multifamily and rental housing, the type more often used by low-income people and jurisdictions.[11]

Analysts like Joel Kotkin see suburban growth as simply resulting from "how Americans prefer to live," criticizing political elites who want to "destroy" the suburban way of life.[12] Historian Kenneth Jackson agrees the dominant residential drift in American cities had been toward the periphery for at least a century before the New Deal: "suburbanization was not willed on an innocent peasantry."[13] But consumer choices were and still are shaped by federal and state policy and metropolitan political organization. Initially small suburban communities had significant powers and independence, granted and enforced by state government, which allowed them to shape housing, public education, and the race and class of their residents.[14]

By the 1950s, the suburbs were growing much faster than cities. Between 1950 and 1970, suburbs increased their share of the U.S. population by 14.3 percent, a 61 percent growth rate, and by 1970, suburbs had a higher share of national population than either central cities or rural areas.[15] In the 1970s, many central cities were losing population, but "in contrast, suburban growth stayed relatively strong through the end of the century."[16] Cities like Los Angeles had low housing density through a combination of single-tract homes, networks of highways, and regulations such as those requiring residential apartments and businesses to provide free parking for customers, often in ground-level lots.

Cities also were mostly blocked from annexing the new suburbs springing up around them. Some newer cities grew—, Phoenix went from seventeen to 248 square miles by annexing neighboring areas, capturing around 75 percent of metropolitan growth. But most suburban growth took place outside established city political boundaries, government taxing power, and education systems. As historian Jon Teaford says, "By the early twentieth century, suburbanites had begun carving up the metropolis, and the states had handed them the knife."[17]

Cities were also at a disadvantage because new construction and land at the urban fringe often is cheaper than rehabilitating or replacing existing urban housing. The FHA and VA supported new suburban housing, in effect downgrading virtually all existing housing relative to new construction that followed FHA construction standards. The Federal National Mortgage Association (FNMA, or "Fannie Mae"), created in 1938, purchased insured and conforming mortgages from banks, freeing up capital and allowing more lending for new housing construction. This facilitated a national capital market in housing, allowing investment capital to flow from older Northern cities to suburban development and the growing West and South.

Transportation policy also facilitated suburban growth. Auto dealerships, gas stations, and repair shops expanded rapidly, fueling domestic consumption. address pent-up demand, industry and unions prioritized converting defense production to domestic vehicles; servicing and accommodating new suburbs was a side effect. A 1945 report, *Automobiles in the Postwar Economy*, barely mentions suburban residential patterns as a possible spur for automotive production,[18] even while the car enabled new and often wealthy suburbs across the country, like Grosse Pointe outside Detroit, the Country Club district of Kansas City, Evanston and Elwood Park next to Chicago, and Los Angeles and Orange County.

Along with finance, state policy, and cars, house-building techniques and new real estate business models fed suburban expansion. The Levitt family, homebuilders who started on Long Island outside New York City, developed new standardized construction techniques when they built military housing. They used those techniques in developing Long Island potato farms in a project named "Island Trees" but then changed to "Levittown." Small, standardized houses sold quickly at mass production prices with easy credit—capped interest rates, thirty-year mortgages, insured lending, and high loan-to-value ratios. Many urban renters became suburban buyers. After 1949, Levittown allowed no rentals, only purchases—and only white buyers.[19]

Suburbs came to symbolize American success. Senator Joe McCarthy (D-WI) called urban public housing a "breeding ground for Communists" while praising Levittown's private sector orientation as a superior form of living.[20] In 1959, then vice president Richard Nixon confronted Soviet premier Nikita Khrushchev at a Moscow exposition. In what became known as the "kitchen debate," held in a mock-up of an American suburban house, Nixon argued, "We have many different manufacturers and many different kinds of washing machines so that the housewives have a choice . . . Would it not be better to compete in the relative merits of washing machines than in the strength of rockets?"[21]

Many developers took advantage of interlocking policy supports, and suburbs mushroomed around central cities across the country, spurring demand for refrigerators, furniture, and washing machines. Real spending on consumer durable goods shot up by 160 percent between 1945 and 1950.[22] Although lower-density suburbs developed retail and service sector employment, most jobs were still in core cities. At first, suburban residents commuted into the central city for work. But over time, jobs grew in the new communities as transportation costs fell for trucks hauling freight using the new free highways, and manufacturing and logistics jobs dispersed with these lower transportation costs, thus facilitating the use of trucks instead of railroads or water transport.

In a self-reinforcing process, "firms followed growing suburban consumer demand and lower suburban wages and land costs."[23] People left cities to live nearer to new jobs and take advantage of new schools and houses, eventually creating what urbanist Joel Garreau labeled "edge cities"—large employment centers, often based on the beltways surrounding central cities, which featured not only retail jobs but higher-end professional service employment.[24]

Metropolitan transportation networks couldn't keep up with demand, especially because commuters in less-dense housing areas used cars, while public policy tilted away from rail and streetcars in favor of buses and private cars. Between 1919 and 1939, with financing from General Motors (GM), Firestone Tire and Rubber, and other companies, New York City reduced its 1,344 miles of trolley tracks to 337 miles. By 1950, GM had replaced over 100 streetcar systems across the country with their buses, supported by industries that made and serviced tires and vehicles and distributed gasoline. Streetcar lines went bankrupt, and cars made city streets more congested; historian Peter Norton estimates that if only 10 percent of riders were in private cars, the resulting congestion would have kept streetcars from running on schedule. But sprawling housing sharply reduced population density in the suburbs, further advantaging cars over mass transit.[25]

Pro-commuter pressure and Cold War fears of nuclear attack led to authorization in 1956 of the "The National System of Interstate and Defense Highways," which continued favoring suburbs over cities.[26] Highway building in part reflected a legacy of rural areas seeking transportation improvements for agricultural production and connecting isolated rural communities. But it also increasingly created infrastructure favoring suburban commuters and bypassing central cities to improve traffic speed and long-distance truck traffic.

State and local subsidies to move jobs out of the cities also favored suburbs, feeding more central city decline. Suburban jurisdictions competed aggressively for employers with property tax breaks, zoning and regulatory relief, rail and road transportation connections, and specialized and subsidized infrastructure. State development agencies directed subsidies away from central cities toward suburban industrialization and new one-story "greenfield" plants. Although the city of Detroit is identified with the motor vehicle industry, production was moving out of the city: "between 1945 and 1957 the Big Three auto companies built twenty-five new plants in the metropolitan Detroit area, all of them in suburban communities."[27]

RACIAL SEGREGATION AND THE GROWTH OF "TWO SOCIETIES—ONE BLACK, ONE WHITE"

Despite American leaders' and manufacturers' claims that suburbia is a superior way of life, the Soviets—and many Americans—noted that racial discrimination was strengthened by the suburbs and pro-suburb policies.[28] As suburbs developed, they increased racial segregation in urban areas, making American central cities poorer, with substandard public goods such as housing and education.

A typical American metropolitan region developed into a poor, disproportionately minority central city ringed by often hostile, wealthier, and dominantly white suburbs. These suburbs captured gains in property values, rising household incomes, and employment while leaving the city to deal with the negative side effects of wealth creation. Federal and state policies facilitated this process, leaving cities to address concentrated social problems largely on their own. Economists sometimes view metropolitan areas as being composed of cities and suburbs working in partnership to obtain the economic benefits of cities. But American metros in practice distribute the costs and benefits of urban production and consumption unequally, with suburbs taking many of the benefits and leaving the costs to cities.[29]

Residential real estate financing policies and regulations that emerged from the 1930s and 1940s addressed problems of recessionary demand and the collapse of banking institutions. But the system also hardwired racial discrimination into housing through redlining, racially restrictive deed covenants, and exclusionary zoning. When the postwar surge of housing finance driven by easy mortgage money, including the G.I. Bill, flowed through this system, it produced highly segregated housing in America's metropolitan areas.[30]

Racial restrictions on federal housing finance were so pervasive that the specter of integrated neighborhoods could halt federal support. Richard Rothstein found that "if a Black family could afford to buy into a white neighborhood without government help, the FHA would refuse to insure future mortgages even to whites in that neighborhood, because it [the neighborhood] was now threatened with integration."[31]

Racially discriminatory housing policies were implemented daily by the residential real estate industry. Brokers in Chicago, San Francisco, New York, and other metropolitan areas engaged in a variety of discriminatory practices, from emphasizing a potential home's defects only to Black buyers to requiring excessive initial financial paperwork from Blacks (but often not whites) and then delaying processing the paperwork, to outright refusals to sell to Black buyers. Only 8 percent of ninety Chicago-area brokers surveyed in 1968 said that they would sell to Blacks without any restrictions, while 83 percent said they would never represent or help Blacks buy a home in an all-white area.[32]

Brokers' professional industry relationships also contributed to racial segregation. White-dominated professional associations controlled the agent-licensing process, and Blacks were effectively blocked from getting or using real estate licenses. Black real estate brokers who finally managed to obtain a license were excluded from suburban associations, and white brokers told researchers of their personal unwillingness to work with Black brokers. A 1962 national survey of American real estate brokerage associations reported only eighteen boards with one or more Black members, out of 1,410 associations.[33]

Brokers working with homebuyers and their communities of mostly first-time white homeowners found and generated resistance to racially integrated housing. This was not only because of long-standing bigotry or loyalty to another ethnic group but also in part because of rational economic reasons—having Black homeowners in their communities created fears of lower white-owned property values as a result of racism's impacts on housing values.

Private neighborhood associations incorporated all these biases, often becoming a vehicle for racial fears and exclusion, both at the community level and increasingly as a political force. J. C. Nichols, the pathbreaking developer in the Kansas City metro, required racially restrictive resale covenants and homeowner membership in associations that enforced those covenants. Suburban housing was sold both as physical and as social shelter and as a new segregated community for residents. As sociologist Kevin Gotham writes, the "entire package" would "include schools, churches, hospitals and health care, entertainment values and other cultural amenities in an all-white, racially homogenous neighborhood."[34]

In Detroit, many white homeowner associations often were ethnically similar and mapped closely to Catholic parish boundaries, increasing their social solidarity. They became central to mayoral elections, eager to protect their housing values, homogenous neighborhoods, and schools. Historian Thomas Sugrue notes in Detroit that "hundreds of thousands of working-class whites became homeowners for the first time" and many "feared . . . an influx of Blacks would imperil their precarious investments." This fear was stoked by real estate agents who adopted so-called blockbusting techniques to increase their profits. Selling or rumors about selling just one house to a Black family would break up all-white blocks and neighborhoods by panicking white homeowners into selling cheaply, with agents profiting when the house was resold.[35]

Suburban racial segregation was reinforced not only by home associations and real estate brokers but also by controlling public schools. A key suburban attraction was keeping control over racially exclusive public schools. This became more pressing for whites after the landmark 1954 Supreme Court case of *Brown v. Board of Education*, where "separate but equal" schools were ruled unconstitutional. *Brown* did not cover suburban schools in politically separate, virtually all-white communities, so metropolitan de facto school segregation could be maintained when politically independent suburbs controlled their schools.

Local school financing also furthered racial segregation. American K–12 public education is heavily funded by local property taxes and with some state aid. Rapidly increasing suburban housing and property values allowed generous funding for suburban schools. But the forces that inflated funding for suburban schools deflated them for city schools. City property tax revenues stagnated and fell, undercutting public education spending and all municipal services, which in turn drove down city fiscal capacity through economic stagnation.

In addition to real estate sales practices, racial segregation was also reinforced by suburban exclusionary zoning, which limited multifamily housing, required large lot sizes, and charged high development and related fees. Because property taxes and mortgage interest payments are deductible from state and federal income taxes, the federal tax code in effect subsidized suburbs over cities.

Racial segregation was also reinforced by public housing policies. Housing assistance for the poor was largely confined to cities and not allowed in suburbs. Federal public housing programs were linked to "slum clearance," by definition putting them with existing concentrations of substandard housing, not greenfield suburbs. Receipt of federal funds was conditioned on a local jurisdiction forming a housing agency, which as Jackson notes, many suburban leaders didn't do. "A suburb that did not wish to tarnish its exclusive image by having public housing within its precincts could simply refuse to create a housing agency, and no local housing authority from another jurisdiction and no national official could force it to do otherwise."[36]

So a wide range of economic and cultural factors encouraged white suburban growth and entrenched racially exclusionary housing finance, economic development, tax policy, and education policies in American metros. By the 1960s, metropolitan areas were highly segregated, both within cities and between cities and suburbs. Between 1940 and 1970, racial segregation indexes in thirty large U.S. cities remained very high, at over 85 percent. And racial segregation increased as whites left cities when Blacks moved in. Economist Leah Boustan found that between 1940 and 1970, each Black arrival in a city was associated with 2.7 white people leaving, most of them moving to nearby suburbs.[37]

So America's economic golden age after World War II, with sustained high economic growth, simultaneously produced a nation of highly unequal and racially segregated metropolitan areas, with wealthier white suburbs surrounding troubled central cities. It was a recipe for conflict, and the 1960s brought both the Civil Rights movement and urban rioting and insurrection to metropolitan areas.

By the 1960s, metropolitan racial segregation had hardened. The "spatial organization of American cities in the years after World War II" was based on race and white privilege.[38] But the 1960s were also a time of hope for cities when America's race problem was confronted by a broad-based Civil Rights movement personified by Dr. Martin Luther King, Jr., a movement that aimed to obtain economic fairness for Black workers and the poor and political rights for excluded Blacks.[39]

The 1950s had brought hope that conditions would improve for workers and the poor. In 1958, liberal economist John Kenneth Galbraith observed that only about 8 percent of the U.S. population was in poverty, saying poverty was "no longer . . . a universal or massive affliction."[40] But in 1962, Michael Harrington's *The Other America* estimated that 25 percent of Americans lived in poverty. President John F. Kennedy began focusing on the issue, planning for a "war on poverty" largely focused on white rural poverty. Kennedy's initial planning neglected cities.[41]

In his 1964 State of the Union address, President Lyndon Johnson announced an "unconditional war on poverty." Johnson was a young New Dealer under Franklin Roosevelt, getting his political start administering youth employment programs in Texas, and his ambition was to continue the New Deal's sweeping work. But Johnson's program, dubbed the Great Society, was inspired, pushed, and pressured to do more by the Civil Rights movement. The movement first focused on equalizing legal rights—voting rights; desegregating public schools; access to public accommodations in transportation, hotels, and restaurants; and the formal end of Jim Crow laws. But ending housing, employment, and economic segregation rose rapidly on the agenda, and the movement's emphasis on actions to combat concentrated Black poverty became a major force, pushing Johnson to more aggressive action.

Racial and gender discrimination—patriarchal policies that consistently assigned unpaid family care and education to women while reserving the best jobs for white men—also was part of America's economic golden age, with its seeming paradox of increased national wealth and persistent poverty. Women and Blacks were blocked from much of the growing economy's benefits through direct employment discrimination, substandard education, and lack of educational opportunities.

The G.I. Bill, which provided mostly male and white veterans with higher education and occupational training, widened the racial education gap. States controlled implementation and Southern Jim Crow states refused Black access to white colleges and universities, confining them to underfunded historically Black colleges and universities (HBCUs).[42] States also would not allow integrated on-the-job training for skilled crafts and restricted Black enrollment in higher-level technical schools. The segregated housing and suburban policies discussed earlier reduced city tax revenue for public schools and also prevented Blacks from crossing political boundaries to attend better-funded white suburban schools.

Unionization and tight labor markets helped improve overall Black employment outcomes. In the 1950s, Black male earnings in the Detroit metropolitan area were about 80 percent of white male wages because of industrial growth along with high levels of unionization through the United Auto Workers (UAW).[43] Detroit boasted one of the highest ratios of Black–white wages in the postwar period. The UAW and other industrial unions pushed the American Federation of Labor and Congress of Industrial Unions (AFL-CIO) to adopt strong antidiscrimination policy. But other unions, especially in construction and the building trades, continued to practice racially exclusionary policies. And even in unionized manufacturing, Blacks were relegated to the lowest-paying and most dangerous jobs.[44]

The combination of labor market discrimination and suburban racial segregation led to accumulated disadvantage. The 1940–1970 migration of southern Blacks to Northern cities "reduced upward mobility in northern cities in the long run, with the largest effects on black men." Whites moved from integrated cities and put their children into segregated suburban public or private schools, concentrating Black families in poorer neighborhoods with worse schools and leading to longer-term negative impacts on Black children. Over the 120 years between 1880 and 2000, white children were more likely to be upwardly mobile with far better chances of escaping the bottom of the income distribution than were Black children.[45]

The economists, policy planners, and social scientists in the Kennedy and Johnson administrations recognized the existence of racial discrimination. Relying in part on standard economic theory, however, they explained persistent poverty more through two other factors that were linked to the social impacts of discrimination—a lack of adequate education among Blacks, and a "culture of poverty," which was seen to undercut motivation and a desire to work and succeed. Believing racial employment discrimination to be economically irrational, policies focused more on improving the individual human capital of excluded Blacks and others so rational employers would hire them. There also were more general appeals to reduce bigotry.[46]

Still, Johnson's historic program was the most sweeping since the New Deal. The Civil Rights Act of 1964 established voting rights and outlawed racial discrimination in transportation, public accommodations, and employment. It included the Economic Opportunity Act, which created the Job Corps and innovative local programs. In 1965, further Great Society programs created a new cabinet agency, the Department of Housing and Urban Development (HUD); passed the Voting Rights Act, which subjected discriminatory voting districts to federal oversight; and passed Medicare (federal health insurance for people over age sixty-five) and Medicaid (health insurance for the poor). Federal welfare policies also expanded—the number of families receiving Aid to Dependent Families with Children (AFDC) almost tripled in the decade between 1963 and 1973 through a combination of administrative changes and increased funding.[47]

Reducing poverty, especially through increasing education for the poor and fighting racial discrimination, was seen as compatible with steady macroeconomic growth. In 1966, Walter Heller, the head of Johnson's Council of Economic Advisers (CEA) declared "the age of the economist," envisioning higher overall productivity and growth flowing from increased education and racial inclusion.[48] Better educated individuals would contribute to macroeconomic growth through higher productivity and optimal use of the nation's labor force, without any specific focus on cities' economic role.

Programs emerging from Congress paid some attention to cities, through the creation of HUD, funding for education in low-income districts, and the Model Cities program. But the Great Society didn't change home mortgage subsidies and racially exclusionary housing policies, tax-favored treatment for single-family homeowners, or highway and suburban road building. Nor did it support much direct job creation. The dollar value of policies and tax subsidies going to suburbs, along with the regulations and polices favoring them, vastly outweighed the targeted spending for new antipoverty programs.

Cities were further isolated by disturbances starting in the early 1960s, peaking in the "long hot summer" of 1967 (including forty-three people killed in Detroit) and after King's assassination in April 1968. Coming at a time when the U.S. economy was slowing down and the golden age was coming to an end, concentrated economic problems and social and political isolation became the norm for many American cities.

The Civil Rights movement was expanding its focus to include Northern economic and housing segregation, meeting with hostile and sometimes violent responses from white residents. In August 1966, King's fair housing march in Chicago's all-white Marquette Park neighborhood was met by hostile whites, with one person carrying a sign saying, "King would look good with a knife in his back." A rock struck King in the head, and he later said, "I have seen many demonstrations in the South, but I have never seen anything so hostile and so hateful as I've seen here today."[49]

The economic, housing, and social trends of the 1950s and 1960s were leading to what sociologists Douglas Massey and Nancy Denton labeled "hypersegregation," measured by the "dissimilarity index"—"the percentage of Blacks who would have to move to achieve . . . the racial composition of the metropolitan area as a whole." By 1970, the dissimilarity index for regions with the thirty largest Black populations averaged 75.3 percent, and it was higher for many large metros—New York (81 percent), Boston (81 percent), Atlanta (82 percent), Detroit (88 percent), Los Angeles (91 percent), and Chicago (92 percent). To achieve racial representation mirroring the percentage of Blacks in the overall region, 80 percent to 90 percent of Black households would have needed to move.[50]

The Johnson administration responded in 1966 with a proposed federal ban against discrimination in the sale and rental of housing, which would have pushed federal law deeply into state and local powers over real estate and provided a major counterweight against suburban racial segregation.[51] Congress had passed previous civil rights legislation but balked when it came to housing desegregation. Suburban homeowners, the real estate industry, and mayors and governors all objected.

Big-city Democratic mayors began defecting from Johnson over his antipoverty and housing programs. New federal antipoverty programs sometimes bypassed mayors and governors, awarding funds directly to community organizations. Chicago Mayor Richard Daley, a key Johnson ally, resisted these community policies and sought injunctions against King's Chicago fair housing campaign.[52] The agitation against fair housing laws grew so strong that long-time liberal Illinois Democratic senator Paul Douglas attributed his 1966 Senate loss to white ethnic opposition to fair housing.[53] A much weaker version of Johnson's fair housing bill eventually passed in 1968, but it has been viewed by some scholars as "intentionally designed" to not work.[54]

Similar dynamics played out in states. Many states opposed expanding fair housing laws and desegregating schools beyond central city boundaries. In 1969, Nelson Rockefeller, the moderate Republican governor of New York, signed the nation's first statewide antibusing legislation, although it was overturned by a federal court one year later. Strong suburban and rural alliances in the New York legislature overturned efforts to limit desegregation at state colleges. A similar process played out with Rockefeller's attempts to build desegregated suburban public housing, and he eventually signed legislation allowing villages and towns to veto housing projects.[55]

Many states took no positive action or actively fought school desegregation and suburban public housing. Governor William Milliken led Michigan to overturn a lower court order to desegregate Detroit metropolitan area schools through cross-jurisdictional busing. In the 1974 *Milliken v. Bradley* case, a 5–4 majority of the Supreme Court ruled that in spite of *Brown v. Board of Education*, busing couldn't be ordered in the absence of explicit on-the-record policies allowing racial segregation.[56]

The reluctance to fight housing desegregation underscores the Great Society's constraints on urban policy. There was little focus on direct job creation or on vigorous antidiscrimination efforts in employment. Suburban communities were not desegregated; racially discriminatory real estate practices remained in place; and public housing was effectively confined to poor, often Black urban neighborhoods.

Residential segregation meant public schooling, dependent on property taxes and local school board control, remained segregated because de facto segregation was permitted by the *Milliken* decision. Transportation policy emphasized road building, not urban mass transit or connecting city residents with suburban jobs. And urban economic development focused on the most economically deprived areas of central cities through narrowly targeted community development corporations (CDCs) and other Office of Economic Opportunity (OEO)–related efforts. These areas were among the least promising places to expand employment and investment.

Stung by urban riots, in 1968, President Johnson's National Advisory Commission on Civil Disorders, better known as the Kerner Commission, warned the nation was heading toward a "system of apartheid" and toward "two societies, one Black, one white—separate and unequal."[57]

Despite calls for prompt action, the nation backed away from the challenge of greater equality, driven in part by the end of the economic golden age and in part by political forces rejecting any stronger federal role for addressing the problems the Kerner Commission so eloquently identified.

Slowing prosperity after 1970 also meant federal and state governments reduced support to cities, even though suburbs depended economically on their overall metropolitan economy. Innovation, economies of scale, agglomeration—all the benefits economists see from cities—were taking place throughout this period. It was the residence of many workers that changed—between 1960 and 1990, "the percent[age] of workers who worked outside of their county of residence grew by over 200 percent."[58]

Where wealth was created became increasingly separated from where wealth was consumed. Commuters had higher-income jobs than city residents.[59] Although jobs grew rapidly in the suburbs, they initially were mostly household-related service and retail employment, with higher-paying business service employment emerging as the suburbs matured. Cities' fiscal problem, reinforced by state and federal policy, was that suburbs benefitted from metropolitan economic strengths, while core cities lost tax and fiscal capacity to the suburbs, especially for education but also for other public services. Although metropolitan areas were generating jobs, the rewards went primarily to suburban residents.[60]

THE END OF THE GOLDEN AGE AND THE ISOLATION OF CITIES

By the late 1960s, cracks were appearing in America's golden age. Inflation rose, driven budgetarily by Johnson's deficit financing of Great Society programs and defense spending for the Vietnam War. But economic problems were not only budgetary, and the changing structure and position of the U.S. economy helped limit options for the nation and cities. These economic changes were coupled with political disruption and white reaction against civil rights, housing and schooling integration, and the Great Society. Together, they locked America's cities into an isolated position, leaving them largely on their own to face economic stagnation, growing social distress, segregation and poverty, and an indifferent or hostile political and policy environment.

Richard Nixon was elected president in 1968 with a margin of less than 1 percent of the popular vote after Johnson didn't run. Issues of race were prominent in the overall campaign, with segregationist Democrat governor George Wallace of Alabama winning 13.5 percent of the vote as an independent candidate.

Nixon immediately began reversing many of Johnson's Great Society programs, reducing a direct federal role in favor of empowering states and emphasizing revenue sharing through block grants rather than categorical programs. Eligibility for revenue sharing, especially in the Community Development Block Grant (CDBG) program, was expanded to smaller suburban and rural towns. In addition to reduced spending, separately funding individual jurisdictions in a metropolitan area contributed to fragmentation and city isolation. Suburban growth had caused the number of local governments in standard metropolitan statistical areas (SMSAs) to mushroom. In 1972, there were 272 local governments in the Denver SMSA, 304 in Houston, 698 in Pittsburgh, and 1,172 in Chicago.[61]

The weak U.S. economy also hurt cities as inflation rose to 6.2 percent in 1971, the highest since 1947. Nixon's Secretary of Agriculture, Earl Butz, implemented a dramatic set of subsidies to large-scale agriculture to increase supply and hold down price increases.[62] Inflation and unemployment occurred together for the first time, challenging conventional economics and Keynesian policies. The recession started in 1969, but prices didn't fall. Stagflation—persistent inflation occurring with slow or negative economic growth—was made worse by the 1973 oil shock recession when the Organization of Arab Petroleum Exporting States' (OAPEC) oil embargo after Israel's victory in the 1973 Arab-Israeli War spiked oil prices[63]. The persistence of inflation puzzled economists and the Nixon administration, driving them to go off the gold standard and impose economy-wide wage and price controls in August 1971.

Although the oil shock had major impacts on the economy, the end of the golden age already was emerging because slow labor productivity growth and rising input costs squeezed corporate profits. Demographic changes and inflation boosted Social Security and Medicare spending. The combination of anti-inflation policies, moderating food prices, and increased social welfare spending helped Nixon achieve his 1972 landslide reelection, but it also set the stage for further economic deterioration when the oil shock hit in 1973.[64]

Nixon's hostility to cities continued. After his reelection, he instructed aides to "flush Model Cities" and wind down Johnson's urban development and Great Society programs.[65] Nixon's policies hurt cities' fiscal capacity and ability to raise revenue, while their costs grew. Suburbs captured the lion's share of metropolitan property and other taxes, while their expenditures were heavily concentrated in education relative to central cities' more widespread service demands. If cities reacted by raising taxes, they risked increasing white flight to suburbs, further concentrating the urban poor and reducing their property values and tax base.[66]

Nixon emphasized "Black capitalism" rather than government programs for aiding cities (his 1968 Democratic opponent, Hubert Humphrey, had called for a multibillion-dollar domestic "Marshall Plan.") Nixon's economic adviser Alan Greenspan, later chair of the Federal Reserve, wrote that Black militancy was "an attack on America's system of free enterprise and individual rights," reinforcing Nixon's desire to eliminate race-specific compensatory programs. Nixon did support minority business ownership and created the Office of Minority Business Enterprise.[67]

Federal spending focused not on direct funding to cities but on broader revenue sharing among states and local governments, including many affluent suburbs. Block grants spread available funds over a wider pool of jurisdictions, including many suburbs that didn't cooperate with central cities on policies and spending, especially in housing and education.

Limited federal funds were further diluted by state and local governments using them to substitute for their own revenues rather than increasing their own efforts. States eventually used an average of 64.3 percent of their revenue-sharing funds for tax or revenue substitution, while the four most urban states (California, Illinois, Massachusetts, and New York) "used 100 percent of their revenue sharing funds for substitution purposes," not for expansion of urban programs.[68] Suburban power in state legislatures meant much of this spending went to more affluent areas. In effect, the revenue pie was shrinking while also being redistributed to smaller and often more affluent governments at the expense of cities.

In addition to continued political and fiscal isolation, cities were hurt by cyclical and structural economic shocks. Several negative macroeconomic factors hit urban economies: rapid declines in manufacturing output and employment, high costs from the oil shock inflation, increasing foreign competition in sectors like steel and motor vehicles, stagnant productivity and profit margins, loss of more affluent households and overall population to suburbs and the Sunbelt, disinvestment in older cities by U.S. firms, and a deep cyclical recession in the mid-1970s. Domestic U.S. steel production fell by 32 percent between 1970 and 1985. By 1980, U.S. auto firms were losing billions, while "the industry had . . . moved 37.2 percent of its production abroad."[69]

The oil shocks and growing international economic competition also revealed that the postwar international system dominated by the United States was running out of steam. (Robert Beauregard refers to the period between 1945 and the 1973 recession as "the short American Century" in a sardonic echo of Henry Luce's earlier claims of American global dominance.[70]) Faced with slowing or even declining productivity growth, falling profits, inflation, and domestic pressures for social welfare spending and wage increases, the leading Western nations found their interests diverging more and more, with the "breakdown of the post-war system of international regulation" that had been established at Bretton Woods.[71] These economic uncertainties unsettled the U.S. economy, fueling a range of problems from volatile capital markets to contentious labor negotiations, to consumer anger at higher inflation and economic recession.

Cities took a double hit: they lost government revenue while suffering major negative effects from cyclical and structural economic forces. Job losses hit cities not only in the aggregate but also in relation to their suburban metropolitan neighbors. Between 1977 and 1987, U.S. central cities saw their manufacturing jobs decline by 22.9 percent, while suburban manufacturing declined by only 4.6 percent.[72] In the Chicago metropolitan area, overall manufacturing jobs fell by 33 percent, while the city's regional share of manufacturing employment sank by 52 percent.

Faced with indifferent or hostile federal and state governments, uncooperative suburbs, and sharp changes in the macroeconomy and their own industrial structure, cities were forced inward for economic development. Antipoverty efforts rooted in the Great Society emphasized neighborhood community and economic development, including creating neighborhood-focused CDCs. Exemplified by the Bedford-Stuyvesant Restoration Corporation in Brooklyn (a project advocated by Robert Kennedy and supported by the Ford Foundation), CDCs became a key element in urban development strategy.[73]

CDCs hoped to attract investment and create jobs for local residents, but over time they were driven by tax policy and weak results in business and job creation to move more into housing construction and rehabilitation. From the start, CDCs were bound to fail in their goal to create substantial local employment, aiming to create jobs in economically depressed areas. Journalist Nicholas Lemann wrote, "[U]rban slums have never been home to many businesses . . . to try to create a lot of new economic activity in the poor neighborhoods is to swim against the great sweeping tide of urban life in America."[74]

Along with CDCs, cities used tax relief to attract investment, both by reducing property and other tax rates and also by offering company-specific tax breaks, copying policies pioneered by Southern states to lure companies away from the North. Newark, New Jersey used all of its initial federal revenue-sharing allocation to cut property taxes, hoping (and largely failing) to lure new investment and housing development. Federal and state governments increasingly turned to tax policy rather than direct investment or job creation for both housing and economic development. Critics saw these as stripping current and future revenue from city budgets while failing to produce large economic impacts, but cities had few other economic tools at their disposal.

John Mollenkopf pointed to a persistent tension in these city growth strategies. Successful urban renewal programs to build highways and large office concentrations and raze poor slum neighborhoods required "sufficiently strong local coalitions" and increased government powers. But those powers were used by a city's "pro-growth coalition" to place "tremendous costs on central city residents," which in turn "triggered severe tensions both within and outside the growth alliance." Budgetary austerity, or at least shifting funds from social spending to economic development and social control, created further tensions in cities trying to grow their downtown office sectors and simultaneously manage social disruption related to poverty.[75]

By the late 1970s, the national impulse to help cities through the Great Society programs had diminished. New York City teetered on the verge of bankruptcy in 1975, when its economy declined and its expenditures outstripped revenues. Even though many analysts feared the impact of bankruptcy on national credit and financial markets, President Gerald Ford initially refused any federal assistance (leading to the famous headline in the tabloid New York *Daily News*: "Ford to City: Drop Dead.")

But there was bipartisan skepticism about cities. Compare the Kerner Commission's stark warnings in 1968 about an emerging American "apartheid" that could result in "two nations—one Black, one white" with the 1980 report—just twelve years later—from Democratic President Jimmy Carter's Commission for a National Agenda for the Eighties. In the latter commission's analysis of urban issues, it stated that "there are no 'national urban problems' only an endless variety of local ones." The commission was "skeptical of narrowly defined, local economic development efforts" and recommended that the government should remove "barriers to mobility" that prevented migration out of cities and even provide "migration assistance to those who wish and need it."[76]

CONCLUSION

American cities, extolled by urban economists as the drivers of prosperity and the source of economic innovation, didn't capture the full benefits of postwar metropolitan economic growth. Cities couldn't tap rising property values or superior public education systems in their surrounding and sometimes hostile suburbs. Many feared taxing suburban residents or were prevented from doing so by their state legislatures, often controlled by rural and suburban interests. Cities were prevented from annexing surrounding developments, while the creation of new suburbs increased metropolitan political and economic fragmentation. Through spending cuts and revenue sharing, federal and state governments had dispersed limited fiscal resources to other governments.

Metropolitan problems—crime, pollution, and substandard housing and education—were concentrated in core cities. These problems were exacerbated and partly caused by deep and wide racial segregation in employment and housing. Slowing economic growth and industrial and employment changes put many working households under stress. And cities and metropolitan areas—from Boston to Charlotte, to Louisville, to Detroit—became bitterly divided over housing segregation and the closely associated problem of de facto segregated metropolitan public schooling, battling over proposed remedies, including school busing across political boundaries.[77] Faced with economic change, inadequate federal resources and policy, hostile suburban and state governments, and continuing structural racism, cities were increasingly left on their own when macroeconomic growth slowed. They responded in different ways when they tried to devise resilient equitable policies and quality jobs.

We now turn to three important cities that attempted to increase equality—New York City, Detroit, and Los Angeles—to illustrate how cities responded to these complex challenges. Assessing their successes and failures will help us understand and assess their future options—and the options for the nation—to achieve a more equitable and economically sustainable future.

4

NEW YORK CITY

From Social Democracy to "A Tale of Two Cities"

In September 2008, the Municipal Assistance Corporation (MAC, known popularly as Big MAC) voted itself out of existence. MAC and the Emergency Financial Control Board (EFCB) were created to prevent New York City's bankruptcy in 1975 by marketing debt and controlling budgetary actions by New York's elected officials. Critics saw MAC and New York's austerity policies as an antidemocratic Wall Street tool, signaling the "real locus of power in the budgetary process has shifted to financial and business elites."[1]

But to the public, New York remained one of the country's most liberal cities. How does that reputation square with the city's postcrisis fiscal experience? Even though a later mayor, Bill de Blasio, focused on inequality, he lacked a coherent progressive economic development strategy. And while the city struggled with the COVID-19 pandemic, Eric Adams's 2021 mayoral victory came while unions, community groups, and other progressive advocates argued over housing regulation, jobs, and economic development without a unified agenda.

THE FISCAL CRISIS, AUSTERITY, THE RISE OF FINANCE, AND RACIAL DIVISION

Late on October 16, 1975, New York City Mayor Abe Beame approved a statement to default on bonds and file for bankruptcy in state court.

MAC had aimed to reassure investors by converting some city taxes to state revenues and dedicating them to bond repayments. But private capital hadn't filled the investment gap, and MAC couldn't sell enough of the restructured longer-term debt. By September, no large banks, including those in New York City, would purchase MAC paper even at ever-higher interest rates.[2] Fearing abrogation of their labor contracts and collective bargaining rights, the United Federation of Teachers (UFT) stepped in to avoid city bankruptcy. Last-minute negotiations led to the UFT pension fund purchasing $150 million of MAC bonds, allowing the city to pay bills due the next day, so Mayor Beame didn't issue the already-approved bankruptcy statement.[3]

Budget overseers had already ordered city spending cuts, including the first-ever tuition at the city university, raising subway fares, and wage freezes and layoffs. In June 1975, firefighters staged sickouts, while sanitation workers conducted wildcat strikes, leaving hundreds of trash fires burning around the city. Off-duty police officers rallied at City Hall, with around 300 of them blocking traffic on the nearby Brooklyn Bridge.[4]

No matter how deep the austerity, private investors rejected MAC bonds, and the federal government continued withholding assistance. In September 1975, the state-created EFCB had brought sweeping powers over city government and finances, including "the power to remove the mayor and other officials if they defied its policies."[5] But private investment stability did not return until December, after reluctant federal approval of loan guarantees tied to Treasury Department oversight of the city budget.

The turmoil was blamed on irresponsible spending and budget practices going back to the 1950s and Mayor Robert Wagner (1954–1965). Budgets relied on one-shot revenues, manipulating the timing of tax receipts and city expenditures, and short-term borrowing to cover operating revenues and satisfy political demands. These practices were exacerbated by Mayor John Lindsay's (1966–1973) increased spending on Black and Hispanic communities along with generous union settlements, until the fiscal crisis erupted in 1975.[6]

But major economic shifts lay behind the crisis, not just the lack of budgetary discipline. Prior to the crisis, New York's economy was battered by two national recessions (December 1969 to November 1970, and November 1973 to March 1975), which came during a period of deep structural economic change. Between 1969 and 1976, the city lost "a sixth

of the city's employment base." All industries lost jobs, especially manufacturing, which fell by over 300,000 jobs.[7]

These economic shifts were coupled with dramatic population change,
driven by two factors: suburban growth and immigration. Like other
postwar American cities, the New York region saw explosive suburban growth. The archetypal suburb of Levittown grew out of a former
Long Island potato farm thirty-two miles from Times Square. Highway
construction and state assistance to the privately owned Long Island
Railroad (LIRR) facilitated commuting into the city, aiding suburban
development.

Suburban growth was directly linked to a significant change in the
city's population, with more affluent white families increasingly living in
the suburbs and parallel growth of the nonwhite, poorer population in the
city. Although the city's total population held relatively steady between
1950 and 1970, the white population fell from 90.2 percent to 76.6 percent,
with nonwhite in-migration and natural increase offsetting the white
decline. Around 684,000 Puerto Ricans migrated to New York as well,
while Blacks had migrated to New York in successive waves.

Economic development subsidies also hurt the city. Manufacturing
employment in New York collapsed, while corporate offices relocated to
suburban locations—"a giant sucking sound," according to the Regional
Plan Association (RPA). Between 1955 and 1980, firms like IBM, Texaco,
Xerox, and PepsiCo moved to suburban locations, often assisted by local
and state governments. Nonetheless, the city retained a significant corporate sector, especially in finance and banking and their ancillary services
(legal, accounting, printing).[8]

New York shared these tensions of manufacturing loss and industrial
change, rapid suburbanization, and increasing racial polarization with
other American cities. To pay for operations and expanding government
employment and city services, New York used unsustainable financial
practices. Between 1961 and 1975, total city debt almost tripled. But even
worse, short-term debt increased from 2.3 percent of the total in 1961 to
36.9 percent in 1975. Short-term debt covered operational expenses, while
bonds were continually refinanced into a semipermanent and expensive
debt pool.

The city also depended on state and federal aid that by 1976 paid for
roughly one-half of the budget.[9] Some of this paid for state and federal

mandates, including welfare and Medicaid (New York was the only state requiring local governments to pay a large share of Medicaid costs). In response to two recessions, the city increased support for health and welfare and negotiated more expensive labor contracts. The Temporary Commission on City Finances called this the "Depression Period" and it had dire effects. The city suffered record losses in population (net out-migration rose 500,000 between 1970 and 1975) and increased taxes, with political conflict over jobs, benefits, and social spending.

For decades, unions, both public and private, advocated higher pay and more housing, employment, transportation, and education to make New York City "the standard-bearer for urban liberalism and the idea of a welfare state."[10] But as manufacturing eroded and private sector unions along with it, public employees took a bigger role in the city's labor movement. Private union membership became concentrated in construction and the building trades, which hadn't been welcoming to Black and Latino members, while more nonwhites joined expanding municipal and health-care unions. Between 1950 and 1992, unionized manufacturing employment fell from 33 percent of the city's jobs to 9 percent, while finance doubled its presence. Although New York remained the most unionized American city, public sector and publicly funded health-care workers increasingly outnumbered private sector union members.

As a result, New York City's labor movement focused more and more on government as an employer, directly or indirectly, as in health care, where funds for wages and benefits were increasingly tied to public budgets. Victor Gotbaum of the municipal worker union DC 37 bragged during the fiscal crisis that "we (unions) have the ability, in a sense, to elect our own boss."[11] Increasing public union power ran into fiscal crisis austerity, but it also contributed to fracturing progressive coalitions, with a weakened union voice in manufacturing and none in the growing finance sector.

Even though their pension funds rescued the city, unions were blamed for New York's fiscal problems. They took the investment risk partly fearing bankruptcy would threaten their pensions and collective bargaining rights, resulting in pension funds holding too much city debt. By 1978, 38 percent of city pension assets were in New York City debt, from below 5 percent in 1974. A union financial adviser later admitted that "we shot crap with the assets of 350,000 pension fund members."[12]

Union leaders hoped the fiscal crisis and labor's financial involvement would trigger a tripartite partnership among unions, business, and city government. But a new politics of austerity replaced any partnership when mayors started attacking public sector unions. Liberal congressional representative Ed Koch followed Beame as mayor and blamed unions for the fiscal crisis. When transit workers struck in 1980, Koch led the opposition, greeting walking commuters on the Brooklyn Bridge and yelling, "Walk over the bridge! We're not going to let these bastards bring us to our knees."[13]

John Mollenkopf notes that, while other American mayors combined cross-racial alliances with neighborhood development, Koch deliberately broke up the old Democratic coalition of unions and minorities. By exploiting "long-standing racial cleavages," Koch "veered away from minority empowerment and a renewed urban liberalism," pitting constituencies against each other and making it difficult to form a broad anti-austerity coalition.[14] The state and federal government's new veto powers over the city budget strengthened Koch's strategy.

By 1985, New York City abandoned special MAC financing because the city's private creditworthiness increased.[15] Finances improved partly due to fiscal austerity but more because of the post-1976 economic rebound in which the city's economy grew faster than the nation's.[16] The employment base changed significantly because services, finance, and construction grew while the city suffered "massive employment losses in manufacturing."[17]

New York City's economy profited from the global financialization boom. Finance services expanded rapidly in the 1980s, sparked by deregulation, increasing global integration, and consumer demand for debt as real household incomes stagnated. Financial services grew from 4.9 percent of gross domestic product (GDP) to 7.9 percent between 1980 and 2007, pulling other related sectors with it. In the 1980s, these sectors grew nearly twice as fast as the U.S. economy.[18]

New York's existing preeminence in finance allowed it to ride this structural shift and unequal economic boom. New York had the sector's highest paying jobs with its financial headquarters, the New York Stock Exchange, and supporting services such as law, consulting, printing, and accounting. In 1980, the city had around 9 percent of the nation's financial sector jobs compared to 4 percent of all private sector jobs and 3 percent of the nation's population.[19]

Financialization generated wealth but also inequality. In 1980, the typical financial services employee earned about the same wages as their counterparts in other industries, but by 2006 they averaged 70 percent more. Unions are nonexistent in the finance sector. And financial wealth paid for successful lobbying for regulatory and political advantages, further weakening progressive opponents.[20]

Proposed regulatory or tax increases on finance produced threats by firms to relocate so New York politicians nurtured business-friendly policies. New York began providing major incentives for real estate and economic development through a complex web of tax incentives, zoning changes, and infrastructure development. Major Manhattan-centered real estate projects, such as the Times Square redevelopment and construction of Battery Park City and the Javits Convention Center, were launched in cooperation with New York State, which had its own opaque list of probusiness subsidies and incentives. These projects were insulated from regular political oversight and control by using public authorities that allowed increasing debt beyond legal limits on the state.[21]

Housing subsidy programs, especially the 421(a) property tax exemption program, offered tax breaks for housing construction and helped to underwrite upper-income housing while low-income housing support stagnated. White working and middle-class out-migration to the suburbs continued, while the growing affluent financial services workforce developed residential enclaves in Manhattan and Brooklyn.[22] New York City was becoming a more unequal city.

Fiscal oversight constrained the city's budget, and postcrisis policy became focused on "corporate revival in the urban core."[23] Economic development was pulled into the city's complex geographic politics, emphasizing neighborhood special projects and localized benefits rather than a broad citywide movement for progressive economic growth and job creation.

Gradually increasing tax revenues led to partial relaxation of the city's fiscal discipline. Because Koch cultivated traditional Democratic Party machines in the Bronx and Queens rather than minority communities or labor unions, city contracts flowed to Democratic machines, and public employment grew 22.5 percent, "becoming the city's fastest growing industry sector after investment banking."[24]

Facing a huge backlog of abandoned residential properties, housing took center stage in Koch's third term. Rather than seeing distressed buildings as liabilities, Koch's policies saw them as potential assets. The program dramatically reduced the city's abandoned housing even while the Reagan administration was cutting overall federal support for housing by two-thirds. It created tens of thousands of new housing units; increased property values, including in distressed neighborhoods; and "has generally been viewed as the greatest success of his (Koch's) twelve-year mayoralty."[25]

An apparent break in austerity and racial policies came in 1989 when Black politician David Dinkins defeated Republican Rudolph Giuliani in a surprisingly close election to become New York's first (and only, until Eric Adams' 2021 election) nonwhite mayor. But Dinkins couldn't fulfill activists' hopes for a more progressive regime. The total number of jobs in the city economy peaked in April 1989, with an eventual loss of over 330,000 jobs in a national recession. Higher value-added services had accounted for around two-thirds of all job growth between 1975 and 1988, but around 100,000 jobs were lost in the downturn.

The recession beginning in July 1990 increased fiscal pressure. Federal aid had fallen from 10.2 percent of general expenditures in 1980 to 4.2 percent in 1989 under Reagan's anti-urban budgets. And the state Financial Control Board reasserted its authority over Dinkins.[26] The recession caused job losses in the restaurant industry, transportation, real estate, and other services, slowing tax revenues and stressing city budgets.[27]

Crime also commanded attention. In 1990, violent contestation of crack cocaine markets pushed murders to a then-record number: 2,245, up 17.8 percent from the previous year's record level. New York State governor Mario Cuomo called for hiring 5,000 new police officers without offering to pay for them. Meanwhile, the Financial Control Board (dominated by the governor's appointees) criticized Dinkins for budget deficits and overspending.[28]

New York State's interventions underscore the state's control over the city. State politicians criticized spending, even though they imposed unfunded mandates on the city, for example, requiring local payment for up to 80 percent of the local Medicaid share, repeatedly increasing pension payments for city employees without providing revenues, and blocking tax increases on city businesses or residents.[29]

Under pressure, Dinkins'1992 budget proposed a large increase in the number of police at an annual cost of $600 million while shrinking other parts of the city workforce, raising new taxes, and cutting capital spending. Union leaders attacked Dinkins, dividing his base and weakening hopes for a united progressive coalition. One critical scholar concluded that "by the end of its four-year term, the Dinkins administration showed few signs of having pursued a policy agenda much different from that of its predecessor, let alone having forged a progressive regime."[30]

Republican Giuliani won a rematch in 1993, inheriting a city with a fragmented opposition and a rising city economy based on finance. From the February 1991 employment trough nationally to its peak in March 2001, financial employment grew almost four times faster than overall private employment, making the city dependent on the financial sector. Between 1992 and 1997, finance directly accounted for 20.5 percent of the city's average annual employment growth and 51 percent of aggregate earning growth. Average salaries were almost 4.5 times higher than in nonfinancial jobs. And the indirect economic and job creation effects of finance, supporting jobs in law, accounting, and business services along with consumption spending for restaurants, retail, personal services, and real estate, meant New York had become "a Wall Street City."[31]

Giuliani's economic development policies largely focused on large Manhattan-based projects, including the redevelopment of Times Square. He also tried (and failed) to put major sports facilities on Manhattan's West Side, from a new Yankee Stadium to a proposed domed football stadium to an exploration for the 2008 Summer Olympics, an initiative picked up by his successor, Michael Bloomberg.

Population increases helped the city, with immigration feeding labor force growth, small business start-ups, and homeownership. After the earlier increase in the numbers of southern Blacks and Hispanics, especially from Puerto Rico, New York continued as the nation's immigration capital. The non-Hispanic white share of the city's population fell steadily, from 62.5 percent in 1970 to 43.4 percent in 1990. The Black share rose from 19.4 percent in 1970 to 25.6 percent in 1990. And the Hispanic share grew throughout the latter part of the twentieth century, from 16.2 percent in 1970 to 23.7 percent in 1990.[32] By March 2000, just over half of the city's population was either foreign born (34.8 percent) or children of immigrants (15.8 percent), the highest level since the early 1900s great immigration wave.[33]

Immigrants encountered a complex system of racial and ethnic political organizations stretching back to the nineteenth century. Newcomers found a political system organized for "mobilization along ethnic group lines" that "encourage[d] . . . ethnic politics" and squeezed out broader progressive alliances.[34] This immigrant culture fit the localized orientation of city politics, which also inhibited citywide movements seeking to unite varied ethnic groups.

New York's ethnic and geographically based city politics, combined with seemingly permanent fiscal austerity, the economic dominance of finance, and state political control, inhibited any citywide progressive economic coalition. Although remembered as a national liberal leader, Democratic governor Cuomo cut state aid to the city while approving tax cuts for the wealthy.[35] And when Cuomo was defeated in 1994 by an obscure Republican state senator, George Pataki, the new (and eventually three-term) conservative governor had little interest in economic equity or helping New York City, other than identifying with post-9/11 building to fuel a potential presidential campaign.

Cuomo's tax policies and their impact on state and city budgets reflected the long-standing control of the state, which was strengthened after the fiscal crisis. Other than the property tax, the state oversaw virtually any other tax change, while expenses like pension increases were regularly enacted over the city's objections.

Many city policies are deeply tied to the state's transactional politics. A state authority controls the city's mass transit system, including capital expenditures and fare increases. And New York State's K–12 education funding is known for baroque formulas favoring rural and wealthy suburban districts over cities. In spite of decades of advocacy and litigation, a 2014 study found "funding equity for public elementary and secondary education in New York State [was] forty-second in the nation, or eighth from the bottom."[36] Wealthier suburban towns ally with rural areas to preserve their state education and other funding shares at cities' expense.

In neither of Giuliani's election victories in 1993 and 1997 "did economic issues play a significant role. Liberals and conservatives alike rarely acknowledged that working-class New York was stuck in something that looked like permanent stagnation," with elections fought instead over racial friction (including welfare reform), policing and crime, and hous-ing costs.[37] Crime, policing, and race were central to Giuliani's political strategy; he rejected civilian oversight into police misconduct despite criticisms from Black leaders protesting dramatic police brutality cases.[38] This kept crime and racial division at center stage at the expense of eco-nomic development, good-quality jobs, and the fight against inequality.

9/11 AND AFTER: MICHAEL BLOOMBERG AND THE POSTINDUSTRIAL CITY

The 2001 mayoral election initially seemed to promise more progressive economic policies. But the 9/11 terrorist attack on the World Trade Center overshadowed the election. Public advocate Mark Green won a bitter pri-mary Democratic runoff against Latino candidate and Bronx Borough President Fernando Ferrer, but he alienated nonwhite voters in the pro-cess. Green then narrowly lost the general election to billionaire Michael Bloomberg.[39]

Arguing New York City was in a global competition for finance-related and other high-value jobs, Bloomberg defined the mayor's role as bal-ancing budgets and using modern management to make data-driven policy decisions. He sought increased powers, including taking control of city schools from the elected board of education, continuing Giuliani's aggressive policing on quality-of-life crimes (the broken windows policy), making government information accessible through a 311 num-ber, and more. In his 2003 State of the City address, Bloomberg said, "New Yorkers expect me to run City government in much the same way I ran my company."[40]

Bloomberg's economic development framework echoed Richard Florida's theory of the "creative class"—in 2003, the mayor said, "New York is in a fierce, worldwide competition; our strategy must be to hone our competitive advantages . . . New York is the city where the world's best and brightest want to live and work." Julian Brash summarizes this as "the Bloomberg Way: the mayor as CEO, the city government as a corporation, valued businesses as clients, citizens as customers, and the city itself as a product." Bloomberg departed from austerity at times; defending higher property taxes to finance services, he said, "Taxes and frugality are far better than crime, filth, and abandonment."[41]

Economic development followed this template. Bloomberg built on continued growth in finance and emphasized large projects, including the continuing obsession for a football or Olympic stadium on Manhattan's West Side and appointing hedge fund investor Daniel Doctoroff as deputy mayor for economic development. Doctoroff used the Olympic bid to push through zoning reforms to free up development on the West Side.[42] In Lower Manhattan, World Trade Center reconstruction didn't start until 2006 because it was mired in battles over funding, insurance payments, design, and community involvement. Post-9/11 rebuilding downtown was largely controlled by the governor along with the Port Authority of New York and New Jersey (the site's owners), leaving the city with little direct control.[43]

Housing affordability remained central to city politics, with advocates for the homeless making common cause with renters seeking low regulated apartment rents. Bloomberg's housing policy (again following Giuliani's lead) was tied to aggressive rezoning. Although Blomberg changed land use from manufacturing to office, commercial, and residential use in some areas (so-called upzoning), much of Bloomberg's rezoning restricted development through downzoning that reduced potential development in many neighborhoods, especially ones with high concentrations of homeowners who voted for the mayor.

Between 2003 and 2007, 23 percent of all lots in New York City underwent some type of zoning change. By the end of Bloomberg's third term, almost 40 percent of the city was rezoned, but total residential capacity increased by only 1.7 percent. Homeowners in low-density neighborhoods were protected from development (which also protected their housing values), but this protective antidensity zoning occurred more often in neighborhoods with "non-Hispanic white residents."[44]

Although some advocates called for preserving manufacturing, many supported Bloomberg's development and zoning policies as adapting to a postindustrial economy where real estate equates with economic development. Progressive activism continued focusing on crime and police mistreatment of Blacks and other minorities, along with residential rent regulation and neighborhood-specific projects. But progressives did not offer a coherent alternative economic vision.[45]

One example of this progressive weakness was the lack of a systemic community benefit agreement (CBA) policy, a tool used in Los Angeles and other cities tying enforceable benefits to development subsidies or rezoning. Bloomberg opposed linking equity or labor market policies to New York's booming real estate market via CBAs. The occasional isolated CBA either failed to obtain significant benefits or became mired in divisions among community groups. Unlike Los Angeles and other cities, progressives did not generate consistent citywide pressure for stronger CBAs or monitoring impacts in return for city subsidies and development actions. In 2010, a New York City Bar Association committee urged "the City to clearly and firmly reject any consideration of CBAs in the land use approval process" while expressing concerns over potential corruption and conflicts of interest for all CBAs, a conclusion embraced by Bloomberg.[46]

On job quality, although Bloomberg eventually supported increasing the state minimum wage, he opposed mandatory paid sick leave and vetoed living-wage and prevailing-wage laws requiring higher wages for workers at large subsidized projects. When the city council overrode him, Bloomberg litigated both laws (getting the prevailing-wage law overturned), arguing that state law preempted city action. In effect, the mayor advocated reducing the city's power over economic returns for work, in contrast to his seeking more authority in education, economic development, and other spheres.[47] The council also passed a mandatory paid sick leave law over Bloomberg's veto.

Bloomberg attended more to poverty and inequality than Giuliani by coordinating existing policies and launching new ones in 2006 through his new Center for Economic Opportunity (CEO), which developed a new empirical, city-specific poverty standard. CEO's activities focused on the labor supply side, ranging from family conditional cash transfer (CCT) payments to encourage children's school attendance, support for remedial education, and aid to poor City University of New York (CUNY) students. CEO also encouraged low-wage workers to supplement their incomes through benefits such as health care, child care, food stamps, and the earned income tax credit (EITC). CEO launched several initiatives but few of them scaled up to a significant level.

Bloomberg's opposition to CBAs, his leveraging more benefits for real estate developments while downzoning residential neighborhoods, and his concentrating on education effectively constituted a trickle-down theory of equity. Encouraging development through subsidies and rezoning would bring rising real estate values and subsequent tax revenue (reduced in part by subsidies), jobs, higher-income residents, and physical improvements. Consistent with an economist's human capital approach, poverty would be fought largely on the supply side of worker education, behavior, and income supplements, with the focus on education mirroring Bloomberg's successful efforts to take control from the elected board of education.[48]

Bloomberg's critics argued that he equated real estate development with economic development and unduly supported New York's most privileged residents, while too few benefits of growth were "reaching the less-wealthy 80 percent of the population."[49] But he won relatively easy reelection in 2005, and he was allowed to bypass New York's term limits law and win again in 2009 in part because opponents didn't build an effective citywide progressive coalition.

Claiming a need for job retention, New York continued subsidizing major corporations, most notably with a 2005 deal for Goldman Sachs to build its new headquarters near the 9/11 site. One of the most profitable financial companies in the world, Goldman received $1.7 billion in tax-exempt Liberty Bond financing, "one-fifth of all those special, triple tax-exempt post-9/11 bonds" along with other subsidies. And between 2006 and 2009, the city provided $1.8 billion for new stadiums for the Yankees and Mets baseball teams, in spite of those teams' profitability and evidence that sports stadiums are poor economic development investments.[50]

Bloomberg made management reforms while cultivating an image of a supermanager who turned the city around. But many of the city's gains came more from the continuing sectoral shift of the U.S. economy to finance. Between 1980 and 2006, finance's share of GDP rose from 4.9 to 8.3 percent, almost a 70 percent increase. New York City in turn became more and more dependent on tax revenues from high-profit firms and their high-income jobs and from rising real estate values and associated taxes. Overall tax revenues shot up by 75 percent between 2002 and 2007, creating a $5 billion surplus. Revenues from wages, bonuses, and capital gains made up 45 percent of the increased income tax base between 2003 and 2007, while "profits from Wall Street and real estate" drove a

165 percent increase in business income taxes. And residential real estate prices after 9/11 resulted in tripling of revenues from two real estate transfer taxes alone, with total returns "increasing by . . . more than $2 billion."[51]

This growth was accompanied by rising inequality. Although the number of high-paying jobs in finance increased, many other jobs were in low-paying service work. Finance jobs pulled average annual wages in Manhattan above $90,000 in 2006, more than 130 percent higher than average wages in the other four boroughs of the city. But half of New York's households eared less than $50,000 annually, below the estimated income needed to be self-sufficient. These low-income jobs were created while real estate prices shot upward. In the decade leading up to 2006, overall housing prices in New York rose by 124 percent, with a 185 percent increase in Manhattan, and spectacular increases in outlying areas of the city—261 percent in Fort Greene/Brooklyn Heights, 270 percent in Central Harlem, and almost 500 percent in East Harlem.[52]

New York City and the state had to depend more on their own resources under President George W. Bush, who spent the Clinton administration's budget surplus on tax cuts for the wealthy and increased military spending after 9/11 and on the Iraq War. Domestic spending tilted to public safety and antiterrorism under the new Department of Homeland Security, while federal housing support and Medicaid failed to keep pace with rising real estate and health-care costs. The federal share of the New York State budget fell from 38 percent in 2004 to 28.7 percent in 2008, with the state in turn reducing its commitment to the city.[53]

Although higher-paying finance and related jobs increased in the city and attracted some wealthy residents, suburban residents, especially whites, continued to benefit. In 2010, 17.9 percent of all New York City jobs were held by white, native-born commuters, who also had the highest annual household incomes of any subgroup. They often resided in relatively racially homogenous suburbs created and supported with decades of tax subsidies and other policies, electing representatives who could join with upstate and rural interests to block or control city policies.[54]

Meanwhile the city continued attracting immigrants. By 2013, immigrants made up 37 percent of New York's population, "the highest share in 100 years." But the countries of origin had changed, from 64 percent European-born in 1970 to only 15 percent in 2013. In the same period, the share of immigrant Latin Americans went from 15 percent to 33 percent.

Caribbean-born New Yorkers more than doubled their share, from 8 to 19 percent. The Asian immigrant share quadrupled from 7 to 28 percent. Immigrants made up over 40 percent of the city's workforce. They transformed neighborhoods, especially in Brooklyn and Queens, where immigrants made up over 48 percent of the population in ten neighborhoods. This diversity may have inhibited broad progressive citywide coalitions because newly arrived immigrants once again fell into New York's existing patterns of strong ethnic and neighborhood political loyalties.[55]

BILL DE BLASIO, A "TALE OF TWO CITIES," AND THE PANDEMIC

Even though inequality continued to increase, by Bloomberg's third term, crime and racial discrimination by police took center stage, as it had periodically ever since the fiscal crisis. Bloomberg increasingly was criticized over stop-and-frisk policies that disproportionately targeted young minority men, justified as an effort to reduce violent street crime. The city's rising and visible inequality was becoming an increasingly important issue, with the 2013 elections wide open due to term limits for all citywide offices.

Earlier that year, council member Brad Lander and City University professor John Mollenkopf articulated a sweeping progressive agenda, including more infrastructure investment, better education from early childhood through college, support for economic diversification and manufacturing, addressing housing costs and homelessness, and building on Bloomberg's pro-environmental legacy. They praised Bloomberg for careful budgeting and overall managerial competence, with the long shadow of the fiscal crisis still hovering over New York politics.

Many progressive politicians won in 2013, but it was not through a unified citywide movement with a coordinated policy agenda. Recognizing New York's fragmented politics and electoral processes, Lander and Mollenkopf concluded that "the large number of progressive issue advocacy groups and organized interest groups" could not be "realistically expect(ed)" to "agree on a larger number of specific initiatives." The election and its aftermath underscored this lack of coordination.[56]

In a crowded Democratic primary, public advocate Bill de Blasio focused on inequality, referring to New York's unequal growth as a "tale of two cities." He called for taxing the wealthy to support universal pre-kindergarten programs while blaming Bloomberg for not attending to neighborhood and community groups and failing to increase affordable housing. He opposed stop-and-frisk policing, and in an election moving the city to the left, and after a narrow win in the Democratic primary, he swept into office with over 73 percent of the vote. Forty-eight out of fifty-one elected city council members were Democrats, twenty of them members of the Progressive Caucus.

A more progressive mayor and city council enacted new policies: expanding mandatory paid sick leave for city-based businesses, pushing for more affordable housing construction (de Blasio pledged to add 200,000 units by 2024), and instituting mandatory prekindergarten education for all four-year-olds. On crime, de Blasio reappointed Bill Bratton, Giuliani's former police commissioner, but he also ended stop-and-frisk by settling an August 2013 federal court case. On housing costs, the mayor successfully advocated a rent freeze on city-regulated private apartments.

De Blasio also settled over 150 outstanding municipal labor contracts left by Bloomberg, who never prioritized labor relations. The city's economy grew throughout de Blasio's first term, much like the U.S. economy—steady increases in jobs but very slow gains in wages. In fact, city employment grew faster than the nation's—11 percent between 2012 and 2016 compared to 8 percent nationally. Finance jobs remained key, constituting 12 percent of total city employment. Yet real city spending did not expand, only keeping up with the national inflation rate between 2014 and 2018.[57]

More progressive labor policies were on de Blasio's agenda, dovetailing with progress made by construction trade unions. For decades, many building trade unions and contractors had resisted integration of their workforce, with a 1993 report to Mayor Dinkins saying that "the construction industry offers a textbook study . . . of institutionalized exclusion." But the 2000s saw progress from a combination of legal pressure and advocacy, new progressive union leadership, and the changing racial and ethnic demographics of the workforce. By 2014, Black representation in higher-paying unionized construction jobs exceeded that in the non-union sector, and nonwhites were over 60 percent of union apprentices compared to 36 percent in 1994 (women's representation, however, hovered just above 10 percent).[58] De Blasio also supported wage standards for workers at subsidized economic development projects and expanded the living-wage agreement.

Much of this required funding, with de Blasio tapping revenues from the growing economy, especially from wealthy New Yorkers. Critics noted city government employment grew by 6.1 percent in de Blasio's first two years, with total expenditures growing faster than Bloomberg's last years in office (although slower than Bloomberg's spending increases in his first six years prior to the Great Recession). Rising expenditures continued during de Blasio's two terms, pushed by a progressive city council and increasing revenues.[59]

There also was pressure to improve low job quality. After the 2007 financial crisis and the Great Recession, New York City recovered a higher percentage of jobs than the nation, but the number of jobs for city residents grew more slowly than for commuters. And the jobs were of worse quality. Over 50 percent of jobs lost in the recession were in higher-wage industries, compared to only 22.7 percent of jobs created in the recovery. According to the city comptroller, in the recovery, "jobs in low-wage industries accounted for 61.5 percent of all the new private-sector jobs in the city" while commuters continued to be disproportionately employed in higher-wage sectors.[60]

De Blasio hoped to become a national progressive leader, but he faced political challenges at home. He fought constantly with Democratic governor Andrew Cuomo over taxes and development, education initiatives, and the subway system. Cuomo initially opposed a city-specific minimum-wage increase (eventually supporting a statewide raise), often using the state's power to constrain the mayor's ambitions.[61]

But state-city friction is a structural political feature, not just a personality struggle. The conflict is embedded in the state-level strength of suburban and rural jurisdictions, the desire of Democratic governors to have a politically divided legislature (fearing an all-Democratic one dominated by New York City), and the state's strengthened oversight and control rooted in the fiscal crisis. Like many states, New York State exercises significant control and preemption of city policies, sometimes in very specific domains. Bloomberg was unable to get congestion pricing for Manhattan, de Blasio couldn't ban plastic shopping bags (and at first couldn't get a minimum-wage increase), and state Republicans insisted on more city-based charter schools in exchange for continuing mayoral control of schools.[62]

After Donald Trump's surprise presidential victory in 2016, de Blasio turned his rhetorical fire against Trump. Continuing battles with the governor obscured their mutual cooperation in reelection campaigns, de Blasio's in 2017 and Cuomo's in 2018. In the 2017 mayoral election, de Blasio won with 66.5 percent of the vote, and in his inaugural address he envisioned New York as "the fairest big city in America." The new city council was more tied to traditional borough political organizations, and some saw the overall electoral result as one where "progressives lost and the party establishment won."[63]

Through all the intragovernmental friction, battles with the Trump administration, and the continuing economic dominance of the finance and real estate sectors, New York kept building more expensive real estate. Residences in the "eternally expensive" supertall building at 432 Park continued to break sales records,[64] while ten other supertalls were either under construction or in the proposal stage (including Brooklyn's first, which began sales in 2022). Several of these clustered on midtown Manhattan's 57th Street just south of Central Park, which was known as Billionaire's Row.

Under Trump, the federal government increased its hostility to cities, in immigration, budgets, and tax policy. Criticism also came from the left, with some progressives opposing real estate for the wealthy, although the city's economy and budget depended heavily on them. Around 50 percent of city tax revenues come from the property tax and other real estate taxes. Another 23 percent of tax revenue in 2018 came from the personal income tax, with around 50 percent paid by households in the top 1 percent. Job growth slowed in high-wage sectors, while low-paying home health-care jobs alone accounted for 43 percent of employment growth in 2018.[65]

De Blasio also increased spending. Total spending hit $92 billion in fiscal year (FY) 2019, "a 26.4 percent increase from $72.8 billion in fiscal year 2014, Mayor de Blasio's first year in office." Spending went up primarily in education (for the new universal prekindergarten program and teacher salaries and benefits), labor costs for contract settlements, and increased numbers of city employees (a 9.9 percent increase over the period.)[66] And state control over city actions remained powerful, not only from the governor but also from legislative actions affecting education, infrastructure, housing regulation, and employee pensions and benefits.

De Blasio's economic development strategy lacked any consistent theme or direct connection with fighting inequality. In May 2019, the $25 billion Hudson Yards project, criticized for providing more luxury housing, opened on Manhattan's West Side. It was built over railroad tracks on a platform originally intended by Bloomberg for an Olympic stadium. Critics noted the project cost more than advertised, with the true costs hidden from public scrutiny.[67] But Hudson Yards continued New York's economic development focus on high-end office support for a few global sectors and expensive housing for wealthier residents.

Elsewhere, progressives stopped another megaproject—Amazon's HQ2, a second headquarters for the retailing giant to be shared with the Washington, DC, region. Although Amazon was invited into New York by de Blasio, Cuomo, and many state and city officials, some progressives rebelled when the bid revealed a cost of $3.4 billion in subsidies. Political agitation led to Amazon's withdrawal, even though many labor unions and some progressives hoped for a renegotiated deal. But activists focusing on housing and subsidies carried the day, with de Blasio and others withdrawing their support. A similar process played out in 2020, with opponents defeating development of Brooklyn's thirty-five-acre Industry City complex, a project that claimed it would produce up to 20,000 new jobs. The mayor once again was absent from efforts to craft a deal, leaving the local city council member to oppose the eventually cancelled project.[68]

Housing costs also remained a problem. Arguing that luxury developments were causing gentrification, advocates opposed significant new private housing construction or upzoning to allow denser development. In June 2019, the state legislature strengthened renters' rights by limiting rent increases on vacated apartments, making evictions harder, and eliminating deregulation for all tenants, even those with incomes over $200,000. Driven by new Democratic majorities in the state legislature, the laws underscored housing's continued domination of city politics. But while New York focused on rent regulation, it built very little housing, with the lack of supply driving up purchase and rental costs. "Between 2010 and 2018 New York City's jobs base increased 22 percent, while its housing stock increased only 4 percent, resulting in the addition of only 0.19 new housing units for every new job created."[69]

Against this background, the COVID-19 pandemic hit New York forcefully. The city was the initial epicenter of the disease and suffered high case numbers and death rates, leading some to conclude incorrectly that the pandemic was driven by urban density. Later infections in rural areas showed that wasn't true, but New York's economy remained hard hit. Office work fell off sharply, pulling down lower-paying service jobs. Tourism, hospitality (restaurants and hotels), and theaters and arts all were damaged and hadn't recovered by the end of 2021, when overall employment was still 413,000 jobs below pre-pandemic levels.[70]

In many ways, the pandemic's shock and economic harm just highlighted New York's inequalities while damaging the slow gains that low-income households were making. In February 2020, just before the pandemic, unemployment in the city hit a forty-year low of 3.4 percent. Along with a minimum-wage increase to $15 per hour at the end of 2019 (an increase of 114 percent in six years), this led to real wage and income gains for the bottom 50 percent and people of color. Poverty fell five years in a row between 2014 and 2019, although still "1.3 million New Yorkers lived at or below the official federal poverty level."[71]

In December 2021, as the mayor was leaving office, his administration produced a report: *The de Blasio Years: The Tale of a More Equal City*. It pointed to a declining poverty rate, a growing wage share for the lowest paid 50 percent of workers, implementation of paid sick and family leave, helping immigrants (both documented and undocumented), universal prekindergarten, and other accomplishments. The report concluded that "the progress of the de Blasio Administration shows fundamentally addressing income inequality is possible, urgent, and necessary."[72]

But the pandemic recession halted or reversed many of those gains, most heavily in minority and low-income neighborhoods. During the initial wave of the virus, the death rate for Blacks and Latinos was double that for whites. New York lost 631,000 jobs in 2020, the biggest one-year decline since modern data have been kept. Lower-wage workers had begun to see some gains, but the pandemic wiped those out. Losses were especially high in the leisure and hospitality sector, which lost 250,000 jobs, over half the prepandemic total.[73]

At the other end of the income scale, fears grew about an exodus of higher-income households. Stories abounded of suburban flight as housing prices dropped in the city and rose in the suburbs, although that fear abated after city housing prices stabilized. New York (like most cities) sees a constant turnover of residents. The city's population peaked in 2017 and had been declining slightly prior to the pandemic, with high taxes and living costs blamed by some analysts; the 2020 Census did show a surprising jump to 8.8 million. The net losses were tied to lower birth rates, an aging population, and declining immigration driven by the Trump administration's restrictive policies and the pandemic recession.[74]

The pandemic recession initially put pressure on the city's budget, which depends in part on high-income taxpayers and business taxes; personal income taxes alone on earners making over $1 million annually was "6.4 percent of City-funded spending in fiscal year 2016." But although the city's budget was strained, a combination of higher-than-expected revenues and budget cuts were keeping the city afloat. At one point, de Blasio proposed short-term borrowing to cover budget gaps, raising the specter of pre–fiscal crisis borrowing practices to cover operating expenses.[75]

In October 2020, the RPA issued *New York's Next Comeback*, underscoring the city's history of rebounding from crises, and finding "reasons to be hopeful" even with a second COVID-19 wave, slow economic recovery, and growing budget gaps. It cited major threats, including the financial crisis of the Metropolitan Transit Authority (MTA), which operates the region's mass transit systems. And RPA feared "widespread evictions and business failures" that "would fall heaviest on the poor." But it still expected a rebound based on the economic advantages of urban density and agglomeration, concentration and diversity of people and skills, and reduced real estate costs.[76]

With the 2021 citywide elections looming, New York's politics remained locked in a complex web of alliances but without a unifying economic policy breaking through the splintered political system. Fighting over Hudson Yards, Amazon, and Industry City had pitted progressive community advocates against many unions. State legislative fights over rent regulation were carried forward by housing advocates, with little engagement from organized labor, environmentalists, or other progressives. Otherwise-liberal community groups battled against denser housing development, including de Blasio's efforts to rezone Soho (perhaps the city's wealthiest neighborhood) to permit more affordable housing construction.

Many observers expected New York to rebound, drawing on its strengths as a financial center, its emerging role in tech, and its global importance. But the pandemic recession accentuated several longer-term negative economic trends, including continuing inequality concentrated in Black and Hispanic households, a lack of affordable housing, a crisis in mass transit financing, and high levels of overall spending in an economy already characterized by high taxes. The pandemic recession put downward pressure on commercial and residential real estate prices, but tech giants like Facebook and Google took advantage, snapping up long-term leases on large amounts of office space.

With COVID-19 vaccinations finally widely available, the pandemic's medical effects began to recede, even after the spike from the Omicron variants. But New York's economy, especially for low-income workers, suffered from the deep recession. Although housing took a sharp hit from the pandemic, sales and prices bounced back quickly, with "sales and rental markets . . . approaching, or in some cases, exceeding pre-pandemic prices." Apartment rents, heavily discounted during the pandemic's early stages, rebounded, and renters faced double-digit increases on expiring leases. New York's long-term failure to construct new housing supply now was driving up rents and sales prices, with little prospect of immediate relief.[77]

The biggest immediate economic threat came from empty offices. As companies kept pushing back dates for office workers to return, buildings stayed empty. This in turn kept mass transit ridership well below the level needed to finance the system. Underused offices meant fewer service and support jobs in sectors like office security, restaurants, janitorial services, and sales to commuters. Broadway and other theaters opened and closed sporadically, and overall tourism was slow to come back, costing more service jobs. Many of those jobs had been held by low-income workers, further amplifying the pandemic's impact on inequality.

Brooklyn Democrat Eric Adams won the 2021 mayoral race, becoming only the second Black mayor in the city's history. Adams, a former police captain, ran as a self-described working-class candidate, winning with substantial labor union and Black community support. In the Democratic primary, Adams won in Assembly districts with an average median income of around $55,000, compared to his closest opponent, Kathryn Garcia, who won in districts with an average income of $111,000[78]

Adams faced immediate challenges in public safety (two police officers were killed during his first weeks in office) and in the continuing slump of the office-based economy. Although inheriting a budget in relatively strong shape, Adams faced longer-term challenges tied to de Blasio's increases in the city's workforce to the highest level ever, with many positions paid for by noncity revenues. With key labor contracts up for negotiation, including unions among Adams's major supporters, he will face challenging labor negotiations.

But budgetary issues were overshadowed by the twin problems of restoring the office sector and the continuing inequality that comes with a city dependent on finance. As Paul Krugman says, New York's economy "is pretty much a monoculture" dependent on financial services.[79] If those high-paying jobs don't return, that hurts the tax base, the commercial real estate market, and by extension the large nonwhite and immigrant labor force working in service jobs. And even if those jobs come back, many are low-paying and unstable, while the continuing low levels of immigration hurts the city's overall population.[80] Without an economic development strategy emphasizing both job growth and equity, and not just redistribution and regulation, New York is likely to remain a wealthy—but unequal—city.

CONCLUSION

Prior to the fiscal crisis in 1975, New York City pursued a labor movement–driven "social democracy" with a "far more extensive web of social benefits" than the rest of America.[81] But the fiscal crisis inaugurated over thirty years of budget discipline, increased state and federal oversight and control, fractured and often divisive racial politics, and rising inequality and income polarization as finance replaced manufacturing. This sectoral shift reduced private sector unionization in the city, leaving the labor movement dominated by construction trades, quasi–public sector workers in health care and services, and unionized government workers. The affluent suburbs surrounding the city continued getting a disproportionate share of the region's economic output while pushing attendant social problems onto the city.

Significant individual progressive policy gains, such as expanded prekindergarten, a higher minimum wage and paid sick leave, or apartment rent regulation, haven't added up to a larger cohesive movement. Mollenkopf and Lander's 2013 insight remains valid: New York's "large number of progressive issue advocacy groups" tend "to work in parallel or even [at] cross purposes" so political leaders can't "realistically expect that they will agree on a large number of specific initiatives."[82] Political battles over policing along with a focus on housing regulation (not construction) remained central to New York's progressives, with relatively little focus on the economy, job creation and quality, and equity.

New York's pre–fiscal crisis, labor-driven policies cannot be restored. But as the fight over Amazon, continuing opposition to housing construction, and an emphasis on rent regulations show, New York progressives lack a coherent approach to economic development and growth. This highlights the lack of a broad movement focusing on how to transform the city's fragmented politics and unequal economy. Splintered politics focused on redistribution and regulation without a strategy for economic growth and housing construction won't provide the jobs and revenues needed for more equitable growth.

5

DETROIT

From the "Arsenal of Democracy" to

Record-Breaking Bankruptcy

A lthough New York may have seemed the most likely progressive economic city in the postwar period, Detroit had great potential. New York's key industries, especially garment and light manufacturing, didn't produce as much profit as the high-productivity automotive sector. And although New York had many unions, Detroit was home to the very large and progressive United Auto Workers (UAW). But Detroit fell a long way, ending up in the largest municipal bankruptcy in U.S. history.

How did Detroit fall so far? Analysts blame a toxic mix of poor strategy from auto companies, unsustainable pay and benefits for unions, a racially polarized region, manipulative Wall Street financing, a lack of comprehensive urban and regional planning, state and federal government indifference, and poor city leadership. But many other U.S. cities also faced bad leadership, industrial change, harmful federal policies, hostility from suburban and state governments, and racial conflict. Yet few fell so hard as Detroit. In particular, Detroit shows the pernicious effects of structural racism, which has poisoned the region's politics and economy for decades. Detroit's collapse is a cautionary tale, showing how far things can go wrong when cities are left on their own with structural racism, economics, and public policy all tilted against them.

THE MOTOR CITY: ECONOMIC CHANGE
AND RACIAL CONFLICT

At the end of World War II, the Detroit region was the center of America's "Arsenal of Democracy." Mass production of complex products like cars, trucks, tanks, and airplanes required innovative methods; supplier chains for raw materials and components; transportation to move raw materials and finished products; a large skilled labor force (including professional management and engineering skills); industrial design; and law, accounting, and finance expertise. Detroit's preexisting lead in the complex mass production of motor vehicles meant war production grew there rapidly.[1]

Motor vehicle plants converted to military production and new factories were created, including the 1,500+-acre Willow Run Bomber Plant and the Chrysler Tank Plant. These large plants supported a complex network of smaller machine shops and other suppliers. But foreshadowing problems that would increasingly confront the city, those factories—and housing for in-migrating workers—were built outside the city. Between April 1940 and June 1944, the population of Detroit's four adjacent suburban counties increased by 200,000, compared to only 30,000 in the city.[2]

This exurban greenfield construction partially reflected more efficient horizontal plant designs with dedicated rail and road connections. New construction in virtually nonexistent towns also meant companies could control construction, land use, taxation, and infrastructure. And new construction boomed outside the city. Between 1941 and 1956, General Motors, Ford, and Chrysler—the big three—built twenty-five new plants in the metropolitan region, all outside Detroit's city limits.[3]

Auto companies were expanding nationally, locating production near growing customer populations. Historian Thomas Sugrue points out that "decentralization was not simply a response to the inexorable demands of the market; it was an outgrowth of the social relations of production itself."[4] Dispersing production allowed companies to resist unions, undercutting plant-level militancy and supporting antilabor politicians. Going to new communities provided opportunities to press local and state governments for favorable taxes and regulation and to implement new technologies.

Production dispersed before the war. Henry Ford's Rouge complex in 1917 and Ford's corporate headquarters in Dearborn were both outside the

Detroit city limits. By 1939, more than half of the region's auto jobs were located outside the city.[5] Detroit's postwar prosperity was already undercut by companies locating production and population across the region and nation. Dispersing large assembly plants also meant dispersing many small supplier companies and their workers.

But the city and region still grew. Autos were central to U.S. prosperity, and the industry fueled massive growth in the city's and the region's population. In 1910, Detroit city's population was 465,766, 15 percent below Pittsburgh. And while Pittsburgh's population grew 25 percent in the next twenty years, Detroit grew by a staggering 237 percent, to 1,568,662 in 1930.[6]

The booming auto industry and a strong union provided high-paying jobs with retirement and health benefits. The landmark 1950 UAW contract, labeled the Treaty of Detroit in *Fortune* magazine, influenced all other American industrial unions. Autoworkers achieved inflation-adjusted wages, health and pension benefits, and profit sharing. In turn, the UAW yielded decision making on production, plant location and investment, and other management prerogatives. Detroit worker incomes soared above national levels; in the 1950s, the metro region had the nation's highest per capita income.[7]

Prosperity even reached Black workers, although they still faced pervasive discrimination. Blacks held the lowest-paying and most dangerous jobs, lacked promotional opportunities, and encountered daily hostility from some white coworkers and managers. Researchers note that "35 percent of the metropolitan population lived below the poverty line in 1950—a time when Detroit's factories dominated auto production."[8] But the industry's growth and the UAW's commitment to integration (driven in part by Black activism) pushed Black wages above the national average. On average, wages for Blacks in Detroit in the early 1950s were 81 percent of whites, while in the nation they were only 57 percent.[9]

Even with relatively high incomes, Blacks were excluded from better housing, especially the low-density housing dispersed in the city and region. Unlike major eastern cities, Detroit adopted the single-family house as its primary housing form—at least for whites—for several reasons: flat topography, dispersed production, and the auto industry's pressure to create wide boulevards and a street grid encouraging car ownership while discouraging mass transit.[10] Foreshadowing the postwar American metropolitan pattern, Detroit's white single-family homes were in outlying neighborhoods, with multifamily housing centrally located in high-density poor Black neighborhoods with worse government services. In 1961, urbanist Jane Jacobs wrote, "Detroit is largely composed, today, of seemingly endless square miles of low-density failure."[11]

By 1960, over half of Detroit homes were owner-occupied. Many white neighborhoods were organized around churches that often provided positive community functions, from organizing dances to advocacy for better trash pickup. But these racially homogenous neighborhoods also enforced racially restrictive covenants that kept Blacks from buying homes.

Sugrue notes that "the working-class hold on affluence was tenuous," especially as the auto industry went through significant layoffs, dropping by almost half in the late 1950s mainly because of industry consolidation, relocation, and restructuring.[12] Most household wealth was the home, and workers focused on maintaining its value—"to a generation that had struggled through the Great Depression, the specter of foreclosure and eviction was very real."[13] Many were of Eastern European origin or they were southern white migrants who came north seeking war industry jobs.[14] Excluding Blacks was an expression of racism, but it was also seen as protection for whites' home values.

Relatively affluent Blacks wanted to move from Detroit's ghettos to better neighborhoods in the city's outskirts and growing suburbs. Detroit's Black population doubled in the decade after 1940, driven by southern migrants seeking war production jobs. And as Blacks sought housing in the city's all-white neighborhoods, blockbusting real estate agents stoked fear among whites, scaring them into below-market panic sales and then reselling houses at a premium to Black buyers. Agents hired Black women to walk baby carriages through white neighborhoods and had Black children go door to door, handing out flyers saying it was a good time for whites to sell.[15]

Racial anger and fear of Blacks was also stoked by politicians. In 1943, violent racial conflict caused by housing, employment, and political discrimination resulted in whites and Blacks fighting in Detroit's streets. Thirty-four people died, and President Franklin Roosevelt sent in federal troops. Although the violence was widespread, deaths, injuries, and arrests fell heavily on Black residents.

The violence, continuing racial fearmongering, and activism from Black civil rights organizations drove white residents to organize. Between 1943 and 1965, 192 homeowner associations were formed, and some white politicians quickly saw their electoral potential. In the 1949 mayoral election, city treasurer Albert Cobo defeated a former UAW organizer by pledging to prevent a so-called Negro invasion of white neighborhoods. Once in office, Cobo attacked public housing programs and antidiscrimination efforts.[16] His success encouraged future mayors to downplay housing desegregation efforts and concentrate public housing in Black areas.

Suburban growth and industrial workers' affluence sharpened regional, spatial, and racial divisions. The city's population declined from its 1950s peak by 338,086 in 1970, while the suburbs grew by 1,526,332.[17] Suburban growth was predominantly white, while the city's population became primarily Black. In 1950, Blacks were 16.2 percent of Detroit's population, growing to 43.7 percent in 1970. Michigan's home rule law enabled suburban growth and independence in creating new, small, and "highly independent governments;" discouraged cooperation with adjacent governments; and "made annexations and mergers extremely difficult or impossible."[18]

Although many commentators use the term "Detroit" to refer interchangeably to the city, the region, and the American auto industry, the fortunes of each have diverged since 1950. The city of Detroit has declined, while the metro area and the auto industry prospered. The motor vehicle industry helped the city somewhat because many residents worked in it. But by the 1950s, the city of Detroit increasingly lost population and jobs, suffered a reduced tax base, and experienced bitter racial division from neighborhood battles over housing to citywide elections.

On June 23, 1963—the twentieth anniversary of the 1943 disturbances—125,000 people, led by Dr. Martin Luther King, Jr. and Reverend C.L. Franklin, joined the "Walk to Freedom" down Woodward Avenue. King spoke in Cobo Hall, giving the first version of his legendary "I Have a Dream" speech.[19] An alliance of Black churches, labor organizations, and the city's white liberal mayor (elected with substantial Black support) promised a hopeful integrated future for Detroit. But four years later, on July 23, 1967, violent civil disturbances shook Detroit for three days.[20] It ended with 8,000 National Guard troops and over 4,000 regular U.S. army soldiers deployed, forty-three people dead, over 7,200 arrested, and estimated property damage of over $40 million.

The hopeful alliance that emerged in 1963 didn't solve Detroit's deep racial divide, and white opposition to desegregation was still growing. Mayor Jerome Cavanaugh had obtained federal Great Society funding, but in October 1963 his proposed housing antidiscrimination ordinance was defeated by the Detroit Common Council, backed by white homeowner associations. They instead proposed a Homeowners' Rights Ordinance allowing owners "the right to choose [their] own friends and associates" and to control real estate sales or rentals."[21] That ordinance passed on the 1964 primary ballot by 55 percent to 45 percent but was later declared unconstitutional.

Economic strains also appeared. Although the auto industry provided good-paying unionized jobs and created a large group of professional managers, engineers, and white-collar workers, industrial conflict increased. The Treaty of Detroit gave management control of production in exchange for higher compensation, and companies now pushed for ever-higher productivity. In response, workers defended themselves through more complex sets of work rules, trying to restrain management's push to speed up production.

Tensions fell hardest on Black workers, whose auto jobs, such as foundry, blast furnace, and painting work, were the hardest, dirtiest, and lowest paid. Blacks got little technical on-the-job training and received limited education outside the factory. As a result, in 1966, Blacks in the region held unskilled jobs at twice the rate of whites, while whites held a seven-to-one advantage in professional and technical jobs.

Conflicts around management's speeding up of production and economic downturns slowed overall job growth. Coupled with dispersed production to the suburbs and other regions, Detroit's Black workers fell further behind. Between 1950 and 1970, overall employment increased in Detroit's suburbs by 31.7 percent while it fell in the city by 26.1 percent as the city's population became increasingly Black.[22]

The loss of businesses and higher-earning white homeowners strained Detroit's budget. Although Detroit instituted a city income tax in 1962 (four years before New York City), city finances would only worsen. Real assessed property value peaked in 1958, but by 1970, it had fallen by 25 percent, and by 1980, real property value in the city was only one-third of the 1958 peak.

In labor relations, plant-level production pressure along with rising Black militancy led to more radical Black labor organizations—the National Negro Labor Council (1951) and the Trade Union Leadership Council (1957), whose members included future mayor Coleman Young. In the late 1960s, Black workers at the notoriously unsafe Dodge Main plant formed the Dodge Revolutionary Union Movement (DRUM) movement, which grew into the influential League of Black Revolutionary Workers.[23] An increasing number of wildcat strikes brought them into conflict with UAW leaders, who were torn between enforcing their contract and responding to the militants' demands.

Black nationalism and militancy grew throughout the city, including the popular Shrine of the Black Madonna (which envisioned Jesus as a Black revolutionary) and other militant voices questioning integration-based solutions. And racial polarization grew among many whites. In 1968, Alabama segregationist governor George Wallace, running for president, gave a downtown speech ending in fistfights between his supporters and protestors. In 1972, Wallace won Michigan's Democratic presidential primary, "sweeping every predominantly white ward in Detroit" along with suburban counties around the city.[24]

In 1973, Detroit elected its first Black mayor—state senator Coleman Young, who would dominate city politics for decades. Young was a former autoworker and militant labor activist who served with the Tuskegee Airmen during World War II. Brought before the House Un-American Activities Committee (HUAC) in 1952 for Communist Party affiliations, he rebuked the committee, saying, "I can assure you I have had no part in the hanging or bombing of Negroes in the South." His election showed the city's sharp racial divide—Young got 92 percent of Black votes while white former police commissioner John Nichols won 91 percent of white votes.[25]

Young dominated regional politics for twenty years during five mayoral terms. Critics called him racially divisive, giving the city's tax base to unionized government employees along with welfare benefits to poor Blacks while undercutting police efforts at public safety. In 2013, a *Wall Street Journal* columnist claimed Young oversaw "a virtual collapse" of city government whose plan was to "go to war with the city's major institutions" that "drove out the white and Black middle classes."[26]

Young did blame many of Detroit's problems on racism. But in his first inaugural address, he called for regional cooperation, saying, "the suburbs cannot live without the city. The white population of this city cannot live while its Black people suffer discrimination and poverty." He disbanded an elite police anticrime unit that had killed twenty-four suspects in its three-and-a-half-year existence; twenty-two of them were Black.

Young's inaugural included a divisive flash point: "to all dope pushers, to all ripoff artists, to all muggers: It's time to leave Detroit, hit Eight Mile Road. And I don't give a damn if they are Black or white, or if they wear Superfly suits or blue uniforms with silver badges: Hit the road." Eight Mile Road is Detroit's northern border with white suburbs, and many suburbanites saw Young threatening to somehow export Black crime. Equating so-called Superfly drug dealers with police further inflamed tensions with Detroit's majority white police department.[27]

But Young also was a tight-fisted fiscal manager who initially balanced budgets by laying off workers and cutting spending. He was helped by a 1982 rise in the city's income tax rate, although city property tax revenue continued to fall. By 1985, Young had restored the city's bond rating to investment grade.

Detroit's finances also suffered when President Ronald Reagan cut aid to cities. Between 1980 and 1988, federal aid as a share of large city budgets fell from 22 percent to 6 percent.[28] And Young's budget challenges came during two severe national recessions, including the double-dip recessions in 1980 and 1981, the worst since the Great Depression.

The recessions struck Detroit particularly hard because both were driven by oil price shocks. Trade policy and foreign competition also hurt the industry. For years, Detroit's big three downplayed threats from low-priced and higher-mileage Japanese cars; however, they lost market share while Japanese cars gained a reputation for reliability and fuel economy, and American markets were exposed by national trade policy and a high dollar.[29]

Oil price shocks coincided with a rising environmental movement. From the first Earth Day in 1970, activists called for greater fuel efficiency. Rather than raise gasoline taxes, politicians prescribed ever-higher fuel efficiency for automobile fleets. As the big three automakers complained about meeting fuel efficiency standards, the UAW was pushed to the opposite side of the growing and progressive environmental movement.

Foreign automakers also enjoyed lower labor costs. America's corporations provided health and retirement benefits, while foreign governments, not companies, provided those same benefits. The UAW advocated national health insurance and higher Social Security benefits to lower U.S. labor costs, but the United States failed to do either, putting American firms at a disadvantage in global competition. By 1980, auto imports surged while auto production moved to the nonunion South, and "Detroit-area factories produced fewer vehicles than they had in twenty years."[30] And the city could not capture taxes from regional auto production; no new auto plant had been built in the Detroit city limits since the 1930s.

Detroit didn't just lose motor vehicles. Motown Records, founded in 1958 by Berry Gordy Jr., produced artists like the Supremes, the Temptations, Marvin Gaye, and Stevie Wonder, but moved to Los Angeles in 1972. The Lions football team left in 1975 followed by the Pistons basketball team in 1978, both to the suburban "Silverdome" in Pontiac, where construction was financed by public bonds and other tax subsidies.

At the federal level, President Reagan had no love for unions or cities. His administration cut welfare state programs, fought unions, and allowed states to spend federal funds in suburban jurisdictions at the expense of central cities. Faced with this policy hostility and economic risks, Mayor Young gambled on reviving auto production in the city. He committed significant tax dollars and city powers to attract the new General Motors (GM) Poletown plant (so-called because of the large number of Polish immigrants who settled in the area). Poletown became part of a bitter political battle, with the city demolishing private houses and businesses while diverting federal housing and community development funds, issuing new bonds, and giving GM large tax abatements. In effect, Young gambled his budget gains on bringing auto production back into the city. But only about half of the projected jobs were created: the full economic benefits never materialized, while the increased borrowing cost the city.[31]

Young also pursued downtown projects, including the massive Renaissance Center, which never achieved economic success and inhibited development by blocking access to the riverfront. Young used Community Development Block Grants (CDBGs) and tax abatements to fund these projects, further eroding the tax base. But Young remained popular by emphasizing white hostility to the city and criticizing opponents for lacking militancy.[32]

For many Blacks, Young's focus on white racism rang true given the region's long history of deep racial conflict. Suburban politicians often won with racial hostility. Dearborn mayor Orville Hubbard won fifteen times between 1942 and 1975 by supporting segregation, saying in 1968 "I favor segregation" so the country wouldn't end up with "a mongrel race."[33]

Young's politics appealed to Detroit's ever-increasing share of Black residents. Between 1980 and 1990, the city's Black population rose to 75 percent—the highest of any major city in America—while the overall population fell by over 14 percent, with ever-fewer white residents and very little immigration. As the big three automakers stagnated regionally, Black workers at the bottom of the industrial pyramid suffered the most. Younger workers could no longer count on industrial jobs as good-paying sectors shrank in the city. And city services suffered as the population, tax base, and revenues all declined.

DECLINE AND FALL—CASINOS, THE HIP-HOP MAYOR AND BANKRUPTCY

After dominating politics for twenty years, Young left office in 1994. Race was central to Detroit politics, and Black leaders feared criticizing Young would validate white suburban hostility. But emphasizing racial identify stifled multiracial progressive political reform efforts.[34] Detroit's large Black majority meant elections were fought along racial unity lines, while economic development concentrated on the automobile industry and large downtown projects.

These development strategies failed. Although national manufacturing employment peaked in 1979, motor vehicle and parts production still grew until June 2000 in the region, but not in the city. The city's share of regional manufacturing employment fell from 34 percent in 1970 to 13 percent in 2000.[35] The city's property values and tax base continued falling, and city residents became poorer and poorer.

In 1994, Dennis Archer became mayor when regional, but not city, motor vehicle employment was still growing. While the region grew by 4.8 percent between 1990 and 2000, the city lost 7.5 percent of its population.[36] Seeking jobs and revenues, the city pursued casino gambling, even though casinos lower property values, don't create good jobs, and often don't deliver consistent tax revenues.[37] Religious and community opposition had defeated casinos four times, but continuing decline and a new casino across the river in Windsor, Ontario, led to casinos winning a 1996 statewide referendum.[38]

Archer envisioned a casino district like the Las Vegas strip, but community and political demands resulted in scattering casinos in different neighborhoods. Archer then faced a recall election for not awarding any casino licenses to Black-owned businesses. Detroit also spent public money for the Detroit Tigers' new baseball stadium in 2000 and football's Detroit Lions Ford Field in 2002, using about $355 million in financing from public sources, even though research shows stadiums are not good uses of public funding.[39]

Initial casino revenues, a growing national economy, and rebounding big three auto and truck sales helped city revenues. By 2000, Detroit had stabilized its budget—general fund revenues grew in real terms by 9 percent between 1995 and 2000. But long-term debt still mounted, and there weren't adequate reserves for future retiree pensions and health benefits. State and federal support also declined. In 1998, Archer agreed to cut Detroit's income tax rate in exchange for increased state revenue sharing. But the state reneged when the 2001 recession squeezed Michigan's revenues. Detroit lost about $700 million between lowering its income taxes and the state's broken promise of increased revenue sharing.[40]

As in many metropolitan areas, Detroit faced continued tax-subsidized, suburban competition for jobs, housing, and residents. Urban economist George Galster describes a decades-long regional "housing disassembly line" where suburbs built more housing than population growth required, tying Detroit's blight to "a speculative, uncontrolled residential development process in the suburbs." Subsidized by tax and regulatory breaks, these suburbs drew homeowners further away from the city, while older housing stock—concentrated in Detroit—declined in value. Falling home values and incomes and Detroit's high property taxes further increased housing disinvestment; as Allan Mallach and Andre Perry note, this further injured stable Black neighborhoods.[41]

Much regional housing remained off-limits to Blacks, and racial polarization remained a winning political strategy in Detroit's suburbs. Racial conflict supported the long political career of L. Brooks Patterson, who came to political prominence in the 1970s fighting regional school busing.

The resulting Supreme Court case, *Milliken v. Bradley*,[42] overturned cross-boundary busing and other desegregation remedies, confining Black students to de facto segregated schools with less resources.

Patterson used *Milliken* to gain a lifetime in public office, first as Oakland County prosecutor and then county executive. A proponent of real estate development, once saying, "I love sprawl . . . Oakland County can't get enough of it," he resisted Blacks moving into the county. He constantly attacked Detroit and its Black leadership, often using directly racist rhetoric. In 2014, Patterson said, "What we're gonna do is turn Detroit into an Indian reservation, where we herd all the Indians into the city, build a fence around it, and then throw in the blankets and the corn." Even with such rhetoric, Patterson was reelected in 2016 to his seventh term.[43]

Suburban sprawl drained more of Detroit's population. Between 1990 and 2000, the metropolitan region grew by 5.2 percent, while the city's population fell by 7.5 percent. And city-suburban cooperation was virtually nonexistent. Schedules and fares for Detroit's separate bus system were uncoordinated with suburban lines, adding hours to the commutes of carless Detroit residents with or seeking jobs in the suburbs. But creating better transit coordination in the region failed dozens of times in the state legislature or on regional ballot initiatives.

For decades, Michigan's state economic development policy subsidized suburban locations at Detroit's expense. A 2006 study found state subsidies were "shortchanging central cities and actively subsidizing new development in thinly populated, newly developing, or already prosperous areas." Between 2001 and 2004, the Detroit nine-county region got 85 percent of the $939 million state development tax credits from the Michigan Economic Growth Authority (MEGA). But only one of the eighty-one MEGA deals went to the city, which suffered the highest number of plant closings and mass layoffs.[44]

Even though revenues stabilized during Archer's two terms, Detroit's long-term future didn't improve. Jobs and residents continued to be lost, subsidized by state economic development policies. Job sprawl put 78 percent of the region's jobs more than ten miles away from the central business district, the second most dispersed among the 100 largest U.S. metropolitan areas.[45] Growing suburban economic power and continuing racial hostility meant the city couldn't find regional or state-level partners, and its population continued falling while becoming increasingly Black and poor.

The brief stabilization of Detroit's revenues soon disappeared, along with any semblance of effective government. In 2002, thirty-one-year-old Kwame Kilpatrick, the son of U.S. congressional representative Carolyn Kilpatrick, was elected mayor. Kilpatrick's use of rap lyrics in his speeches led comedian Chris Rock to call him "America's first hip-hop mayor."

But Detroit continued declining. The long-term trends hurting Detroit—housing and job sprawl, deindustrialization, racial isolation, and increasing urban poverty—continued. And the city's basic functioning was now at risk. Archer increased government employment but didn't improve performance. In 1999, he took control of Detroit's indebted and poorly performing public schools from the separately elected school board. But neither student performance nor school finance improved, with the system showing a $200 million annual deficit by 2004.[46]

Government performance suffered across the board. In 2004, Detroit police resolved only 11 percent of major crimes reported to the Federal Bureau of Investigation (FBI), well below the level for other major U.S. cities.[47] While property tax revenues declined, the city couldn't distinguish residential, commercial, and industrial property tax revenues until 2003. Kilpatrick made substantial layoffs, but these worsened city services while adding to Detroit's retiree pension and health systems costs as laid-off workers claimed their benefits.[48]

As population and revenues fell, the city couldn't deliver essential services—police, fire, sanitation, transportation, utilities, education—across its low-density footprint. Detroit's physical area is 142.9 square miles, enough to fit Boston, San Francisco, and Manhattan within its borders. Those three cities had a 2020 combined population of over 3 million, but Detroit's population peaked at 1.8 million in 1950, and in 2020, it hit 639,000, 21 percent of the three-city total in a larger physical space. Neighborhood political resistance prevented geographic consolidation, so services kept declining, in turn feeding further blight.

City government became more dysfunctional under these pressures. The city council fought the mayor's proposal for a land bank, an innovative way to clear abandoned properties for redevelopment, at a time when around 10 percent of Detroit's land parcels already were seized for nonpayment of taxes.[49] The resulting political deadlock limited the city's ability to clear increasingly blighted neighborhoods.

The nonprofit sector also experienced disorganization. The city government, foundations, and nonprofit development institutions introduced three separate neighborhood development strategies that sometimes outlined different neighborhood boundaries. Similar disjunctions took place in economic development, with a variety of commissions, boards, business organizations, foundation initiatives, and government agency-led proposals that didn't come together on a common strategy.

Even in the face of declining revenues; regional and state hostility; job loss; growing residential poverty; and several scandals, both personal and financial, Kilpatrick was reelected in 2005. He used aggressive racial identity themes in the runoff election—some supporters ran advertisements comparing criticism of Kilpatrick to lynching.[50]

By 2005, city finances had reached a critical stage. Desperate for revenue, Kilpatrick made a fateful decision that would push city finances over the edge. For years, Detroit had underfunded its pension plans and not funded pledges for retiree health care. Pension plans also had lost investment value, making the funding problem critical as payouts to retirees began growing. With guidance from UBS, Merrill Lynch, and other investment firms, Kilpatrick proposed funding the pension gap with $1.4 billion in risky pension obligations certificates of participation (COPs). Because the city's borrowing capacity was tapped out, the deal was carried out by newly created, supposedly independent public authorities, and the COPs were insured by two private bond insurance companies.

After negotiating with the city's public employee unions, Kilpatrick's COP deal passed in February 2005. The city then moved all variable funds to fixed interest rates (which were relatively high at the time) through insured interest-rate swaps. Wall Street hailed the complex set of deals, and the COPs were rated at the highest possible level. In December 2005, the reelected mayor accepted a crystal pyramid at a New York City dinner, awarded by *Bond Buyer* magazine for the "Midwest Regional Deal of the Year."[51]

But in less than two years, it all fell apart. In 2007, Kilpatrick was sued by former police officers alleging illegal dismissals to hide an investigation into the mayor's personal conduct. The city settled the suit for $8.4 million rather than reveal text messages that would have confirmed the charges. In January 2008, those messages and the city's four-year attempt to hide them were revealed, and in September Kilpatrick pled guilty to two felonies. After further federal extortion and bribery convictions, he received a twenty-eight-year federal prison sentence.[52]

Kilpatrick's scandals shouldn't divert attention away from Detroit's continuing structural economic problems. Population continued falling, while the regional population fluctuated and sprawl grew. With an ever-smaller population, declining property values, and increasing housing blight, the city's residents became ever poorer. Vital services declined along with revenues, while budget demands rose from the increasing number of retirees. Detroit's elected leadership focused on Black-white conflict and paid little attention to government operations and reform. And suburban governments remained hostile, with open racism from some, while state and federal governments didn't provide significant new aid.

These factors might have caused the city's bankruptcy even in normal economic times. But starting in late 2007, in what became known as the Great Recession, the manufacturing sector and U.S. auto companies took a steep dive. Over several years, financial firms building complex debt structures of poorly understood securities and derivatives had created a massive financial bubble. When American housing prices slowed, this financial house of cards fell, taking major Wall Street firms down with it.[53] The crash rapidly spread into the real economy, causing the worst economic slump since the Great Depression. The auto industry virtually collapsed, with GM and Chrysler facing bankruptcy.

This Great Recession pushed Detroit's fragile municipal finances to insolvency. Detroit continued laying off workers, worsening its already weak services and increasing pension and retiree health-care outlays. As revenues fell, the true costs of Kilpatrick's debt deal were revealed. In January 2009, rating agencies marked Detroit's debt down to junk bond levels, requiring an over $300 million payment on the older swap contracts, close to 10 percent of Detroit's annual general revenue.

In 2009, the city desperately pledged casino gambling revenue, its most reliable, to guarantee the swap payments. The revenues would be held by a third-party bank to ensure that Detroit wouldn't default on the swaps. The swap contracts were also restructured so that Detroit couldn't reduce its obligations even if other interest rates fell. These maneuvers gave the city a little breathing room but soon made things worse.

State politics also played a role because state finances disintegrated along with the city's. Across the state, revenues to municipalities went down 31 percent in the decade after 2000. In Detroit, state officials began to experiment with more direct control. Between 1999 and 2004, the Detroit Public Schools (DPS) were placed under mayoral control with state oversight. Control was restored to the elected school board in 2004, but by 2008, DPS was losing money and students through mismanagement and revenue losses to an aggressive charter school program passed by state Republicans. By 2014, only 47 percent of Detroit's K–12 students were enrolled in DPS, and "money followed the student" to charter schools. Democratic governor Jennifer Granholm put DPS under a state emergency manager in 2009, but revenue and attendance losses continued.

In spite of political pressure, Granholm resisted putting the entire city government under an emergency manager. It was difficult for a white Democrat to take power away from a majority Black city that also was a reliable source of votes, and administering and being responsible for the city's finances wasn't a solution any politician willingly sought.

Things changed with the 2010 election of Republican governor Rick Snyder. A self-described nerd, Snyder had made a fortune as president of Gateway Computers and had served on the board of the New Economy Initiative (NEI), a philanthropically funded effort to help turn Detroit's economy around. Snyder took a tough line on Detroit, including contemplating an emergency manager to assume most powers held by elected officials. The city signed a consent agreement in 2012 to carry out reforms under a state watchdog advisory body, but little was accomplished.

Like all issues in Detroit, an emergency manager was viewed through the long-standing prism of racial distrust. Because of the high concentration of poverty among Blacks and their being hemmed into central cities across the state, appointing emergency managers for Detroit along with other financially troubled Michigan cities could mean almost half of the state's Black residents would be living where power had been taken away from their elected officials.[54]

The state already had placed four cities and three school districts (including Detroit's) under emergency managers. In November 2012, the American Federation of State, County, and Municipal Employees (AFSCME) union led a ballot initiative overturning the state's emergency manager law. A postelection, Republican-led legislative session enacted a new manager law and prevented it from being overturned by voters. In March 2013, Snyder appointed an emergency manager for Detroit—Kevyn

Orr, an African American bankruptcy lawyer. Orr assumed many powers from elected officials, including newly elected Detroit mayor Dave Bing, a businessman and former professional basketball star.

Orr concluded that Detroit was running out of money and unable to provide basic services. The number of employed residents had fallen over 53 percent since 1970, with an especially deep plunge after the 2008 Great Recession. Police were clearing 11 percent of murders, compared to 35 percent in Cleveland and 66 percent in St. Louis. The city had cut around 40 percent of its police force, and it took an average of fifty-eight minutes for police to respond to priority calls compared to a national average of eleven minutes. Forty percent of the city's streetlights didn't work. Firefighters didn't use hydraulic ladders unless a life was at stake because the ladders hadn't been inspected.

Extensive blight drove down property values and taxes. Property tax revenues fell over 19 percent after 2008, leading to a downward spiral of more abandonment, less rehabilitation, lower revenues, and declining city services. But the city lacked the funds and capacity to respond effectively. A 2012 Internal Revenue Service (IRS) audit described the city's income tax system as "catastrophic." The city wasn't paying its bills, especially to its pension and retiree health system. Proposing to defer over $100 million of pension contributions while continuing layoffs of city workers meant rising overall pension and retiree health-care payments. And Kilpatrick's prize-winning Wall Street debt deal was requiring ever-higher interest payments: the city had not reduced the principal at all because the deal initially required interest-only payments.[55]

Orr convened the city's creditors, including banks, bond insurers, and union representatives of workers and pensioners, and threatened not to pay on the COPs bonds and thus put the city in default. Orr argued that Detroit should direct its limited revenues to failing city services. Secured creditors were protected, but unsecured creditors felt they were being forced into losses of up to fifty cents on the dollar. They concluded that Orr "wanted to vaporize their holdings and use the leftovers to upgrade city services."[56]

The creditors balked. The bond insurers didn't want to pay investors, and retiree representatives couldn't agree to Orr's proposed deep pension cuts; the initial restructuring proposal meant retirees would get as little as sixteen cents on the dollar. In spite of rhetoric about high pensions, the average police officer's annual pension was around $30,000 in 2011, lower than many other cities. And the average municipal worker pension was just over $18,000, below the $24,008 federal poverty level for a household of four. Retired Detroit workers were not in Social Security so modest city pensions were the sole income for many.

Orr targeted Detroit's pension and retiree health benefits. Just four budget categories—annual payouts for retiree health care, contributions to the pension funds, principal and interest on the COPs, and premiums on the swaps insurance—already were 27.2 percent of the city's revenues in fiscal year (FY) 2012. Orr's projections for FY 2016—only four years away—showed these four categories alone rising to over 50 percent of city revenues, with a continuing steady tax revenue decline.[57] Orr also proposed deep cuts to unsecured investors. He announced Detroit wouldn't cover the unsecured pension COPs, triggering an immediate downgrade of the city's financial status and panicking the two firms who had insured the COPs, now on the hook to pay investors.[58]

Bankruptcy appeared as the only route to fiscal stabilization. The federal government refused to help Detroit, in contrast to $80 billion for the auto industry in the federal bank bailout bill, the Troubled Asset Relief Program (TARP). In May 2013, Orr notified the state treasurer that Detroit was insolvent, meaning it couldn't borrow. Governor Snyder and the Republican state legislature wouldn't help the city not only because Michigan's finances were also in critical condition but also because many of them saw Detroit's problems as self-inflicted. Oakland County's Brooks Patterson tried to separate his county's future from Detroit's, saying, "I'm just done sending cold, hard cash to the city, especially when it's going to go right down a rathole."[59]

Although there was plenty of mismanagement in Detroit, bankruptcy was ultimately caused by the decades-long decline in the city's economy and population and the decades-long failure of state and federal governments to help the city. Former Goldman Sachs investment banker Wallace Turbeville concluded, "Detroit's bankruptcy was primarily caused by a severe decline in revenue and exacerbated by complicated Wall Street deals."[60]

Detroit filed for federal Chapter 9 bankruptcy in July 2013 the largest municipal bankruptcy in American history. This suspended debt payments and protected fiscal and operational restructuring from creditors who now faced significant financial losses. Being in federal court gave Orr several advantages, especially in relation to pensions. Michigan's state constitution explicitly protected accrued public employee pension benefits. A state judge ruled against Orr, but the federal bankruptcy judge found federal law overrode the state constitution.

The complex politics of bankruptcy drove Detroit's retirees into alliance with the Wall Street bond insurers because both faced substantial losses under Orr's proposal. Together, the two groups accounted for close to 90 percent of the city's total unsecured liabilities and thus held enormous leverage in negotiations. Without approval by creditors, the bankruptcy could not be easily or quickly resolved. So the plight of Detroit retirees, many living only on their pensions and without Social Security, became a central political battleground.

In addition to litigation by the bond insurers and unions representing retirees, political resistance in Detroit was growing. Orr and the governor were attacked, especially over the deep cuts proposed for retirees—up to 34 percent of the modest pensions of former city employees, many of whom were African American. Creditors wanted other revenues to relieve the financial pressure.

Unlike a corporation in bankruptcy, cities can't sell all of their assets to pay creditors. The city must still provide police, fire, sanitation, health, education, and other services. But individual assets can be sold, and creditors found a new potential revenue source—the city-owned Detroit Institute of Arts (DIA). Unlike most museums, with collections owned by nonprofit organizations, the DIA's world-class art and building was owned directly by the city. In December 2013, Christie's estimated selling the best parts of the collection could raise up to $866 million, while an informal survey by the *Detroit Free Press* estimated the most important pieces could fetch up to $2.5 billion.[61]

The chief negotiator appointed by federal bankruptcy judge Steven Rhodes feared the DIA collection would be sold, and he approached private philanthropic foundations for funding to avoid the sale. But some of the foundations, especially those committed to racial and social justice, were skeptical about seeming to put artwork ahead of pensioner and city needs. Rip Rapson, president of the Kresge Foundation, reportedly told Rosen not to "put the foundations in the position of seeming to come to the rescue of the art institute . . . we also can't be seen as coming to the rescue of the pensioners." Under Rapson's leadership, Kresge had made substantial investments in building community capacity, trust, and leadership in the city, and a divisive bankruptcy could reverse that work, especially in poor Black neighborhoods. Resolving the bankruptcy faster and more equitably would be in the interest of the city, its citizens, and the pensioners. And such a move could politically isolate the bond insurers from their potential allies among Detroit's retirees.[62]

A consortium of foundations, including the Kresge, Ford, Mott, and Knight Foundations, which had earlier funded the $100 million NEI, joined a "grand bargain." Foundations (using their tax-exempt dollars) would contribute over $350 million, most of which came from Kresge and Ford. The state also would contribute, while pensioners would get smaller pension cuts but have their cost-of-living increases eliminated and promised retiree health care aggressively phased out. In turn, the DIA and its art collection would be transferred to nonprofit ownership, insulating it from future claims against the city. Judge Rhodes accepted the grand bargain, as did the Detroit retirees in a vote because the pension cuts were less onerous than originally proposed.

The grand bargain remains controversial. Although the agreement blurred it, the bargain favored a set of unsecured creditors (pensioners) over the bond insurers, one of which tried (and failed) to litigate this issue. And while foundations often are praised for the bargain, it is estimated that close to 75 percent of the retirement liabilities reduction came not from philanthropic or government funds but from Detroit's retirees accepting smaller pensions, even though many lived close to poverty.[63] It is an open question whether some artwork could or should have been sold to get a financial contribution that would lessen the burden on retirees. The foundations had (and continue to have) strong, ongoing commitments to social equity in Detroit and in effect the grand bargain could also be seen as diverting funds from those efforts.

Government also played a reduced role. The state of Michigan made a relatively small contribution to the grand bargain while at the same time approving $440 million in economic development bonds for a new hockey and basketball arena in Detroit, in effect subsidizing billionaire owner Mike Ilitch. The federal government made no financial contribution. Its impact was limited to the legal bankruptcy framework that claimed preemption of Michigan's constitutional protections for pensions, and the de facto subsidy of the philanthropic contribution through the federal tax code, because foundations are tax-free entities.

Seventy-three percent of general city workers approved the deal to keep the bankruptcy and restructuring on track. Solutions were found to other issues, including the proposed privatization of the municipal water system and awarding valuable city-owned property and development rights to the unsecured bond insurers, who then dropped their litigation threats. Judge Rhodes approved the city's plan of adjustment covering both financial restructuring and future spending, with Orr presenting a bare bones service delivery plan along with modest revenue projections. The city exited bankruptcy on November 7, 2014.

DETROIT'S FUTURE AND THE PANDEMIC'S TOLL

By then, Detroit had a new mayor—Mike Duggan, a former county official and CEO of the Detroit Medical Center. He won the 2013 election in spite of mixed support from unions. Duggan was Detroit's first white mayor in forty years. His well-funded campaign presented him as a committed, experienced financial manager seeking to dismiss or rein in emergency manager Kevyn Orr.[64]

Some hoped for an economic turnaround. Quicken Loans, owned by Detroit native Dan Gilbert, purchased over 2.6 million square feet of office space and relocated over 7,000 jobs to downtown Detroit. Rents and condominium prices in the city's central business district were rising. Backed by private, public, and philanthropic investment, a light rail system opened along Woodward Avenue in May 2017, although the line stopped almost six miles short of the city's northern border. And the NEI claimed responsibility for 17,490 new direct and indirect jobs in seven years, although those estimates were for the entire region, not just the city.[65]

Both the sports arena and the transit process were criticized for lacking public input, with advocates arguing the money could have been better spent on neighborhood development and on bus service.[66] One analysis concluded that in spite of high-visibility projects, the city continued to struggle economically while suffering "increasing inequality."[67]

Duggan was reelected in 2017, and in December 2018—after three consecutive balanced budgets and four years after exiting bankruptcy—the city reentered the credit market with bonds to fund economic development. Bankruptcy reduced debt payments but also pension obligations, helping stabilize the budget. State oversight would continue, but the city could now take budgetary steps without official state preclearance.[68]

But this fiscal stabilization must be set against Detroit's larger trends, which continued to lag behind the rest of the nation. The Census Bureau estimated that the city's population between 2015 and 2019 fell by almost 70,000 residents. Detroit's unemployment rate remained consistently the worst among America's fifty largest cities, with its 2019 rate of 8.8 percent more than 50 percent higher than the forty-ninth worst city, Fresno, California. The 2019 poverty rate was 30.6 percent, more than double the rate in the surrounding metropolitan area and significantly higher than all other large American cities. And population kept falling, dropping by 38,000 people, or 5.6 percent of the total, between 2015 and 2020.[69]

The region remained politically fragmented, with economic development and other programs tilted against the city and patterns of poor governance haunting it. It took forty years and twenty-three attempts to finally establish a regional transit authority in 2012. But continuing the decades-long conflict between Detroit and its suburbs, a 2016 regional ballot initiative to fund more transit failed, and in 2018, suburban counties blocked the authority from even considering another ballot proposal. Mayor Duggan moved aggressively to address Detroit's housing blight, but in 2016 a major corruption scandal in the Land Bank Authority jeopardized the antiblight program. In 2019, the median value of Detroit's owner-occupied housing units was about one-third of units in the metropolitan area. And after spending $324 million in public funds to build the new sports arena, the adjacent affordable housing and mixed-use project (District Detroit) repeatedly missed deadlines and construction and jobs targets.[70]

So even after exiting bankruptcy and reentering the credit markets, decades-long structural barriers continued to plague Detroit. The city still faced declining industries and weak employment growth, slumping property values and a constricted tax base, racial tension in the region and state, the failure of state and national governments to provide ongoing support, and a combative us-against-them mentality in the city and region. The region's racially charged hostility has long suppressed or diverted energies that could have gone to new political organization and reform, and innovative economic development strategies. Racial tensions were underscored in 2020 when Republicans on the Wayne County Board of Canvassers initially refused to certify the city of Detroit's presidential election votes in favor of Joe Biden, an action quickly reversed under charges of racism.[71]

One progressive development strategy, which copied innovations in Los Angeles and elsewhere, was a 2016 law requiring a community benefit agreement (CBA) for projects over $75 million receiving over $1 million in public subsidies. The winning ballot ordinance was developed in order to displace another, more aggressive CBA ordinance. One review found that by the end of 2018, "the first year of Detroit's Community Benefits ordinance yielded almost no community benefits that the city can enforce." The city council made some revisions to the ordinance in 2021, mostly expanding community consultation and public meetings.[72]

Prior to the pandemic, Mayor Duggan faced pressure to increase opportunities for community organizations and Black-owned businesses. A 2019 survey of 100 leading Detroit Black-owned firms found 67.8 percent of them did not "feel included and able to fully participate in the economic growth happening in the city of Detroit." Duggan formed a Detroit Equity Council to link Black-owned firms to city contracts and private development.[73] The city also launched a new Strategic Neighborhood Fund with ten target areas outside the downtown area aimed at neighborhood stabilization and housing. Initial reports from neighborhood residents found "greater overall neighborhood satisfaction" in the first wave coupled with "fears of being displaced due to rising housing costs."[74]

The city finally began attracting automobile manufacturing. A major parts supplier for Ford built a new $160 million plant, and the city subsidized a new Jeep assembly plant, although one critic called the deal "corporate welfare . . . tantamount to a shakedown." Major central downtown projects were built, many funded by Gilbert of Quicken Loans, with over 15 million square feet and ninety buildings in a growing portfolio.[75] Both the Jeep plant and several major real estate projects are covered by the city's CBA legislation. The Ford Motor Company expanded its rehabilitation of the ruined iconic Michigan Central railroad under a detailed CBA, planning a major mixed-use "mobility innovation district" anchored by the station. And the city counted twenty-two major residential projects being built prior to the pandemic.[76]

Detroit's recovery efforts were harmed by the COVID-19 pandemic recession. Michigan's first two cases were in the Detroit metropolitan area, and by April 2020, with only 6.8 percent of the state's population, Detroit accounted for 29 percent of all COVID-19 deaths. The recession battered the city's economy. Detroit's unemployment rates were only slightly higher than the nation's at the end of 2019; by the end of 2020, the rates were much higher than the national average.[77]

As in many cities, COVID-19 exacerbated Detroit's economic and political fragility, furthering inequality and accelerating preexisting negative trends. The city lost population and its tax base even when the region grew slightly. And the city's economy suffered for decades, until the cumulative negative conditions seemed almost unsolvable.

Like other cities, Detroit's city budget suffered deeply from the pandemic recession. The city's budget relies on income taxes, casino revenues, and state aid, with over 60 percent of its general fund projected to come from those three sources. All three sources were sharply reduced by the recession, with little hope for alternative funds from the federal government. In April 2020, the city projected a 16.4 percent reduction in general fund revenues and feared budget overruns would result in reimposition of state financial controls. Detroit's high concentration of essential workers with few financial resources—many of whom are Blacks facing higher COVID-19 risks—and an already stressed municipal budget and health system meant the city faced a very challenging winter in 2020. Rising case counts caused a virtual economic shutdown, including the city's casinos, hurting working households but also opening deeper holes in the city's budget, with reduced spending and further employee furloughs and layoffs looming.[78]

In August 2021, Mayor Duggan was overwhelmingly elected to a third term with 75 percent of the vote. He emphasized economic development, citing projects like the Jeep plant and a new Amazon warehouse under construction. His opposition expressed fears of gentrification and a belief that Detroit neighborhoods don't benefit from overall economic development efforts. But even national economic recovery leaves Detroit facing ongoing structural problems—a low tax base and high poverty, racial and economic tensions with surrounding suburbs, and a continuing policy tilt against cities at both the state and national level.

Detroit still performs poorly on a variety of metrics. The 2020 census found that the city lost 10.5 percent of its population, around 75,000 people, between 2010 and 2020. In 2019, it had the second highest poverty rate of any U.S. city with a population over 100,000. Earnings for those working also were low. A University of Michigan study found that "less than 30 percent of Detroit residents working full-time earned enough to sustain a family of three at a middle-class standard of living in 2019." This reflected the city's long-term economic challenges; Detroit's gross city product (GCP) rose only 9 percent between 1997 and 2019, compared with growth in the nation's gross domestic product (GDP) of 66 percent.[79]

CONCLUSION

When it was flush with success and revenue in the 1950s, Detroit tried to provide welfare state benefits to city employees and residents even when the state and nation didn't, moving forward (often out of necessity) without regional, state, or national support. But the city's revenue base couldn't support the efforts on its own, especially as economic circumstances changed the city's budget capacity as metropolitan fragmentation and suburbanization worked actively against the city, while racial conflict grew. Detroit provides a sobering example for America, serving as what economist Rob Johnson calls the "canary in the coal mine." Its collapse warns us about how cities can suffer when economic shifts are coupled with racial hostility and negative public policy.[80]

Although overt regional hostility has abated somewhat, structural economic and racial divides remain. Given the region's toxic history when it comes to race, the collapse of the old industrial economy, and a political system that seems stuck in regional fragmentation and noncooperation, it isn't clear what the path forward is for the once-vibrant Motor City. The city's motto is "Speramus meliora, resurget cineribus," usually translated as "We hope for better things; it will arise from the ashes." But without substantial political change in the city, region, and state, and perhaps nationally, that rising will be delayed or suppressed.

6

LOS ANGELES

Progressive Coalitions in a Changing Economy

I n November 2008, with the nation entering the worst economic crisis since the Great Depression, Los Angeles County voters approved raising their sales tax by one-half cent to 8.75 percent, one of the nation's highest. The increased tax—called Measure R—would be devoted largely to mass transit, with projected revenues over $30 billion.

Tax increases are never popular. Measure R also needed a two-thirds supermajority, a condition imposed by the 1978 state constitutional amendment, Proposition 13. It limited property tax increases but also created a supermajority requirement for passing tax increases in the state legislature or local governments in special elections. In spite of these barriers and in the face of a sharply declining economy, Measure R was backed by labor unions, communities of color, environmental groups, and even the chamber of commerce. It passed by 67.2 percent, just over the necessary threshold.

This surprising result reflected the strong political coalition built through years of political and economic organizing and advocacy centered in the city of Los Angeles (LA). Like New York and Detroit, LA suffered from industrial change, state and federal policies favoring suburbs over cities, racial and ethnic divisions amid major demographic shifts, and structural racism in housing and employment. LA's creation of a coalition supporting progressive economic measures stands in contrast to fiscal decline and conflict in many U.S. cities and offers important lessons for future progressive efforts in cities and urban regions.

When the COVID-19 pandemic struck, LA's progressives responded quickly, with a group of philanthropists, community organizations, elected officials, and activist scholars forming the Committee for Greater LA. In under six months, they researched, wrote, discussed with stakeholders, and produced a remarkable report, *No Going Back: Together for an Equitable and Inclusive Los Angeles.*[1] The report analyzed inequities and recommended policy actions in fifteen domains, from economic development to housing affordability, to immigration, and will likely form the basis for progressive advocacy and politics in the coming years. The rapidity and quality of this effort testifies to the ongoing strength of LA's progressive coalition and the ability of its members to work together even under crisis conditions.

THE 1990s: RACIAL CONFLICT, ECONOMIC CHANGE, AND PROGRESSIVE ORGANIZING

Understanding LA's movement for equity, growth, and environmental quality requires looking back to the troubled 1990s, when two sets of issues—one political, one economic—illustrated the city's troubles. First, in April 1992, the Rodney King riots shook the city, state, and nation after police officers were acquitted of misconduct in King's earlier arrest. On March 3, 1991, King, an African American construction worker, was arrested and then beaten, kicked, and Tasered after a high-speed car chase. A video of the arrest ignited outrage against the Los Angeles Police Department (LAPD) officers who abused King and claimed he was resisting arrest while on drugs, although later drug tests were negative. King was on parole from the California prison system and said he feared returning to prison for a parole violation.

The case received widespread media coverage, and four officers were indicted. Their lawyers won a change of venue to nearby Simi Valley, and in April 1992 the jury acquitted all officers of some charges, only deadlocking on one officer charged with excessive force. Protests and conflict broke out immediately, especially in the largely Black South Central neighborhood. Over 13,000 National Guard. U.S. Army, and Marine troops eventually were deployed, and the disturbances largely stopped after six days. Sixty-three people died and estimated economic losses reached over $1 billion.

The disturbances are still largely remembered as Blacks angrily protesting racist treatment by the LAPD. That certainly was a core factor, but there also was Latino involvement, especially Central American and Mexican immigrants later seen to be protesting economic conditions. Social critic Mike Davis points out that "36 percent of the riot arrestees were African-American, while 52 percent had Spanish surnames and 10 percent were white."[2]

Activists and scholars who helped launch LA's new equity movement saw the violence not only as evidence of racial polarization but also as linked to a backdrop of economic recession, industrial restructuring, and government austerity. The King riots took place during a painful transition in LA's economy as the aerospace, defense, and manufacturing sectors underwent a sharp decline that rippled throughout the entire region. In 1990, with job declines already underway, aerospace employment was 26 percent of all manufacturing and 6 percent of total employment in Los Angeles County, compared to a national level around 8 percent of manufacturing and 2 percent of total jobs.[3] The county had around 10 percent of all aerospace jobs in the nation.

Manufacturing in general, and aerospace in particular, also had high-value multiplier effects, supporting smaller machine shops, contractors, design firms, and other related jobs, along with higher wages that helped sustain overall prosperity. Defense spending supported many of LA's aerospace jobs, but the fading of the Cold War reduced the defense share of the federal budget. Defense procurement often is highly specialized, and firms and workers could not easily adapt to other lines of work, especially in the face of sharply falling overall demand.[4] In the decade after 1986, aerospace industry employment fell in Los Angeles County by 122,700 jobs, a 54.6 percent loss.[5]

Total manufacturing didn't fall as dramatically. In fact, numerical job losses in aerospace were closely matched by growth in clothing and apparel. But the new jobs were significantly lower paid, providing less of a regional economic boost. The sophisticated supplier networks of the aerospace industry also supported high-paying jobs, not only in direct production but also in engineering, product design, and related occupations. With annual median wages for an aerospace job at $45,000 but at only $17,000 in apparel, "it took 2.5 garment jobs to equal the purchasing power of a single aerospace job." These income reductions affected household and consumer spending and reduced government tax revenues.[6]

LA's rapidly shifting demographics, principally white out-migration and Latino in-migration, reflected this economic transition. Over 800,000 whites left as a result of the recession.[7] As the industrial base shifted, large numbers of Latino migrants entered nondurable manufacturing industries like clothing and also low-paid service work.

In addition to racism, the Rodney King disturbances should be viewed against this rapid structural economic change, especially higher-paid manufacturing work being replaced by lower-paid jobs. Accompanied by white departures and a large inflow of Latino immigrants, the disturbances also came at a regional demographic turning point. This not only reemphasized the long-standing problems of low-income Black communities but also the fracturing of the city's economy and its inability to cope with major population shifts and the new wave of immigrants, many of them facing discrimination and poverty.

This wasn't the future envisioned by LA's political and business leadership. In 1988, the Los Angeles 2000 Committee, whose members were appointed by Black mayor Tom Bradley, produced a visionary, optimistic view of the city's future, stating, "Just as New York, London and Paris stood as symbols of past centuries, Los Angeles will be THE city of the 21st century."[8] But the 1992 disturbances shook the confidence of the city's elites, and their worries became central in the 1993 election to replace the term-limited Bradley.

The top two mayoral candidates had very different views of how to address the city's problems. Democrat Mike Woo adopted a broad range of progressive views, saying that he would fire LAPD chief Daryl Gates, steer capital investment into damaged South Central and other minority communities, and appoint a gay member to the police commission. Woo's opponent, Republican businessman and lawyer Richard Riordan, emphasized law and order and a more conservative economic platform, saying that LA was "increasingly the enemy of business." He advocated leasing the publicly owned Los Angeles International Airport (LAX) to private business and using the funds to hire more police officers, cutting regulations, and relaxing business taxes and permitting policies.[9] Riordan won the June election with 54 percent of the vote.

But the 1990s also saw a variety of progressive activists engaging with LA's changing economy and demography. They sought broad coalitions on diverse issues with two consistent themes: embedding each issue in a larger vision of regional economic change and equity, and reaching out across ethnic and racial lines. Activist scholars linked their research with emerging social movements and specific issue campaigns. They also analyzed how LA's transforming industrial structure was affecting organized labor and how unions might work with the new activists and immigrants.[10] These new coalitions, later joined by environmentalists, would provide the organizational vision and muscle for the progressive policy experiments that made Los Angeles a national leader in linking economic and social justice.

Several key organizations emerged from this initial period. The Bus Riders Union formed a multiethnic and racial alliance that successfully changed how LA spent its public transit money by forcing more spending on bus lines serving poor neighborhoods. Action for Grassroots Empowerment and Neighborhood Development Alternatives (AGENDA) grew out of community organizing in South Los Angeles, anchored in a strong Black base but with a vision including "consciousness-raising, community organizing, and direct action with sophisticated research, strong coalitions, and long-term alliances" and a focus on the city's place in the regional economy.[11]

A third key organization focusing on economic conditions for workers was central to many successful campaigns in the coming years—the Los Angeles Alliance for a New Economy (LAANE). LAANE grew out of the Tourism Industry Development Council (TIDC) formed in 1993 with the leadership of three people: Miguel Contreras, an organizer for the UNITE-HERE union; Maria Elena Durazo, president of the LA hotel workers union local; and Madeline Janis, an activist attorney with roots in the immigrant and refugee rights movement. They were sobered by the King riots but saw how the structural transformation of LA's economy was worsening wages and job conditions for immigrant and other low-income workers. The organization initially was funded by the hotel workers' union to concentrate on improving working conditions and incomes in that industry and also to promote a better image for LA's less well-known ethnic neighborhoods.[12]

LAANE quickly entered other battles. In 1995, some workers at LAX were going to lose unionized jobs as the city awarded new food service contracts to low-wage, nonunion franchises. LAANE worked with the LA city council to help these workers retain their jobs, with a law enacted over Mayor Riordan's veto. But they realized simple job retention wasn't enough. As Durazo noted, the campaign's analysis and talking with workers at the airport revealed that "the new hires at LAX didn't have union wages or any benefits. We realized we couldn't just win worker retention. We had to create a living wage."[13]

LA's labor activists began fighting for a policy like Baltimore's 1994 living-wage law, which established a new wage 16 percent higher than the federal minimum wage for some city contractors. The city council again overrode a mayoral veto on a 1997 bill, backed by a broad coalition of labor unions, minority community organizations, liberal council members, and religious leaders. The law was expanded in 1999 to ensure coverage of city-owned and -operated facilities like LAX.

The living-wage campaign was not the only major activist initiative during the Riordan years, but it was the one most focused on wages and job quality. The campaign opened a new front for low-income workers by using the city's contracting and regulatory powers to create better jobs as part of obtaining contracts and benefits with the city. In 1998, LAANE helped incorporate living-wage, job-training, and health-care provisions into a Hollywood real estate development deal. As Harold Myerson notes, "What Janis realized was that local government's contracts with and assistance to private companies gave cities and counties the legal authority to raise wages and create benefits selectively in the private sector."[14]

This new energy in community and economic organizing affected union politics. LAANE cofounder Miguel Contreras won election as secretary-treasurer of the Los Angeles County Labor Federation, the first Latino in that position.[15] The aerospace decline and the rise of lower-paid manufacturing and service jobs sparked a change in union politics and policies. Contreras focused not only on classic union bread-and-butter issues but also on more aggressive political support of progressive candidates and initiatives, including the critical issue of immigration, because Latino workers were the fastest growing group in LA's workforce.

In 1998, this growing labor and community coalition anchored a broad coalition on the proposed expansion of Universal Studios. The coalition advocated multiple benefits in exchange for public subsidies and zoning and land-use approval. In addition to seeking better job conditions and living wages, organizers linked with environmental groups concerned about land use and water quality, and they advocated project jobs for low-income community residents. This style of incrementally adding new benefits and expanding coalitions was emerging as the LA strategy, winning concrete benefits and bridging the sometimes large gaps in trust and outlook between communities and people of color, labor unions, and environmental activists.

The proposed expansion of the downtown sport and convention Staples Center proved a watershed for these movements. The original center broke ground in 1998, but with a long-term vision of commercial and housing development to help revitalize the area, a priority for Riordan. In 2001, LA's growing community coalitions entered the negotiations for a hotel, theater, and apartments, and an expansion of the convention center requiring a city subsidy worth over $70 million. LAANE and Strategic Actions for a Just Economy (SAJE)[16] were the lead negotiators for the Figueroa Corridor Coalition for Economic Justice, which included twenty-eight community organizations and five unions.

Riordan's last year in office was 2001, and developers eventually agreed to a historic set of concessions, fearing a new mayor and city council could set the project back for years. The final agreement included a goal that at least 70 percent of jobs in the project would pay living wages and that the project would include community skill training and access to those new jobs, creation of parks and open spaces in consultation with the community, and affordable housing.[17] The agreement also included monitoring through quarterly meetings between the developer and an oversight committee. Greg LeRoy, the head of Good Jobs First, a national advocate for linking public economic development subsidies to enforceable community benefits, said, "I've never heard of an agreement as comprehensive as this."[18]

The Staples Center agreement exemplified what were now being called community benefit agreements (CBAs). For years, scholars and activists had decried cities' awarding tax subsidies and other benefits to private firms for economic development, arguing such policies often gave away limited tax resources without getting adequate benefits in return, especially for low-income people and communities of color.[19]

Traditional urban development theory assumed that zoning and other regulatory policies were the best way to govern private firm behavior and that incentives and subsidies were needed to get private capital investment, especially in economically distressed areas. The development supposedly induced by the incentives would then benefit the city more broadly, through jobs, tax revenues, and higher property values.

But CBA advocates saw those subsidies as increasingly captured by private interests, draining scarce tax revenues and starving essential services without producing the promised jobs and economic benefits for poor city and community residents. LAANE's pioneering insight was linking the city's contracting, zoning, and taxation powers and subsidies to concrete, measurable outcomes from private investors. This allowed building broad coalitions that could negotiate with both the city and investors. These coalitions had strong and diverse political support, giving them credible threats to use voting and litigation to delay or stop projects unless developers negotiated.

Supported in part by philanthropic funding, interest in CBAs grew rapidly among progressive urban groups.[20] The final Staples Center agreement showed the possibilities for such negotiations. Rather than concentrating only on one dimension—affordable housing, parks and open spaces, job creation, training, or improved job conditions including wages and benefits—the Staples Center deal included all of these and showed that CBAs could address a wide range of concerns. This range meant that broader CBA coalitions could be built, bringing what often were single-issue organizations (unions, people of color, community and neighborhood groups, environmentalists) under a bigger tent where each one's chance of advancing its specific issue was strengthened by the broader alliance.

FROM INDIVIDUAL BATTLES TO A PROGRESSIVE POLITICAL COALITION

LA's 2001 mayoral election reflected the electoral potential of these broader CBA coalitions but also showed they had some distance to go. The election was fought against the backdrop of a national recession exacerbated by the uncertainty caused by the 9/11 attacks in New York City; Washington, DC; and Pennsylvania. In California, the bursting of the dot-com bubble initially hurt the LA region less than the San Francisco region, which had a higher concentration of information technology (IT) jobs and investment.[21]

Southern California began suffering aggregate job loss in the fourth quarter of 2001. The region's structural economic shift away from aerospace continued, with that sector's higher-paid employment falling at a 15 percent annual level. In the three years between 2002 and 2005, overall manufacturing employment in LA County fell by 62,500 jobs across both durable and nondurable sectors. Apparel jobs, which peaked in 1996, fell in the three-year period by 15.2 percent, or 11,100 jobs.[22]

But the most dramatic change continued to be demographic. It was driven by the steady influx of younger Latinos to the region, many of whom in turn formed households and had children. In the twenty years between 1990 and 2010, LA County's population grew by slightly over 1 million, but the white population declined by 886,792, a 24.5 percent reduction. The county's Black population also fell, by 73,758 (7.9 percent). But the Latino population increased in twenty years by over 1.3 million, a 39.2 percent increase. By 2010, Latinos were 47.4 percent of all county residents, a share that stabilized at 48.6 percent in 2020.[23]

The 2001 mayoral election took place in the midst of these continuing economic and demographic shifts. Riordan was term-limited and the early favorite (and eventual winner) was city attorney James Hahn. Although white, Hahn had strong Black voter support rooted in his father's civil rights advocacy during forty years on the Los Angeles County Board of Supervisors. None of the six candidates won a majority in the first round, with Hahn coming in second behind Antonio Villaraigosa, the former California State Assembly Speaker who began his political career as a teachers' union organizer.

The county American Federation of Labor and Congress of Industrial Unions (AFL-CIO) supported Villaraigosa, and their support combined with Latino voter registration and turnout made him the top of the two finalists. But the city's public sector unions supported Hahn, and in the two-person runoff election, Hahn positioned himself as the law-and-order candidate, citing his prosecution of gangs and winning the endorsement of the police union. In a city still traumatized by the King disturbances and fears of crime, this brought Hahn victory, with an unusual coalition of white voters, police and public sector unions, and strong African American voter support.[24]

Villaraigosa's surprising strength and his support from private sector unions showed how coalition building from the CBA and related movements was foreshadowing a change in LA's politics. The emerging political movement had major analytic and advocacy support from the Progressive Los Angeles Network (PLAN), an umbrella group of policy scholars and political activists with ties to the living-wage and CBA movement and to the county AFL-CIO.[25]

The CBA coalition continued targeting new opportunities. One of Hahn's major priorities was expanding and modernizing LAX airport, a plan conceived after the 9/11 attacks. The plan faced environmental concerns and community opposition from neighborhoods nearest the airport, those most affected by airport noise, pollution, and other environmental hazards. Drawing on their Staples Center experience, CBA advocates formed a new umbrella coalition, the LAX Coalition for Economic, Environmental, and Educational Justice. The coalition eventually included twenty-five groups, once again emphasizing quality job opportunities for minority and poor workers along with other community benefits.

The LAX coalition was strengthened by including environmental organizations and the threat of using environmental impact statements and laws to stop the expansion if LAX, and the city wouldn't negotiate. Although environmental issues had been one element of previous CBAs and of the progressive movement in general,[26] in the 2004 LAX fight, they became more prominent, with six environmental organizations joining the coalition.

Faced with costly and lengthy litigation (including regarding health impacts on children in nearby minority communities) and political opposition from community and labor groups, in 2004, Los Angeles reached agreement on another landmark CBA. If LAX kept its part of the bargain (a monitoring group including coalition members would oversee the agreement), the coalition agreed not to sue to stop the expansion, although they could do so if future implementation was compromised.[27]

The LAX deal again broke new ground in CBAs. On the economic side, it included living-wage provisions for workers at the airport, local hiring for neighborhood residents and low-income people, $15 million in job-training funds, and business opportunities for minority and women-owned firms. But it also included extensive environmental provisions, including soundproofing for nearby schools and houses, clean air retrofits to construction and working vehicles at the airport, and research funds to investigate health impacts in adjacent residential areas.[28]

Continuing pressure for CBAs and other progressive labor policies took place during ongoing structural economic and social change. Two of LA's three key economic sectors in the 1980s—manufacturing and financial services—continued losing jobs. Manufacturing now was losing jobs not only in aerospace and other high-value jobs but also in lower-paid apparel industry work. Jobs were growing in logistics, driven by surging Asian imports through the Port of Los Angeles and from U.S. trade policy, but those jobs "did not create the stimulus that locally produced manufacturing exports provide."[29]

Between 1978 and 2005, higher-paid durable manufacturing jobs in aerospace, automobiles, and other sectors in Los Angeles County declined by 64 percent. Social, public service, and educational employment (driven in part by mandated class size reductions in schools) rose by 49 percent, and jobs in low-paid services rose by 43 percent, making "low paid routine service jobs" in retail, accommodation, and food services "LA's biggest industry sector."[30] Individual CBAs, even historic ones like the LAX agreement, could not change these overall economic dynamics at sufficient scale.

LAANE and other progressive organizations brought these issues to the forefront of the 2005 mayoral campaign, which ended up as a rematch between incumbent James Hahn and Antonio Villaraigosa, who this time beat Hahn by 59 percent to 41 percent. Villaraigosa held his strong advantage among Latino voters and increased his share of whites by 9 percent to split that group 50:50. But his biggest gain was among Blacks. Hahn still won them by 52 percent to 48 percent, but in 2001, Hahn had won Black votes by an 80:20 margin.[31] Turnout for the election versus 2001 fell from 38 percent to 34 percent, so voters as a whole seemed less energized, but Villaraigosa improved with key constituencies. Although he didn't win the endorsement of the Los Angeles AFL-CIO and other unions that viewed Hahn as friendly to labor, Villaraigosa got more votes from union members.[32]

Villaraigosa had strong ties to the progressive coalition, and his mayoralty embraced many of their goals and policy ideas. In his first term, he supported unionizing low-wage security guards in the city, enacted a $100 million affordable housing trust fund, and pushed the city's

Community Redevelopment Agency to negotiate harder with companies, seeking better jobs, wages, and benefits in return for city subsidies. And he tried (but failed) to get more control over LA's public schools.[33]

On the economic front, his first term was marked by several important victories for jobs with equity: a 2008 agreement with the Port of Los Angeles that would provide environmental, community, and labor benefits; expansion of the LAX living-wage agreement to cover hotels near the airport, and then to provide health insurance for workers at the airport; and passage in 2008 of a half-cent addition to the county sales tax (Measure R) that would produce $40 billion in new transit spending, with a substantial amount directed to mass transit.

The negotiations around the port expansion illustrate the growing scope and vision of the jobs with equity movement but also the challenges in meeting the diverse needs of all its members. The Port of Los Angeles is owned by the city. Rapid increases in imports from China and Asia drove the port's traffic up, along with the traffic at the adjacent Port of Long Beach. The two ports together are the biggest shipping complex in the Western Hemisphere; in 2019 they together had $366.2 billion of international trade shipments: the nation's highest total.[34]

Logistics and the transport of goods were an economic bright spot for Los Angeles, but both came at a substantial environmental cost. Shipping containers have to be downloaded onto railcars or trucks, and the ports have a large amount of truck traffic. Logistical backups and inadequate infrastructure meant substantial delays in loading trucks, and increased security policies after the 9/11 attacks added to delays. And trucks come and go on crowded freeways, often stuck in traffic jams. Taken together, these factors made the over 16,000 diesel trucks working in the two ports a major source of severe air pollution, not only for the ports themselves but also for the predominantly poor and minority residential communities near them.

To handle expanding Asian trade, the Ports of Los Angeles and Long Beach proposed a major expansion. But the expansion would require political support and passage through California's increasingly rigorous environmental impact process. Taking a page from their successful LAX campaign, which blocked the airport's expansion plans until both environmental and jobs issues were addressed, LAANE and others organized the Coalition for Clean Ports, an umbrella organization of over forty community, labor, and environmental organizations. The coalition sought to force the ports to negotiate a CBA or face substantial delays and possible defeat of the expansion plans through environmental litigation and other tactics.[35]

After prolonged negotiation, in 2008, the ports adopted a three-part agreement with important benefits for communities, environmentalists, and labor. Port trucks would be retrofitted to use natural gas or meet a low-emissions standard, funds would be made available through a trust for community programs to abate harm from pollution, and firms would have to classify and hire truck drivers as regular employees rather than the prevailing practice of labeling them as independent contractors. This latter provision was key for labor unions, who were protesting that low-paid "independent" drivers were really de facto employees of large firms who couldn't afford to keep their trucks clean and safe while facing dirty and dangerous jobs. Classifying them as regular employees would open up unionization campaigns for drivers and other trucking company workers.

LAANE conducted detailed research documenting the harm from current port practices and the potential overall environmental and economic benefits of a clean air action plan (CAAP) with three core elements. They estimated total five-year benefits of over $4 billion through health impacts from reduced air pollution, and community and worker benefits through higher wages and health-care benefits as truckers became regular employees. LAANE's work showed many drivers were Latino immigrants, often living in the same communities suffering from the port's pollution, so the research made an explicit link between improving drivers' labor status and working conditions and the broader environmental and community benefits.[36]

The labor provisions were the most controversial parts of the agreement. The Teamsters Union did not have a strong record of working with environmental groups, but the union became a key part of the port coalition, hoping that changing the drivers' status to regular employees would make it possible to organize them. The American Trucking Association, the national trade association of private trucking firms, argued that federal law preempted many of CAAP's core elements, and a federal court eventually agreed, removing the agreement's labor provisions.[37]

Trucking companies also litigated the environmental provisions all the way to the U.S. Supreme Court, which in 2013 did not address the case on the environmental issues, although the labor provisions remained eliminated. In response, and in addition to unionization drives, labor advocates shifted to slower, more cumbersome company-by-company proceedings, arguing that trucking firms were violating labor laws by wrongly classifying drivers as independent contractors.[38]

Labor issues continued as a flashpoint at the port. In 2014, drivers at the Los Angeles and Long Beach ports engaged in rolling work stoppages to protest misclassification, underpayment or withholding of wages, and other labor law violations. In 2015, the dockworkers' union engaged in work stoppages and slowdowns over wages, automation, and working conditions. And in 2019, California's passage of a new law (AB5) against classifying workers as independent contractors gave new life to the driver classification issue. That law was plunged into litigation, with state courts upholding most of it, but federal courts giving mixed rulings while a 2020 ballot initiative exempted ride-share drivers.

The continuing fight at the port shows how the three-pronged coalition—community groups, environmentalists, and labor unions—supported each other's issues. Environmentalists pushed for the transition to clean, low-emission trucks, and community organizations received a variety of program grants. The Sierra Club also supported the AB5 classification bill in order to make trucking companies responsible for reducing truck pollution.[39] And the overall coalition held together in support of labor provisions, even with ongoing tensions between the low-income drivers classified as independent contractors and the unionized port workers. In 2018, a state investigation found some drivers had been misclassified as independent contractors and awarded $1.2 million in additional wages; if trucking companies don't pay, a new state law can hold retailers hiring such companies financially responsible for labor violations.[40]

Some criticized LAANE and its partners for going industry-by-industry and not taking on broader or national policy issues. But Janis argued that this focused strategy can win concrete victories and help build trusted partnerships for future, broader efforts: "The left tends to focus on the economy from sixty thousand feet high . . . It leaves progressives with no sense of what they can do to change it."[41]

The other major political and economic battle of Villaraigosa's first term was voter approval in November 2008 of Measure R, adding half a cent to the Los Angeles County sales tax with funds dedicated to transportation.

Even with projected revenues of $40 billion over thirty years and over 75 percent of the funds dedicated to mass transit, three of the five members of the county board of supervisors opposed it. But Villaraigosa was a major supporter, and the measure just passed the necessary two-thirds voter threshold with 67.2 percent of the vote.[42]

The mayor easily won a second term in 2009, during the depths of the Great Recession, the nation's worst economic decline since the Great Depression. The slumping national economy constrained much of his second term. As with virtually every city in the United States, Los Angeles's finances (along with the state's) suffered from the deep recession as businesses slowed, unemployment rose, and taxes—from business, sales, labor, and property—fell below predicted levels. By 2012, city forecasters' four-year budget outlook foresaw spending increases outpacing a predicted 2.8 percent annual revenue growth, held down by the continuing economic slump.[43]

Opponents blamed Villaraigosa for not battling more with unions over labor costs, citing a 2007 labor contract that resulted in a cumulative 24.5 percent raise over five years for unions other than those for the police and firefighters.[44] With spending outstripping revenue growth, bond ratings fell and borrowing costs rose. This meant little new infrastructure spending from traditional sources, mirroring the experience of virtually all the nation's largest cities.[45]

These constrained municipal finances made the infrastructure spending funded by Measure R even more significant. LAANE and others had supported the measure. They helped devise plans to create unionized training and other programs and to ensure that jobs created by the new spending would be covered by living-wage and other agreements, and that they would be made available to low-income and minority workers. Again bringing together the interests of low-income workers and labor unions (environmental groups broadly supported Measure R due to its emphasis on mass transit), in January 2012, their coalition got the Los Angeles County Metropolitan Transit Authority (Metro) to adopt a broad project labor agreement (PLA) to achieve these goals.[46]

PLAs are used in complex unionized construction projects, where many different skills and types of work are required, to create an umbrella group for resolving disputes and keeping projects on track and to respect the wide variety of work rules and practices of different unions. Under the Metro PLA, the Los Angeles/Orange County Building Trades Council became "the primary source of all craft labor employed on the construction contracts for the various projects," mainly but not exclusively those funded by Measure R. And the unions in turn agreed that "40 percent of the work hours be performed by workers who live in economically disadvantaged neighborhoods, with 10 percent of the work hours going to individuals who are struggling with poverty, chronic unemployment and other hardships." This provided an apprenticeship training pathway to a unionized construction career for disadvantaged and minority workers.[47]

Initially used for dispute resolution, PLAs in recent years have included provisions on health and safety and on job access for low-income workers, as in the LA Metro case.[48] Although some unions worry PLAs can restrict their ability to strike and impose outside equity practices on union hiring and employment practices, they often support them to keep public projects unionized. The LA Metro PLA struck a balance between traditional union interests in maintaining job quality and controlling membership versus community advocates' desire to put disadvantaged workers into higher-paying union jobs. LAANE's work outlining a union construction careers policy for young minority workers was instrumental in building broad political support for the agreement.[49]

LAANE's diverse industry campaigns combined several factors its members now view as critical for success: (1) research on the industry, its positives and negatives, and how jobs could be improved; (2) policy development and advocacy "grounded in reality"—proposals that have a chance of winning; (3) community organizing to build grassroots support and to ensure the policy addresses real needs of low-income people; (4) coalition building, reaching out beyond traditional liberal or progressive groups; (5) communications not only to coalition members but also to elected officials and the public; and (6) capacity to draft laws and regulations that can withstand legal and technical objections to initial proposals and later implementation.[50]

Improving economic conditions industry by industry and city agency by city agency might seem slow to activists seeking sweeping and systemic changes. But LAANE and others argue success only comes from this type of campaign-specific work involving many different stakeholders. Executive Director Roxana Tynan says, "Our real message is that power gets built in place and gets built through long-standing coalitions and through leadership development. And it gets built through the day-to-day work of organizing folks through permanent institutions. There is no shortcut to that."[51]

THE LIMITS TO ONE-CITY POLICIES?

Los Angeles prepared to elect a new mayor in 2013, with the city in a paradoxical position. Progressive reforms advocated by LAANE and others had helped build a political movement that now was a major force in electoral politics. Mayoral and other candidates now had to declare their position on a variety of progressive ideas. The top two runoff candidates, Comptroller Wendy Gruel and City Council President Eric Garcetti, both had progressive and union backing, leading a journalist to observe that "the labor divide in the mayoral contest is largely a matter of where the public employee and private sector unions are placing their bets."[52] The County Federation of Labor endorsed Gruel, while Garcetti's wife had been a member of LAANE's advisory board for years.

Garcetti won the runoff with 54 percent of the vote, taking office in June 2013. His campaign had emphasized better public management, budget efficiency, and "making LA the best-run city in America." But he soon faced debates over bigger issues. In 2013, the city council president had commissioned a Los Angeles 2020 Commission led by former U.S. Secretary of Commerce Mickey Kantor. Their December 2013 report, *A Time for Truth*, painted a dystopian picture of the city's future, saying, "Los Angeles is barely treading water while the rest of the world is moving forward" with income distribution shaped like a "barbell," "more typical of developing world cities, like Sao Paulo, than a major American urban area."[53]

The commission highlighted negative economic trends. Total jobs in Los Angeles had declined since 1990 compared to other large cities. Since the Great Recession began in late 2007, LA had added more poor people than any other city with a population of over 1 million. The commission catalogued other dire problems in education, municipal finance (especially public pensions), and economic development. But given the dire tone of the analysis, the commission's recommendations were much less sweeping than expected, focusing on process issues such as municipal election dates, merging the ports, rationalizing tourism offices, and appointing another commission to study municipal pension funding.[54]

Meanwhile, LA's progressive coalition continued advocating larger actions. In April 2014, its members successfully supported a zero-waste proposal that rationalized private trash collection and recycling, encouraged a recycling industry, and improved jobs (with possible unionization) for private sanitation workers. In September, the city enacted a law raising the minimum wage for hotel workers well above the state and federal minimum wage. Garcetti had first advocated a smaller citywide minimum wage increase but switched to supporting a $15 minimum wage, which passed in June 2015 to be phased in over five years. And in November 2016, 71.1 percent of county voters approved Measure M for mass transit, indefinitely extending the original sales tax increase and adding another 0.5 percent to generate an estimated $120 billion over the next forty years. Voters also approved bonds under Proposition HHH to generate $1.2 billion for homeless housing and services.

Each Los Angeles campaign had been resisted by opposing economic interests and increasingly involved the detailed campaign steps outlined by LAANE. And this approach has another objective: building and sustaining broad coalitions of diverse advocacy groups that will support each other. In the Los Angeles case, three diverse groups—labor unions, environmental advocates, and community organizations—have been able to overcome historic divisions and seemingly competing interests to unite around common objectives. Those diverse political groups in turn influenced the mayor and city council to support more aggressive policy steps.[55]

For example, Teamsters union leaders found a way to work with environmental advocates around the waste and recycling issues central to the city's new garbage policy.[56] And when courts struck down the port agreement's labor provisions, the environmental and community partners still cooperated with the unions. Community organizations representing people of color have worked with construction trade unions to find mutually agreeable practices in PLAs. These help the growth of union jobs and also make more of those good-paying jobs available to people who historically have been shut out from them on mass transit projects that are central to environmental goals.

These coalition experiences by no means ensure that these diverse groups will always work together. Each campaign brings up new issues and potential divisions, although built-up trust and working relationships facilitate more cooperation. Garcetti was not endorsed originally by the County Federation of Labor and public sector unions, but he did have strong support from several private sector unions. Although his election theme of "back to basics" was seen by some as a criticism of Villaraigosa's management style, Garcetti moved forward aggressively with the new waste management plan, endorsed a city council measure to raise wages for hotel workers, and supported raising the city's minimum wage above the existing federal and state level.

The recycling and waste management program shows how labor standards and job quality have been central to many of LA's initiatives. The plan's most controversial elements included labor standards and job quality in trash and recycling jobs along with encouraging contractors to have labor peace agreements with unions, the basis for opponents' claims that the request for proposal (RFP) encouraged unionization in the trash industry.[57] Opponents saw this as favoring unionized contractors and virtually requiring nonunionized firms to enter into negotiations over employee representation.

Proponents of the new plan in turn claimed the old system supported small, undercapitalized trash companies and low-paying, dangerous, and polluting jobs. They argued that upgrading job quality, especially through unionization, for trash haulers and later for recycling jobs should be central not only to waste management but also to all the city's procurement and regulation. But they also stressed that quality jobs should go to economically and racially disadvantaged communities. In this type of mutually supportive model, unions, communities of color, and environmentalists all got some of what they wanted.

Garcetti was overwhelmingly reelected in 2017 with 81.4 percent of the vote, and LA seemed poised to continue with broad reforms. The city also had been part of statewide progressive efforts, including funding for public education. On the 2012 ballot, local progressive organizations in alliance with state teachers' unions successfully pushed for Proposition 30 to raise funds for education through increasing sales and a millionaire's tax. In 2016, Proposition 55 extended the millionaire's tax but not the sales tax.[58]

Garcetti did face criticism. A coalition called Fix LA and led by public sector unions called for restoration of public sector jobs in basic services like street repair and trash pickup. The city's new franchise trash system, where firms won exclusive commercial trash contracts for specific city neighborhoods tied to aggressive recycling and ultimately zero waste, got off to a rocky start, although making recycling free and rebating fees to some customers helped stabilize the program.

But Los Angeles remained poor and unequal. In 2016, Los Angeles was "the seventh most unequal among the largest 150 metro regions" with ongoing racial and income gaps in education, housing, and employment. Nevertheless, Garcetti felt strong enough politically to explore an eventually unsuccessful 2020 run for president, while former mayor Villaraigosa tried (and failed) to leverage his successful LA leadership to win the 2018 election as California's governor.[59]

Economist Manuel Pastor, considering the strengths and weaknesses of LA's approach, says that a mixed record on progressive state ballot and other legislative initiatives, especially in housing, underscored that "California progressives had realized that they could not give up on huge swaths of the state and expect to wield power."[60] Los Angeles and other urban centers needed to assemble larger statewide coalitions that brought in suburban and rural areas, working initially on shared problems such as inadequate school financing.

LA's economy and politics encountered two issues facing many American cities: inadequate education funding (in spite of the state ballot initiatives) and housing costs and homelessness. In 2019, after prolonged contract negotiations, striking teachers in LA eventually won higher pay, smaller class sizes, and more support personnel in schools. Because the majority of California's local school funding comes from the state, the political negotiations were complex, with Garcetti playing a mediator role (LA's mayor does not control the schools, something Villaraigosa failed to achieve). LAANE and other progressive organizations actively supported the teachers' union, adapting lessons from their earlier fights and helping to build Reclaim Our Schools LA, a broad coalition of community, labor, and other organizations.

Other major conflicts in LA swirled around housing: both the rise and persistence of homelessness, and the generally high cost of housing. Implementation of new homeless housing services was slower and more expensive than expected, while homelessness continued rising. Between 2013 and 2019, the number of individuals experiencing homelessness in the city rose by over 13,000 people, or 59 percent. Advocates claimed much of the increase was directly related to rising housing costs, while others pointed to relatively slow housing development compared to earlier decades. In the LA metro, the share of homes that median-income households could afford was 12.7 percent, with the number of low-rent units falling by 34.5 percent between 2011 and 2017. The housing burden was tied not only to higher costs but also to stagnant and unequal incomes; in the third quarter of 2019, only 25 percent of LA County households could afford a median-priced, single-family home.[61]

Housing issues divided LA's progressives. The state of California passed laws allowing more dense development in cities and towns with restrictive single-family zoning. Although the laws were aimed in part at wealthy exclusionary suburbs, they were resisted in some large cities, including Los Angeles. Randy Shaw describes LA as "the epicenter of homeowner support for single-family zoning," with multifamily housing sharply limited or banned in much of the city.

Under pressure from homeowner groups, the LA city council voted to oppose the state's housing legislation, while progressive city council member Kevin DeLeon based his 2022 mayoral campaign in part on opposing the state laws allowing more density.[62] Although a 2016 ballot measure authorized $1.2 billion in bonds for permanent housing for people experiencing homelessness, the city's ongoing crisis led to divisions over clearing homeless encampments and other policy options.

The COVID-19 pandemic hit the city very hard. As in other cities, the virus hit low-income and nonwhite people disproportionately. Death rates per 100,000 for LA County in mid-September 2020 were sixty-four per 100,000 for Latinos and seventy-three per 100,000 for Blacks, with an overall rate of fifty. Nonwhite workers were more likely to be high-risk and essential workers—21 percent for Blacks and 29 percent for both U.S.-born and immigrant Latino workers, compared to 17 percent of whites. In contrast, almost half of white workers—47 percent—were in the safest category—nonessential and lower risk. LA's undocumented population suffered even more economically because they were not eligible for extended unemployment insurance, small business assistance, or the tax rebate checks distributed by the federal government.[63]

LA County made some initial progress in controlling the pandemic, although rates were much higher among poor and nonwhite residents, as is true across the country. But a second wave threatened to overwhelm the health-care system, with cases, hospitalizations, and deaths all spiking, requiring severe shutdown measures. For several weeks, there were no available intensive-care beds, and the county had to lift air quality restrictions on cremation to accommodate the backlog of deaths.

Like other cities, the pandemic recession hit nonwhite workers and neighborhoods the hardest, furthering racial and ethnic inequity in job and income losses. Initially, four times as many residents in Latino neighborhoods had been infected compared to affluent areas like Santa Monica. LA's large undocumented immigrant population was hurt even worse, although the state did provide a $500 cash payment for undocumented workers. And the pandemic recession hammered the city's budget and resources, with rising expenses and falling revenues from sales and hotel taxes, port revenues from lower international trade, and state assistance.

LA's long-term work in building progressive coalitions brought a quick response. In September 2020, only six months after the pandemic started, the newly formed Committee for Greater LA issued a detailed analysis of COVID-19's impact and a set of progressive principles and policy proposals. Led by scholars at the University of Southern California and the University of California at Los Angeles, the work was funded by a broad coalition of foundations. The analysis and recommendations drew heavily on LA's decades-long work in combining racial and ethnic justice with economic analysis and policy proposals, and sought to maintain the gains they had achieved.

The report noted that LA faced many challenges around inequality and discrimination prior to the pandemic: "COVID-19 is the disease that has revealed our social illnesses of anti-Black racism, precarious employment, sharp racial gaps in wealth and digital access, unaffordable housing, growing homelessness, unresponsive government, and so much more." The report detailed inequities and provided a policy agenda in fifteen different domains to form the basis for future advocacy, organizing, and electoral politics.

CONCLUSION

Although LA's progressive coalition faces structural economic and racial challenges and conflicts around affordable housing policy, fighting for more and better jobs and economic equity now seems to be a permanent part of the political landscape for the city. Diversity remains at the heart of the region's progressive coalition, with non-Hispanic whites making up less than 30 percent of the city's population. But the coalition now faces issues it wasn't originally designed to address, especially housing costs and development, educational quality, and public health and COVID-19.

Although LA's turbulent political history might still produce surprises, the progressive coalition looks to be central to the city's and region's economic and political future, with increasing influence on state government as well. But ongoing economic inequality and racial and ethnic inequity show the limits for Los Angeles—or any city—in taking on the large problems of shifting economics and industries given the failure of federal policy and the entrenched structural racism that continues to hamper our cities.

7

ECONOMICS AND EQUITY

N ew York City, Detroit, and Los Angeles hoped to provide a better life for their residents by advancing policies focused on equity. Despite their efforts and those of other cities, America continues battling high levels of urban poverty and inequality. The COVID-19 pandemic and accompanying recession highlighted and exacerbated class and racial inequalities already present in income, housing, jobs, education, and health care and other public services. Without state and federal support, cities can't fulfill growth and equity missions on their own.

Economists correctly credit cities and urban areas as driving economic growth, innovation, and national prosperity. However, market-oriented approaches don't adequately explain the worsening inequality even during periods of economic growth. Nobel laureate Joseph Stiglitz calls this "market fundamentalism"—"the argument that firms (and individuals) who pursue their self-interest . . . would lead . . . to general societal well being."[1] Much of urban economics is based on these individual choice models, which distort economists' policy recommendations. Effective policies for achieving both growth and equality need to include structural and institutional factors that lay outside conventional economics.

LESSONS FROM THE THREE CITIES

The case studies of the cities in chapters 4 to 6 showed that New York City, Detroit, and Los Angeles, like most American cities, underwent significant structural economic change, faced inadequate or hostile state and federal policies, experienced metropolitan political fragmentation, and endured structural racism. These factors constrained their fiscal base and their ability to implement adequate equity policies on their own.

New York City entered virtual bankruptcy in 1975, inaugurating a long run of austerity and limits on pro-equity economic policies. The rise of finance as the dominant industry and the city's inability to tap suburban prosperity meant less support for essential services, lower wages and benefits for its workforce, and inadequate social programs. The decline of manufacturing undercut the power of private sector unions, and although the public sector remained organized, union policies increasingly focused on wage and benefit struggles with government, not on broader economic prosperity and social change.

Detroit underwent a significant industrial shift, losing much of its high-valued-added manufacturing. But unlike the automotive sector, New York's manufacturing was concentrated in lower-paying garment, apparel, and other sectors. In the run-up to the 1970s fiscal crisis, New York lost more than one-sixth of its jobs, while public sector costs rose. The fiscal crisis and resulting state control and austerity slowed the budget problems but exacerbated economic and racial tensions in education, social services, housing, and budgetary support.

Like other cities after World War II, New York suffered from federal and state pro-suburban policy. Segregated suburbs like Levittown on Long Island benefitted from racially discriminatory housing subsidies and public support for automobiles and commuter rail lines. Growing suburbs weakened New York City's political strength at the state level. Yet New York didn't make common cause with Buffalo, Rochester, Syracuse, and other older cities also suffering from industrial change, declining populations, falling revenues, and little state and federal assistance.

Racial tensions infused New York City politics. Racialized battles over public schools, blackout looting in 1977, and violence in Crown Heights and elsewhere were flashpoints of ongoing racial division. David Dinkins had been New York's only Black mayor until Eric Adams took office in

2022. Dinkins held office for only one contentious term and was then defeated by Rudolph Giuliani, who campaigned on crime, disorder, and anti-Black sentiments.

Despite these pressures, New York's shift to a financialized economy in the 1980s favored New York above other American cities. Ironically, New York City's very size and new economic strength may have fostered the false feeling it could prosper on its own because the finance-led revival brought prosperity to wealthier parts of the city.

But the new financial economy brought stark inequality, fostering higher housing and other costs of living. Housing affordability became a central political issue in New York since the fiscal crisis. All mayors since the 1970s addressed housing—dealing with abandoned buildings, and supporting ongoing rent regulation, public housing, and rent subsidy programs. But housing costs have outpaced incomes, and housing problems differ by group. Some neighborhoods fear gentrification; other residents want new housing or public housing. New immigrants, the elderly, and the homeless want more housing from city policy and limited budgets, while some progressives resist new development.

New York's economic health was aided by something Detroit lacked in the postwar period—immigrants. New York City's role as America's historic portal for immigration has always fueled economic strength. In 2019, 36.8 percent of the city's population was foreign-born, second in history only to the record in 1910 of 40.8 percent during the nation's great immigration wave. In contrast, 33.5 percent of Detroit's population was foreign-born in 1910, but it was only 6.2 percent in 2019.[2]

Immigrants filled many jobs, especially in services and health care, and also bolstered neighborhoods and real estate outside the wealthy Manhattan core. But immigrants did not join larger progressive movements, falling instead into long-standing patterns focused on nationality and neighborhoods, while native-born Black New Yorkers remained largely locked into their geographic power bases.

Although the population shifted from majority white, in the over forty years after the fiscal crisis, New York City had a nonwhite mayor for only one term (and never a woman). In 2019, Blacks were 24.3 percent of the city's population, and non-Hispanic whites were 32.1 percent. Relatively centrist or conservative white leaders dominated the mayoralty through 2013, along with a city council tied to traditional party organizations rooted in the city's boroughs.[3] This changed in 2013, with Democrat Bill de Blasio elected twice along with a progressive city council. But major divisions over economic development, characterized by fights over the Hudson Yards development and the rejection of Amazon's second head-quarters and the Industry City project, divided progressives, with some still resisting housing and economic development.

Unlike New York, Detroit's economic woes resulted in the nation's larg-est municipal bankruptcy. State governments took control of both cities' budgets and policies, preempting elected officials' authority and pushing both cities into a policy framework that required appeasing private capital markets and subordinating equity goals. Although Detroit is now Amer-ica's poster child for urban poverty and dysfunction, it fell from a very prosperous position. Detroit and its metropolitan region thrived during the 1950s as the center of the thriving motor vehicle industry.

The United Auto Workers (UAW) obtained a share of the rising sector's wealth for their members, which spilled over into the rest of the region. Massachusetts Institute of Technology (MIT) economists Frank Levy and Peter Temin dubbed this economic dynamic the Treaty of Detroit, pro-ducing "an expanding middle class," "mass upward mobility," and a "safety net" beyond the minimal federal floor. This shared prosperity (including unemployment insurance, health care, and pensions) allowed companies to control and change production processes and output, with workers get-ting rising incomes and benefits.[4]

The treaty's major flaw was persistent racial inequality. Black residents and workers were confined to the worst neighborhoods and the dirtiest, lowest-paid jobs. Unionized Black workers' income rose relative to other Black workers, but they still had substantially less income and wealth than whites. And even with economic prosperity, racial division persisted in the Detroit region. Bitter battles were fought over neighborhood integra-tion. Fueled by discriminatory lending and housing policies, the rapid postwar growth of segregated suburbs induced whites to exit the city, eventually making the Detroit metro one of the nation's most racially seg-regated regions.

Because Blacks continued facing discrimination, racial income and wealth gaps grew. Affluent suburbs built healthier neighborhoods and better schools based on rising property taxes. The Supreme Court rejected legal bids to allow city children to attend suburban schools, leaving

Detroit to pay for its increasing share of the region's social problems with an ever-shrinking tax base. New automobile plant construction outside the city's borders attracted supplier firms to the suburbs and to states with more antiunion governments.

Racial conflict and suburban power grew steadily in the postwar period, sometimes directed by overtly racist elected officials and an increasingly hostile state government. In a pattern repeated across the nation, the Detroit metropolitan region fragmented into hundreds of independent and often racially exclusionary governments. Mayor Coleman Young and other city leaders responded with Black pride and political assertiveness.

Although Young and other mayors balanced city budgets, they were blamed for the city's decline, which was largely caused by the auto industry shifting jobs from the city and region. Detroit adopted risky municipal financing to cope with its ever-increasing debt, failing when the Great Recession starting in late 2007 drove Detroit into the largest municipal bankruptcy in American history.

After 1970 the city's population fell dramatically and became poorer and more Black. The city went from the nation's fifth largest in 1970 to tenth in 2000, nineteenth in 2010, and twenty-fourth in 2019, losing almost 25 percent of its population in one decade. But the surrounding metropolitan region's population stabilized and actually increased in some years. After bankruptcy, overt racial discord in the city's politics abated, but despite downtown real estate development, the city' economy stagnated and the population remained largely Black and poor. In 2019, 78.3 percent of Detroit residents were Black, and 10.5 percent were non-Hispanic whites.

Economic shifts, racial tension, and demographic transitions also changed Los Angeles. The city and region were a major manufacturing center, but high-paying and high-value-added aerospace and related manufacturing declined sharply in the 1990s, while lower-paid manufacturing sectors grew, especially in the garment industry. Median annual wages in aerospace were 2.6 times higher than in the garment industry.

The garment industry's rise coincided with white out-migration and record Latino in-migration, mostly from Mexico. Hispanics were 30 percent of LA's population in 1980, rising to 40 percent in 1990 and reaching 48.5 percent by 2019. By 2018, 13.2 percent of the nation's entire Hispanic population lived in just three adjacent counties—Los Angeles, Riverside, and San Bernardino. In contrast, LA's non-Hispanic white population fell from over 50 percent in 1980 to 28.5 percent in 2019. Further enhancing LA's diversity, the Asian share of the population rose sharply, from 6 percent in 1980 to 11.6 percent in 2019. And like New York, foreign-born residents became a significant share of LA's population, rising to over one-third in 1990 and reaching 36.9 percent in 2019.[5]

LA's Black population, in contrast, remained relatively stable—12 percent in 1980 to 9 percent in 2019. But Black-white relations went through several phases of racially charged conflict, from deadly violence in Watts in 1965 up to the violence after the police officers who beat Rodney King were acquitted in 1992.

Rapid economic and population transformations shook LA's economy and politics, and spurred a progressive coalition of groups often divided in urban politics—minority communities, immigrants, labor unions, and environmentalists. This coalition did not spring magically into being but was intentionally created in reaction to economic change, increased diversity in the city's population, and the need to combine progressive forces rather than compete in a zero-sum battle over scarce resources.

Organizations like the Los Angeles Alliance for a New Economy (LAANE), with strong labor union ties and Strategic Concepts in Organizing and Policy Education (SCOPE), which grew after the Rodney King disturbances, advocated and negotiated enforceable community benefit agreements (CBAs) with private developers and went on to build voting power. The coalition helped Antonio Villaraigosa win the mayor's race in 2005 and enact progressive hikes in living and minimum wages, CBAs, and career access to unionized construction jobs for poor and minority residents. The progressive strategy was ongoing internal negotiations and movement building to develop win-win solutions for disparate groups, especially by linking organized labor, nonwhite communities, and environmentalists.[6]

The coalition supported successful ballot initiatives to increase sales taxes to fund mass transit construction tied to inclusive union apprenticeships and job programs. California law requires a two-thirds vote to pass taxes on the ballot, and LA achieved this high standard in 2008, even during the Great Recession. A 2012 campaign just missed the vote target (66.1 percent approval, needing 66.7 percent), but organizers won increased sales taxes for transit in 2016, with over 70 percent voter approval. Later, recycling and waste management contracts were negotiated to link job quality with environmental goals.

The COVID-19 pandemic and recession hit all three cities hard. With higher concentrations of poor and nonwhite residents, cities' public health, social welfare, and education systems were stressed, while federal aid helped stabilize services. But many of the pandemic's inequalities were in place and growing prior to the outbreak. COVID-19 accelerated and deepened urban inequality, worsening trends that were emerging prior to the pandemic.

FACTORS SHAPING UNEQUAL ECONOMIES

Part of American cities' poor performance on reducing inequality simply comes from being in the United States, a nation where inequality and poverty are high compared to other advanced economies. The Organization of Economic Cooperation and Development (OECD) in 2020 ranked the United States tied with Turkey as the sixth most unequal member country, only better than Bulgaria, Mexico, Chile, Costa Rica, and South Africa.[7] Countries as varied as Canada, South Korea, Greece, Germany, Romania, and Ireland are more equal.

U.S. inequality is fueled by high pretax earnings and the ever-increasing capital incomes of the very wealthy. Government taxes and transfers do less to reduce inequality than in other nations. France and Germany have approximately the same pretax and transfer inequality as the United States, but their inequality falls much further after taxes and transfers.[8] When national policies contribute so strongly to inequality and poverty, cities are hampered in achieving greater equality on their own. The problem is exacerbated by states and cities competing with each other on lower taxes and regulations, in a "race to the bottom" that erodes equity.

Although every city is different, four common factors deserve more attention in urban economic analysis and policy debates: sectoral economic change and disruption, federal anti-urban bias, state control of cities which fosters regional government fragmentation, and structural racism.

STRUCTURAL ECONOMIC DISRUPTION MATTERS

All three cities experienced wrenching deindustrialization. New York City transformed from a manufacturing and logistical center to a postindustrial financial capital. Detroit lost automotive and related manufacturing jobs with little to replace them. And Los Angeles lost high-end aerospace and other manufacturing and gained lower valued-added garment manufacturing. In all three cities, manufacturing employment fell. Losing high-end jobs contributed significantly to inequality. Historically, manufacturing wages are higher than other sectors primarily because unionization boosts relative wages for non-college-educated workers.[9] Cities that shifted to other sectors (as New York did with finance) or were hubs of new industries (like Seattle and San Jose in technology) grew, but still experienced rising inequality.

The structural move away from manufacturing was coincident with income and wealth gains at the very top—what economists Bennett Harrison and Barry Bluestone called "the Great U-turn." No one factor is the sole cause of inequality. Bluestone argued that "every major economic trend in the US contributes" to inequality, calling it "the Inequality Express" (after the Agatha Christie novel, *Murder on the Orient Express*, where twelve suspects all participate in one murder).[10]

In the aftermath of the Great Recession, the lost jobs were eventually replaced by worse jobs. Nationally, 41 percent of jobs lost in 2007 to 2009 were in higher-wage industries, but only 30 percent of jobs in the recovery were in those industries. And jobs in lower-wage industries were 22 percent of the losses but comprised 44 percent of jobs created during the recovery.[11]

Total employment didn't recover until May 2014, and city budgets didn't recover until much later. And then the pandemic recession starting in 2020 hit hard and fast. The COVID-19 virus spread widely into the economy during March 2020, and by the end of April, the resulting economic damage had wiped out 22.7 million jobs, more than the 22.2 million jobs added since the Great Recession. Jobs came back strongly during President Biden's first year in office with over 6 million new jobs created. But as of January 2022, the economy was still 2.9 million jobs below pre-pandemic levels, with disproportionate job losses among lower-income and nonwhite workers. Larger metro areas had the most job loss, with employment rates dropping by 14.1 percent in metros with over 5 million people compared to an 8.4 percent drop in other areas.[12]

On their own, cities can't overcome such longer-term structural and industrial changes, fight increasing income and wealth inequality, or generate enough jobs in the face of the Great Recession and the subsequent COVID-19 collapse. Cities need robust state and federal policy responses to reduce inequality and economic decline. But federal and state policies often make things worse for cities and actively contribute to urban isolation and decline.

FEDERAL ANTI-URBAN BIAS MATTERS

With decades of urban decline, the federal and state governments might have helped cities instead of enacting indifferent or sometimes hostile federal and state policies furthering their decline. Earlier chapters detailed the consistent anti-urban bias in housing, transportation, and economic federal policies that enabled suburban prosperity and racial exclusion.

Cities have long been harmed by the basic design of the U.S. government, which favors states and rural areas over cities. With two senators for each state, sixty-two senators represent about 25 percent of the U.S. population, the same percentage as the six senators from California, New York, and Florida. In the House of Representatives, members from small states like Wyoming, Vermont, and North Dakota represent many fewer people than those from New York, Texas, and California, giving small state residents around 3.5 times the representation of a large state voter, an advantage reproduced in the Electoral College.[13]

This power imbalance flows through to federal policy. Each policy dimension—macroeconomic policy, federal and state budgetary aid, taxation, international trade, innovation, housing, economic development, and labor market institutions—works against cities. Edward Glaeser acknowledges that many federal policies can seem "almost intentionally designed to hurt the cities."[14]

The anti-city bias isn't confined to federal spending. Take macroeconomic policy. For decades, the major focus was controlling inflation at the cost of faster wage and job growth. Economics promoted monetarism, whose core belief was that the "natural" unemployment rate cannot be reduced and any effort to do so through monetary policy will cause inflation, giving the Federal Reserve (the Fed) a theoretical justification to slow growth. Indeed, until the Great Recession, the Fed's policy directives were "reluctant to mention employment as a separate policy objective, preferring instead to state that maximum employment could best be achieved by achieving price stability".[15] This anti-employment bias slowed job and income growth, especially for those at the back end of the employment queue, which disproportionately includes women, minorities, and less-educated workers.[16]

Slower growth also slows government tax revenue. States are required to balance their budgets; thus, lower revenues mean contractionary state fiscal policy, making recessions worse and reducing aid to cities.[17] In recessions, state balanced budget requirements work against federal deficit-funded economic stimulus, leading economist Paul Krugman to say that states during recessions are "50 Herbert Hoovers," referring to President Hoover's policies of cutting government spending and exacerbating the Great Depression.[18]

The composition of federal and state budget aid to cities has changed significantly, and the small state and rural advantage appears in every budget category. For example, after the 9/11 attacks, congressional appropriations meant that "Wyoming received $38 per person while New York received less than $5.50 per person from the largest pot of federal homeland security funding."[19] This federal rural and small state bias is partly why federal aid, as a direct share of city budgets, has fallen since the 1980s. In 2017, direct federal funding as a percentage of total revenues was 4.6 percent in New York City, 4.5 percent in Los Angeles, and 6.1 percent in Detroit.[20]

Another source of urban disadvantage is that most federal aid goes to states, not cities, and states, in turn, favor rural areas and suburbs. Ever since the Reagan administration eliminated federal revenue sharing to cities in 1986, direct federal aid to cities has been a small share of their general revenues. The federal-aid share of state budgets also declined from around 22 percent in 1977 to about 16 percent in 1989. Since then, federal aid to states and cities trended back up to above 30 percent, peaking at 35.5 percent in 2010.

But these funds increasingly were driven by mandatory health spending, while discretionary grants fell; health care represents around

60 percent of federal intergovernmental aid, mostly Medicaid, as federal dollars in cities have shifted from "places" to "people." And states, not cities, are the major recipients of federal intergovernmental monies. Because these funding streams to states "are large and very durable features of the U.S. fiscal system," it is unlikely cities will see significant new direct federal funding.[21]

The Great Recession and resulting state budget reductions put further fiscal pressure on cities. State revenues allocated to cities remained flat or fell in thirty-seven of the fifty states. As federal and state budgets have tightened under political pressures to reduce spending, cities have to depend on their own stressed revenue bases. Between 2000 and 2017, budget revenues from sources controlled by cities rose by 29 percent, while state assistance to cities increased by only 10 percent. And just as cities climbed out of that budget hole, the COVID-19 pandemic struck, pushing state and city budgets back down.[22]

Battles over fiscal aid to cities and states underscore the federal anti-city bias. The Trump administration labeled some American cities as "anarchist jurisdictions" and tried to block their federal funds. Trump called Baltimore a "disgusting, rat and rodent infested mess," and once retweeted a message saying, "[L]eave Democrat cities. Let them rot." Federal fiscal aid for COVID-19 relief was held up for months because Republicans refused to fund cash-strapped cities and states.[23]

The pandemic was initially estimated to cause average city revenue shortfalls between 5.5 and 9 percent, with the "hardest hit cities fac[ing] revenue losses of 15 percent or more." Although cities took major revenue losses, significant federal spending directly helped their budgets and also helped their economies through aid to small businesses, expanded unemployment insurance, the Federal Reserve's stabilization of the municipal bond market, and other actions.[24] These were welcome, but they didn't change the fundamental policy of federal fiscal aid passing through states.

Anti-city biases are found elsewhere in policy. Trade policy damaged urban economies, especially in older industrial cities. For cities with low-income light manufacturing like Los Angeles, Chinese import competition significantly reduced employment. More advanced manufacturing regions like Detroit suffered from "multiple existential crises" ranging from increased Asian auto imports to exchange rate fluctuations, to high

corporate health costs, to U.S. policies subsidizing manufacturing relocation in Southern right-to-work states.[25]

Federal military spending favors the Sunbelt over older Northern
urban areas. Total federal spending continues to give much more to
rural areas than they pay in taxes. Between 2015 and 2018, the top four
"giver" states paying more to the federal government than they received
were the urbanized states of Connecticut, New Jersey, New York, and
Massachusetts, while "taker" states were dominated by small rural states.
Analysts found that "over four years, New York taxpayers have given
$116.2 billion more to the federal government than they received back in
federal spending."[26]

Federal policies also support labor market inequality through weak
union rights enforcement, which reduces labor's ability to bargain over
productivity gains. The Economic Policy Institute documents that hourly
compensation gains closely tracked productivity gains between 1948 and
1979, when productivity rose by 108.1 percent and hourly compensation
rose by 93.2 percent. But between 1979 and 2018, productivity went up by
69.6 percent while hourly compensation rose by only 11.6 percent.[27] This
productivity-pay gap provided the income gains to the wealthy that have
fueled inequality.

Union membership declined, the real value of the federal minimum
wage did not keep pace with overall compensation (with small and
Republican states blocking any increase), and changes in pension coverage have resulted in barely 50 percent of the workforce having any private
pension coverage.[28] Deregulation reduced airline and trucking wages, and
rising health-care costs due to America's inefficient health-care system
suppressed wage gains for most workers. Marginal tax rates fell for the
wealthiest Americans, and financialization of corporations boosted executive compensation, not only reducing the overall wage share of income
but also lowering investment in innovation, which in turn helped slow
overall productivity growth.[29]

All of these factors disproportionately hurt cities by suppressing wages
and benefits for the majority of American households. Combined with
long-standing federal anti-urban policies in housing, education, and
transportation, the cumulative effects have left cities pushing uphill to
achieve economic growth while struggling on their own to deal with the
costs generated by low income and urbanization.

STATE GOVERNMENT AND METROPOLITAN
FRAGMENTATION MATTER

Anti-urban bias is compounded by America's federal structure, especially because of the pivotal role of state governments. Although federal policies significantly affect housing and transportation, programs are primarily controlled, regulated, and administered by state governments. States have long-standing and frequently adversarial relationships with their cities, so housing, education, and transportation money shifts to the suburbs. Margaret Weir has analyzed how the governance of regional economies, the distribution of political power within states, and changes in state politics that made it harder for cities to build coalitions also put cities at a disadvantage.[30]

Legislative malapportionment favoring rural legislative districts has worked against cities through much of American history. It wasn't until the 1960s that the Supreme Court made state legislative districts abide by "one man [sic], one vote." In 1964, Utah's smallest legislative district had 165 people, while the largest had over 32,000; in Vermont, one district had thirty-six people compared to the largest, at around 35,000; and Los Angeles County, with 6,000,000 residents, had one state senator, the same as a rural county with 14,000 people.[31]

This political imbalance cemented rural state legislative dominance over cities. As wealthy suburbs' population and influence grew after World War II, state politics moved toward what Weir calls "defensive localism." Rather than innovative statewide policy solutions, governments moved to "limit State action in addressing urban economic and social problems" by "push[ing] costs and responsibilities down to local governments."[32]

State government power over cities matters because, as described in chapter 2, the nineteenth-century battle over city sovereignty and independent political and economic action was largely resolved in favor of state control, which was reflected in the eponymous Dillon's Rule.[33] States routinely override—or preempt—cities on a variety of policies, including equity and labor policies. Since 2013, forty-four states have enacted preemption laws stopping cities from passing minimum or prevailing and living wages, unionization protections, paid sick and family leave, and classification of gig economy workers as employees rather than contractors.[34]

State control of cities facilitated the growth of independent suburbs in the same regional economy. A single regional economy is comprised of literally hundreds of fragmented and sovereign political jurisdictions, each with their own laws, rules, taxation, housing and land-use regulation, police and courts, and education systems. The result is inefficiency and unfairness because suburbs reap the benefits of the urban economy and cities pay the costs.

The misalignment can be seen in our case studies: the Los Angeles economy sits in a five-county region with over 190 separate city governments; Detroit's economy is the heart of a ten-county region with over 300 local governments; and the New York economic region is governed by twenty-seven county governments, three states, and over 750 local governments. In addition to separate city governments, American regions also contain hundreds of special-purpose bodies with their own governmental powers—mostly school districts, but also water and sewer, transportation, utilities, and other functions.[35]

This political fragmentation and resulting economic misalignment are more pronounced in the United States than elsewhere. America's metropolitan boundaries are political choices, not lines flowing from the regional economy. People commute across boundaries daily; goods and services flow freely from one to another; and regional residents all use airports, seaports, highways, transit systems, water and electric utilities, parks, and universities and cultural institutions. But the single large regional economy operates in a fragmented political world. This often racially biased fragmentation produces inequality and inefficiency.

Regional fragmentation allows suburbs to separate themselves from urban problems while benefiting from metropolitan concentration and innovation. Through refusing annexation and building their own legislative power bases, enacting restrictive housing policies to keep out higher-density residential buildings and nonwhite residents, suburbs isolated themselves from overcrowding, density, and poverty. They also used their independent political status to prevent city minority students from attending better-funded suburban schools and to enforce racially restrictive covenants preventing nonwhite homeownership in their communities.

Suburbs also have allied with rural areas to obtain a disproportionate share of state resources. Although the U.S. population increasingly lives in metropolitan areas, the sharp divisions between city and suburb have worked against increasing the overall political power of metropolitan areas. Suburbs have significant policy control within those economic regions so that, in policies ranging from education funding to economic development, core cities often get less than their fair share.

Cities' budget assistance from their state governments has declined over time. In 2017, the state share of large city budgets averaged 23 percent, an 8.2 percent drop from 2000, with a significant share going to K–12 education. Federal revenues constitute more of city budgets mainly because of increased Medicaid and other mandated spending, not general revenue assistance to cities. As a result, cities must depend on their own strapped revenues. In 2017, median own-source revenues were 51 percent of city budgets, a 12.8 percent increase from 2000.[36]

States administer a good deal of federal assistance as the bridge between federal and local governments. But aid to local governments does not equal aid to cities. There are over 90,000 local governments in the United States, including school districts, towns, counties, and special-purpose districts. Over 50 percent of state fiscal transfers to local governments don't go to cities. They go to disproportionately wealthier suburban school districts that also have stronger property tax bases for funding their local schools. [37]

Spending for schools compounds inequality. In general, K–12 public education spending is dominated by local property taxes, which favors wealthier suburbs. And large numbers of affluent children attend private schools, leaving public schools with higher levels of poverty. In 2016, 24 percent of the nation's public school students were from high-poverty households, but only 8 percent of whites fell into this category compared to 44 percent of Blacks and 45 percent of Hispanics. Since the 1980s, state funding for K–12 education rose, with the state share rising from 39 percent in 1976 to around 48 percent in 1986 to the present, but that funding isn't directed to poor districts. Overall federal funding as a share has been stable for decades, hovering between 8 and 9 percent.[38]

Other policies underscore city disadvantages. Many state economic development programs work against cities. In examining over 4,000 company-specific economic development deals, Good Jobs First found state incentives "directed jobs and industry away from Michigan's core areas" feeding a "mismatch . . . shortchanging the central cities while favoring more affluent outlying areas." The city of Detroit "consistently received a disproportionately low share of subsidies," even though it had the highest number of plant and business closures.[39]

Regional political fragmentation in the same regional economy, enabled by state law, pits local governments against each other. Companies spark bidding wars for projects like Amazon's second headquarters (HQ2). It drew 238 initial bids, resulting in twenty finalist cities, at least four of which offered $5 billion in incentives. Finalists were required to sign nondisclosure agreements limiting how much they could reveal to the public about negotiations.[40]

Even towns in the same regional economy get into subsidy wars. Kansas City suburbs fought over the Applebee's restaurant chain headquarters starting in 2007. The company got $26 million in subsidies to move its offices ten miles within the bistate economic region, while staying on the Kansas side. In 2011, the state of Missouri then provided $12.5 million to move the offices eight more miles, still within the region but across the state border. And in 2015, having saved millions of dollars in Kansas and then Missouri taxes, Applebee's moved its headquarters and the associated jobs to Glendale, California, as part of a corporate consolidation.[41]

STRUCTURAL RACISM MATTERS

The economic and political fragmentation of American metropolitan areas and the alignment of political power against central cities aren't random outcomes—they are part of America's structural racism infused in urban and metropolitan policies. Douglas S. Massey and Nancy A. Denton argue that white suburbs battling with the very cities at the heart of their economic region was "manufactured by whites earlier in the century to isolate and control growing urban black populations."[42]

Scholars have documented conscious, persistent efforts to segregate metropolitan regions, including explicit loan and mortgage conditions prohibiting home sales or resales to Blacks, redlining (denying federally insured mortgages) in neighborhoods that were either nonwhite or might become so, discriminatory zoning (first based explicitly on race and later excluding multifamily housing, requiring building lots of large minimum size and therefore higher cost, etc.), and the practices of real estate brokers who often would either steer Black purchasers away from homes in white areas or use blockbusting tactics to change neighborhoods rapidly from white to Black.[43] For Blacks who somehow managed to buy homes, they were overcharged for substandard houses in weak, segregated submarkets—what Keeanga-Yamahtta Taylor calls "predatory inclusion."[44]

The cumulative weight of these laws and practices, along with the value for many whites of maintaining their racial identity and preserving their segregated housing values, made the postwar suburban boom largely a white one. Economist Leah Boustan is cautious when identifying the underlying cause of the postwar white-flight suburbanization, but she estimates each Black arrival from the South to Northern cities was associated with 2.7 white departures between 1940 and 1970. She attributes this to decisions by whites to leave, not decisions of Black migrants to live separately from whites, or market effects of migration on housing prices. Others have found a deeper pattern of white flight and racism: "segregation and its rise over the first half of the twentieth century was a truly national phenomenon occurring in both the cities people were moving to and the rural areas they left."[45]

Persistent economic discrimination maintained racial wealth and income gaps. Black households' lower incomes and lack of inherited wealth blocked home purchases, while stagnant job growth blocked employment advances. Between 1970 and 2000, Black men in fourteen major U.S. cities "experienced a significant decrease in their rates of employment" and became more detached from the labor force when "their average number of annual weeks of work and annual earnings relative to white men decreased dramatically." One economic analysis concluded that "there appeared to be virtually no progress of Black men in the labor markets between 1970 and 2000."[46]

Not only are Blacks less attached to the labor force but they also suffer more turnover and longer spells of looking for work. Prior to the pandemic, in December 2019 (one of the hottest labor markets in sixty years), Black unemployment at 5.9 percent was within three-tenths of a percent of its all-time measured low, and it was falling faster than white unemployment. But that was still over 80 percent higher than the white unemployment rate of 3.2 percent. Blacks encounter continuing bias in hiring; a 2017 metareview of twenty-eight studies found "no change in the levels of discrimination against African Americans since 1989" based on callback and interview field experiments that use identical résumés for Black and white job applicants. This long-term discrimination undergirds and reproduces continuing wealth inequality, and lower generational levels of Black household wealth and homeownership result in white high school graduates having higher household wealth than Black households headed by an advanced degree holder.[47]

The pandemic recession made racial gaps worse. Nonwhite workers experienced higher and more persistent unemployment, and slower rehiring or reentry into the labor force than whites. In January 2022, white unemployment was 3.4 percent compared to 6.9 percent for Blacks and 4.9 percent for Hispanics. Nonwhite workers facing unemployment have less cushion than whites because they have lower levels of household savings and more debt. Nonwhites face more food insecurity and struggle to pay rent. The pandemic highlighted and worsened "harsh, longstanding inequities—often stemming from structural racism."[48] And they are concentrated in cities that struggle to provide adequate services and housing.

Before the pandemic, deindustrialization hit Black men harder than whites. The automotive industry in the 1950s was among the highest-paying manufacturing sectors, and Black unionized autoworkers did better economically than other Black workers. But they still lagged behind comparable white workers through worse job assignments, lack of seniority, and discrimination on the shop floor. In the service sectors, Black and Latino workers are overrepresented in the lowest-paying jobs. When government austerity hit cities, especially after the Great Recession and then in the pandemic recession, Black workers suffered disproportionate losses as the public sector shrank, with Black women more likely to lose public or nonprofit jobs.[49]

The geography of metropolitan employment also favors whites, as seen in an index of the share of jobs within three miles of an area's downtown. Between 1998 and 2006, "95 out of 98 metro areas saw a decrease in the share of jobs located within three miles of downtown." Job sprawl favors affluent suburbs, which generate demand for service jobs near wealthier households. Los Angeles and Detroit rank among the worst of U.S. metropolitan areas on job sprawl. A lack of mass transit from the city to suburbs makes it harder for residents to work outside central cities, and political fragmentation is correlated with higher levels of job sprawl.[50]

The COVID-19 pandemic hurt central city jobs because affluent office workers worked more at home and spent less money on city restaurants and retail. There will likely be some lasting impact on downtown job density even if a major transformation of office-based work doesn't happen.[51]

Some argue that racial and ethnic economic disparities stem from poor education, with improved educational outcomes seen as the long-term solution. Yet the same segregated housing patterns that have excluded or marginalized nonwhites also puts them in worse schools and thus perpetuates multigenerational inequality. The landmark 1974 *Milliken* Supreme Court decision allowing Detroit's suburbs to avoid regional school desegregation forced educational improvement onto core cities' lower tax bases and higher poverty levels, even though research confirms that higher per pupil spending at the K–12 level results in more education, higher wages, and lower levels of poverty later in life. Surveying the long-intertwined history of public K–12 education and residential segregation, Richard Rothstein concluded, "[I]t is not possible to desegregate schools without desegregating both low-income and affluent neighborhoods."[52]

Although racially unequal education hurts nonwhite employment prospects and thus cities, equalizing educational achievement wouldn't eliminate racial economic disparities. Some economists have documented persistent gaps in employment, underemployment, wages and incomes, and wealth between whites and nonwhites with the same education credentials. These racial gaps, controlling for education, persist even in high-demand occupations such as engineering and other science-related jobs. Compared to other college graduates in the economic recovery after the Great Recession, "black recent college graduates were more likely . . . to be unemployed or to be in low-paying jobs." This was true "even for black graduates . . . in STEM [science, technology, engineering, mathematics] majors." Such findings, consistent with a great deal of other research, underscore that "racial discrimination remains an important factor in contemporary labor markets."[53]

Substantial research shows that protracted spells of unemployment, especially when a person is young, reduces future earnings and increases collateral effects, such as lower homeownership rates and anemic wealth accumulation. Nonwhites are also blocked from accumulating wealth by redlining and other racially discriminatory housing policies. Long-term lower homeownership leads to less intergenerational wealth, which in turn causes more decline. Although there has been some change in metropolitan racial segregation, neighborhood segregation levels "are still quite prevalent" and "white Americans continue to reside in mostly (and often largely) white neighborhoods." These cumulative disadvantages for non-whites, especially for Blacks, perpetuate racial wealth, income, education, and mobility gaps and keep central cities economically disadvantaged.[54]

ECONOMISTS' VIEWS OF CITIES

Even with these four common factors—sectoral change and disruption, federal anti-urban bias, state control of cities and metropolitan government fragmentation, and structural racism—it is difficult to generalize about urban development across the wide diversity of cities. But as Michael Storper writes, cities and regions are "forward-moving development processes," and analysts should be able to answer key questions: "Why do some regions grow and others decline? What are the principal regularities in urban and regional growth?"[55]

Market-oriented urban economists have clear answers to Storper's questions. For them, theory leads to policy. Economists of all stripes hold cities in high regard as sources of economic output, innovation, and productivity. But there are major differences between market-oriented and institutionalist economists in analyzing cities, and these differences lead to differences in policy recommendations. Market-oriented economists focus on individual factors to explain urban growth, while institutionalists focus on differences in industrial composition, political geography, and racial divisions.

Urban economics has been shaped and explained in recent years through the work of Edward Glaeser, a distinguished, prolific scholar and a popular writer. His best-selling 2011 book *Triumph of the City* won distinction from the *Economist* magazine and the *Financial Times*/McKinsey Business Book of the Year contest. Gary Becker, Nobel Prize winner in economics, once said that "urban economics was dried up" prior to Glaeser's work.[56]

Glaser's work is firmly rooted in market-oriented economic theory, which places individual choice in response to incentives at center stage. For cities, this economic theory posits that forces of supply and demand and rational individual self-interest will eventually yield acceptable, fair, and efficient economic outcomes for workers, firms, households, housing, and cities. Individual choice is central, and government intervention should be temporary, with a preference for market-based solutions over laws and regulations. It would answer Storper's question, "What are the principal regularities in urban and regional growth?" with three key factors: (1) free mobility of private factors of production, especially labor and capital; (2) political arrangements, like taxes and regulations, that don't create negative incentives for private economic actors; and (3) minimal government interventions that should be invoked only when markets fail to achieve some specific necessary objective like public safety, education, or pollution control.

With this individual choice framework, economists like Glaeser are skeptical of geographically targeted public policies. They see the role of policy as enhancing private individual choice and the free mobility of capital and labor. As Glaeser argues, "[T]he goal of policy is to increase the choices available to people. The most important part of this assumption is that people, not places, are the important outcomes."[57]

This economic approach generates specific analytic predictions about cities, including that economic outcomes converge over time as mobile capital and labor move from less preferred to more preferred locations (driven both by costs and amenities like weather), eventually resulting in an equilibrium balancing costs and benefits. Some analysts argued that urban externalities and increased mobility meant cities would shrink and become much less economically important as changing communication technology and production logistics took away locational advantages and increased the mobility of both capital and labor.[58]

But shrinking cities and convergence predictions were wrong. Cities and urban regions kept growing, both in size and overall economic importance. In 2018, U.S. metropolitan areas accounted for 91 percent of U.S. gross domestic product (GDP), with the twenty-five largest alone accounting for 51.8 percent. The combined total GDP of the ten largest metro areas exceeded the combined GDP of thirty-eight small states. In some states, metros contribute virtually all GDP—98.9 percent in California, 98.1 percent in Florida, 97.4 percent in New York, and 93.1 percent in Texas. In 2018, there were only four states—Montana, North Dakota, Wyoming, and Vermont, together with less than 10 percent of the nation's population—where metropolitan activity was less than 50 percent of GDP.[59]

Even more surprising, prosperous metros kept growing economically, with little convergence in good job creation and income. This lack of convergence runs counter to market-oriented urban economic predictions. Even rising housing costs in more prosperous regions, a trend that has persisted for twenty-plus years, didn't seem to slow growth. The COVID-19 pandemic seems to have sparked some relocation of wealthier households to suburbs, especially in the New York City region. But those moves may have been primarily an adjustment to already unsustainably high housing prices; in 2020, the Manhattan housing market began to stabilize. Despite an increase in remote work, many economists believe urban areas will remain the center of economic activity. The biggest economic threat from COVID-19, if high-level office jobs do deconcentrate somewhat, is to low-wage service employment that once served high-income urban and commuting workers.[60]

In the ten years ending in 2020, population grew in forty-six of the nation's fifty largest cities at an average of 8.5 percent. Population growth slowed because of restrictive federal immigration policies, "resulting in the lowest levels of international migration in decades." The pandemic spurred urban households with children to hasten their relocation to the suburbs. In some metro regions, population declined in 2020 because of the lack of foreign newcomers and domestic migrants moving out. But overall U.S. population isn't growing because of reduced immigration, lower fertility, and an aging population, with "a slower rate than in any other year since the founding of the nation."[61] The pandemic temporarily reversed metropolitan and city population trends. Demographer William Frey says Census data "make plain that the pandemic exerted a negative impact on America's population growth, especially in its biggest metro areas and urban cores." Whether this is temporary or tied to more permanent changes driven by COVID-19 and rising work from home remains to be seen.[62]

Economist Enrico Moretti called the continuing lack of convergence among urban regions the Great Divergence, considering it "one of the most important developments" in the past thirty years. He explains the divergence by using the central urban economics idea of externalities and spillovers.[63] A region's higher educated and skilled labor force increases growth through (1) their own contributions to productivity; (2) attracting companies that use such labor, creating a "thick" high-skilled labor market; (3) providing informal on-the-job and career learning to less skilled people; and (4) increasing the wages of lower-skilled people through more aggregate demand. These positive forces are found empirically to outweigh the negative effects of higher wages and even the drag of high housing prices. Other scholars see the decline in income convergence as tied paradoxically to higher housing prices and restrictions on home building.[64]

Moretti calls innovative regions "brain hubs" and is skeptical that public policy can do much to have a positive impact on their development. In keeping with the emphasis on education and skills as the core determinants of regional growth and inequality, he also sees weak childhood education and peer effects in poor neighborhoods, not increasingly high costs and student debt burdens, as reasons poor people don't pursue college.[65] Moretti calls for more federal and state aid to increase public funding for higher education.

Moretti's call for more education spending is consistent with the market-oriented economists' interpretation of the outcomes both within and between cities as grounded in educational and skill differences between individuals. Of course, education and skills matter for the well-being of individuals, cities, and regions. But the market-oriented framework discounts how the four important institutional factors—sectoral change and disruption, federal anti-urban bias, state control of cities and metropolitan government fragmentation, and structural racism—shape cities and inequality.

Another crucial mistake made by many economists and urban analysts is to use the terms *regions, metropolitan areas*, and *cities* interchangeably, which obscures their critical political and institutional differences. A region's core city is not the same as the region or metropolitan area. The core city is a smaller unit in the region that usually ends up with most of the negative economic and social spillovers (poverty, lower tax bases, lower education levels, crime, pollution, substandard housing) from population and density, innovation, specialization, and public investment. And the region's suburbs disproportionately benefit from agglomeration and other benefits of density.

Mainstream economics actually endorses governmental fragmentation, seeing multiple governments as promoting beneficial competition on taxes and amenities in a manner similar to private market competition among firms. The idea is that many competing governments will, in theory at least, produce an optimal combination of taxes and quality public services.[66] But empirical analyses cast doubt on the theory. One study found that government fragmentation reduces economic growth, negates positive regional agglomeration effects, and lowers productivity in the fragmented regions by 3 to 4 percent. Others have argued that mobile workers, especially higher-paid and higher educated workers, consider not only city-specific but regional amenities, including transportation, housing, recreation, and education, making regional cooperation increasingly important for the success of individual cities.[67]

One key driver of urban growth—innovation—is deeply intertwined with public policy. Consider how innovation forms and how regional high-technology sectors grow. For market-oriented economists, the initial location of an innovative industry is viewed as serendipitous, tied in part to where entrepreneurs decide to live. Moretti writes that it "was not a business decision" when Bill Gates and Paul Allen moved their already successful company—Microsoft—from Albuquerque to Seattle, to live in their hometown. The growth of Silicon Valley is seen as tied to William Shockley, inventor of the transistor. Moretti encourages regions to attract and retain individual innovators and not tax them too heavily, arguing that "state taxes can have significant effects on the geographical location of start scientists and possibly other highly skilled workers."[68]

This focus on individuals and innovation doesn't engage with the rich literature on how regional innovation clusters actually develop and prosper. One central factor is that government policy and investment lay the groundwork for innovation clusters. Rather than seeing high-tech innovation as serendipitous, this research emphasizes the institutional networks and government funding that supports and maintains these sectors.

In Silicon Valley, Stanford University received substantial federal government support for high-technology defense and weapons development. Coupled with Stanford's land ownership in the region, these public funds supported the emergence of Silicon Valley. Stanford's provost (who was building science research capacity supported by defense contracts) recruited Shockley, whose career was supported by defense funding. Although the aerospace industry and its hub firm, Boeing, slowed in the early 1970s, Seattle was still the regional hub of growing high-technology industries, fueled in significant part by federal defense spending.[69]

When economists pay attention to nonmarket factors, they concentrate on the negative effects of regulation—taxes, labor markets, or patent policies. But the history of innovation shows how growth and industrial structure receive powerful positive support from government, along with other institutional and political factors, which market-oriented economists often downplay. Analyses of innovation show how it is driven by positive public sector factors such as direct government spending, private licensing of publicly funded scientific innovation, and rules enabling investment and profit making by corporate finance and venture capital.

Mariana Mazzucato has documented the significant and essential role of government spending in the growth of innovative consumer electronics, while economist and venture capitalist William Janeway emphasizes how government spending allows for necessary financial "waste" as new technologies are tried and often fail.[70] Some urban regions are well positioned, often with defense or other government spending, to become the economic hubs of these new industries.

But perhaps the most problematic issue downplayed by market-oriented urban economists is race. As shown in Detroit, New York, and Los Angeles and in decades of analysis and history, city formation, economies, regional political organization, and urban futures in the United States cannot be understood without race. White suburbs, aided and abetted by a wide range of federal and state policies, formed in significant part as ways for whites to avoid living with Blacks.

Labor market discrimination, not just education, explains a significant portion of the racial earnings and wealth gap. Housing patterns and public education are deeply intertwined with racial discrimination. Transportation infrastructure disproportionately hurts nonwhites, from the mix of public versus private resources to the location and quality of the infrastructure, extending even to such details as the economic ability to buy automobiles.

City evacuation plans for disasters like Hurricane Katrina that rely on private car ownership disproportionately harm Blacks.[71] Formal redlining of Black neighborhoods beginning in the 1930s limited the ability of Blacks to become homeowners, "directly contributed to disinvestment in poor urban American neighborhoods," and continued to affect housing segregation "almost three quarters of a century later." Black and Latino urban residents are significantly more exposed to environmental toxins and poor air quality, contributing to poor health and shorter life spans.[72]

Race also is central for explaining access to and payoffs from education. Nonwhites are segregated into central city high-poverty neighborhoods with lower-quality schools. When Blacks obtain a college degree, they receive much lower returns to their education than comparable whites, resulting in lower lifetime incomes, homeownership, and wealth accumulation, and these trends persist over generations.[73] Racial violence has even been shown to affect the number of patents and inventions; Lisa Cook's work shows that "valuable patents decline in response to major riots and segregation laws," with losses not only for Black inventors but also for the overall economy through lost productivity.[74]

Under consistent prodding from Black and other economists who are producing strong empirical work on the intertwining of race and economics, economists have begun paying more attention to race, with empirical work on white flight, lynching, redlining, wealth accumulation, patents and innovation, and minimum wages; all this work treats race and discrimination as independent factors explaining unequal economic outcomes. The prestigious National Bureau of Economic Research in November 2020 launched a new working group on race and stratification in the economy, calling for explicit attention to other social science perspectives and public policy.[75]

But even with this recent attention to race in empirical studies, market-oriented economists continue to view poverty and inequality as primarily a function of unequal human capital and as a necessary price to pay for urban economic growth. When displaced agricultural workers moved to cities in the early stages of industrialization, their large numbers and low initial productivity produced low wages and poverty, but eventually everyone was better off. The mainstream narrative is that growth over time will reduce those negative inequalities as industry becomes more productive and workers' skills eventually capture a larger share of national income.[76]

But the market-oriented theory hasn't been supported by the data: inequality has continued to increase. In 2013, in the Detroit region, the ratio of the income of the top 1 percent to that of the bottom 99 percent was 22.8 to 1; in the Los Angeles region, it was 30.3 percent; and in the New York region, it was 39.4—thirteenth worst in the nation. As discussed above, the Economic Policy Institute famously documented how productivity and pay grew together between 1948 and 1973 and then diverged sharply, with wages lagging far behind productivity. RAND Corporation researchers found that if income equality had remained at pre-1975 levels, income for the bottom 90 percent of the population "would have been $2.5 trillion higher in 2018."[77]

Mainstream economists have not yet incorporated in their theory the power dynamics that divert economic gains into "the pockets of extraordinarily highly paid managers and owners of capital" as a result of the breakdown in unions and successful lobbying by the wealthy for policies that increase their income share.[78] But the data may lead theory eventually; there is beginning to be some recognition about these empirical patterns of inequality and institutional factors that cause them. Harvard economists Anna Stansbury and Lawrence Summers recently argued that "declining worker power" explains "sluggish wage growth" and the "declining labor share of income" better than more conventional explanations.[79]

Some social scientists place inequality at the center of their economic research. Chris Benner and Manuel Pastor critique "economic models that cast fairness as either a secondary concern or one that actually hurts the economy." They show that pro-equity policies can foster regional economic growth. While they agree educated workforces are associated with prosperity, they find growth associated with reduced government fragmentation and consolidation, ethnic and racial diversity, a robust public sector, economic development roles for higher education, industrial diversity, and what they call "epistemic communities"—efforts to create shared understandings and equity-seeking actions among different political and social groups [80] Their detailed empirical work parallels international studies at the International Monetary Fund (IMF), OECD, and elsewhere.[81]

Emphasizing collective action undergirds their departure from a conventional economics framework where "atomistic individuals maximizing their own utility" produce the best social outcome. Benner and Pastor link their work to that of Elinor Ostrom, the 2009 Nobel Prize winner in economics, who stressed the positive economic role of collective action, trust, and cooperation. They argue atomistic self-interest, instead of producing optimal results, may instead cause "fragmented competition," which in turn produces unequal outcomes that undercut "cooperation

and solidarity." This leads both to collective underinvestment and to political and social division, which they characterize as "squabbling over the
spoils by those who feel consistently left out."[82]

While focusing on many of the same core issues addressed by market-oriented economists, Benner and Pastor's empirical work emphasizes collective action, institutions, and politics, providing a different and
richer view of growth, inequality, and prosperity in America's metropolitan regions. It is disappointing these two perspectives haven't engaged
with each other. Benner and Pastor are not referenced in the best sellers
written by Glaeser or Moretti. Moretti is not cited in two books by Benner
and Pastor, and Glaeser's work receives only one citation in their 2012
book. Urban economics research and analysis needs engagement across
these theoretical frameworks for better analysis and more effective policy
recommendations.

CONCLUSION

These four factors—sectoral economic change and disruption, federal
anti-urban bias; state control of cities and metropolitan government
fragmentation; and structural racism—have fed persistent and growing
inequality across the American economy, among regions, and within metropolitan areas and cities themselves. Without attention to these structural
factors, market-oriented policies fall short in addressing inequality in cities.

Policymakers and the public face considerable difficulties if they turn to
economics for advice on inequality and urban economies. Differing views
on how inequality affects growth result in very different policy responses.
We have already noted differing points of view on whether regional governmental fragmentation is good or bad for growth; where innovation
clusters come from; and how much education and human capital can be
expected to increase regional prosperity, especially given racial discrimination in obtaining education and differential racial payoffs to education
once obtained.

Fortunately, policymakers can draw from economists' agreement that
cities are the growth engines of modern societies. Policy divisions differ
on how much and what active roles for government are in contrast to

attention to individuals (largely advocating human capital acquisition). Should policy be place-based or people-based? As mayors and elected officials, community and labor advocates, and the public struggle to understand what cities can do on their own, it is important to sort through the confusing range of economic advice. The dominant individualized focus of market-oriented economists can obscure alternative economic analyses, and lead to policy recommendations that are at best partial and at worst counterproductive for addressing inequality.

8

ECONOMICS AND POLICY

What Can Cities Do?

R ising inequality didn't shake the leadership position of the field of economics when it came to advising on government policy until the global economic crisis of the Great Recession, starting in late 2007, the worst downturn since the Great Depression. Briefed at the London School of Economics (LSE), Queen Elizabeth II famously asked, "Why did nobody notice it?" LSE economists replied that they thought "banks knew what they were doing," telling the queen that economists failed to understand systemic risks and admitting "it is difficult to recall a greater example of wishful thinking combined with hubris."[1]

In urban economics, close attention to data has overturned several theoretical ideas that were held to be fundamental by market economics. Increased minimum wages don't automatically reduce employment. Better educational credentials don't eliminate racial and gender earnings and employment discrimination. More expensive cities can maintain economic advantages over time and not converge with lower-cost ones. And more urban equality can spur growth through shared prosperity.[2]

Market-oriented economists claim their theory shows that interventionist government policy stymies urban growth. Edward Glaeser writes that "economists remain more skeptical of many forms of government intervention than representatives of many other disciplines" and that "is particularly important in debates about activist economic policy." In market-oriented theory, cities are modeled as maximizing entities, akin to profit-making firms, so governments should be fostering "competition between cities, each of which is trying to attract people and firms."[3]

Other economists question how well these models of maximization describe reality. Institutionalist economists emphasize the role of institutions, power, and the historical development and evolution of economies. An institutionalist perspective is not averse to theory, but it relies heavily on empirical analysis to make conclusions. Institutionalists caution policymakers to not rely on economic theory for automatic policy prescriptions but to consider alternative explanations and options.

Policy options to solve urban inequality differ for strong or weak market cities. Troubled cities like Detroit often face different leverage points than growing ones like New York or Los Angeles. But all urban economic policies must recognize the four factors that constrain equity policies: sectoral change and disruption, federal anti-urban bias, state control of cities and metropolitan government fragmentation, and structural racism.

In spite of their theoretical differences, urban economists agree on several policies. This chapter reviews three policy dimensions central to urban prosperity and equity: economic development and job creation, job quality and labor market regulation, and housing. Although economists sometimes reach consensus on policy (even though their theoretical underpinnings may differ), public officials and advocates sometimes disregard these consensus views, especially in economic and housing development.[4]

ECONOMIC DEVELOPMENT AND JOB CREATION

Virtually all economists dislike cities' routine use of company-specific tax subsidies to attract or retain businesses. Market-oriented economists (those who root their understanding in individual maximization models) argue that "targeted economic development subsidies usually fail" and "are likely to further depress tax revenues." Institutional economists would emphasize what Greg LeRoy calls "the great American jobs scam," where corporations drain revenue from cities through subsidies while reinforcing their political power over local communities. Despite the widespread use of subsidies, there's no evidence that they help. Institutional economists and the market-oriented economists agree: "economic development incentives have little or no impact on firm location and investment decisions."[5]

But economists' consensus against subsidies is often ignored by pol-icymakers. In 2017, cities and states fought over Amazon's second head-quarters (HQ2), with 238 subsidy bids offered to the highly profitable corporation. Cities also routinely bid for Amazon's warehouse operations, even though new distribution centers often result in lower wages with no net overall gain in county employment.[6] These problems aren't limited to Amazon. In 2016, Wisconsin awarded $3 billion in subsidies to Foxconn for an electronics plant that was never built, and Nevada and Texas have given Elon Musk's Tesla Motors (whose market capitalization in late 2021 exceeded $1 trillion) billions in subsidies. The state of Florida spent over $1 billion in subsidies in a failed attempt to increase biotechnology invest-ment. And the list goes on and on.

Driven by a mistaken belief that taxes are central to firms' location decisions, almost all state and local governments routinely use subsidies. Lobbyists and corporate executives instill this fear to get windfall subsi-dies. Justifying $320 million in tax subsidies for a United Airlines facility, which closed just ten years later, Indiana's then-governor Joseph Kernan said, "Indiana, like virtually every other state, is not going to unilaterally disarm" and would continue offering subsidies to corporations in order to compete with other states.[7]

Most research finds subsidies don't have a major impact on location decisions. One line of research does argue that counties winning million-dollar plants with subsidies have higher total factor productivity over time. But that is countered by other research finding overall manufac-turing location decisions aren't affected, or may be slightly negatively affected, by subsidies—"firms favor states with low corporate taxes, right-to-work laws, low unionization, and (most surprisingly) small incentives," and subsidized plants don't stay longer than nonsubsidized ones.[8]

Economists also dislike geographically targeted, tax-advantaged investment programs. Research finds that enterprise zones (EZs) and the Trump-era Opportunity Zones (OZs) are ineffective for job creation, especially in the poor communities often used to justify the programs.[9] In congressional testimony, the Brookings Institution scholar David Wessel concluded that Opportunity Zones did more to cut taxes for the wealthy "than to improve the lives of people who live in the zones."[10]

Economists are divided about policy when the debate moves past firm-specific subsidies. Many economists endorse competition among cities, even in the same metropolitan economic region, because their models argue that lower taxes and less regulation attract mobile capital and labor. In this framework, governments are like for-profit companies competing in a textbook free market. Thus, at the same time market economists have called for Congress to end the "economic war among the states" by banning firm-specific subsidies, they also want state and local governments to compete with each other by cutting tax and spending programs to produce "the right level of public goods."[11]

Economists use the individual choice models to argue against place-based policies because those policies are seen to inhibit capital and labor mobility across jurisdictions and industries. Glaeser writes that policies should "increase the choices available to people," wondering if after Hurricane Katrina, "500,000 residents of New Orleans" would prefer "200,000 dollars apiece or 100 billion dollars' worth of government infrastructure." Enrico Moretti has called for a portion of unemployment insurance to come "in the form of a mobility voucher that would cover some of the costs of moving to a different area."[12]

In contrast, economist Timothy Bartik favors place-based economic development, noting people often don't relocate due to family obligations, an inability to sell devalued houses, and high transactions and housing costs for relocating. Place-based policies can address involuntary unemployment, target industries that produce multiplier benefits, and provide general business and workforce services along with public infrastructure and land development. All of these are more cost-effective than firm-specific subsidies. Even Glaeser now accepts some limited place-based policy, although he still focuses on individuals through employment subsidies such as a higher earned income tax credit (EITC) rather than infrastructure investment or larger financial transfers to troubled regions.[13]

In a recent dialogue, Bartik and economist David Neumark agreed that capital subsidies to businesses or investors aren't effective. Neumark argues subsidies might be even more expensive than realized because there is no evidence they create jobs. But while they agree on rejecting standard business tax subsidies, they differ on scale. Neumark advocates targeting private employment subsidies to poor residents in poor neighborhoods, while Bartik argues for broader use of vouchers in cities or regions, saying that "neighborhoods are not labor markets."[14]

Economists' broad antisubsidy consensus has little traction in most cities, which often use inducements to attract or retain companies and jobs. Progressive policy advocates also recognize that unrestricted subsidies don't create good jobs for city residents and cost far too much. But given the persistent use of subsidies, practical advocates seek to link them with concrete, verifiable benefits while also calling out overly expensive tax cuts where the revenue could be spent effectively on items like infrastructure and education.

Los Angeles pioneered tying public development assistance to legally specified goals—job creation, hiring of subaltern and excluded workers, small business procurement, environmental standards—through community benefit agreements (CBAs). CBAs using legally binding and monitored contracts with strong involvement from the affected community are central to progressive development strategies. How-to guides for CBAs now are widespread, and even troubled cities like Detroit use CBAs for major subsidized development projects. Critics argue that CBAs interfere with city zoning and development processes, making negotiations long and unrealistic, while advocates fear the process can be captured by developers to limit community benefits. But well-crafted and enforceable CBAs can save cities money and produce observable benefits in exchange for subsidies and move the process into regular contract law while generating political support for development projects.[15]

CBAs are just one type of development linkage (or exaction) used by cities. Progressives also call for minimum labor standards on jobs—higher wages and benefits, unionization, and affirmative hiring for low-income and minority workers and contractors. Other strategies, such as those pioneered by Jobs to Move America in the transportation field, seek to incentivize better outcomes from companies and bar low-road companies from city contracts.[16]

Cities also are using impact or land value capture fees where land prices are increasing, with the increased land value caused partly from public infrastructure and services not fully captured by tax revenues. Cities have enacted local-source agreements that require local resident hiring, or first-source policies that use people referred through city labor agencies or nonprofits as the first source of potential hires. These hiring programs work best when linked to broader CBAs, unions, or other empowered organizations.[17]

Cities also direct economic development support to industry clusters rather than single firms, including Baltimore's fledgling biotech cluster based on health-care research at Johns Hopkins and New York City's digitally based industry program in cooperation with the new Cornell Tech. Harvard Business School professor Michael Porter advocates for industry cluster policies based on his analysis of corporate competitive advantage. Perhaps because Porter works with case studies and not formal economic theory, market economists haven't engaged very much with industry cluster approaches.[18]

Market-oriented economists generally disapprove of city interventions in economic development and prefer reducing or eliminating targeted government policies in favor of lower taxes and less regulation. Their theory argues that private capital flows and decisions, along with labor market mobility for individuals, will provide the optimal economic outcome for a city. Government actions would interfere and make outcomes worse.

But subsidies won't go away because of policymakers' strong support and state autonomy in setting tax policy. In 2004, a federal appeals court ruled an Ohio investment tax credit violated the federal Commerce Clause, encouraging subsidy critics. A unanimous Supreme Court overturned the decision, and Congress immediately moved to eliminate the basis for the appellate decision and legally enshrine state use of subsidies.[19] Although many progressives dislike corporate subsidies, their economic criticisms aren't grounded in market fundamentalism but in how subsidies contribute to unequal economic outcomes. In order to address this, some CBA advocates suggest routine inclusion of CBAs in all city land-use policies such as zoning and broader city planning rather than using them only on a deal-by-deal basis.[20]

Job creation programs also can be linked to other policies, especially transit and environmental policies. Many cities are pursuing environmental green policies to create good jobs, including retrofitting buildings and making new development environmentally sound, increasing mass transit, shifting power generation to renewables, mitigation of sea-level rise and urban heat islands, and electrification of public transportation. In *Greenovation: Urban Leadership on Climate Change*, Joan Fitzgerald details the promise and complexity of these efforts, showing the need for an overarching vision, political leadership, and ongoing transparency and dialogue among a wide group of stakeholders. Using CBA-type mechanisms, new green jobs can be unionized and opened to subaltern and subordinated minority and women workers.[21]

On job creation, some advocates have called for a national universal jobs guarantee with adequate pay and benefits to put pressure on low-road jobs and businesses. Some even call for a municipal job guarantee if national policy cannot be implemented, although paying for that would be daunting, especially in smaller and economically troubled cities.[22]

There are calls for process changes that emphasize more community input into development decisions and, at the extreme, giving communities power over any projects in their geographic area. But while increasing community voice is central to progressive strategies because it gives people a stake in outcomes and brings in the views of those most directly affected, community veto power goes too far, seeing the city's economy as nothing more than a collection of discrete neighborhoods. It could result in an even more balkanized city economy that is unable to coordinate resources and powers at an adequate scale for equitable growth, as happened with New York City's rejection of the admittedly flawed Amazon HQ2 and Industry City projects. A more visionary opposition perhaps could have negotiated better deals from those two megaprojects rather than kill them.[23]

JOB QUALITY AND LABOR MARKET REGULATION

While most economists reject firm-specific subsidies for job creation, they disagree about whether labor market regulations are effective in improving job quality. Market-oriented economists prefer using education and training to improve workers' job prospects and minimizing government's role in decisions about hiring and firing, compensation, benefits, and labor market organization. But institutional economists see a range of possibilities for more city regulation of labor markets, especially improving work for the lowest-paid and marginalized workers.

Job training as an antipoverty measure has been emphasized for decades. It is based on the market-oriented economic proposition that unemployment and low wages are caused primarily by workers lacking education and skills. But effective training needs effective institutions. Training works best when it includes more extensive support services; focuses on industry sectors; and engages intermediary organizations ranging from labor unions to community colleges, to nonprofits, with a dual-customer focus on both workers and businesses. Without these aspects, training isn't very promising.[24]

Community colleges are the most important national source of formal training, and there are hundreds in large and midsize cities. Community college students are disproportionately minority, and they concentrate on vocational courses and sectors (such as information technology and health care) with very low costs relative to four-year institutions. But community colleges have low graduation rates and are often disconnected from labor market needs. Innovative institutions and programs often fail to reach scale individually.[25]

Although institutional economists argue that education and training help shrink inequality, human capital formation alone isn't sufficient. Shrinking labor unions, especially in the private sector, and policies of active wage suppression by employers has led these economists to support a variety of active interventions to raise wages and incomes and improve job quality.[26]

Market-oriented economists believe that shaping or interfering in private contracts usually produces worse outcomes, so they are indifferent to or oppose unions, health and safety regulation, regulation of benefits, and minimum wages. Free-market economist and Nobel Prize winner Milton Friedman wrote, "[I]nsofar as minimum wage laws have any effect at all, their effect is clearly to increase poverty . . . The effect of the minimum wage is therefore to make unemployment higher than it otherwise would be."[27] A similar market-oriented logic is used to oppose other labor market interventions.

This anti-minimum-wage consensus has been shaken by an expanding body of empirical literature, beginning in 1994 with a finding of no job losses in fast-food labor markets spanning two states with different minimum wages. Several states and cities have since raised their minimum wages above the federal level, giving economists natural experiments on the impacts.[28] A comprehensive review found higher minimum wages "significantly increase the earnings of low-paid workers," while the "overall evidence base suggests an employment impact of close to zero." Faced with this evidence, many economists are agnostic on whether market theory can explain minimum-wage and employment effects, although some still believe higher minimum wages cost jobs, especially for younger workers.[29]

The federal minimum wage was last raised in 2009, but thirty states and the District of Columbia were above the federal level by 2022, and over forty local governments raised minimum wages above their own state level. Starting with Baltimore in 1993, cities also have explored living-wage policies, requiring city contractors or developers receiving government assistance to pay higher wages. Many cities, including Los Angeles, Detroit, and New York, have adopted some kind of living-wage policy.[30]

More cities want to raise minimum wages, but states often want to block them.[31] As of January 2022, twenty-six states had forbidden their cities to raise minimum wages—in other words, states preempted their cities from acting. And state labor preemptions aren't limited to wages. States also have blocked cities from requiring paid sick leave, scheduling work shifts to accommodate workers with caregiver responsibilities, and adopting prevailing-wage and project labor agreements with unions in return for city development subsidies.[32]

Unionization is another job quality strategy. Some cities work with unions to bring in formerly excluded workers. Direct economic benefits come from union jobs, and mobilizing unions' political strength can help in elections and enacting legislation. The progressive movement in Los Angeles has substantial union engagement, helping low-income and minority workers get unionized jobs at the city-owned airport, in mass transit construction, and in trash pickup and recycling. Private sector unions in other cities also are working with community organizations to help diversify their membership and build broader political coalitions, working to overcome a history in some places of racial exclusion by unions, especially in the building trades.

Some market fundamentalist economists advocate eliminating all labor market regulation—minimum and living wages, pro-unionization policies, and mandated benefits like family leave and paid sick days. These economists have also taken aim at occupational licensing, with conservative economist Tyler Cowen suggesting that the federal government preempt state and local occupational licensing.[33] In contrast, institutional economists' focus on licensing and hiring practices has concentrated on criminal justice records, with thirty-seven states and more than 150 cities adopting ban-the-box laws, which regulate or end inquiries on criminal records for initial employment applications and in occupational licensing. To reduce wage discrimination, cities and states are also regulating questions about salary history and considering requiring pay transparency disclosures when employers interview for jobs to help reduce wage gaps for women and nonwhite workers.[34]

Progressives often want to expand cities' role in regulating labor markets well beyond hiring practices. Instead of seeing excessive regulation as a barrier to prosperity, these economists see labor markets as highly concentrated by location and occupation, often with unequal power between companies and workers. Employer power suppresses wages and working conditions both within firms and across labor markets—what economists call a monopsony market.[35] Monopsony in turn is seen as contributing to a declining rate of new businesses, entrepreneurialism, and innovation, in contrast to market-oriented economists who blame such declines on excessive regulation.

Advocates endorse a broad range of policies to raise the floor for low-wage work, and these policies are centered on a higher minimum wage. They also want cities to use other regulatory powers, principally contracting and economic development deals, to require living wages and mandatory paid family and sick leave for any employer doing business with the city, if not for all employers in a city.

Several cities now engage in industry or occupation-specific regulation. New York, Seattle, and San Francisco provide protections for fast-food workers to prevent scheduling abuses and protection against layoffs. Prior to a more general wage increase, Los Angeles and Long Beach adopted industry-specific minimum wages for hotel workers. And hundreds of cities and counties have enacted some version of a living wage, requiring city contractors or firms receiving tax benefits to pay an administratively determined living wage. Although these provisions make labor law more complex, they represent efforts by progressives to mobilize government power to win concrete victories while seeking to spread equity policies to the larger economy and labor market.[36]

Advocates stress proworker policies that promote racial and gender equity, arguing that cities can implement them without federal action, although many state legislatures have prevented cities from taking such equity measures. A project tracking equitable labor market strategies in ten cities calls for both "raising racial equity" and "raising the floor on low-wage jobs" across the labor market and argues that helping poor and minority families will also increase shared prosperity for all.[37]

HOUSING

Housing quality and affordability is a core issue for all cities. In cities like Los Angeles and New York, affordable housing is a volatile economic and political issue. In declining cities like Detroit, blighted housing and falling property values consume administrative attention and resources, and contribute to a downward spiral of abandonment and blight.

Economists share a broad consensus on housing: cities should encourage more density and supply. Restricting density and development rewards incumbent homeowners, increasing their home's value by limiting supply while raising the overall cost of owner-owned and rental housing. Glaeser puts it succinctly: "An increase in the supply of houses, or anything else, drives prices down while restricting the supply of real estate keeps prices high."[38] Far to Glaeser's left, Matson Boyd of the Center for Popular Economics agrees: "no radical vision for a progressive city can become a success" until homeowners blocking higher density "are challenged."[39]

More affordable housing is central to increasing some city populations, especially for workers and immigrants. Metropolitan areas saw population growth in the early part of the last decade, but growth rates declined after 2015. Much of the decline preceded the pandemic, driven by domestic out-migration, declining international in-migration because of Trump administration policies, and declining birth rates as the population ages. There also was very slow housing construction in many major urban areas, with low numbers of building permits issued for new construction because of opposition to new development and increasingly complex permitting processes.[40]

San Francisco area housing activists, with their organization called YIMBY (Yes In My Back Yard), aggressively advocate for development to help reduce sale and rental price pressures. Many YIMBY advocates see expanding supply as complementing equity regulations and policies supporting low-income and displaced families. Other progressives with an environmental focus concentrate on increasing density near mass transit sites and using transportation to increase job equity in a policy called transit-oriented development (TOD).[41]

As with firm-specific economic development subsidies, a wide spectrum of economists agree that we should reduce restrictive housing legislation and increase supply. In writing about NIMBYism (Not In My Back Yard), Nobel Prize winner Paul Krugman said that it "is bad for working families and the US economy as a whole, strangling growth precisely where workers are most productive."[42]

Most economists favor increased density and housing construction, and limits on housing regulations that limit supply—single-family zoning, height restrictions, caps on units in a project or area, unwarranted design restrictions, parking requirements, minimum lot sizes, using environmental reviews to block building, restrictions on alternative dwelling units, and excessive historic preservation. Market economists also would do away with most rental and affordability regulations, but institutionalists see a potential equity role for impact fees and other developer payments, affordability requirements, anti-eviction policies, and possible rent regulation. Many economists also question subsidizing private developers to encourage construction, a common feature of many city housing policies. Community benefit advocates would link subsidies to specific measurable outcomes.

Many local housing regulation policies are viewed as reducing supply and increasing cost. A literature survey concluded that "the vast majority of studies have found that locations with more regulation have higher house prices and less construction." Perhaps it will come as a surprise that the review found costs of construction—labor (including unionization) and materials, often blamed for high housing costs—were not a major negative influence on housing supply. Instead, regulatory impacts on land "that restrict the size and type of housing units that can be built on a given amount of land" are the key factors in limiting supply. The review also didn't find a strong correlation between homeownership and regulation. The strongest influence on current land-use patterns is simply previous land use.[43]

Many progressive housing advocates, including YIMBY members, part company with some economists' rejection of all housing regulation,

arguing instead for a mix of rent and price regulation, eviction protections, public housing construction and ownership, and rental or
purchasing subsidies for low-income households. YIMBY advocates
sometimes are attacked by other progressives who want to restrict
private development and density and regulate prices. These advocates
worry about gentrification that would further racial discrimination,
arguing for more community control of private development and more
public housing. For example, the San Francisco Democratic Social-
ists of America called the San Francisco YIMBY organization a "pro-
development, pro-gentrification, pro-landlord organization." But many
YIMBY members also support policies such as "public housing, rent
control, anti-eviction measures" in what economist Noah Smith calls a
"do all the things" housing policy.[44]

What about housing in weaker market cities like Detroit? The problem
in these cities isn't high land costs but blight. Sustained economic growth
can reduce or even reverse blight. In the late 1970s, New York City owned
over 100,000 housing units because of abandonment and tax foreclosures.
Through a combination of dedicated policy staff with mayoral support,
capital investment, resale to private owners, and a growing economy and
immigrant population, New York no longer has a backlog of abandoned
housing. But it took a combination of aggressive public intervention and
a growing economy and population to solve the problem.[45]

Weaker cities often cannot deal quickly with blight because abandoned properties often have complex title and ownership issues, which
block sale or demolition. Following the example of Flint, Michigan, cities
are creating land banks, which allow for the clearing of titles and the
disposal of blighted property more rapidly. But Detroit and other cities
have found political infighting and fears of neighborhood displacement
have blocked such programs or have run them inefficiently. Detroit's land
bank also has been accused of corrupt property resales and bidding for
demolition work.[46]

Federal and state governments neglect housing in cities. A 2015 study
compares the federal government's annual budget of around $40 billion
on low-income housing subsidies and $6 billion in tax expenditures
through the Low-Income Housing Tax Credit to the "roughly $195 bil-
lion" that "goes towards subsidizing homeowners through the tax code."
The study notes that adding the "non-taxation of imputed rent" means

homeowner subsidies are effectively around $600 billion,[47] most of which flow to higher-income families and suburban residents.

What extreme housing policies might economists argue for? Market-oriented economists point to Houston, a city without formal zoning, as evidence that development can self-manage. But others see even Houston as having the "*de facto* equivalency of a traditional zoning system" expressed through minimum lot sizes, parking requirements, deed restrictions, land-use designations and variances, landscaping and buffer policies, and a variety of other ordinances.[48]

What about sharp reductions in existing regulation, especially land-use controls? Glaeser provocatively argues that "coastal California could house many millions more than it already does" if environmental and other regulations were reduced or eliminated. Other economists have estimated very large negative impacts from housing regulation. Chang-Tai Hsieh and Enrico Moretti estimate that adjusting housing regulations to the median national level between 1964 and 2009 in just three cities—New York, San Francisco, and San Jose—would have increased total national gross domestic product (GDP) by up to 8.9 percent in 2009. In their estimate, job growth in the New York metropolitan area alone would have risen by 318 percent, and even the troubled city of Flint, Michigan would have seen a 161 percent increase in employment.[49]

Such provocative estimates aside, prosperous cities and regions often restrict housing to the detriment of renters; low-income households; and the city, regional, and national economies. San Francisco has some of the highest housing prices in the nation but a significantly lower population density than New York. If San Francisco's residential density were the same as Manhattan, in 2020 its population of 873,965 would have been 3.48 million. If its density were simply as high as Brooklyn, San Francisco would have had over 1.8 million residents.

In many cities, including New York, housing development hasn't kept pace with the economy: "between 2010 and 2018, New York City's job base increased 22 percent, while its housing stock only increased 4 percent." In 2019, California experienced the "most severe" reduction in housing permits "since the Great Depression." Analysts fault low-density policies, downzoning, excessive historic landmarking, caps on building heights, and community review powers that cause delay and raise cost while giving the advantage to existing homeowners.[50]

Housing restrictions combined with long-standing suburban practices (limiting multifamily housing, large lot zoning, racial and other development barriers, lack of regional mass transit) lead to regional housing shortages and pricing barriers. New York University's Furman Center notes that, despite its liberal reputation, the New York region is among the most segregated in the nation and that New York State "has the most exclusionary zoning in the country."[51]

Some cities with strong real estate markets use zoning reform to expand affordable housing. Although some advocates favor inclusionary zoning (IZ) requiring affordable housing to be part of market-rate construction projects, research finds that IZ may "restrict development or raise prices." Many housing advocates now favor affordable housing overlays, which provide financial and regulatory incentives for affordable housing production in addition to existing zoning rules.[52]

Glaeser and other economists see affordable housing provisions as an "implicit tax on development" that will limit construction. But other analysts find incentives for affordable housing to be effective and more politically feasible than striving for politically challenging, comprehensive zoning reform or more equitable taxation of homeownership, which could then fund low-income housing subsidies.[53]

Many progressive advocates want more than reconfigured zoning. They criticize subsidies to private developers, such as New York's 421(a) tax abatement program, estimated to have cost billions in foregone tax revenues. Advocates prefer direct subsidies to low-income households along with construction of publicly owned housing, while opposing development that doesn't expand affordable housing.[54]

Otherwise progressive cities can have strong antidevelopment politics, making it hard to expand housing supply.[55] In his 2021 mayoral campaign, New York City comptroller Scott Stringer called for tight limits on private housing development, decrying a "gentrification-industrial complex" while elected supervisors in San Francisco regularly limit the city's market-rate housing construction, including ones combining affordable housing with market-rate units. Some tenant advocacy groups there and in Los Angeles also have fought state legislation to increase density and TOD.

In 2017, California passed fifteen bills to increase affordable housing, including increasing state funds for construction, expanding inclusionary housing, and fighting against local NIMBY practices. Facing continuing resistance from smaller cities, wealthier suburbs, and even some larger cites, in 2021 the state enacted stronger laws and incentives to break down zoning restrictions and build affordable housing.[56]

A California study found "homeownership . . . is associated with opposition to new housing of all kinds, even as it has little influence on attitudes about other policies." Although it is not surprising homeowners want less supply to preserve their asset values, it may be surprising that equity-focused housing advocates ally with wealthier homeowners. In these cases, progressives oppose private housing development, including projects incorporating affordable housing, despite research concluding that a lack of affordable housing particularly hurts low-income and minority households. For example, the local New York City chapter of the progressive climate organization, Sunrise Movement, joined a coalition to oppose upzoning in Soho, one of the city's wealthiest neighborhoods, even though it would mandate around 25 percent affordable units in construction.[57]

David Schleicher argues that policies opposing housing development are caused by a lack of political party competition in cities that in turn creates "noncompetitive legislatures" where "members end up with an outsized degree of control over issues in their districts," especially land use and zoning. Housing advocate Randy Shaw finds progressives endorsing exclusionary zoning and other antidensity policies, even in liberal cities like Cambridge, Austin, and San Francisco. In contrast, progressives in Minneapolis, Portland, and Seattle have pushed for major prodensity zoning reforms.[58] In 2022, in addition to support for unions and the Green New Deal, Courage to Change, the political action committee (PAC) associated with New York congressional representative Alexandria Ocasio-Cortez, called on candidates to "end exclusionary zoning" even if local neighborhood officials were opposed.[59]

These progressive stances in favor of housing development aim to counter fears that development will displace poor and minority residents by building luxury housing they believe increases all housing rents and prices. But recent economic research finds that shortages of market-rate housing push higher-income buyers into adjacent lower-income neighborhoods, pushing up prices there. And some research also finds current residents and children actually may benefit from higher-income households moving into their neighborhood if supply also increases.[60]

CAN ECONOMISTS HELP CITIES FIGHT INEQUALITY?

As this review shows, there's no sweeping consensus version of economics to guide city policies on inequality, even though there is agreement on a number of specific ideas. Economists agree that firm-specific development subsidies don't work, while policies to create more housing and more density are good and necessary. Institutional economists are more comfortable with economic interventions to promote equitable growth through CBAs and other development mechanisms, housing and price regulations combined with more construction, and other nonmarket mechanisms. They also disagree with market economists on labor market policy and cities regulating wages, hiring, firing, and other working conditions.

Different opinions about policy stem from different interpretations of empirical evidence and major differences in how economists frame urban problems. Market-oriented urban economists, like Glaeser, argue that an economics approach should aim to "increase the choices available to people" because "people, not places, are the important outcomes." For Glaeser, government intervention is downplayed based on the framework's "doubts about the competence and benevolence of government."[61]

But basing policy options on what economists call the theoretical microfoundations of rational individual self-interest doesn't exclude economists who support active government interventions. Economist Paul Krugman, winner of the Nobel Prize for work in trade and economic geography, has endorsed higher minimum wages, more labor unions, infrastructure investment financed by higher federal deficits, more taxation of the wealthy, and other interventionist policies. Yet Krugman claims the "New Economic Geography" (inspired by his work) is theoretically grounded in "full microfoundations," which means outcomes are presumed to be equilibrium results of maximizing individuals interacting. He is careful to say (as other economists are not) that the model isn't a "literal description of the economy."[62]

In response, economic geographer Michael Storper argued that Krugman's reliance on microfoundation models can lead economists (Storper excepted Krugman) to lose sight of how their models and metaphors can confuse "the models for real explanation." That confusion undergirds sweeping statements like Glaeser's about urban economic theory ruling out place-based strategies or his broad skepticism about government interventions.[63]

Institutional urban economists don't rely on theories of individual maximization. For example, Chris Benner and Manuel Pastor's framework of solidarity economics focuses on reducing inequality based on their empirically rooted urban research. They believe "standard economic models of human behavior" are "outdated," relying heavily on self-interest to explain people's economic activity and justifying inequality. They note empirical research finds "high levels of income disparities, racial segregation, and social fragmentation" undercut sustainable job and income growth. In order to achieve outcomes that favor growth and equity, policies need to support "security and community."[64] In related critiques of individual-choice models, economist Emanuel Saez argues that without incorporating "the social nature of humans," which is "absent from the standard economic model," we cannot understand why "concerns about inequality are so pervasive" or how to address it.[65]

Another perspective relevant to urban economics is stratification economics. Observing persistent intergroup race and gender economic and social inequalities, "stratification economics presumes the rationality of discrimination, that discrimination is functional in promoting the privileged group's relative status." Stratification economics differs from individualized models that explain group-based inequalities as irrational distortions to be eroded by market forces.

Economists such as Darrick Hamilton, William Darity, Jr., Stephanie Seguino, and Nancy Folbre point to persistent and growing racial and gender inequalities in wages and income, wealth, employment, housing, and other outcomes that cannot be explained by subaltern groups' individual educational achievement, skills, or behavior. Rather, outcomes are explained by systemic "stratification processes," which are "characterized by the dominance of whites and males, with women and racial/ethnic 'minorities' the subordinate groups."[66]

In 2020, the prestigious National Bureau of Economic Research established a working group on race and stratification in the economy (although not on gender). By using newly available data and methodologies on urban growth, industry, employment, and housing patterns in cities, including residential segregation, empirical stratification research can help illuminate how systemic stratification and subordination reproduce and maintain markets and the distribution of privilege and power.

Storper describes the intellectual challenge facing urbanists and economists: "[C]ities or regions . . . have complex economic development processes shaped by an almost-infinite range of forces" beyond the scope of "any single discipline or theory, even the 'economic' ones."[67] Empirical work in stratification, economic geography, economic history, and urban economics, grounded in critical perspectives and open to insights and methods from other disciplines, is the best way forward for understanding cities and inequality, although crafting policy still requires seeking regularities and not defaulting to overly discrete or unique analyses.[68]

In urban economics, we have learned that data matters. Studies stand or fall on their data adequacy, selection of methodologies, and plausibility in relation to other knowledge about how outcomes are determined. Practical evidence-based policy needs honest discourse about empirical findings and multifaceted explanations, and it should not be captive to supposedly higher-level validation of economic models. Theoretical claims may have value for academic economists, but they aren't good guides to policy and sometimes blur more complex realities for policymakers and the public. Empirical work does not require a full microfoundations theory, especially if it comes by excluding institutional and historical insights along with analyses of power and influence.

Many urban economic ideas—agglomeration, externalities and spillovers, and cities as hubs of innovation—are widely and sensibly accepted. Market-oriented and institutional economists agree increased housing supply increases affordability. Economists' findings that early childhood education can increase lifetime income and security encouraged cities to provide universal prekindergarten. And virtually all economists argue against tax subsidies for specific companies or sports stadiums, or locational tax breaks like enterprise zones or Opportunity Zones, as a waste of taxpayer dollars because they starve tight budgets and do not produce any lasting economic development benefits.

But these policy ideas don't require a universal theory of human behavior. Perhaps regrettably for policymakers, there is no automatic theoretical shortcut to assess policy impact, including those to reduce inequality. Empirical analyses, case studies, insights, and tests of predictions from a variety of models, perspectives, and disciplines all help in figuring out what works.

Economics sensibly questions overly elaborate theories or policy claims for simple questions about how people, firms, and institutions respond to incentives. Resistance to housing development and increased density can be explained by property owners protecting their property values rather than complex arguments about their preserving neighborhood "character." Instead of explaining street crime through a "culture of poverty," economists look for how criminal behavior responds to perceived costs and benefits.

But economists need to be humble, as when they admitted to the queen of England, about their theoretical rigidities. For example, the definition of "public goods"—areas where government intervenes to provide what private markets fail to provide—is not in reality defined by theory but by ongoing struggles over the proper role of government. What are now commonly accepted as public goods—universal public education, workplace health and safety standards, environmental regulation, and antidiscrimination regulations—were once dismissed as unnecessary interference with markets. As June Sekera points out, market economics sees the very existence of public goods as driven by "market failure" rather than seeing collective action as complementary and necessary for prosperity.[69]

Of course, attention to changing norms and politics doesn't mean every government intervention is justified. It only means the value of proposed urban policies cannot be judged by how well they conform to theoretical maximization models. Economists' empirical strengths, as in minimum-wage studies, sway policy debates even though a mandated minimum wage is always judged suboptimal by models grounded in individual choice.

In spite of a desire for simple solutions, there's no single way economists think about cities, prosperity, and equity. The market-oriented individual maximization framework leaves out history, institutions, and power, while institutionalists can get mired in exceptions or details that can't engage with policy formation. This book argues that policies promoting equity and growth can incorporate insights from market economics. But accurate analysis and effective policy must incorporate four dimensions that urban economists downplay or ignore: sectoral change and disruption, federal anti-urban bias, state control of cities and metropolitan government fragmentation; and structural racism. For cities, regions, states, and the nation to address inequality, these structural factors need to be understood with wide-ranging empirical analyses of urban economies and policies while questioning the theoretical claims of market fundamentalism.

9

EPILOGUE

Can Cities Fight Inequality On Their Own?

Donald Trump's 2016 election underscored the political threats to American cities. Although Joe Biden's 2020 election was a relief, it didn't change cities' fundamental problems in addressing inequality. America's unequal urban structure and related problems are too deeply rooted for a single close presidential election to transform them.

Although Trump's real estate business was based in New York, his campaign rhetoric described cities as gang-dominated "war zones," "ruled" by Democrats, where "you get shot walking to the store." Trump and Republicans pursued deep cuts in housing, mass transit, community banking, food aid, Medicaid and health spending, transportation and infrastructure, economic development and minority business support, aid for seniors, and job training. Republicans also revived long-standing efforts to convert federal programs into state-controlled block grants, which would further disadvantage cities. Trump had little urban support in 2016 (Hillary Clinton won 111 of the nation's 137 counties with populations over 500,000), so his administration's hostility wasn't surprising.[1]

Perhaps the most intense conflicts came around immigration. Attacks on undocumented workers and immigrants were central to Trump's political rise. Some cities refused to cooperate with aggressive federal arrest and deportation policies, declaring themselves sanctuary cities where undocumented immigrants would be protected. In 2017, the administration issued an executive order barring federal grants to sanctuary cities

and threatening to arrest mayors and hold them personally accountable for noncompliance. The order met a wave of litigation with no
full resolution by 2020, and Biden rescinded the executive order on his
first day in office.[2]

In September 2020, responding to disorder around police killings of
Blacks, Trump ordered the attorney general to label some cities as anarchist jurisdictions in order to withhold federal funds from them. Trump's
campaign also highlighted barely concealed racial attacks on fair housing
policies, claiming such policies could "easily spread" urban crime to the
suburbs and threaten the safety of "suburban women."[3]

The COVID-19 pandemic and the accompanying deep recession also
put many cities in peril. The pandemic hit hardest first in major cities, and
it was wrongly thought that urban density made cities uniquely vulnerable. But as the disease progressed, it became clear the virus could thrive in
urban, suburban, and rural areas. And even as vaccines were rolled out,
the virus was battering inadequate public health systems that had been
further harmed by a year of delays, missteps, and inaction by the Trump
administration.

States and cities were forced to compete with each other for protective
equipment, and accurate public health information wasn't communicated
while Trump popularized false treatments. Legislative resistance from the
Republican Party meant state and city budgets didn't receive adequate
federal funds to replace lost revenues.

In addition to being a health crisis in its own right, the pandemic was
an accelerator—heightening preexisting economic and racial inequalities. The initial shock of the pandemic brought the economy to a virtual
halt by April 2020, but by the fall, higher-income workers had mostly
regained their lost jobs and income, in a so-called K-shaped recovery.
In contrast, lower-paid workers (disproportionately nonwhite) remained
worse off, suffering from unemployment and lack of income, poor health
care, inadequate and crowded housing and under threat of eviction, and
food shortages.[4]

Black and Hispanic neighborhoods and communities suffered significantly higher COVID-19 case and death rates. Higher levels of poor
health and comorbidities along with more crowded living spaces and less
access to health care contributed to these differences. And labor market
conditions also played a role. Nonwhite workers were more concentrated

in essential occupations like health care and food sales and delivery, with less opportunity to work at home and insufficient savings to buffer the pandemic's economic fallout.[5]

The pandemic also hit city budgets hard. A 2017 survey of city fiscal officers found general fund revenues still hadn't fully recovered from the Great Recession, with many states never restoring the aid to cities that they had cut after 2008. The pandemic accelerated city revenue problems, underscoring how cities don't get their proportionate share of regional revenues. Wealthier suburbs capture more of the tax base (especially property taxes) while not sharing the costs of regional education, infrastructure, environmental costs, criminal justice, anti-poverty programs, and transportation. The Lincoln Institute of Land Policy says that municipal finances are the "invisible challenge" underlying many other urban problems, noting that even as policy demands increase, "cities face a distressing combination of mounting historical debt, increasing costs for providing public goods and services, and diminishing revenues."[6]

In spite of advertising campaigns saying "we are all in this together," the pandemic highlighted inequality, especially based on race and income. And it also showed the inadequacy of generalized growth strategies. The pandemic had a significant impact on urban economies, with increased working from home among higher-income service sector workers depressing office rents, eliminating lower-wage service jobs in cities, and straining city budgets. As the Omicron wave of COVID-19 began to come under control in early 2022, there were mixed signs about how rapidly and how extensively workers would return to offices.

But as with previous pandemics, COVID-19 wasn't likely to dislodge cities from their central economic role. A 2020 McKinsey survey found 15 percent of CEOs saying "at least one-tenth of their employees could work remotely one or two days a week going forward," but only 7 percent of the CEOs being willing to consider three days or more for that minimum one-tenth. There's a big gap with the workforce; a report released in early 2022 found 75 percent of executives saying that they want to work at least three days in the office, compared to 37 percent of nonexecutives.[7] Many of these remote workers are in the same metropolitan economic region as their office. Thus, the impacts of hybrid work may fall more on central city versus suburban job and tax revenue issues within a metropolitan area, and on service jobs that support office workers rather than on job shifts across different metropolitan areas.

But even with these possible increases in hybrid work, cities will remain central to the economy. Urbanist Richard Florida wrote that after the pandemic, "the roster of the world's leading cities" will be largely unchanged. Cities' advantage in terms of "thick" professional labor markets, agglomeration and innovation, and postvaccine amenities would help keep cities at the economy's center.[8]

In spite of some media claims that the pandemic was causing a major population shift from more expensive cities to less expensive locations, demographer William Frey found that "permanent migration levels in the U.S. plummeted to a historically low level during the first year of the pandemic." Some relocations occurred within large and prosperous metro areas—what economists Nicholas Bloom and Arjun Ramani call the "doughnut effect," "making suburbs relatively more popular" but not seeing employees leaving the region altogether. This still hurt cities because they lost tax revenue, service jobs supported by higher-income commuters, and mass transit revenues. And increased working from home, especially for higher-income people, could hurt city property and income taxes if downtown office districts are harmed and other sectors don't pick up the slack.[9]

Even being a growing economic hub doesn't automatically generate greater equality. A 2018 study of inclusive recovery in 274 American cities concluded that "economically healthy cities tend to be more inclusive than distressed ones." The authors advised that local actions should take the long view that inclusion can spur growth, arguing that "building voice and power into economic recovery efforts, allocating resources more fairly, and designing policies that remove structural barriers to opportunity" will pay off.[10]

Although cities obviously prefer broad job expansion, cities having a large number of low-wage and unstable jobs confine many residents in low-paying jobs and inadequate housing, feeding inequality. Because metropolitan areas produce around 90 percent of gross domestic product (GDP), urban inequality reinforces national inequality and its negative economic impacts. In 2016, the Organization for Economic Cooperation and Development (OECD) warned cities were in danger of becoming "inequality traps" if they relied only on aggregate growth to solve their economic and social problems.[11]

Joe Biden's presidential inauguration in 2022 encouraged urban advocates. Biden took immediate action on state and local budget aid, along with naming mayors and progressive urban policy experts to government positions. He issued a flurry of executive orders, including aggressive steps on climate change and requiring all federal agencies to promote and measure policies promoting equity; overturned several anti-urban Trump executive orders; and pressed for more spending and policies to fight COVID-19 and racial inequity. Several Biden proposals weren't limited to cities but would benefit them—tuition-free community colleges, a $15 minimum wage, "Buy American" procurement, support for mass transit and transit-oriented development (TOD) projects, fair housing and fighting exclusionary zoning, and vigorous efforts at racial equity ranging from federal contracting and agency policies to aggressive enforcement of antidiscrimination laws.

But Biden's initial budget aid to cities was a one-shot injection of funds (resisted by Republicans), not a fundamental change in how cities are financed or relief from their fiscal dependence on sometimes hostile state governments. City and state budgets were stronger after the pandemic than first feared, but many observers expect longer-term budget pressures to return without further federal aid. As of spring 2022 there was no prospect of further financial aid to cities, and some of Biden's big pro-urban initiatives looked unlikely to get through Congress. Although Trump used fair housing policies as a scare tactic in the presidential campaign, Biden's proposed restoration of an Obama-era regulation wouldn't by itself have much impact on suburban development. Some advocates hoped for more aggressive administrative actions in favor of fair housing, but pushing suburbs in this direction has been politically charged in the past.[12]

Biden's actions were welcomed after Trump's anti-city hostility, but even if fully enacted they wouldn't by themselves reverse the core long-term structural economic and political urban problems. Without sustained policies promoting equity, cities will continue suffering from inequality, and the national economy will suffer as a result. Biden got more financial aid to states and cities to fight the economic impacts of COVID-19, but some states fought federal prohibitions against using budget aid for tax cuts instead of social and equity spending. Biden's major infrastructure

bill allowed states to spend funds largely without regard to racial or economic equity.[13] Although metropolitan areas are becoming more diverse
as the population changes, segregation is still prevalent in the United
States, with significant public school segregation and whites living mostly
in unintegrated neighborhoods.[14]

Biden did order the Office of Management of Budget (OMB) to study
how to assess equity for underserved communities across the range of federal programs, and OMB reported that "progress towards equity requires
both a sprint and a marathon." Devising appropriate equity measures for
the wide of range of government programs and putting them into regular
budget cycles is a complex task that will take time and experimentation.
In addition to Biden's order, nonprofits like PolicyLink and the Government Alliance on Race and Equity (GARE) are working with cities around
the country to build tools for monitoring and achieving greater equity in
budgets and programs. In philanthropy, the Surdna Foundation also is
working on metrics both to advance equitable economic outcomes and to
conduct a "more equitable form of grantmaking."[15]

But there remain formidable barriers to city equity policies. Low-wage
urban jobs won't improve without more unionization and active labor
market regulation. Regional economies are misaligned with metropolitan political boundaries, weakening cities' tax base while leaving them to
address problems created in the regional economy. But only fundamental political transformation could align metropolitan political power with
economic geography by strengthening cities.

Many state governments remain hostile to federal actions seeking
greater equity. There are overarching equity goals in Biden's $1 trillion
infrastructure bill, the biggest expansion of federal infrastructure spending in over ten years. But most of the money goes directly to states with
no specific requirements for equity provisions or outcomes in the project spending. Some states obtained an injunction against provisions that
prohibited using American Rescue Plan Act (ARPA) funds for tax cuts,
including cuts that would reward the state's wealthier taxpayers. The case
is likely to end up in the Supreme Court, and a ruling allowing financing
of state tax cuts using federal program funds will further states' ability to
ignore federal equity efforts.[16]

Fragmented metropolitan regions also present barriers to equity. But
is increased regional cooperation possible? Dedicated expert advocates

like Bruce Katz and the late Jeremy Nowak have heralded a cooperative "new localism" as a counter to "angry populism." But like other policy experts, their thoughtful calls for action sometimes blur important distinctions between cities and metropolitan areas. Regional cooperation on transit systems, higher education, and water and sewer systems, combined with support of ineffective policies like the Trump-era Opportunity Zones, won't address the fundamental racial and economic divisions that characterize our cities and metropolitan regions. The Biden administration has launched an economic development effort to encourage equitable regional collaboration, focusing especially where older industries have declined.[17] But such efforts leave our fragmented metropolitan governance intact.

Some blue-sky thinkers are questioning the relationship of cities and existing political boundaries. The modern U.S. economy is really made up of metropolitan regions, not states whose boundaries are arbitrary compared to local economies. A 2009 study identified eleven "megaregions" in the United States with 31 percent of all U.S. counties but 74 percent of the nation's population and an estimated 80 percent of employment growth by the year 2025.[18] Others have called for a restoration of cities' annexing powers or greater metropolitan consolidation; reducing suburbs' power over zoning, housing, and de facto segregated school systems; and limiting poor urban residents' access to suburban-based jobs.

But perhaps the most radical idea would replace states with city-states— political regions centered on the real economy of cities and metropolitan areas. This would align regional economies with political boundaries and eliminate states' anti-urban bias and their excessive political influence. A 2016 economic geography analysis sorted the lower forty-eight states into fifty-five economically based regions, each centered on a region's major city and commuting patterns. The map effectively outlines a nation of city-states reflecting America's real economic relationships instead of the noneconomic jurisdictions of counties and states, which favor rural and suburban political power over cities.[19]

Redrawing America into city-states also could lessen the power of suburbs or encourage them to be more cooperative. It would allow better delivery of public services but also lead to more equal sharing of regional economic costs. Simply engaging in this admittedly impractical thought experiment reveals the deep spatial misalignment of America's economics and politics. While cities drive regional and national economic growth, innovation, and prosperity, their political geography means they cannot effectively deal with inequality, poverty, and other social and economic problems.

State restrictions on city autonomy often preempt city policies that promote equity. Can long-standing state hostility to cities be reversed, turning states toward more progressive directions? Drawing on lessons from Los Angeles and elsewhere, Manuel Pastor points to progressive labor, immigration, climate, and voting policies in California that are driven by "intersectional movements" with a long-term "coherent economic vision." Pastor is hopeful, saying that "California is America, only sooner." In New York and New Jersey, unified Democratic control of state governorships and legislatures, rooted in urban votes, has led to more aggressive action on climate, labor, and tenants' rights, although initially doing little on housing construction or equitable economic development.[20]

But other states lag far behind, retaining their anti-urban bias. The so-called Texas Triangle, bounded by Dallas–Fort Worth, Austin–San Antonio, and Houston, produces over 75 percent of the state's GDP and has over 65 percent of the state's population, but it lacks proportionate political power. Given America's history and political infrastructure that puts cities at a disadvantage, federal housing and transportation policies that continue shaping the nation's urban form in favor of sprawl and suburbanization, state political control over cities, and the ever-continuing damage caused by racial segregation and conflict, local steps ultimately will not be enough.

Although voting patterns suggest suburbs in large metros can sometimes align with central cities, that cooperation historically has never included revenue sharing, school desegregation, or widespread housing integration. Some states pursued extensive legislative redistricting after the 2020 census, further weakening city and suburban minority populations by diluting their votes. Using a technique known as "cracking"— splitting city populations into separate districts—Tennessee is allocating Nashville's population across three separate congressional districts, all of which observers expect to be won by Republicans.[21]

There is little prospect of addressing inequality through market economists' prescription of fostering tax and regulatory competition among cities, coupled with their deep skepticism and reluctance to try new public interventions. Economists correctly identify cities as the sources of innovation and economic growth. The big data analyses of Raj Chetty and his colleagues underline the paradox that dense metropolitan areas have higher per capita GDP but often lower intergenerational upward mobility. A decades-long failure to build housing has driven homeownership and rental costs to historic highs. The lack of intergenerational mobility and lost wage premiums for cities are evidence of, and major contributors to, rising urban inequality.[22]

Economists also have documented declining urban wage premiums for less-educated adults, linked to a "hollowing out of middle-skill, non-college, blue-collar production and white-collar administrative support jobs." The growth in lower-paid jobs has characterized urban job markets for some time, and it is documented by economist David Howell in his work on the expansion of "lousy jobs" after 1979. Howell criticizes economists' attachment to skill-based explanations of declining wages and job quality, saying that it ignores "the need to rebalance bargaining power between employers and workers."[23] These lower-paid jobs have been slowest to come back in urban labor markets due to COVID-19, leading to high city unemployment rates, especially for minority and less-educated workers.

Edward Glaeser agrees that "lower urban opportunity remains a major problem for American cities," but he suggests the pathway is changing educational systems and providing human capital, which is consistent with a focus on individual skills. In this view, reform is inhibited by "insiders" such as teachers' unions, wealthy homeowners fighting new housing construction, overregulation of business start-ups, and occupational licensing. These insiders capture city political and policy processes to the long-term detriment of growth.[24]

Institutionalist economists have in turn documented economic stagnation and declining opportunity as driven by changes in private economic power, which is enabled by public policy favoring businesses and higher-income households. Local efforts to change political and economic power, including new or expanded roles for government and collective action, is essential for greater urban equity. But those local movements must have concrete visions of equitable economic growth along with housing and infrastructure development, not just redistribution. Economists can help by including historic and institutional factors and analysis of power relationships to help explain and devise equity policies.[25]

Ultimately, resolving America's urban inequality—which also would boost the entire economy—will require national policy changes aligning cities' central economic role with new political arrangements that can foster shared prosperity. Cities need a stronger governing role in their metropolitan areas to help bring the regional economy and governance into alignment with each other and thus allow more aggressive enforcement of racial and social equity in housing, economic development, labor rights, and education. Cities also should have more representation in their state governments, to accurately reflect the importance of their economic roles.

Increased equity can in turn boost city, regional, and national prosperity in an upward spiral. But creating and sharing that prosperity more equally is a political task that is ultimately national in scope. Paradoxically, what's possible under current political arrangements isn't economically adequate, and what's needed doesn't seem politically possible.

Our political arrangements remain heavily biased against cities, from metropolitan fragmentation to state control of city policy; to legislative gerrymandering; to federal underrepresentation; to lack of proportionate power in the House, Senate, and Electoral College. Cities can point the way through their own policy innovations, even when constrained by state laws and limited fiscal capacity. They must avoid a largely redistributive strategy in favor of fostering equitable economic growth and increased housing production. In some states, they may achieve political power through alliances with larger suburbs and perhaps economically distressed rural areas. But because political arrangements are so tilted against them, they cannot solve economic inequality on their own.

America's cities face a difficult landscape of sectoral change and disruption, federal anti-urban bias, state control of cities and metropolitan government fragmentation, and structural racism. These constraints prevent the full economic potential of cities, well described by economists, from being realized. Progressive advocates need to work across their issue boundaries and find common ground on economic development, job quality, housing, and environmental issues. Coalitions need to be informed by an economics that understands real-world factors, institutions and power, and is skeptical about the broad theoretical claims of market fundamentalism. That will give us the best hope of creating thriving, growing, and equal cities, pushing back against America's long-standing and racially influenced anti-urban bias.

ACKNOWLEDGMENTS

W riting a book is an individual endeavor that draws on the expertise of lots of people. I'm grateful to many people for their knowledge, friendship, and encouragement that helped me with this one.

My studies in economics at the New School for Social Research benefited greatly from working with David Gordon and Robert Heilbroner, who both showed me it was possible to advocate for social change while doing rigorous, critical scholarship.

I started work on the book as a visiting scholar at Manuel Pastor's Program for Environmental and Regional Equity (now the Dornsife Equity Research Institute) at the University of Southern California, and I finished it while affiliated with the Institute for Social Transformation at the University of California at Santa Cruz, directed by Chris Benner. Among the many urbanists who've taught me a lot, John Mollenkopf's knowledge and generosity stand out. I admire their lifetimes of committed scholarship and tireless work for social change.

At the Ford Foundation, I was privileged to work on equitable urban development. I learned a great deal from purposeful and progressive colleagues, including Susan Berresford (who gave me the chance to work in Detroit), Don Chen, John Colborn, Hector Cordero-Guzman, Frank DeGiovanni, Michelle DePass, Pablo Farias, Linetta Gilbert, George McCarthy, Katherine McFate, Marta Tellado, and Luis Ubiñas.

A fair amount of my career has been spent in government and public policy, working with dedicated public servants on practical projects while pursuing the goal of economic equity. Special thanks to Senator Edward M. Kennedy, Representative David Obey, Secretary of Labor Alexis Herman, Ranny Cooper, Joe Crapa, Seth Harris, Sarah Fox, Nick Littlefield, Ed Montgomery, Tony Gaetano, Lee Smith, Alan Sullivan, and Vincent Tese.

At the New School, David Howell is a valued colleague and fellow economist and, along with his wife Lydia Tugendrajch, a lifetime friend. As Dean of the Milano School, Michelle DePass raised the focus on racial, social and environmental justice while working hard on behalf of students. I also want to mention my inspiring friend Darrick Hamilton, whose pioneering scholarship on racial stratification is complemented by his daily work for racial and social justice.

My work on the three case study cities included in this book was generously informed in Los Angeles by Madeline Janis and Roxana Tynan; in Detroit by Tonya Allen, Rip Rapson, and Laura Trudeau; and in New York by John Mollenkopf and Mark Willis. I've learned a lot from many urbanists and advocates, especially, Bruce Katz, Greg LeRoy, Amy Liu, Mitchell Moss, David Perry, and Jennifer Vey. In economics, my thanks go to Rob Johnson and Bill Janeway at the Institute for New Economic Thinking.

A special note of appreciation goes to "The Group," close friends but also serious scholars—Kathleen Gerson, John Mollenkopf, Carol Willis, and Mark Willis. Our regular conversations have sharpened my thinking on a wide range of issues, but especially on New York and other cities. I've learned a lot from Mark through a long-running conversation on cities, housing, policy, and economics. Thanks also to Marcia Marley and Peter Rappoport, and Joan Fitzgerald and Bob Kuttner, for their always thoughtful discussions and their friendship.

At the Columbia University Press, Christian Winting did heroic work in getting the book to the finish line after taking over as my editor. I also benefitted from conversations with Eric Schwartz at the press. And I must thank Bridget Flannery-McCoy, my original editor and an enthusiastic champion of the book.

Earlier versions of some chapters were presented at the Milano School at the New School; the Graduate Program in Political Science, and also at John Jay College, of the City University of New York; the Political Economy

Research Institute at the University of Massachusetts at Amherst; and the Institute for Social Transformation at the University of California at Santa Cruz.

On a more personal note, I want to thank my daughter, Genevieve McGahey. I think about her every day, and admire how she strives to balance her life, work, and exceptional talents. Thanks also to my dear sister Lisa Veghlan, an expert on hospice care who also is a deeply committed citizen and a wonderful parent.

My final and highest thanks go to my wife and partner, Teresa Ghilarducci. I literally could not have finished this book without her. As a first-rate economist, she is a great sounding board, critic, editor, and colleague. As a public intellectual, she demonstrates how to connect scholarship with progressive values and commitment. And as my wife and partner, she enriches my life every day.

NOTES

1. CITIES, THE ECONOMY, AND INEQUALITY

1. The term comes from Carol Willis, "The Logic of Luxury: New York's New Super-Slender Towers" (presentation, 2014 Shanghai Conference of the Council on Tall Buildings and Urban Habitat, Shanghai, China, September 2014), http://global.ctbuh.org/resources/papers/download/1952-the-logic-of-luxury-new-yorks-new-super-slender-towers.pdf; for a great overview of New York's skyscrapers and "supertall" buildings see The Skyscraper Museum, "Supertall! New York City," https://skyscraper.org/supertall/new-york/.

2. Erin Duffin, "U.S. Metro Areas—Ranked by Gross Metropolitan Product (GMP) 2020," *Statista*, October 5, 2020, https://www.statista.com/statistics/183808/gmp-of-the-20-biggest-metro-areas/; Jeff Desjardins, "MAPPED: The US Cities with the Biggest Economies," *Business Insider*, September 27, 2017, https://www.businessinsider.com/us-cities-with-the-biggest-economies-2017-9.

3. Joshua Brown, "Meet the House That Inequality Built: 432 Park Avenue," *Fortune*, November 24, 2014, http://fortune.com/2014/11/24/432-park-avenue-inequality-wealth/.

4. Richard Florida, "Where the Good Jobs Are," *Route Fifty*, September 2, 2016, https://www.routefifty.com/2016/09/where-good-jobs-are/131259/.

5. Edward Glaeser, *Triumph of the City: How Our Greatest Invention Makes Us Richer, Smarter, Greener, Healthier, and Happier* (New York: Penguin Press, 2011), 1.

6. United States Conference of Mayors, *U.S. Metro Economies: GDP and Employment, 2018–2020*, September 2019, Washington DC, https://www.usmayors.org/metro-economies/september-2019/.

7. The Hamilton Project, "Patenting Is Concentrated in Cities and Near Universities," The Brookings Institution, December 13, 2017, https://www.hamiltonproject.org/charts/patenting_is_concentrated_in_cities_and_near_universities.

8. Mark Muro, Eli Byerly Duke, Yang You, and Robert Maxim, "Biden-Voting Counties Equal 70 percent of America's Economy. What Does This Mean for the Nation's Political-Economic Divide?," November 10, 2020 (Washington DC: The Brookings Institution), https://www.brookings.edu/blog/the-avenue/2020/11/09/biden-voting-counties-equal-70-of-americas-economy-what-does-this-mean-for-the-nations-political-economic-divide/; Ron Brownstein, "The Prosperity Paradox Is Dividing America in Two," *CNN*, January 23, 2018.

9. Poverty has spread into some suburban neighborhoods but did not decline significantly in core cities. One study found that 6,547 high-poverty neighborhoods in the United States in 2018 was "almost double the number" from 1980. Thomas J. Cooke, "Residential Mobility of the Poor and the Growth of Poverty in Inner-Ring Suburbs," *Urban Geography* 31, no. 2 (2010): 179–193; August Benzow and Kenan Fikri, *The Expanded Geography of High-Poverty Neighborhoods* (Washington DC: Economic Innovation Group, May 2020.)

10. Peter Drier, John Mollenkopf, and Todd Swanstrom, *Place Matters: Metropolitics for the Twenty-First Century* (Lawrence: University Press of Kansas, 2014). For a view claiming rising affluence in city centers, see Richard Florida, Zara Matheson, Patrick Adler, and Taylor Brydges, *The Divided City and the Shape of the New Metropolis* (Toronto: University of Toronto, 2014). For an analysis finding continuing advantages for suburbs, see Whitney Airgood-Obrycki, "Suburban Status and Neighborhood Change," *Urban Studies* 56, no. 14 (November 2019): 2935–2952.

11. Edward L. Glaeser, "Why the Anti-Urban Bias?," *Boston Globe*, March 5, 2010.

12. National League of Cities, *2012 National Municipal Policy and Resolutions* (Washington, DC: National League of Cities, 2011), 1.

13. Glaeser, *Triumph of the City*, 70. Emphasis in original.

14. Glaeser, *Triumph of the City*, 6.

15. Edward L. Glaeser, José A. Scheinkman, and Andrei Shleifer, "Economic Growth in a Cross-Section of Cities," *Journal of Monetary Economics* 36, no. 1 (August 1995): 117–143.

16. Gabriel M. Ahlfeldt and Elisabetta Pietrostefani, "The Economic Effects of Density: A Synthesis," *Journal of Urban Economics* 111(C) (May 2019): 93–107.

17. Masahisa Fujita and Jacques Thisse, *Economics of Agglomeration: Cities, Industrial Location, and Economic Growth*, 2nd ed. (New York: Cambridge University Press, 2013).

18. John M. Quigley, "Urban Diversity and Economic Growth," *Journal of Economic Perspectives* 12, no. 2 (1998): 130.

19. Antonio Ciccone and Robert E. Hall, "Productivity and the Density of Economic Activity," *American Economic Review* 86, no. 1 (March 1996): 55.

20. Gilles Duranton and Diego Puga, "Micro-Foundations of Urban Agglomeration Economies," Working Paper 9931, National Bureau of Economic Research, September 2003.

21. Edward L. Glaeser and Matthew G. Resseger, "The Complementarity Between Cities and Skills," *Journal of Regional Science* 50, no. 1 (February 2010): 221–244.

22. José Lobo, Kevin Stolarick, and Richard Florida, "Growth Without Growth: Population and Productivity Change in U.S. Metropolitan Areas, 1980–2006," (Toronto: University of Toronto, 2010), 14.

23. Robert D. Atkinson and Stephen J. Ezell, *Innovation Economics: The Race for Global Advantage* (New Haven, CT: Yale University Press, 2012).

24. Enrico Moretti, "The Effect of High-Tech Clusters on the Productivity of Top Inventors," Working Paper 26270, National Bureau of Economic Research, September 2019.

25. David Raths, "Will the Chief Innovation Officer Transform Government?," *Government Technology*, January 21, 2013, http://www.govtech.com/e-government/Will-the-Chief-Innovation-Officer-Transform-Government.html.

26. Bruce Katz and Julie Wagner, *The Rise of Innovation Districts: A New Geography of Innovation in America* (Washington, DC: Brookings Institution, 2014).

27. Richard Florida, *The Rise of the Creative Class, Revisited* (New York: Basic Books, 2012).

28. Richard Florida, "The Creative Class Is Alive and Well," interview by Jonathan Fowler and Elizabeth Rodd, *BigThink*, March 24, 2013, http://bigthink.com/videos/the-creative-class-is-alive-and-well. Author's calculation of percentages using U.S. labor force in March 2013 as the denominator.

29. Ann Markusen, "Urban Development and the Politics of a Creative Class: Evidence from a Study of Artists," *Environment and Planning A: Economy and Space* 38, no. 10 (October 2006): 1921–1940.

30. Michele Hoyman and Christopher Faricy, "It Takes a Village: A Test of the Creative Class, Social Capital, and Human Capital Theories," *Urban Affairs Review* 44, no. 3 (January 2009): 323.

31. Edward L. Glaeser, review of *The Rise of the Creative Class* by Richard Florida, *Regional Science and Urban Economics* 35, no. 5 (September 2005): 594.

32. Rebecca Diamond, "The Determinants and Welfare Implications of US Workers' Diverging Location Choices by Skill," *American Economic Review* 106, no. 3 (March 2016): 479–524.

33. The Alonso-Muth-Mills approach concentrates on commuting costs and household location choice, while the Rosen-Roback model focuses on spatial equilibria between cities based on overall amenities, especially housing quality and price. William Alonso, *Location and Land Use: Towards a General Theory of Land Rent* (Cambridge, MA: Harvard University Press, 1964); Richard F. Muth, *Cities and Housing* (Chicago: University of Chicago Press, 1969); Edwin S. Mills, "An Aggregate Model of Resource Allocation in a Metropolitan Area," *American Economic Review* 57, no. 2 (May 1967): 197–210.

34. Adam Smith, *An Inquiry Into the Nature and Causes of the Wealth of Nations*, ed. Edwin Cannan (London: Methuen, 1904), 25.

35. Alfred Marshall, *Principles of Economics*, 8th ed. (London: Macmillan, 1920): 225.

36. Edward L. Glaeser, Hedi D. Kallal, José A. Scheinkman, and Andrei Shleifer, "Growth in Cities," *Journal of Political Economy* 100, no. 6 (December 1992): 1150. The authors note that during the period they examined, American "traditional manufacturing" cities, which were highly specialized, were doing poorly.

37. Vernon Henderson, Ari Kuncoro, and Matt Turner, "Industrial Development in Cities," *Journal of Political Economy* 103, no. 5 (October 1995): 1067–1090.

38. Gilles Duranton and Diego Puga, "Diversity and Specialisation in Cities: Why, Where and When Does It Matter?," *Urban Studies* 37, no. 2 (2000): 553.

39.   Mark J. Perry, "Understanding America's Enormous $20.6T Economy by Comparing US Metro Area GDPs to Entire Countries," *Carpe Diem* (blog), American Enterprise Institute, December 18, 2019, https://www.aei.org/carpe-diem/understanding-americas-enormous-20-6t-economy-by-comparing-us-metro-area-gdps-to-entire-countries/.

40.   Some analysts argue that increased work from home as a result of the COVID-19 pandemic will spread jobs to lower-cost regions. See Adam Ozimek, *The New Geography of Remote Work*, Upwork, March 22, 2022, https://www.upwork.com/press/releases/the-new-geography-of-remote-work.

41.   Dave Donaldson, "Lecture 6: Economic Geography and Path Dependence," 2020 Lectures on Urban Economics, Urban Economics Association, July 16, 2020, http://www.urbaneconomics.org/meetings/lectures2020/slides/UEA_Lectures_Donaldson.pdf; Gilles Duranton and Diego Puga, "Urban Growth and Its Aggregate Implications," Working Paper 26591, National Bureau of Economic Research, December 2019.

42.   Smith, *An Inquiry Into the Nature and Causes of the Wealth of Nations*, 183.

43.   Edward L. Glaeser, "The Economics Approach to Cities." NBER Working Paper 13696, National Bureau of Economic Research, Cambridge, MA, December 2007, 28. This echoes the work of James Buchanan, winner of the 1986 Nobel Prize for his "public choice" economics, which included viewing government as a "Leviathan" maximizing power by extracting taxes and exerting regulatory control.

44.   June Sekera, "Why Aren't We Talking About Public Goods?," Demos, September 23, 2013. https://www.demos.org/blog/why-arent-we-talking-about-public-goods.

45.   In formal analysis, economists distinguish more narrowly defined "public goods" from the broader category of public services. Some would limit interventions in the market only to public goods, but much of policy debate focuses on public services and regulatory interventions in markets.

46.   Richard A. Greenwald, *The Triangle Fire, the Protocols of Peace, and Industrial Democracy in Progressive New York* (Philadelphia: Temple University Press, 2005), 36.

47.   U.S. Conference of Mayors, "U.S. Metro Areas Expected to See Real Economic Growth in 2014," January 22, 2014, http://legacy.usmayors.org/pressreleases/uploads/2014/0122-release-metroeconomies.pdf.

48.   Obama for America, "Barack Obama: Supporting Urban Prosperity," January 16, 2008, https://www.readkong.com/page/barack-obama-supporting-urban-prosperity-714351.

49.   Jim Clifton, "Forget Washington—Cities Will Win or Lose America," *Chairman's Blog, Gallup*, November 14, 2012, http://www.gallup.com/opinion/chairman/169136/forget-washington-cities-win-lose-america.aspx.

50.   Parag Khanna, "When Cities Rule the World," *McKinsey and Company*, February 2011, https://www.mckinsey.com/featured-insights/urbanization/when-cities-rule-the-world.

51.   Joe Cortright, "Big City Metros Are Driving the National Economy," *City Observatory*, March 23, 2017, http://cityobservatory.org/big-city-metros-driving/; Michael B. Sauter, "Ten Years Later, These 28 US Cities Never Recovered from the Great Recession," *USA Today*, October 12, 2018, https://www.usatoday.com/story/money/economy/2018/10/12/cities-never-recovered-great-recession/38094325/.

52. John D. Landis, "The COVID-19 Recession: Which Urban Economies Have Performed Better or Worse and Why," Penn IUR Policy Brief, Penn Institute for Urban Research, University of Pennsylvania, October 2021, 6.

53. Lawrence Mishel and Jori Kandra, "Wages for the Top 1 Percent Skyrocketed 160 Percent Since 1979 While the Share of Wages for the Bottom 90 Percent Shrunk," *Working Economics* (blog), Economic Policy Institute, December 1, 2020, https://www.epi.org/blog/wages-for-the-top-1-skyrocketed-160-since-1979-while-the-share-of-wages-for-the-bottom-90-shrunk-time-to-remake-wage-pattern-with-economic-policies-that-generate-robust-wage-growth-for-vast-majority/.

54. Emmanuel Saez and Gabriel Zucman, "Wealth Inequality in the United States Since 1913: Evidence from Capitalized Income Tax Data," *Quarterly Journal of Economics* 131, no. 2 (2016): 519–578; Howard R. Gold, "Never Mind the 1 Percent. Let's Talk About the 0.01 Percent," *Chicago Booth Review*, November 29, 2017.

55. FRED Economic Data, "Share of Total Net Worth Held by the Top 1 percent (99th to 100th Wealth Percentiles)", Economic Research, Federal Reserve Bank of St. Louis, https://fred.stlouisfed.org/series/WFRBST01134.

56. Michael Batty, Ella Deeken, and Alice Henriques Volz, "Wealth Inequality and COVID-19: Evidence from the Distributional Financial Accounts," *Feds Notes*, Board of Governors of the Federal Reserve System, August 30, 2021.

57. Brian Thiede, David L. Brown, Jaclyn Butler, and Leif Jensen, "Income Inequality Is Getting Worse in US Urban Areas," *The Conversation*, April 14, 2020, https://theconversation.com/income-inequality-is-getting-worse-in-us-urban-areas-132417.

58. Jonathan D. Ostry, Andrew Berg, and Charalambos G. Tsangarides, *Redistribution, Inequality, and Growth* (Washington, DC: International Monetary Fund, 2014), 4; Heather Boushey, *Unbound: How Inequality Constricts Our Economy and What We Can Do About It* (Cambridge MA: Harvard University Press, 2019).

59. On debt's role in the economic collapse, see Atif Mian and Amir Sufi, *House of Debt: How They (and You) Caused the Great Recession, and How We Can Prevent It from Happening Again* (Chicago: University of Chicago Press, 2014).

60. Joseph E. Stiglitz, "Inequality Is Holding Back the Recovery," *Opinionator* (blog), *New York Times*, January 19, 2013. For the broader argument, see Joseph E. Stiglitz, *The Price of Inequality: How Today's Divided Society Endangers Our Future* (New York: Norton, 2012).

61. Martin Gilens and Benjamin I. Page, "Testing Theories of American Politics: Elites, Interest Groups, and Average Citizens," *Perspectives on Politics* 12, no. 3 (2014): 576.

62. Richard Florida, *The New Urban Crisis: How Our Cities Are Increasing Inequality, Deepening Segregation, and Failing the Middle Class—And What We Can Do About It,* (New York: Basic Books, 2017), 186.

63. Edward Glaeser and David Cutler, *Survival of the City: Living and Thriving in an Age of Isolation* (New York: Penguin Press, 2021), 320.

64. Simon Kuznets, "Economic Growth and Income Inequality," *American Economic Review* 45, no. 1 (March 1955): 1–28. Kuznets recognized severe data limitations but said his "excuse for building an elaborate structure on a such a shaky foundation is a deep interest in the subject." Kuznets, "Economic Growth," 26.

65.   Glaeser, *Triumph of the City*, 81.

66.   Raj Chetty, Nathaniel Hendren, Patrick Kline, and Emmanuel Saez, "Where Is the Land of Opportunity? The Geography of Intergenerational Mobility in the United States," *Quarterly Journal of Economics* 129, no. 4 (2014), 1620.

67.   Alessandra Fogli and Veronica Guerrieri, "The End of the American Dream? Inequality and Segregation in US Cities," Working Paper 26143, National Bureau of Economic Research, August 2019; Leah Platt Boustan, "Race, Migration, and Cities," 2020 Lectures on Urban Economics, Urban Economics Association, June 18, 2020, http://www.urban economics.org/meetings/lectures2020/slides/UEA_Lectures_Boustan.pdf.

68.   OECD, *Does Income Inequality Hurt Economic Growth?*, December 2014, http://www.oecd .org/els/soc/Focus-Inequality-and-Growth-2014.pdf.

69.   Ostry, Berg, and Tsangarides, *Redistribution, Inequality, and Growth*, 25–26; Markus Brueckner and Daniel Lederman, "Effect of Income Inequality on Aggregate Output," Policy Research Working Paper 7317, World Bank Group, June 2015.

70.   Joe Maguire, *How Increasing Income Inequality Is Dampening U.S. Economic Growth, and Possible Ways to Change the Tide* (New York: Standard & Poor's, 2014); Heather Boushey and Carter C. Price, "How Are Economic Inequality and Growth Connected? A Review of Recent Research," Washington Center for Equitable Growth, October 2014.

71.   For a list of stories, see James Brausell, "The Media Can't Stop Talking About the End of Cities," *Planetizen*, September 2, 2020, https://www.planetizen.com/blogs/110403-media -cant-stop-talking-about-end-cities.

72.   Caroline Pryor and Donald Tomaskovic-Devy, "How COVID Exposes Healthcare Defects for Black Workers," Center for Employment Equity, University of Massachusetts at Amherst, August 2020, https://www.umass.edu/employmentequity/how-covid-exposes -healthcare-deficits-black-workers. The Biden administration issued an emergency health standard for large employers through the Occupational Health and Safety Administration (OSHA), but it was stayed by the Supreme Court and withdrawn on January 25, 2022.

73.   Raj Chetty, John N. Friedman, Nathaniel Hendren, and Michael Stepner, "The Economic Impacts of COVID-19: Evidence from a New Public Database Built Using Private Sector Data," Opportunity Insights, November 2020, https://opportunityinsights.org/wp-content /uploads/2020/05/tracker_paper.pdf; Valerie Wilson, "Inequities Exposed: How COVID-19 Widened Racial Inequities in Education, Health, and the Workforce," testimony before the U.S. House of Representatives Committee on Education and Labor, June 22, 2020, https://www.epi.org/publication/covid-19-inequities-wilson-testimony/; Joseph A. Benitez, Charles J. Courtemanche, and Aaron Yelowitz, "Racial and Ethnic Disparities in COVID-19: Evidence from Six Large Cities," Working Paper 27592, National Bureau of Economic Research, July 2020.

74.   Richard McGahey, "Unemployment Benefits, Stimulus Checks, and State and City Aid Needed as Economy Slows," *Forbes*, July 24, 2020, https://www.forbes.com/sites/richard mcgahey/2020/07/24/#30de786e2ba8; Richard McGahey, "Monetary and Fiscal Policy Under Covid-19: The Case of the Fed's Municipal Liquidity Facility," *Forbes*, July 21, 2020, https://www.forbes.com/sites/richardmcgahey/#7734dc4d44a2.

2. AMERICA'S HOSTILITY TOWARD CITIES: "PESTILENTIAL TO THE MORALS, THE HEALTH, AND THE LIBERTIES OF MAN"

1. Richard Hofstadter, *The Age of Reform: From Bryan to F.D.R.* (New York: Vintage, 1955), 1; see also Richard Hofstadter, "The Myth of the Happy Yeoman," *American Heritage* 7, no. 3 (April 1956): 42–47.

2. Jarrett Murphy, "Are Cities on Candidates' Minds?: Where They Are on Urban Issues," *City Limits*, May 29, 2007, http://citylimits.org/2007/05/29/are-cities-on-candidates-minds-where-they-are-on-urban-issues/.

3. John McClaughry, "Jefferson's Vision," *New York Times*, April 13, 1982, http://www.nytimes.com/1982/04/13/opinion/jefferson-s-vision.html.

4. Barack Obama, "Remarks by President Obama and President Hollande of France After Touring Thomas Jefferson's Monticello," February 10, 2014, The White House, transcript, https://obamawhitehouse.archives.gov/the-press-office/2014/02/10/remarks-president-obama-and-president-hollande-france-after-touring-thom.

5. Thomas Jefferson, *Notes on the State of Virginia* (Richmond, VA: J.W. Randolph, 1853), 175–177, https://archive.org/details/notesonstateofvio1jeff.

6. Thomas Jefferson to Dr. Benjamin Rush, September 23, 1800, in *The Letters of Thomas Jefferson, 1743–1826*, http://www.let.rug.nl/usa/presidents/thomas-jefferson/letters-of-thomas-jefferson/jefl134.php.

7. Benjamin L. Carp, *Rebels Rising: Cities and the American Revolution* (New York: Oxford University Press, 2007), 213.

8. George Washington, letter to Marquis de Lafayette, July 28, 1791, in *The Papers of George Washington*, ed. Mark A. Mastromarino (Charlottesville: University Press of Virginia, 1999), 238–241.

9. J. David Hacker, "From '20. and Odd' to 10 Million: The Growth of the Slave Population in the United States," *Slavery and Abolition* 41, no. 4, (May 2020): 840–855.

10. Campbell Gibson, "Population of the 100 Largest Cities and Other Urban Places in the United States: 1790 to 1990," Working Paper, Population Division, United States Census Bureau, Washington, DC, 1998.

11. Robert J. Bennett, "SN 7154—Urban Population Database, 1801–1911," Working Paper, University of Cambridge, 2012, http://doc.ukdataservice.ac.uk/doc/7154/mrdoc/pdf/guide.pdf.

12. Christian Montes, *American Capitals: A Historical Geography* (Chicago: University of Chicago Press, 2014), 68–69.

13. Paul Kantor, "The Dependent City: The Changing Political Economy of Urban Economic Development in the United States," *Urban Affairs Review* 22, no. 4 (June 1987): 493–520.

14. Thomas Bender, *The Unfinished City: New York and the Metropolitan Idea* (New York: New York University Press, 2007), 170.

15. Kenneth T. Jackson, *Crabgrass Frontier: The Suburbanization of the United States* (New York: Oxford University Press, 1985).

16. The term *suburb* is very old, appearing in Chaucer's *Canterbury Tales*, where the yeoman lives "in the suburbes of a town."

17. Jackson, *Crabgrass Frontier*, 20.

18. Jackson, *Crabgrass Frontier*, 140. Data from table 8–2.

19. See Michael Rawson, *Eden on the Charles: The Making of Boston* (Cambridge, MA: Harvard University Press, 2010), 169. See also "Annexation Spurned: Brookline's 1873 Rejection of Boston," Brighton-Allston Historical Society, last modified August 28, 2005, http://www.bahistory.org/HistoryAnnexBrookline.html.

20. Jackson, *Crabgrass Frontier*, 149.

21. Isabel Wilkerson, *The Warmth of Other Suns: The Epic Story of America's Great Migration* (New York: Random House, 2010); James Gregory, *The Southern Diaspora: How the Great Migrations of Black and White Southerners Transformed America* (Chapel Hill: University of North Carolina Press, 2005).

22. Edwin G. Burrows and Mike Wallace, *Gotham: A History of New York City Until 1898*, (New York: Oxford University Press, 1999), 1219–1236.

23. The City of Clinton v. The Cedar Rapids and Missouri River Railroad Company, 24 Iowa 455 (1868). Joan Williams sees Dillon as one of a new breed of lawyers specializing in corporate law. After his judicial career, he moved to New York and worked for the Union Pacific railroad, Western Union, and other large companies.

24. Clayton P. Gillette, "In Partial Praise of Dillon's Rule, or, Can Public Choice Theory Justify Local Government Law?," *Chicago-Kent Law Review* 67, no. 3 (October 1991): 963. Emphasis in original.

25. Christopher Cotter, "Off the Rails: The Real Effects of Railroad Bond Defaults following the Panic of 1983," *AEA Papers and Proceedings 2021*, 111: 509.

26. Joan C. Williams, "The Constitutional Vulnerability of American Local Government: The Politics of City Status in American Law," *University of Wisconsin Law Review* 1986, no. 1 (1986): 83–153.

27. Williams, "The Constitutional Vulnerability of American Local Government," 94.

28. A fascinating discussion of Chicago's development, especially in relation to the ecology and environment, can be found in William Cronon, *Nature's Metropolis: Chicago and the Great West*, (New York: Norton, 1991).

29. David R. Meyer, "Midwestern Industrialization and the American Manufacturing Belt in the Nineteenth Century," *Journal* of Economic History 49, no. 4 (December 1989), 921–937.

30. Stephen Klepper, "The Evolution of the U.S. Automobile Industry and Detroit as Its Capital," Working Paper, Department of Social & Decision Sciences, Carnegie Mellon University, January 2001, 4, https://www.researchgate.net/scientific-contributions/Steven-Klepper-9626536.

31. Otis demonstrated his invention at the 1854 World's Fair in New York, when he rode up on an elevating platform and had a workman cut the cable; the platform dropped a little, then was held in place by the safety brake.

32. Carol Willis, *Form Follows Finance: Skyscrapers and Skylines in New York and Chicago* (New York: Princeton Architectural Press, 1995), 162.

33. Clay Jenkinson, "Thomas Jefferson, Epidemics, and His Vision for American Cities," *Governing*, April 1, 2020, https://www.governing.com/context/Thomas-Jefferson-Epidemics-and-His-Vision-for-American-Cities.html.

34. Karen Clay, Joshua Lewis, and Edson Severnini, "What Explains Cross-City Variation in Mortality During the 1918 Influenza Pandemic?: Evidence from 438 U.S. Cities," *Economics and Human Biology*, 35, December 2019: 47; Thomas A. Garrett, "Economic Effects of the 1918 Influenza Pandemic: Implications for a Modern-day Pandemic," Federal Reserve Bank of St. Louis, November 2007, https://www.stlouisfed.org/~/media/files/pdfs/community -development/research-reports/pandemic_flu_report.pdf.

35. Anne Garner, "Cholera Comes to New York City," The New York Academy of Medicine, February 3, 2015, https://nyamcenterforhistory.org/2015/02/03/cholera-comes-to-new -york-city/.

36. Campbell J. Gibson and Emily Lennon, "Historical Census Statistics on the Foreign-Born Population of the United States: 1850–1990," Working Paper, Population Division, United States Census Bureau, Washington, DC, 1999.

37. Charles Hirschman and Elizabeth Mogford, "Immigration and the American Industrial Revolution from 1880 to 1920," *Social Science Research* 38, no. 4 (December 2009): 897–920, https://www.ncbi.nlm.nih.gov/pmc/articles/PMC2760060/.

38. Hirschman and Mogford, "Immigration and the American Industrial Revolution," 898.

39. Peter Drier, John Mollenkopf, and Todd Swanstrom, *Place Matters: Metropolitics for the Twenty-First Century* (Lawrence: University Press of Kansas, 2014), 169–170.

40. The vast majority of America's Black population were ex-slaves and their descendants. In 1910, three-quarters of blacks lived in rural areas compared to 54 percent of the total U.S. population, and 90 percent of black Americans lived in states that were part of the former Confederacy. Between 1915 and 1918, 500,000 moved out of the South, with another 1.3 million following between 1920 and 1930. Frank Hobbs and Nicole Stoops, *Demographic Trends in the 20th Century: Census 2000 Special Reports* (Washington, DC: United States Census Bureau, 2002), 77, 83, 93.

41. "The Great Migration," Digital History, http://www.digitalhistory.uh.edu/disp_textbook .cfm?smtID=2&psid=3385.

42. See Douglas S. Massey and Nancy A. Denton, *American Apartheid: Segregation and the Making of the Underclass* (Cambridge, MA: Harvard University Press, 1993), and Robert M. Adelman and James Clarke Gocker, "Racial Residential Segregation in Urban America," *Sociological Compass* 1, no. 1 (2007): 404–423.

43. The real estate and racial tensions of this transition are discussed in Kevin McGruder, *Race and Real Estate: Conflict and Cooperation in Harlem, 1890–1920* (New York: Columbia University Press, 2015). On the rise and evolution of northern ghettos, see Lance Freeman, *A Haven and a Hell: The Ghetto in Black America*. New York: Columbia University Press, 2019.

44. Michael Jones-Correa, "American Riots: Structures, Institutions and History," Working Paper 148, Russell Sage Foundation, 1999, 31.

45. Michael B. Katz, *In the Shadow of the Poorhouse: A Social History of Welfare in America* (New York: Basic Books, 1996). See especially chapters 3 and 6.

46. Steven Conn, *Americans Against the City: Anti-Urbanism in the Twentieth Century* (New York: Oxford University Press, 2014), 63.

47. Conn, *Americans Against the City*, 65.

48. David M. Cutler and Grant Miller, "The Role of Public Health Improvements in Health Advances: The Twentieth-Century United States," *Demography* 42, no. 1 (February 2005): 1–22.

49. Leah Platt Boustan, Devin Bunten, and Owen Hearey, "Urbanization in the United States, 1800–2000," Working Paper 19041, National Bureau of Economic Research, May 2013, 6–7. The authors found that "by 1920, 69 percent of manufacturing employment occurred in a metropolitan setting, compared to only 43 percent of general work activity." Urban wage premiums fell in this period, partly attributed to reduced risk from urban health problems.

50. Hobbs and Stoops, *Demographic Trends in the 20th Century*, 33.

51. Richard Rothstein, *The Color of Law: A Forgotten History of How Our Government Segregated America* (New York: Norton, 2017), 78; Marc A. Weiss, "Urban Land Developers and the Origins of Zoning Law: The Case of Berkeley," *Berkeley Planning Journal* 3, no. 1 (1986): 18.

52. Conn, *Americans Against the City*, 94; Price Fishback, "How Successful Was the New Deal?: The Microeconomic Impact of New Deal Spending and Lending Policies in the 1930s," *Journal of Economic Literature* 55, no. 4 (2017): 1435–1485.

53. Conn, *Americans Against the City*, 100, 109; see also Amanda Kolson Hurley, "How the Green New Deal Could Retrofit Suburbs," *CityLab*, February 11, 2019, https://www.citylab.com/perspective/2019/02/green-new-deal-greenbelt-suburbs-climate-change/582445/.

54. Richard K. Green and Susan M. Wachter, "The American Mortgage in Historical and International Context," *Journal of Economic Perspectives* 19, no. 4 (2005): 93.

55. Price Fishback, Jonathan Rose, and Kenneth Snowden, *Well Worth Saving: How the New Deal Safeguarded Home Ownership* (Chicago: University of Chicago Press, 2013).

56. Green and Wachter, "The American Mortgage in Historical and International Context."

57. Kristen B. Crossney and David W. Bartelt, "The Legacy of the Home Owners' Loan Corporation," *Housing Policy Debate* 16, no. 3–4 (2005), 552; William S. Chapin, *We the Americans: Our Homes* (Washington, DC: United States Census Bureau, 1993).

58. Jackson, *Crabgrass Frontier*, 196.

59. David C. Wheelock, "The Federal Response to Home Mortgage Distress: Lessons from the Great Depression," Federal Reserve Bank of St. Louis *Review* 90, no. 3, part 1 (May/June 2008): 133–48.

60. The New Deal's racially discriminatory aspects are masterfully analyzed in Ira Katznelson, *When Affirmative Action Was White: An Untold History of Racial Inequality in Twentieth-Century America* (New York: Norton, 2005).

61. Many HOLC loans were made before the actual maps were created, but the patterns were similar, and the redlining practices extended forward into American home lending standards and policies.

62. Jackson, *Crabgrass Frontier*, 201–202. Newark's Weequahic neighborhood was immortalized by Philip Roth in novels like *Portnoy's Complaint*, *Nemesis*, and *The Plot Against America*.

63. Amy E. Hillier, "Who Received Loans?: Home Owners' Loan Corporation Lending and Discrimination in Philadelphia in the 1930s," *Journal of Planning History* 2, no. 1 (2003): 3–24.

64. Price Fishback, Jonathan Rose, Ken Snowden, and Thomas Storrs, "New Evidence on Redlining by Federal Housing Programs in the 1930s," WP2022-01, Federal Reserve Bank of Chicago, January 3, 2022, 3, 7.

3. ISOLATING AMERICA'S CITIES: FROM THE ECONOMIC "GOLDEN AGE" TO "TWO SOCIETIES—ONE BLACK, ONE WHITE"

1. Henry Luce, "The American Century," *Diplomatic History* 23, no. 2 (1999): 159–171; Eric Hobsbawm, *The Age of Extremes: A History of the World, 1914–1991* (New York: Vintage, 1994).

2. John W. Jeffries, "Mobilization and Its Impact," in *World War II and the American Home Front*, ed. Marilyn M. Harper (Washington, DC: National Park Service, 2007), 15.

3. James M. Gregory, "Internal Migration: Twentieth Century and Beyond," in *The Oxford Encyclopedia of American Social History*, ed. Lynn Dumenil (New York: Oxford University Press, 2012), 542.

4. U.S. Department of Commerce, Economic and Statistics Administration, U.S. Census Bureau, *United States Summary: 2010. Population and Housing Unit Counts*, September 2012, table 7, https://www.census.gov/prod/cen2010/cph-2-1.pdf.

5. Claudia D. Goldin, "The Role of World War II in the Rise of Women's Employment," *American Economic Review* 81, no. 4 (September 1991): 755.

6. Andrew Glyn, Alan Hughes, Alain Lipietz, and Ajit Singh, "The Rise and Fall of the Golden Age," in *The Golden Age of Capitalism: Reinterpreting the Postwar Experience*, ed. Stephen A. Marglin and Juliet B. Schor (New York: Oxford University Press, 1992), 39–125.

7. Glyn, Hughes, Lipietz, and Singh, "The Rise and Fall of the Golden Age."

8. Robert Bruce Slater, "The First Black Graduates of the Nation's 50 Flagship State Universities," *The Journal of Blacks in Higher Education*, no. 13 (Autumn 1996): 72–85.

9. Federal Housing Administration, *Underwriting Manual: Underwriting and Valuation Procedure Under Title II of the National Housing* Act (Washington, DC: U.S. Government Printing Office, 1936). Found in Sections 228 and 233.

10. FRED Economic Data, "Private Residential Fixed Investment (PRFIA)," Federal Reserve Bank of St. Louis, https://fred.stlouisfed.org/series/PRFIA, author's calculations.

11. H. V. Savitch, "Encourage, Then Cope: Washington and the Sprawl Machine," in *Urban Sprawl: Causes, Consequences, and Policy Responses*, ed. Gregory D. Squires (Washington, DC: Urban Institute Press, 2002), 148.

12. Joel Kotkin, "Countering Progressives' Assault on Suburbia," *RealClearPolitics*, July 10, 2015, http://www.realclearpolitics.com/articles/2015/07/10/countering_progressives_assault _on_suburbia_127327.html.

13. Kenneth T. Jackson, *Crabgrass Frontier: The Suburbanization of the United States* (New York: Oxford University Press, 1985), 216–217.

14. Alan Altshuler, William Morrill, Harold Wolman, and Faith Mitchell, "Central Cities, Suburbs, and Metropolitan-Area Problems," in *Governance and Opportunity in Metropolitan America*, ed. Alan Altshuler, William Morrill, Harold Wolman, and Faith Mitchell (Washington, DC: National Academy Press, 1999), 29.

15. Frank Hobbs and Nicole Stoops, *Demographic Trends in the 20th Century: Census 2000 Special Reports* (Washington, DC: United States Census Bureau, 2002), 33.

16. Jordan Rappaport, "The Shared Fortunes of Cities and Suburbs," *Economic Review* 90, no. 5 (2005): 35.

17. Jon C. Teaford, *City and Suburb: The Political Fragmentation of Metropolitan America, 1850–1970* (Baltimore, MD: Johns Hopkins University Press, 1979), 31.

18. Frank P. Huddle, *Automobiles in the Postwar Economy* (Washington, DC: CQ Press, 1945).

19. Jackson, *Crabgrass Frontier*, 234–238.

20. Luce, "The American Century"; David Kushner, *Levittown: Two Families, One Tycoon, and the Fight for Civil Rights in America's Legendary Suburb* (New York: Walker & Company, 2009), 30, 45.

21. William Safire, "The Cold War's Hot Kitchen," *New York Times*, July 23, 2018.

22. FRED Economic Data (for DDURRC; accessed November 14, 2019), author's calculations, https://fred.stlouisfed.org/series/PCDGA. Expenditures in 1945 and 1950 were $9.1 billion and $32.4 billion, respectively.

23. Peter Mieszkowski and Edwin S. Mills, "The Causes of Metropolitan Suburbanization," *Journal of Economic Perspectives* 7, no. 3 (August 1993): 136.

24. Joel Garreau, *Edge City: Life on the New Frontier* (New York: Doubleday, 1991).

25. Stanley Mallach, "The Origins of the Decline of Urban Mass Transportation in the United States, 1890–1930," *Urbanism Past and Present* no. 8 (Summer 1979): 1–17; Jackson, *Crabgrass Frontier*, 170; Peter D. Norton, *Fighting Traffic: The Dawn of the Motor Age in the American City* (Cambridge, MA: MIT Press, 2008).

26. Valerie Adams, "Civil Defense," in *Encyclopedia of the Cold War*, ed. Ruud van Dijk (New York: Routledge, 2008), 164.

27. Thomas J. Sugrue, *The Origins of the Urban Crisis: Race and Inequality in Postwar Detroit* (Princeton, NJ: Princeton University Press, 2005), 128.

28. Mary L. Dudziak, *Cold War Civil Rights: Race and the Image of American Democracy* (Princeton, NJ: Princeton University Press, 2000), 159–163.

29. Richard Voith, "City and Suburban Growth: Substitutes or Complements?," *Federal Reserve Bank of Philadelphia Business Review* (October 1992): 21–33.

30. Ira Katznelson, *When Affirmative Action Was White: An Untold History of Racial Inequality in Twentieth-Century America* (New York: Norton, 2005).

31. Richard Rothstein, "Public Housing: Government-Sponsored Segregation," *The American Prospect*, October 11, 2012, http://prospect.org/article/public-housing-government-sponsored-segregation.

32. For Chicago, see Rose Helper, *Racial Policies and Practices of Real Estate Brokers* (Minneapolis: University of Minnesota Press, 1969); for San Francisco, see Douglas S. Massey

and Nancy A. Denton, *American Apartheid: Segregation and the Making of the Under-class* (Cambridge, MA: Harvard University Press, 1993); for New York, National Committee Against Discrimination in Housing, *Jobs and Housing: A Study of Employment and Housing Opportunities for Racial Minorities in Suburban Areas of the New York Metropolitan Area* (New York: National Committee Against Discrimination in Housing, 1970).

33. Helper, *Racial Policies and Practices of Real Estate Brokers*, 287; National Association of Realtors, "Historic Report," https://www.nar.realtor/membership/historic-report.

34. Kevin Fox Gotham, "Urban Space, Restrictive Covenants, and the Origins of Racial Residential Segregation in a US City, 1900–1950," *International Journal of Urban and Regional Research* 24, no. 3 (September 2000): 626.

35. Sugrue, *The Origins of the Urban Crisis*, 213, 215; Amine Ouazad, "Blockbusting: Brokers and the Dynamics of Segregation," *Journal of Economic Theory* 157 (May 2015): 811–841.

36. Kenneth T. Jackson, "Federal Subsidy and the Suburban Dream: The First Quarter-Century of Government Intervention in the Housing Market," *Records of the Columbia Historical Society, Washington DC* 50 (1980): 447, http://ti.org/JacksonFedSubsidies&-Suburbs.pdf.

37. Leah Platt Boustan, "Was Postwar Suburbanization 'White Flight'?: Evidence from the Black Migration," *Quarterly Journal of Economics* 125, no. 1 (February 2010): 417–443.

38. Massey and Denton, *American Apartheid*, 46.

39. Taylor Branch, *Parting the Waters: America in the King Years, 1954–63* (New York: Simon and Schuster, 1988).

40. John Kenneth Galbraith, *The Affluent Society* (Boston: Houghton Mifflin, 1958), 324.

41. Michael Harrington, *The Other America: Poverty in the United States* (New York: Macmillan, 1962).

42. Katznelson, *When Affirmative Action Was White*; Hilary Herbold, "Never a Level Playing Field: Blacks and the GI Bill," *Journal of Blacks in Higher Education* no. 6 (December 1994): 108.

43. Reynolds Farley, Sheldon H. Danziger, and Harry J. Holzer, *Detroit Divided* (New York: Russell Sage Foundation, 2000); Patrick Bayer and Kerwin Kofi Charles, "Divergent Paths: Structural Change, Economic Rank, and the Evolution of Black-White Earnings Differences, 1940–2014," Working Paper 22797, National Bureau of Economic Research, November 2016.

44. Paul Frymer, *Black and Blue: African Americans, the Labor Movement, and the Decline of the Democratic Party* (Princeton, NJ: Princeton University Press, 2008).

45. Ellora Derenoncourt, "Can You Move to Opportunity?: Evidence from the Great Migration," *American Economic Review*, 112 no. 2 (February 2022): 269–408; William J. Collins and Marianne H. Wanamaker, "African American Intergenerational Mobility Since 1880," Working Paper 23395, National Bureau of Economic Research, May 2017.

46. Gary Becker, *Human Capital: A Theoretical and Empirical Analysis with Special Reference to Education* (Chicago: University of Chicago Press, 1994), 23–24.

47. John F. McDonald, *Postwar Urban America: Demography, Politics, and Social Policy* (New York: Routledge, 2015), 127–131.

48.   Walter W. Heller, *New Dimensions of Political Economy* (Cambridge, MA: Harvard University Press, 1966), 2. See Richard M. McGahey, "The Political Economy of Growth and Distribution: Economics, Public Policy, and Politics," in *Economics as Worldly Philosophy: Essays in Honour of Robert L. Heilbroner*, ed. Ron Blackwell, Jaspal Chatha, and Edward J. Nell (New York: St. Martin's Press, 1993), 161–186.

49.   Frank James, "Martin Luther King Jr. in Chicago," in *Chicago Days: 150 Defining Moments in the Life of a Great City*, ed. Stevenson Swanson (Chicago: Contemporary Books, 1997), 202–204.

50.   Massey and Denton, *American Apartheid*, 63–64.

51.   Steven R. Goldzwig, "LBJ, the Rhetoric of Transcendence, and the Civil Rights Act of 1968," *Rhetoric & Public Affairs* 6, no. 1 (2003): 25–53, Johnson quoted at 29. See also Jonathan Zasloff, "The Secret History of the Fair Housing Act," *Harvard Journal on Legislation* 53, no. 1 (January 2016): 247–278.

52.   The program was criticized, and its terms mocked, by Daniel Patrick Moynihan in his book *Maximum Feasible Misunderstanding: Community Action in the War on Poverty* (New York: Free Press, 1969). Daley controlled Chicago's OEO programs, a power not given to most mayors. Zasloff, "The Secret History of the Fair Housing Act," 267.

53.   Rick Perlstein, *Nixonland: The Rise of a President and the Fracturing of America* (New York: Scribner, 2008), 117–120, 164–165.

54.   Massey and Denton, *American Apartheid*, 195; Zasloff, "The Secret History of the Fair Housing Act," views the law's powers more favorably.

55.   Jennifer L. Hochschild and Michael N. Danielson, "The Demise of a Dinosaur: Analyzing School and Housing Desegregation in Yonkers," in *Race, Poverty, and Domestic Policy*, ed. C. Michael Henry (New Haven, CT: Yale University Press, 2004), 221–241; Matthew F. Delmont, *Why Busing Failed: Race, Media, and the National Resistance to School Desegregation* (Oakland: University of California Press, 2016).

56.   Milliken v. Bradley, 418 US 717 (1974).

57.   National Advisory Commission on Civil Disorders, *Report of the National Advisory Commission on Civil Disorders* (Washington, DC: U.S. Government Printing Office, 1968), 1, http://www.eisenhowerfoundation.org/docs/kerner.pdf.

58.   Nancy A. McGuckin and Nanda Srinivasan, *Journey-to-Work Trends in the United States and Its Major Metropolitan Areas, 1960–1990* (Washington, DC: U.S. Department of Transportation, 2003), 2–1, https://rosap.ntl.bts.gov/view/dot/5543.

59.   Diane N. Westcott, "Employment and Commuting Patterns: A Residential Analysis," *Monthly Labor Review* 102, no. 7 (July 1979): 8.

60.   Christopher G. Gellner, "Occupational Characteristics of Urban Workers," *Monthly Labor Review* 94, no. 10 (October 1971): 25.

61.   U.S. Bureau of the Census, *Census of Governments, 1972: Volume 5, Local Government in Metropolitan Areas* (Washington, DC: Department of Commerce, 1974), 3, 32–165.

62.   Nixon blamed food price increases not on farmers but on "chain stores," which he saw as "primarily dominated by Jewish interests." Quoted in Perlstein, *Nixonland*, 471. Butz resigned after racist "jokes" he made were widely circulated in the media.

63. The larger organization, Organization of Petroleum Exporting Countries (OPEC), did not call an embargo, although oil price increases from OAPEC's embargo helped their revenues.

64. A detailed discussion can be found in Glyn, Hughes, Lipietz, and Singh, "The Rise and Fall of the Golden Age," 72–125. Also see Barry Bluestone and Bennett Harrison, *The Great U-Turn: Corporate Restructuring and the Polarizing of America* (New York: Basic Books, 1988).

65. Nicholas Lemann, "The Unfinished War," *The Atlantic Monthly* 263, no. 1 (January 1989): 67.

66. Advisory Commission on Intergovernmental Relations, *Central City-Suburban Fiscal Disparity and City Distress, 1977* (Washington, DC: U.S. Government Printing Office, 1980).

67. On the Greenspan memo, see Mehrsa Baradaran, *The Color of Money: Black Banks and the Racial Wealth Gap* (Cambridge, MA: Harvard University Press, 2017), 209–210; on Nixon's broader strategy, see Dean Kotlowski, "Black Power—Nixon Style: The Nixon Administration and Minority Business Enterprise," *Business History Review* 72, no. 3 (1998): 409–445.

68. Richard Nathan, "The Uses of Shared Revenue," *Journal of Finance* 30, no. 2 (May 1975): 559, 563.

69. Robert K. Schaeffer, *Understanding Globalization: The Social Consequences of Political, Economic, and Environmental Change* (Lanham, MD: Rowman and Littlefield, 2009), 7–8.

70. Robert A. Beauregard, *When America Became Suburban* (Minneapolis: University of Minnesota Press, 2006), 1.

71. Glyn, Hughes, Lipietz, and Singh, "The Rise and Fall of the Golden Age," 114.

72. Dennis R. Judd and Todd Swanstrom, *City Politics: Private Power and Public Policy* (New York: HarperCollins College Publishers, 1994), 345.

73. Ford Foundation, *Community Development Corporations: A Strategy for Depressed Urban and Rural Areas* (New York: Ford Foundation, 1973), http://files.eric.ed.gov/fulltext/ED090328.pdf.

74. Nicholas Lemann, "The Myth of Community Development," *New York Times Magazine*, January 9, 1999, https://www.nytimes.com/1994/01/09/magazine/the-myth-of-community-development.html; see also Alice O'Connor, "Swimming Against the Tide," in *Urban Problems and Community Development*, ed. Ronald F. Ferguson and William T. Dickens (Washington, DC: Brookings Institution, 1999), 11.

75. John H. Mollenkopf, "The Post-War Politics of Urban Development," *Politics and Society* 5, no. 3 (1975): 256–257. Similar themes are discussed, although with less attention to how these trends contributed to urban conflict, in Harvey Molotch, "The City as a Growth Machine: Toward a Political Economy of Place," *American Journal of Sociology*, 82, no. 2 (September 1976): 226–238.

76. Panel on Policies and Prospects for Metropolitan and Nonmetropolitan America, *Urban America in the Eighties: Perspectives and Prospects* (Washington, DC: U.S. Government Printing Office, 1980), 99.

77.   Boston's battles are magnificently described in J. Anthony Lukas, *Common Ground: A Turbulent Decade in the Lives of Three American Families* (New York: Vintage, 1986).

4. NEW YORK CITY: FROM SOCIAL DEMOCRACY TO "A TALE OF TWO CITIES"

1.   Jack Newfield and Paul Du Brul, *The Abuse of Power: The Permanent Government and the Fall of New York* (New York: Viking Press, 1997); Paul Kantor and Stephen David, "The Political Economy of Change in Urban Budgetary Politics: A Framework for Analysis and a Case Study," *British Journal of Political Science* 13, no. 3 (July 1983): 271.

2.   These higher rates also were rippling out to other municipal and state debt markets, where September yields rose to "record levels." Federal Reserve Bank of New York, "The Money and Bond Markets in September 1975," *Monthly Review* 57, no. 10 (October 1975): 240.

3.   The Beame statement can be seen in Jeff Nussbaum, "The Night New York Saved Itself from Bankruptcy," *New Yorker*, October 16, 2015.

4.   Kim Phillips-Fein, *Fear City: New York's Fiscal Crisis and the Rise of Austerity Politics* (New York: Metropolitan Books, 2017), 136. The police union distributed leaflets, "Welcome to Fear City," warning visitors to "stay away from New York City if you possibly can." The leaflet, featuring a grinning skull, can be seen at http://gothamist.com/2013/09/16/the _1970s_pamphlet_aimed_at_keeping.php#photo-2.

5.   Joshua B. Freeman, *Working-Class New York: Life and Labor Since World War II* (New York: New Press, 2000), 265.

6.   Martin Shefter, *Political Crisis, Fiscal Crisis: The Collapse and Revival of New York City* (New York: Columbia University Press, 1992), 60–65.

7.   Samuel M. Ehrenhalt, "Economic and Demographic Change: The Case of New York City," *Monthly Labor Review* 116, no. 2 (February 1993): 41; Temporary Commission on City Finances, *The City in Transition: Prospects and Policies for New York* (New York: Arno Press, 1978), 99, see table V-2.; on government jobs, see Temporary Commission on City Finances, *The City in Transition*, 24.

8.   Christopher Jones, "Border Warfare: Can We Do It Differently This Time?," *Regional Plan Association*, January 26, 2010; Matthew Drennan and Georgia N. Stergiou, "The Local Economy and Local Revenues," in *Setting Municipal Priorities: American Cities and the New York Experience*, ed. Charles Brecher and Raymond D. Horton (New York: New York University Press, 1984), 43–68. On corporation relocations, see Kenneth T. Jackson, *Crabgrass Frontier: The Suburbanization of the United States* (New York: Oxford University Press, 1985), 268.

9.   Temporary Commission on City Finances, *The City in Transition*, 70, see table IV-5; on intergovernmental aid, see Temporary Commission on City Finances, *The City in Transition*, 48.

10.   Freeman, *Working-Class New York*, 272.

11.   Unionstats.com, "Union Membership and Coverage from the CPS," 2020, http://www .unionstats.com/. Data are for the New York metropolitan region. Victor Gotbaum

quoted in Daniel DiSalvo, "How to Approach Public Sector Unions," in *A Time for Governing: Policy Solutions from the Pages of National Affairs*, ed. Yuval Levin and Meghan Clyne (New York: Encounter Books, 2012), 315.

12.   Freeman, *Working-Class New York*, 268–269.

13.   Larry Celona, "Former New York City Mayor Ed Koch Dead at Age 88," *New York Post*, February 1, 2013. The transit workers were actually negotiating with the Metropolitan Transit Authority (MTA), but Koch attacked them partly in preparation for upcoming negotiations with city employees.

14.   John H. Mollenkopf, *A Phoenix in the Ashes: The Rise and Fall of the Koch Coalition in New York City Politics* (Princeton, NJ: Princeton University Press, 1992), 5, 8.

15.   "Treasury Secretary Hails Fiscal Effort," *New York Times*, April 16, 1981.

16.   Matthew Drennan, "Economy," in *The Two New Yorks: State-City Relations in the Changing Federal System*, ed. Gerald Benjamin and Charles Brecher (New York: Russell Sage Foundation, 1988), 57.

17.   Ehrenhalt, "Economic and Demographic Change," 42.

18.   Lois M. Plunkert, "The 1980's: A Decade of Job; Robin Greenwood and David Scharfstein, "The Growth of Finance," *Journal of Economic Perspectives* 27, no. 2 (2013): 3. Growth and Industry Shifts," *Monthly Labor Review* 113, no. 9 (September 1990): 14

19.   Rona B. Stein, "New York City's Economy in 1980," *Federal Reserve Bank of New York Quarterly Review* 6, no. 1 (1981): 1–7.

20.   Christopher Witko, "The Politics of Financialization in the United States," *British Journal of Political Science* 46, no. 2 (April 2016): 349–370.

21.   Daphne A. Kenyon, Adam H. Langley, and Bethany P. Paquin, *Rethinking Property Tax Incentives for Business* (Cambridge, MA: Lincoln Institute of Land Policy, June 2012). These authors, like many others, find "there is little evidence that these tax incentives are an effective instrument to promote economic development." On public authorities, see Charles Brecher and Jo Brill, *Public Authorities in New York State* (New York: Citizens Budget Commission, 2006).

22.   The move to tax expenditures over direct spending grew nationally in housing, health care, social welfare spending, and other spheres. See Christopher Faricy, "The Politics of Social Policy in America: The Causes and Effects of Indirect Versus Direct Social Spending," *Journal of Politics* 73, no. 1 (January 2011): 74–83; on residential enclaves, see John H. Mollenkopf and Manuel Castells, *Dual City: Restructuring New York* (New York: Russell Sage Foundation), 9.

23.   William Sites, "The Limits of Urban Regime Theory: New York City Under Koch, Dinkins, and Giuliani," *Urban Affairs Review* 32, no. 4 (March 1997): 537.

24.   Mollenkopf, *A Phoenix in the Ashes*, 15.

25.   Jonathan Soffer, *Ed Koch and the Rebuilding of New York City* (New York: Columbia University Press, 2012), 304. See also Michael H. Schill, Ingrid Gould Ellen, Amy Ellen Schwartz, and Ioan Voicu, "Revitalizing Inner-City Neighborhoods: New York City's Ten-Year Plan," *Housing Policy Debate* 13, no. 3 (January 2002): 529–566.

26.   J. Phillip Thompson III, *Double Trouble: Black Mayors, Black Communities, and the Call for a Deep Democracy* (New York: Oxford University Press, 2006), 200; Josh Barbanel, "Control Board Is Re-Emerging as Power Focus," *New York Times*, October 9, 1990.

27.   Ehrenhalt, "Economic and Demographic Change," 45.

28.   Elizabeth Kolbert, "Cuomo's Crime Remedy: 'Produce the Police, Period,'" *New York Times*, September 11, 1990.

29.   State control of the city has a long history. George Washington Plunkett, a legendary leader of the nineteenth-century Tammany Hall political machine (who is best known for his definition of "honest graft") said rural legislators in Albany viewed New York City as "pie for the hayseeds." Quoted in Robert B. Ward, *New York State Government* (Albany, NY: Rockefeller Institute Press, 2006), 103.

30.   Sites, "The Limits of Urban Regime Theory," 542.

31.   Office of the State Deputy Comptroller, "New York City's Economic Dependence on Wall Street," *Challenge* 42, no. 2 (March/April 1999): 6–22.

32.   Arun Peter Lobo and Joseph J. Salvo, *The Newest New Yorkers 2000: Immigrant New York in the New Millennium* (New York: New York City Department of City Planning, 2004), 128–129.

33.   John Mollenkopf, David Olson, and Timothy Ross, "Immigrant Political Participation in New York and Los Angeles," in *Governing American Cities: Inter-Ethnic Coalitions, Competition, and Conflict*, ed. Michael Jones-Correa (New York: Russell Sage Foundation, 2001), 20; see table 1.2.

34.   Roger Waldinger, "From Ellis Island to LAX: Immigrant Prospects in the American City," *International Migration Review* 30, no. 4 (1996): 1084.

35.   E. J. McMahon, "Mario Cuomo, Tax Cutter," *City Journal*, January 2, 2015, https://www.city -journal.org/html/mario-cuomo-tax-cutter-11486.html.

36.   Alan Rothstein, "The New York State Legislature: How Albany Controls the City," *Gotham Gazette*, January 29, 2001, https://www.gothamgazette.com/government/1586 -the-new-york-state-legislature-how-albany-controls-the-city; Bruce D. Baker, *School Funding Fairness in New York State: An Update for 2013–14* (Albany, NY: Alliance for Quality Education, 2014).

37.   Freeman, *Working-Class New York*, 332.

38.   Jack Newfield, "The Full Rudy: The Man, the Mayor, the Myth," *The Nation*, May 30, 2002.

39.   John Mollenkopf, "How 9/11 Reshaped the Political Environment in New York," in *Contentious City: The Politics of Recovery in New York*, ed. John Mollenkopf (New York: Russell Sage Foundation, 2005), 205–222.

40.   Michael Bloomberg, "State of the City Address," January 23, 2003, *Gotham Gazette*, transcript, http://www.gothamgazette.com/government/1670-mayor-michael-bloombergs-2003-state -of-the-city-address.

41.   Bloomberg, "State of the City Address"; Julian Brash, *Bloomberg's New York: Class and Governance in the Luxury City* (Athens: University of Georgia Press, 2011), 130.

42.   New York did extensive planning, rezoning, and project design to support the Olympic bid and much of that work fed ongoing development. See Mitchell Moss, *How New York City Won the Olympics* (New York: New York University, 2011).

43.   Mitchell Moss, "The Redevelopment of Lower Manhattan: The Role of the City," in *Contentious City: The Politics of Recovery in New York*, ed. John Mollenkopf (New York: Russell Sage Foundation, 2005), 95–111.

44. Amy Armstrong, Vicki Been, Josiah Madar, and Simon McDonnell, "How Have Recent Rezonings Affected the City's Ability to Grow?" (New York: New York University, 2010), 8–9, http://furmancenter.org/files/publications/Rezonings_Furman_Center_Policy_Brief_March_2010.pdf.

45. Brad Lander and Laura Wolf-Powers, "Remaking New York: Can Prosperity Be Shared and Sustainable?," Working Paper, Center for Community Development, Pratt Institute, 2004, http://repository.upenn.edu/cplan_papers/43/.

46. Vicki Been, Mark A. Levine, Ross Moskowitz, Wesley O'Brien, and Ethel Sheffer, *The Role of Community Benefits Agreements in New York City's Land Use Process* (New York: New York City Bar Association, 2010), 48, TheRoleofCommunityBenefitAgreementsin NYCLandUseProcess.pdf.

47. Aviva Shen, "Mayor Bloomberg Sues to Kill New York's Living Wage Law Before He Leaves Office," *ThinkProgress*, December 16, 2013, https://thinkprogress.org/mayor-bloomberg-sues-to-kill-new-yorks-living-wage-law-before-he-leaves-office-57f1126c2ead/.

48. Michael E. Porter, Christian H. M. Ketels, Anne Habiby, and David Zipper, *New York City: Bloomberg's Strategy for Economic Development* (Cambridge, MA: Harvard Business School, 2009).

49. Lander and Wolf-Powers, "Remaking New York," 1.

50. "Accountable USA—New York," Good Jobs First, http://www.goodjobsfirst.org/states/new-york. On sports stadiums, see (among many others) Scott A. Wolla, "The Economics of Subsidizing Sports Stadiums," *Page One Economics* (blog), May 2017, https://research.stlouisfed.org/publications/page1-econ/2017-05-01/the-economics-of-subsidizing-sports-stadiums/.

51. Greenwood and Scharfstein, "The Growth of Finance," 3; James Parrott, "Neighborhoods and the Fiscal Boom," *Gotham Gazette*, August 7, 2007, http://www.gothamgazette.com/index.php/development/3629-neighborhoods-and-the-fiscal-boom.

52. Amy Armstrong et al., *State of New York's Housing and Neighborhoods, 2008* (New York: Furman Center for Real Estate and Urban Policy, New York University, 2008), 15.

53. The Pew Charitable Trusts, "Federal Share of State Revenue," *Fiscal 50: State Trends and Analysis*, updated October 8, 2019, http://www.pewtrusts.org/en/multimedia/data-visualizations/2014/fiscal-50#ind1.

54. John Mollenkopf, Joseph Pereira, Steven Romalewski, and Lesley Hirsch, "Shifting Shares: Demographic Change, Differential Mobility, and Electoral Trends in New York City, 2000 to 2011," in *Toward a 21st Century City for All: Progressive Policies for New York City in 2013 and Beyond*, ed. John Mollenkopf (New York: City University of New York, 2013), tables 6 and 7.

55. Thomas P. DiNapoli and Kenneth B. Bleiwas, *The Role of Immigrants in the New York City Economy* (New York: Office of the New York State Comptroller, 2015).

56. John Mollenkopf and Brad Lander, "Needed: A Progressive Agenda," in *Toward a 21st Century City for All: Progressive Policies for New York City in 2013 and Beyond*, ed. John Mollenkopf (New York: City University of New York, 2013), 1.

57. Office of the Mayor, "Mayor de Blasio, Speaker Mark-Viverito, and City Council Reach Early Agreement on FY2018 Budget," June 2, 2017, http://www1.nyc.gov/office-of-the-mayor/news/387-17/mayor-de-blasio-speaker-mark-viverito-city-council-reach-early-agreement-fy2018-budget-/#/0.

58. New York City Commission on Human Rights, *Building Barriers: Discrimination in New York City's Construction Trades* (New York: New York City Commission on Human Rights, 1993), http://www.talkinghistory.org/sisters/images/building_barriers.pdf. On progress, see Lawrence Mishel, *Diversity in the New York City Union and Nonunion Construction Sectors* (Washington, DC: Economic Policy Institute, 2017).

59. Citizens' Budget Commission, *Where Is the Money Going?: Mayor DeBlasio's Spending Priorities*, City Budget Report, June 3, 2016; James Parrott, "CityViews: Alarmist Commentary on City Budget Misjudges Responsible Growth," *City Limits*, December 21, 2018, https://citylimits.org/2018/12/21/cityviews-alarmist-commentary-on-city-budget-misjudges-responsible-growth/.

60. Lawrence Mielnicki, Farid Heydarpour, and Orlando Vasquez, *New York City's Labor Market: Evidence from the Recent Expansion* (New York: Office of the New York City Comptroller, 2017).

61. Zack Fink, "Revenge Is Coming: How Everything Fell Apart Between Andrew Cuomo and Bill de Blasio," *City & State New York*, January 16, 2017.

62. Bruce Schaller, "New York City's Congestion Pricing Experience and Implications for Road Pricing Acceptance in the United States," *Transport Policy* 17, no. 1 (August 2010): 266–273. Congestion pricing was approved by the state in 2019, with implementation in 2021. New York State eventually enacted a plastic bag ban.

63. William Neuman and J. David Goodman, "In City Council, Power Shifts Away from Progressives," *New York Times*, February 2, 2018.

64. Liz Lucking, "432 Park Avenue Leads Luxury Real Estate in Another Strong Week," *Mansion Global*, April 9, 2018, https://www.mansionglobal.com/articles/93725-432-park-avenue-leads-luxury-real-estate-in-another-strong-week.

65. New York City Independent Budget Office, *Recession Ahead?: While Concerns Mount, Projections Show Moderate Growth in NYC Tax Revenue for the Upcoming Years* (New York: New York Independent Budget Office, 2019), 5.

66. Citizens Budget Commission. "Less Spending, More Saving: Benchmarks to Assess the NYC Financial Plan," November 13, 2019, Citizens Budget Commission, https://cbcny.org/research/less-spending-more-saving.

67. Bridget Fisher and Flávia Leite, "The Cost of New York City's Hudson Yards Redevelopment Project," Working Paper 2018–2, Schwartz Center for Economic Policy Analysis, The New School.

68. Emma G. Fitzsimmons. 2020. "Progressives Defeat Brooklyn Project That Promised 20,000 Jobs," *New York Times*, September 23, 2020.

69. Vivian Wang, "New Rent Laws Pass in N.Y.: 'The Pendulum Is Swinging' Against Landlords," *New York Times*, June 14, 2019; Citizens Budget Commission, *Strategies to Boost Housing Production in the New York Metropolitan Area*, August 26, 2020, 6.

70. Brad Lander, Krista Olson, and Andrew McWilliam, "New York by the Numbers: Monthly Economic and Fiscal Outlook," Office of the New York City Comptroller, February 2022, table 1, https://comptroller.nyc.gov/newsroom/new-york-by-the-numbers-monthly-economic-and-fiscal-outlook-no-62-february-7th-2022/.

71. Community Service Society, 2020, "Poverty Declined in New York for Fifth Straight Year," September 18, 2020, https://www.cssny.org/news/entry/statement-poverty-declined-in-new-york-city-for-fifth-straight-year-but-cen.

72. City of New York, *The de Blasio Years: The Tale of a More Equal City*, December 2021, https://www1.nyc.gov/assets/home/downloads/pdf/press-releases/2021/Wealth-Transfer-Report.pdf; Emma G. Fitzsimmons and Jefferey C. Mays, "Is New York Still a 'Tale of Two Cities'?", *New York Times*, December 22, 2021.

73. Greg David, "NYC Lost a Record 631,000 Jobs to the Pandemic in 2020: So What's Next?", *The City*, March 14, 2021, https://www.thecity.nyc/economy/2021/3/14/22326414/nyc-lost-record-jobs-to-pandemic-unemployment; James A. Parrott, *Inequality in New York City: Does Local Policy Matter in the Age of the Covid-19 Pandemic?*, June 2020, Center for New York City Affairs, The New School, https://stonecenter.gc.cuny.edu/files/2020/08/Parrott-Stone-Center-Inequality-Workshop-June-2020annotated.pdf.

74. Frank Donnelly, "New York's Population and Migration Trends in the 2010s," WCIB Occasional Paper 21, Weissman Center for International Business, Baruch College, City University of New York, Fall 2020.

75. Citizens Budget Commission, "Personal Incomes Tax Revenues in New York State and City," August 13, 2019, https://cbcny.org/research/personal-income-tax-revenues-new-york-state-and-city; Center for New York City Affairs, "The Pandemic Torpedoed New York City's Budget: Now What?," October 28, 2020, w.centernyc.org/urban-matters-2/2020/10/28/the-pandemic-torpedoed-new-york-citys-budget-now-what.

76. Regional Plan Association, *New York's Next Comeback.*, October 2020, https://rpa.org/work/reports/new-yorks-next-comeback: 38.

77. Stefanos Chen, "In 2021, New York's Housing Market Made a Stunning Comeback," *New York Times*, December 31, 2021.

78. Raeedah Wahid, "Adams Won by Betting on a New York Divided by Race and Income," *Bloomberg*, July 21, 2021, https://www.bloomberg.com/graphics/2021-nyc-mayoral-analysis/.

79. Paul Krugman, "Why a Blue City Is Feeling the Blues," *New York Times*, January 17, 2022.

80. Robert Gebeloff, Dana Goldstein, and Winnie Hu, "Cities Lost Population in 2021, Leading to the Slowest Year of Growth in U.S. History," *New York Times*, March 24, 2022.

81. Freeman, *Working-Class New York*, 334.

82. Mollenkopf and Lander, "Needed: A Progressive Agenda," 1.

5. DETROIT: FROM THE "ARSENAL OF DEMOCRACY" TO RECORD-BREAKING BANKRUPTCY

1. Admiral Isoroku Yamamato, the planner of the Pearl Harbor attacks, spent two years in the United States between 1919 and 1921. After touring Detroit automobile plants and agricultural, oil, and mining sites, he concluded, "Japan lacks the national power for a naval race with America." Ian W. Toll, "A Reluctant Enemy," *New York Times*, December 6, 2011.

2. Sarah Jo Peterson, *Planning the Home Front: Building Bombers and Communities at Willow Run* (Chicago: University of Chicago Press, 2013), 7.

3. Detroit Metropolitan Area Planning Commission, "Study of Expansion Trends in the Automobile Industry with Special Reference to the Detroit Region," Detroit Metropolitan Area Planning Commission, 1956, 11, figure 3, https://babel.hathitrust.org/cgi/pt?id=mdp.35128001565876;view=1up;seq=1.

4. Thomas J. Sugrue, *The Origins of the Urban Crisis: Race and Inequality in Postwar Detroit* (Princeton, NJ: Princeton University Press, 2005), 128.

5. Ford's control of Dearborn was underscored in the 1928s consolidation of Dearborn and the town of Fordson to stave off annexation by Detroit, and the election of his cousin Clyde Ford as Dearborn's first mayor. Heather B. Barrow, " 'The American Disease of Growth': Henry Ford and the Metropolitanization of Detroit, 1920–1940," in *Manufacturing Suburbs: Building Work and Home on the Metropolitan Fringe*, ed. Robert D. Lewis (Philadelphia, PA: Temple University Press, 2004), 200–220.

6. Campbell Gibson, "Population of the 100 Largest Cities and Other Urban Places in the United States," Working Paper POP-WP027, U.S. Bureau of the Census, Washington, DC, 1998, tables 14 and 16, https://www.census.gov/library/working-papers/1998/demo/POP-twps0027.html

7. Frank Levy and Peter Temin, "Inequality and Institutions in 20th Century America," Working Paper 13106, National Bureau of Economic Research, May 2007, 29; Daniel J. Clark, *Disruption in Detroit: Autoworkers and the Elusive Postwar Boom* (Chicago: University of Illinois Press, 2018), 147–165.

8. Reynolds Farley, Mick Couper, and Maria Krysan, *Race and Revitalization in the Rust Belt: A Motor City Story*, PSC Research Report No. 07–620, University of Michigan, April 2007, 22.

9. Reynolds Farley, Sheldon Danziger, and Harry J. Holzer, *Detroit Divided* (New York: Russell Sage Foundation, 2000), 53; David Leonhardt, "The Black-White Wage Gap Is as Big as It Was in 1950," *New York* Times, June 25, 2020, https://www.nytimes.com/2020/06/25/opinion/sunday/race-wage-gap.html.

10. Frances M. Grunow, "A Brief History of Housing in Detroit," *modelD*, November 17, 2015, http://www.modeldmedia.com/features/detroit-housing-pt1-111715.aspx.

11. Jane Jacobs, *The Death and Life of Great American Cities* (New York: Random House, 1961), 204.

12. Donald R. Deskins, "Economic Restructuring, Job Opportunities, and Black Social Dislocation in Detroit," in *Social Polarization in Post-Industrial Metropolises*, ed. John O'Loughlin and Jürgen Friedrichs (New York: De Gruyter, 1996), 260.

13. Sugrue, *The Origins of the Urban Crisis*, 213.

14. John Hartigan Jr., *Racial Situations: Class Predicaments of Whiteness in Detroit* (Princeton, NJ: Princeton University Press, 1999).

15. Sugrue, *The Origins of the Urban Crisis*, 194.

16. Michael R. Glass, "Detroit, MI, 1941–1952," in *Cities in American Political History*, ed. Richardson Dilworth (Los Angeles: Sage, 2011), 512–518.

17. Kurt Metzger and Jason Booza, "African Americans in the United States, Michigan, and Metropolitan Detroit," Working Paper 8, Wayne State University, February 2002, 10, tables 12 and 13.

18. John F. McDonald, "What Happened to and in Detroit?," *Urban Studies* 51, no. 16 (December 2014): 3309–3329; Reynolds Farley, "The Bankruptcy of Detroit: What Role Did Race Play?," *City & Community* 14, no. 2 (June 2015): 122.

19. David Maraniss, *Once in a Great City: A Detroit Story* (New York: Simon and Schuster, 2005), 161–188. Reverend Franklin was head of the New Bethel Baptist Church and a prominent Detroit organizer and voice for civil rights; he was also Aretha Franklin's father.

20. The violence was triggered by a Detroit police raid on a "blind pig," an illegal afterhours drinking club where two black soldiers were being welcomed back after service in the Vietnam War.

21. "N.A.A.C.P. Joins Attack on Detroit Housing Law," *New York Times*, December 22, 1964.

22. McDonald, "What Happened to and in Detroit?," 3317, 3319.

23. George Galster, *Driving Detroit: The Quest for Respect in Motown* (Philadelphia: University of Pennsylvania, 2014), 191–194. The classic source on the league is Dan Georgakas and Marvin Surkin, *Detroit, I Do Mind Dying: A Study in Urban Revolution* (Cambridge, MA: South End Press, 1998).

24. William Kling, "Wallace Clips Detroit Speech Short as Violence Breaks Out," *Chicago Tribune*, October 30, 1968; on the 1972 primary see Sugrue, *The Origins of the Urban Crisis*, 265.

25. John O'Loughlin and Dale A. Berg, "The Election of Black Mayors, 1969 and 1973," *Annals of the Association of American Geographers* 67, no. 2 (June 1977): 223–238.

26. Steve Malanga, "The Real Reason the Once Great City of Detroit Came to Ruin," *Wall Street Journal*, July 26, 2013.

27. Rachel S. Dauenbaugh, "Coleman Young's Detroit: A Vision for a City 1974–1994," thesis, DePauw University, 2014, 28, https://scholarship.depauw.edu/cgi/viewcontent.cgi?article=1006&context=studentresearch.

28. Peter Dreier, "Reagan's Real Legacy," *The Nation*, February 4, 2011.

29. Japanese industry adopted industrial techniques for reliability first developed by U.S. engineer W. Edwards Deming but ignored by the big three—Ford, Chrysler, and General Motors. Alan Goldstein, "Curmudgeon of Quality: U.S. Industry Listens Now When Once-Ignored International Management Wizard Speaks," *Los Angeles Times*, March 31, 1987.

30. Galster, *Driving Detroit*, 128, 133.

31. Todd C. Shaw and Lester K. Spence, "Race and Representation in Detroit's Community Development Coalitions," *Annals of the American Academy of Political and Social Science* 594 (July 2004): 125–142; John J. Bukowczyk, "The Poletown Case and the Future of Detroit's Neighborhoods," *Michigan Quarterly Review*, 25, no. 2 (1986): 449–458.

32. Janice L. Bockmeyer, "A Culture of Distrust: The Impact of Local Political Culture on Participation in the Detroit EZ," *Urban Studies* 37, no. 13 (December 2000): 2423–2425; Isabel Wilkerson, "Primary Will Provide Detroit Mayor a November Opponent," *New York Times*, September 11, 1989; Shaw and Spence, "Race and Representation in Detroit's Community Development Coalitions," 139.

33. Gus Burns, "Controversial Statue of Racist ex-Dearborn Mayor Orville Hubbard Relocated," *MLive*, September 29, 2015.

34. This can be seen in contrast to Harold Washington's 1983 progressive and multiracial coalition victory in Chicago. Progress was cut short by Washington's untimely death in 1987. See Roger Biles, *Mayor Harold Washington: Champion of Race and Reform in Chicago* (Urbana: University of Illinois Press, 2018).

35. FRED Economic Data, Federal Reserve Bank of St. Louis, https://fred.stlouisfed.org /series/SMU26198203133630001A. On regional manufacturing, see McDonald, What Happened to and in Detroit?," 3221, table 4.

36. McDonald, What Happened to and in Detroit?," 3316, table 2.

37. David Frum, "A Good Way to Wreck a Local Economy: Build Casinos," *The Atlantic*, August 7, 2014.

38. David Barkholz, "Casino Foes Set to Play Ace in Hole: Petition Drive Seeks Repeal of Proposal E," *Crain's Detroit Business*, November 17, 1997.

39. Sports stadiums are widely held to be money losers for cities. See Roger G. Noll and Andrew Zimbalist, editors, *Sports, Jobs, and Taxes: The Economic Impact of Sports Teams and Stadiums* (Washington, DC: Brookings Institution, 1997).

40. David Ashenfelter, "Handshake Deal with State Haunts Detroit," *Bridge Magazine*, March 15, 2013, https://www.bridgemi.com/michigan-government/handshake-deal-state -haunts-detroit.

41. Allan Mallach, *The Divided City: Poverty and Prosperity in Urban America* (Washington DC: Island Press, 2018); Andre M. Perry, *Know Your Price: Valuing Black Lives and Property in America's Black Cities* (Washington DC: Brookings Institution Press, 2020).

42. Milliken v. Bradley, 418 U.S. 717 (1974).

43. Paige Williams, "Drop Dead, Detroit!," *New Yorker*, January 19, 2014.

44. Greg LeRoy, Allison Lack, and Karla Walter, with Philip Mattera, *The Geography of Incentives: Economic Development and Land Use in Michigan* (Washington, DC: Good Jobs First, 2006), 2, 36.

45. Edward L. Glaeser and Matthew E. Kahn, "Decentralized Employment and the Transformation of the American City," *Brookings—Wharton Papers on Urban Affairs* (2001): 1–63.

46. "Takeover of Detroit Schools Shows Few Intended Results," *Mackinac Center for Public Policy*, January 19, 2006, https://www.mackinac.org/7556.

47. Michigan State Police, *2004 Uniform Crime Report* (Lansing: Michigan State Police, 2005), 55–69, http://www.michigan.gov/documents/Cb-AgencyClearance04_140083_7 .pdf.

48. Task Force on Local Government Services and Fiscal Stability, *Final Report to the Governor* (Lansing: Michigan Department of Treasury, 2006), https://www.michigan.gov /documents/FINAL_Task_Force_Report_5_23_164361_7.pdf.

49. Nancy Kaffer, "Land Bank Limbo," *Detroit Metro Times*, November 30, 2005.

50. Edward McClelland, "Kwame Kilpatrick Exits, with Barack Obama Holding the Door," *Salon*, September 4, 2008, http://www.salon.com/2008/09/04/detroit_2/.

51. Nathan Bomey, *Detroit Resurrected: To Bankruptcy and Back* (New York: Norton, 2016), 18–35.

52. At the end of his term, former president Trump commuted Kilpatrick's sentence, although the former mayor still has the convictions on his record and owes millions in various financial claims.

53. Financial Crisis Inquiry Commission, *Financial Crisis Inquiry Report: Final Report of the National Commission on the Causes of the Financial and Economic Crisis in the United States* (Washington, DC: U.S. Government Printing Office, 2011).

54. Monica Davey, "For Detroit, a Path to Recovery Under State Oversight," *New York Times*, April 5, 2012.

55. City of Detroit, *Proposal for Creditors*, Detroit, 2013, http://www.detroitmi.gov/Portals/0 /docs/EM/Reports/City%20of%20Detroit%20Proposal%20for%20Creditors1.pdf.

56. Bomey, *Detroit Resurrected*, 49–50.

57. City of Detroit, *Proposal for Creditors*, 34.

58. Bomey, *Detroit Resurrected*, 61–62.

59. Drake Bennett and Mark Niquette, "Detroit Is Dead. Long Live Oakland County," *Bloomberg Businessweek*, July 25, 2013, https://www.bloomberg.com/news/articles/2013 -07-25/detroit-is-dead-dot-long-live-oakland-county.

60. Wallace C. Turbeville, *The Detroit Bankruptcy* (Washington, DC: Demos, 2013), 6.

61. Randy Kennedy, "Christie's Reveals Detroit Art Appraisal," *New York Times*, December 4, 2013.

62. Bomey, *Detroit Resurrected*, 141.

63. Howard Husock, *The Pension Grand Bargain: A New Reform Model for Cities* (New York: Manhattan Institute, 2016). Author's calculations from data in figure 8.

64. Anna Clark, "Racing to Run a City Without a Motor," *American Prospect*, October 2, 2013.

65. Brian Pittelko, Bryan Bommersbach, and George Erickcek, *The Employment Impact of the New Economy Initiative (NEI) on the Detroit Region and the State of Michigan* (Kalamazoo, MI: W.E. Upjohn Institute for Employment Research, 2016), 3.

66. Bill Shea, "How Olympia Financed an Arena in a Bankrupt City," *Crain's Detroit Business*, September 10, 2017; Kate Lowe and Joe Grengs, "Private Donations for Public Transit: The Equity Implications of Detroit's Public–Private Streetcar," *Journal of Planning Education and Research* 40, no. 3 (September 2020): 289–303.

67. Laura A. Reese, Jeanette Eckert, Gary Sands, and Igor Vojnovic, "'It's Safe to Come, We've Got Lattes': Development Disparities in Detroit," *Cities: The International Journal of Urban Policy and Planning* 60, A (February 2017): 367–377.

68. Louis Aguilar, "Detroit Sale of $135M in Bonds to Fund Dozens of Projects," *Detroit News*, December 5, 2018.

69. Bureau of the Census. "American Community Service Demographic and Housing Estimates." https://factfinder.census.gov/faces/tableservices/jsf/pages/productview.xhtml?src=; "Unemployment Rates for the 50 Largest Cities, Annual Averages," Bureau of Labor Statistics, U.S. Department of Labor, https://www.bls.gov/lau/lacilg19.htm.

70. Chastity Pratt, "It's Official: No Vote This Year for Transit Fixes in Southeast Michigan," *Bridge Michigan*, July 19, 2018, https://www.bridgemi.com/detroit-journalism-cooperative /its-official-no-vote-year-transit-fixes-southeast-michigan; Robin Runyan and Aaron

Mondry, "Mapping the District Detroit," *Curbed Detroit*, December 12, 2019, https://detroit
.curbed.com/maps/arena-district-detroit-construction-development-ilitch-olympia;
Bureau of the Census, "Census Reporter: Detroit," https://censusreporter.org/profiles
/16000US2622000-detroit-mi/.

71. Beth LeBlanc, Francis X. Donnelly, and Craig Mauger, "Wayne Co. Canvassers Certify
Election Results After Initial Deadlock," *Detroit News*, November 18, 2020.

72. Daniel Kravitz, *Fighting for Equity in Development: The Story of Detroit's Community
Benefits Ordinance*, Detroit People's Platform and Equitable Detroit Coalition, 2017,
https://buildingmovement.org/wp-content/uploads/2019/08/Fighting-for-Equity
-in-Development-The-Story-of-Detroits-Community-Benefits-Ordinance.pdf; Shelby
Jouppi, "Detroit's Community Benefit Ordinance Yields Hours of Dialogue and Almost
No Community Benefits," *WDET*, March 19, 2018, https://wdet.org/posts/2018/03/19
/86319-detroits-community-benefits-ordinance-yields-hours-of-dialogue-and-almost-no
-community-benefits/.

73. Ken Harris, "Blog: New Survey Finds 80% of Detroit's 100 Top Black-Owned Businesses Feel Left Out of Building Boom," *dBusiness*, November 5, 2019, https://www
.dbusiness.com/daily-news/blog-new-survey-finds-80-of-detroits-top-100-black-owned
-businesses-feel-left-out-of-building-boom/; Annalise Frank, "'Elected by the People Who Stayed': Duggan Targets Equity in State of the City Address," *Crain's Detroit
Business*, February 5, 2020, https://www.crainsdetroit.com/government/elected-people
-who-stayed-duggan-targets-equity-state-city-address.

74. Lydia Wileden and Afton Branche-Wilson, *Detroit's Strategic Neighborhood Fund: A
Baseline Report of Resident Perceptions*, Detroit Metro Area Communities Study, University of Michigan, December 2020, 2.

75. John Gallagher, "FCA's Jeep Assembly Plant Is Coming to Detroit—But City May Have
Paid Too Much," *Detroit Free Press*, May 15, 2019.

76. Robin Runyan and Aaron Moody, "Detroit's New Residential Developments, Mapped,"
Curbed Detroit, January 17, 2020, https://detroit.curbed.com/maps/detroit-building
-construction-new-residential-map; Ford Motor Company, "Ford Reveals Plans for
Inclusive, Vibrant, Walkable Mobility Innovation District Around Michigan Central Station," November 17, 2020, https://media.ford.com/content/fordmedia/fna/us/en/news
/2020/11/17/ford-plans-mobility-innovation-district.html.

77. Detroit Area Summary, U.S. Bureau Of Labor Statistics, https://www.bls.gov/regions
/midwest/summary/blssummary_detroit.pdf.

78. City of Detroit, "Four-Year Financial Plan, FY2021-FY2024," May 29, 2020, A12, https://
detroitmi.gov/sites/detroitmi.localhost/files/2020-06/1%20-%20FY%202021-24%20
Four-Year%20Financial%20Plan%20-%20Section%20A%20Overview%20-%20
Adopted_1.pdf.

79. Andrew DePietro, "U.S. Poverty Rate by City in 2021," *Forbes*, November 26, 2021,
https://www.forbes.com/sites/andrewdepietro/2021/11/26/us-poverty-rate-by-city-in-
2021/?sh=f368e55a544d; Scott A. Brave, Ross Cole, and Paul Traub, "Measuring Detroit's
Economic Progress with the DEAI," *Chicago Fed Letter*, no. 434, Federal Reserve Bank of
Chicago, March 2020; City of Detroit-University Economic Analysis Partnership, "City of

Detroit Economic Outlook 2020–2026," September 2021, https://lsa.umich.edu/content
/dam/econ-assets/Econdocs/RSQE%20PDFs/RSQE_Detroit_CREC_Slides.pdf.

80.   Robert Johnson, "The Climate Crisis and the Global New Deal—Bob Pollin," *Podcast:
Economics and Beyond*, Institute for New Economic Thinking, February 25, 2021, https://
www.ineteconomics.org/perspectives/podcasts?q=pollin.

6. LOS ANGELES: PROGRESSIVE COALITIONS IN A CHANGING ECONOMY

1.   Committee for Greater LA, *No Going Back: Together for an Equitable and Inclusive Los
Angeles* (Los Angeles: USC Dornsife Equity Research Institute, September 2020).

2.   Mike Davis, *Ecology of Fear: Los Angeles and the Imagination of Disaster* (New York:
Metropolitan Books, 1998), 371.

3.   James Dertouzos and Michael Dardia, *Defense Spending, Aerospace, and the California
Economy* (Santa Monica, CA: Rand Corporation, 1993), 6, see figure 1.

4.   Dan Flaming, President, Economic Roundtable, interview with Richard McGahey, July
23, 2014.

5.   Mark Drayse, Daniel Flaming, David Rigby, and Michael Beltramo, *The Gateway Cities Economy: Impacts of Aerospace Restructuring* (Los Angeles: Economic Roundtable,
1998), 4.

6.   Lou Cannon, *Official Negligence: How Rodney King and the Riots Changed Los Angeles
and the LAPD* (New York: Times Books, 1997), 10.

7.   William Frey, "Three Americas: The Rising Significance of Regions," *Journal of the American Planning Association* 68, no. 4 (2002): 352.

8.   Los Angeles 2000 Committee, *LA 2000: Final Report of the Los Angeles 2000 Committee*
(Los Angeles: Los Angeles 2000 Committee, 1988), 59. Emphasis in original.

9.   "Enemy of business" quote in Frank Clifford, "Woo, Riordan Differ on Healing L.A.'s
Economy," November 18, 1992, *Los Angeles Times*, November 11, 1992; Robert Reinhold,
"Distinct Choice in Los Angeles Race," *New York Times*, April 22, 1993.

10.   These developments and their history are well analyzed in Manuel Pastor and Michele
Prichard, *LA Rising: The 1992 Civil Unrest, the Arc of Social Justice Organizing, and the
Lessons for Today's Movement Building* (Los Angeles: Liberty Hill Foundation and USC
Program for Environmental and Regional Equity, 2012).

11.   Manuel Pastor, Jr., Chris Benner, and Martha Matsuoka, *This Could Be the Start of
Something Big: How Social Movements for Regional Equity Are Reshaping Metropolitan
America* (Ithaca, NY: Cornell University Press, 2009), 121. Chapter 4, "Coming Back
Together in Los Angeles," details the interactions of these and other progressive activist
groups.

12.   Leslie Berestein, "Coalition Aims to Show the 'Other' Los Angeles," *Los Angeles Times*,
September 3, 1995.

13.   Quoted in Harold Meyerson, "L.A. Story," *The American Prospect*, August 6, 2013.

14.   Meyerson, "L.A. Story."

15. Stuart Silverstein, "L.A. Federation Labor Vote Divides Along Ethnic Lines," *Los Angeles Times*, April 17, 1996, http://articles.latimes.com/1996-04-17/business/fi-59484_1_county-federation.

16. SAJE's main focus was protecting low-income communities from displacement by real estate development and gentrification. See Pastor, Benner, and Matsuoka, *This Could Be the Start of Something Big*, 126–130.

17. Julian Gross, Greg LeRoy, and Madeline Janis-Aparicio, *Community Benefit Agreements: Making Development Projects Accountable* (Los Angeles: Good Jobs First and the California Partnership for Working Families, 2005), 29–32. Underscoring that the deal was in Los Angeles, the final agreement even included permit parking for neighborhood residents.

18. Lee Romney, "Community, Developers Agree on Staples Plan," *Los Angeles Times*, May 31, 2001.

19. See Greg LeRoy, *The Great American Jobs Scam: Corporate Tax Dodging and the Myth of Job Creation* (San Francisco: Berrett-Koehler, 2005), and Richard McGahey, "Regional Economic Development in Theory and Practice," in *Retooling for Growth: Building a 21st Century Economy in America's Older Industrial Areas*, ed. Richard McGahey and Jennifer Vey (Washington, DC: Brookings Institution, 2008): 3–32.

20. See chapter 8 for a discussion of CBAs as a policy tool.

21. Information technology (IT) jobs were 32 percent of total payroll in the Bay Area compared to 10 percent in Southern California. See Mary Daly and Fred Furlong, "Profile of a Recession: U.S. and California," *FRBSF Economic Letter* no. 2002–4 (2002), https://www.frbsf.org/economic-research/publications/economic-letter/2002/february/profile-of-a-recession-the-us-and-california/.

22. "Employment by Industry Data," for Los Angeles County (Los Angeles-Long Beach-Glendale MD), accessed on November 29, 2019, https://www.labormarketinfo.edd.ca.gov/data/employment-by-industry.html.

23. Kfir Mordechay, *Vast Changes and an Uneasy Future: Racial and Regional Inequality in Southern California* (Los Angeles: Civil Rights Project/Proyecto Derechos Civiles, 2014), 29, table 8.; U.S. Bureau of the Census, *Quick Facts: Los Angeles County, California*, December 2020, https://www.census.gov/quickfacts/fact/table/losangelescountycalifornia/RHI725219.

24. Raphael J. Sonenshein and Susan H. Pinkus, "The Dynamics of Latino Political Incorporation: The 2001 Los Angeles Mayoral Election as Seen in *Los Angeles Times* Exit Polls," *PS: Political Science & Politics* 35, no. 1 (March 2002): 67–74.

25. Robert Gottlieb, Mark Vallianatos, Regina M. Freer, and Peter Dreier, *The Next Los Angeles: The Struggle for a Livable City* (Berkeley: University of California Press, 2005).

26. See Manuel Pastor, Jr., *Racial/Ethnic Inequality in Environmental-Hazard Exposure in Metropolitan Los Angeles* (Berkeley: California Policy Research Center, 2001), 1–38.

27. John M. Broder, "Los Angeles Groups Agree to Airport Growth, for a Price," *New York Times*, December 17, 2004.

28. See Los Angeles World Airports, *Community Benefits Agreement—LAX Master Plan Program*, Los Angeles, 2004, 1–35, https://www.lawa.org/-/media/lawa-web/lawa-our-lax/lax_cba_final.ashx.

29.	Kevin Klowden and Perry Wong, *Los Angeles Economy Project: Executive Summary and Recommendations* (Santa Monica, CA: Milken Institute, 2005), 15.

30.	Daniel Flaming, *Poverty, Inequality, and Justice: A Vanishing Middle Class in Southern California* (Los Angeles: Economic Roundtable, 2006), 3, 8.

31.	Raphael J. Sonenshein and Susan H. Pinkus, "Latino Incorporation Reaches the Urban Summit: How Antonio Villaraigosa Won the 2005 Los Angeles Mayor's Race," *PS: Political Science and Politics* 38, no. 4 (October 2005): 718.

32.	John Mollenkopf, Ana Champeny, Raphael Sonenshein, and Mark Drayse, "Race, Ethnicity, and Immigration in the 2005 Mayoral Elections in Los Angeles and New York," Working Paper 2007–07 (Berkeley: Berkeley Institute of Urban and Regional Development, University of California, December 2006), http://iurd.berkeley.edu/wp/2007-07.pdf; Matea Gold, "Labor to Bolster Hahn Endorsement," *Los Angeles Times*, March 11, 2005.

33.	Villaraigosa also was close to progressive intellectuals around the city and region and had spent time as a fellow at the USC Center for Sustainable Cities. Pastor, Benner, and Matsuoka, *This Could Be the Start of Something Big*, 139, see note 40; Peter Dreier, E.P. Clapp Distinguished Professor of Politics, Politics, Urban and Environmental Policy, Occidental College, interview with Richard McGahey, July 28, 2014. See also Peter Dreier, "Judging Mister Mayor: Los Angeles Magazine's Rip of Antonio Villaraigosa Put in Perspective," *LA Progressive*, June 22, 2009, http://www.laprogressive.com/judging-mister-mayor-los-angeles-magazines-rip-of-antonio-villaraigosa-put-in-perspective/.

34.	Bureau of Transportation Statistics, United States Department of Transportation, "Top U.S. Foreign Trade Gateways by Value of Shipment," table 1–51, December 20, 2020, https://www.bts.gov/content/top-us-foreign-trade-freight-gateways-value-shipments-current-billions. Reflecting U.S. trade imbalances, over 80 percent of the total shipment value through the ports came from imports.

35.	Jessica Durrum, "Building a Sturdy Blue-Green Coalition at the Ports of Los Angeles and Long Beach," *Progressive Planning*, no. 197 (2013): 12–16.

36.	Jon Zerolnick, *The Road to Shared Prosperity: The Regional Economic Benefits of the San Pedro Bay Ports' Clean Trucks Program* (Los Angeles: Los Angeles Alliance for a New Economy, 2007).

37.	American Trucking Association, Inc. v. the City of Los Angeles, 660 F.3d 384 (9th Cir. 2011).

38.	Rebecca Smith, Paul Alexander Marvy, and Jon Zerolnick, *The Big Rig Overhaul: Restoring Middle Class Jobs at America's Ports Through Labor Law Enforcement* (New York: National Employment Law Project, 2014).

39.	Sierra Club California, "Letter from Sacramento: A Bill That Works for the Environment and Workers," August 25, 2019, https://www.sierraclub.org/california/letter-sacramento-bill-works-for-environment-and-workers.

40.	Margot Roosevelt, "As L.A. Ports Automate, Some Workers Are Cheering on the Robots," *Los Angeles Times*, November 7, 2019; International Brotherhood of Teamsters, "California Port Truck Drivers Awarded over $1.2 Million for Wage Theft," *Teamsters News*, April 17, 2019, https://teamster.org/news/2019/04/california-port-truck-drivers-awarded-over-12-million-wage-theft.

41.   Madeline Janis, quoted in Meyerson, "L.A. Story."

42.   The two-thirds requirement is a legacy of 1978's Proposition 13, a sweeping constitutional amendment that capped property taxes and imposed the two-thirds limit for tax approval on the state legislature as well as on local governments.

43.   Miguel A. Santana, *City of Los Angeles: Four-Year Budget Outlook and Update to the Three-Year Plan to Fiscal Sustainability* (Los Angeles: City of Los Angeles, 2012), 46. See attachment 1.

44.   David Zahniser, "L.A. City Employees Receive Last in a Costly Series of Raises," *Los Angeles Times*, January 1, 2014.

45.   Susan K. Urahn, Michael Ettlinger, Kil Huh, Alyssa Lee, and Matt Separa, *Understanding the Great Recession's Impact on City Bond Issuances* (Washington, DC: Pew Charitable Trusts, 2013).

46.   Given the two-thirds vote needed for approval, the labor issues were not negotiated until after the tax increase passed because proponents feared it might hurt the initiative's prospects. Beth Steckler, deputy director, Move LA, interview with Richard McGahey, July 22, 2014.

47.   Los Angeles County Metropolitan Transit Authority, *Project Labor Agreement*, January 26, 2012 (Los Angeles: Los Angeles County Metropolitan Transit Authority, 2012), http://media.metro.net/about_us/pla/images/Project_Labor_Agreement.pdf. For the training and careers provisions, see Los Angeles County Metropolitan Transit Authority, *General Management–Construction Careers Project* (Los Angeles: Los Angeles County Metropolitan Transit Authority, 2012).

48.   Dale Belman and Matthew M. Bodah, *Building Better: A Look at Best Practices for the Design of Project Labor Agreements*, Briefing Paper 274 (Washington, DC: Economic Policy Institute, August 2010).

49.   Other projects in the region also used project labor agreements (PLAs), such as the LAX Airport PLA, which was extended in 2011 and included a 30 percent local hiring preference. See Jackelyn Cornejo, *Moving L.A. Forward: Promoting Construction Careers at Metro* (Los Angeles: Los Angeles Alliance for a New Economy, 2011.)

50.   Madeline Janis, cofounder and national policy director, Los Angeles Alliance for a New Economy, interview with Richard McGahey, July 10, 2014. Roxana Tynan, executive director, Los Angeles Alliance for a New Economy, interview with Richard McGahey, July 16, 2014. See also "*How We Win, What We Do*," Los Angeles Alliance for a New Economy, https://web.archive.org/web/20151127012631/http://www.laane.org/what-we-do/how-we-win/.

51.   Quoted in Steven Greenhouse, *Beaten Down, Worked Up: The Past, Present, and Future of American Labor* (New York: Alfred A. Knopf, 2019), 283.

52.   Michael Finnegan, "Labor Money Starts Flowing in for Garcetti," *Los Angeles Times*, April 6, 2013.

53.   John Buntin, "Does Eric Garcetti Have a Big Enough Vision for L.A.?," *Governing*, August 2014, https://www.governing.com/topics/mgmt/gov-eric-garcetti-los-angeles-mayor.html; Los Angeles 2020 Commission, *A Time for Truth* (Los Angeles: Los Angeles 2020 Commission, 2013), 1, 2, https://zwartztalk.files.wordpress.com/2015/10/2020-commission-time-for-truth.pdf.

54. Los Angeles 2020 Commission, *A Time for Action* (Los Angeles: Los Angeles 2020 Commission, 2014), https://www.socalgrantmakers.org/sites/default/files/resources/A-Time-For-Action%20LA%202020%20Report%20April%202014.pdf.

55. Garcetti appointed Greg Good, who directed LAANE's waste and recycling project, as his Director of Infrastructure, with duties including the implementation of the new trash policy.

56. In 2008, the national Teamsters Union withdrew support for oil drilling in the Arctic National Wildlife Refuge (ANWR). General Secretary James Hoffa said that "our future lies in a green economy," citing the LA port coalition on how labor and environmental groups can work together. See Evelyn Larrubia, "Labor, Environmentalists Unusual Allies," *Los Angeles Times*, November 27, 2008.

57. Los Angeles Bureau of Sanitation, *Request for Proposals: City-Wide Exclusive Franchise System for Municipal Solid Waste Collection and Handling* (Los Angeles: Los Angeles Bureau of Sanitation, 2014), 7, 12.

58. Patrick Murphy and Jennifer Paluch, *Just the Facts: Financing California's Public Schools* (San Francisco: Public Policy Institute of California, 2018).

59. PolicyLink and USC Program for Environmental and Regional Equity, *An Equity Profile of the Los Angeles Region* (Oakland, CA: PolicyLink, 2017), 3.

60. Manuel Pastor, *State of Resistance: What California's Dizzying Descent and Remarkable Resurgence Mean for America's Future* (New York: The New Press, 2018), 162.

61. Joint Center for Housing Studies, *The State of the Nation's Housing 2019* (Cambridge, MA: Joint Center for Housing Studies of Harvard University, 2019); Hadley Mears, "Cranes Proliferated in L.A. But Don't Call It a Building Boom," *Curbed Los Angeles*, January 2, 2020, https://la.curbed.com/2020/1/2/21034785/los-angeles-development-housing-shortage; California Association of Realtors, "Housing Affordability Index—Traditional," December 27, 2020, https://www.car.org/marketdata/data/haitraditional/.

62. Randy Shaw, "California Progressives Split Over SB9 and SB10," *LA Progressive*, August 28, 2021, https://www.laprogressive.com/end-exclusionary-zoning/.

63. City of Los Angeles, "Covid-19: Keeping Los Angeles Safe: Data—Health and Wellness," https://corona-virus.la/data; Committee for Greater LA, *No Going Back*, 23, figure 3; County of Los Angeles, Public Health, *LA County Daily Covid-19 Data*, "Death Rates," December 27, 2020, http://www.ph.lacounty.gov/media/Coronavirus/data/index.htm#.

7. ECONOMICS AND EQUITY

1. Joseph E. Stiglitz, "Moving Beyond Market Fundamentalism to a More Balanced Economy," *Annals of Public and Cooperative Economics* 80, no. 3, 2009: 345.

2. United States Census Bureau, "Quick Facts. Los Angeles city, California; New York city, New York; Detroit city, Michigan," December 28, 2020, https://www.census.gov/quickfacts/fact/table/losangelescitycalifornia,newyorkcitynewyork,detroitcitymichigan,MI/PST045219.

3. William Neuman and J. David Goodman, "In City Council, Power Shifts away from Progressives," *New York Times*, February 2, 2018.

4. Frank Levy and Peter Temin, "Inequality and Institutions in 20th Century America," Working Paper 13106, National Bureau of Economic Research, May 2007. 30.

5. United States Census Bureau, "Quick Facts."

6. Fernando E. Gapasin, "The Los Angeles County Federation of Labor: A Model of Transformation or Traditional Unionism?," in *Central Labor Councils and the Revival of American Unionism: Organizing for Justice in Our Communities*, ed. Immanuel Ness and Stuart Eimer (New York: Routledge, 2001), 79–101.

7. Organization of Economic Cooperation and Development (OECD), "Income inequality," accessed May 19, 2022, https://data.oecd.org/inequality/income-inequality.htm.

8. Max Roser and Esteban Ortiz-Ospina, "Income Inequality," *Our World in Data*, last modified October 2016, https://ourworldindata.org/income-inequality/#redistribution-through-tax-and-transfer-policies.

9. Robert Rowthorn and Ramana Ramaswamy, "Deindustrialization–Its Causes and Implications" (Washington, DC: International Monetary Fund, 1997), https://www.imf.org/EXTERNAL/PUBS/FT/ISSUES10/INDEX.HTM.; Robert E. Scott, *The Manufacturing Footprint and Importance of U.S. Manufacturing Jobs*, Briefing Paper 388, Economic Policy Institute, Washington, DC, January 2015.

10. Barry Bluestone and Bennett Harrison, *The Great U-Turn: Corporate Restructuring and the Polarizing of America* (New York: Basic Books, 1988); Barry Bluestone, "The Inequality Express," *The American Prospect*, December 10, 2001.

11. National Employment Law Project, *The Low-Wage Recovery: Industry Employment and Wages Four Years into the Recovery* (New York: National Employment Law Project, 2014).

12. Seung Jin Cho, Jun Yeong Lee, and John V. Winters. "Employment Impacts of the COVID-19 Pandemic Across Metropolitan Status and Size," IZA Discussion Paper 13468, July 2020.

13. Phillip Bump, "To Avoid Removal, Trump Needs Senators Representing only 7 Percent of the Country to Support Him," *Washington Post*, December 19, 2019.

14. Edward Glaeser, *Triumph of the City: How Our Greatest Invention Makes Us Richer, Smarter, Greener, Healthier, and Happier* (New York: Penguin Press, 2011), 264.

15. Daniel L. Thornton, "The Dual Mandate: Has the Fed Changed Its Objective?," *Review—Federal Reserve Bank of St. Louis* 94, no. 2 (March/April 2012): 117; Aaron Steelman, "The Federal Reserve's 'Dual Mandate': The Evolution of an Idea," Economic Brief EB11-12, Federal Reserve Bank of Richmond, Richmond, VA, December 2011.

16. On Federal Reserve targeting, see James K. Galbraith, Olivier Giovannoni, and Ann J. Russo, "The Fed's *Real* Reaction Function: Monetary Policy, Unemployment, Inequality—and Presidential Politics," Working Paper 511, Levy Economics Institute of Bard College, Bard College, Annandale-on-Hudson, New York, August 2007. Emphasis in original. On labor force impacts, see Seth B. Carpenter and William M. Rodgers III, "The Disparate Labor Market Impacts of Monetary Policy," *Journal of Policy Analysis and Management* 23, no. 4 (September 2004): 813–830.

17. Katherine Bradbury, "State Government Budgets and the Recovery Act," Public Policy Brief 10–1, Federal Reserve Bank of Boston, Boston, MA, February 2010, 2.

18. Paul Krugman, "Fifty Herbert Hoovers," *New York Times*, December 28, 2008.

19. Hillary Rodham Clinton, "Give New York Its Fair Share of Homeland Money," opinion, *New York Times*, August 22, 2004.

20. Sarah Bartlett, "Federal Aid Cutback in '80's Hurt New York City," *New York Times*, May 26, 1991; Nelson A. Rockefeller Institute of Government, *Giving and Getting: Regional Distribution of Revenue and Spending in the New York State Budget, Fiscal Year 2009–10* (Albany: State University of New York at Albany, 2011); Richard McGahey calculations from Lincoln Institute of Land Policy, "Fiscally Standardized Cities," https://www.lincolninst.edu/research-data/data-toolkits/fiscally-standardized-cities.

21. Congressional Research Service, *Federal Grants to State and Local Governments: A Historical Perspective on Contemporary Issues*, updated May 22, 2019, Washington, DC: 2019; David E. Wildasin, "Intergovernmental Transfers to Local Governments," in *Municipal Revenues and Land Policies*, ed. Gregory K. Ingram and Yu-Hung Hong (Cambridge, MA: Lincoln Institute of Land Policy, 2010), 53. Rising federal health care payments do flow partly to cities through the health care system.

22. Mike Maciag and J. B. Wogan, "With Less State Aid, Localities Look for Ways to Cope," *Governing*, February 2017, http://www.governing.com/topics/finance/gov-state-aid-revenue-sharing-intergovernmental-revenue.html.

23. The White House, "Reviewing Federal Funding to State and Local Government Recipients," Washington DC, September 2, 2020, https://www.whitehouse.gov/presidential-actions/memorandum-reviewing-funding-state-local-government-recipients-permitting-anarchy-violence-destruction-american-cities/; Richard McGahey, "Covid's Comeback Means Washington Must Help Red and Blue States—Now," *Forbes*, December 8, 2020, https://www.forbes.com/sites/richardmcgahey/2020/12/08/both-red-and-blue-states-need-federal-money-now/?sh=6448d90c7c64.

24. Howard Chernick, David Copeland, and Andrew Reschovsky, "The Fiscal Effects of the COVID-19 Pandemic on Cities," *National Tax Journal*, 73 no. 3 (September 2020): 699–732; Richard McGahey, "Why Didn't COVID-19 Wreck State and City Budgets?: Federal Spending," *Forbes*, September 1, 2021, https://www.forbes.com/sites/richardmcgahey/?sh=170de00644a2.

25. David Autor, David Dorn, and Gordon H. Hanson, "The China Syndrome: Local Labor Market Effects of Import Competition in the United States," *American Economic Review* 103, no. 6 (October 2013): 2121–2168; Robert E. Scott and Zane Mokhiber, "Growing China Trade Deficit Cost 3.7 Million American Jobs Between 2001 and 2018," Economic Policy Institute, January 30, 2020; Joel Cutcher-Gershenfeld, Dan Brooks, and Martin Mulloy, "The Decline and Resurgence of the U.S. Auto Industry," Briefing Paper 399, Economic Policy Institute, May 2015, 3.

26. David C. Perry and Alfred J. Watkins, *The Rise of the Sunbelt Cities* (Beverly Hills, CA: Sage, 1977); Laura Schultz and Michelle Cummings, "Giving or Getting?: New York's Balance of Payments with the Federal Government," SUNY Rockefeller Institute of Government, January 2020, table 7, 20, https://rockinst.org/wp-content/uploads/2020/01/1-22-20-Balance-of-Payments.pdf.

27. Economic Policy Institute, "The Productivity-Pay Gap," updated August 2021, http://www.epi.org/productivity-pay-gap/.

28. Siavash Radpour and Teresa Ghilarducci, *Gaps in Retirement Savings Based on Race, Ethnicity, and Gender*, Testimony to 2021 Advisory Council on Employee Welfare and Pension Benefit Plans, US Department of Labor, Washington DC, August 26, 2021.

29. On executive compensation and corporate policies, see William Lazonick, "Labor in the Twenty-First Century: The Top 0.1 Percent and the Disappearing Middle Class," Working Paper 4, Institute for New Economic Thinking, New York City, February 2015.

30. Margaret Weir, "Central Cities' Loss of Power in State Politics," *Cityscape: A Journal of Policy Development and Research* 2, no. 2 (May 1996): 23–40.

31. Reynolds v. Sims, 377 U.S. 533 (1964); Morris K. Udall, "Reapportionment I: 'One Man, One Vote' . . . That's All She Wrote!," October 14, 1964, Special Collections at the University of Arizona Libraries, University of Arizona, transcript, http://speccoll.library .arizona.edu/online-exhibits/files/original/11ac559f0063813f0a80bed401b4597f.pdf.

32. Weir, "Central Cities' Loss of Power in State Politics," 23.

33. John Forrest Dillon, *Treatise on the Law of Municipal Corporations* (Chicago: James Cockroft, 1872), https://babel.hathitrust.org/cgi/pt?id=inu.39000007582039;view=1up; seq=4.

34. Economic Policy Institute, "Worker Rights Preemption in the U.S.," August 2019, https:// www.epi.org/preemption-map/.

35. Myron Orfield, *American Metropolitics: The New Suburban Reality* (Washington, DC: Brookings Institution, 2002), 132, see table 7–1.

36. Richard McGahey calculations from Lincoln Institute of Land Policy, "Fiscally Standardized Cities Data Base," accessed December 28, 2020, https://www.lincolninst.edu /research-data/data-toolkits/fiscally-standardized-cities.

37. Orfield, *American Metropolitics*, 55; Urban Institute, *State and Local Finance Initiative* (Washington DC: Urban Institute, 2019), https://www.urban.org/policy-centers/cross -center-initiatives/state-and-local-finance-initiative/about.

38. National Center for Education Statistics, "Concentration of Public School Students Eligible for Free or Reduced-Price Lunch," Institute for Education Studies, https://nces.ed.gov /programs/coe/indicator_clb.asp; Sheila E. Murray, Kim Rueben, and Carol Rosenberg, "State Education Spending: Current Pressures and Future Trends," *National Tax Journal* 60, no. 2 (June 2007): 325, https://www.urban.org/sites/default/files/publication /31091/1001132-State-Education-Spending-Current-Pressures-and-Future-Trends.PDF, see table 1.

39. Greg LeRoy, Allison Lack, and Karla Walter, with Philip Mattera, *The Geography of Incentives: Economic Development and Land Use in Michigan* (Washington, DC: Good Jobs First, 2006), 1, 39. They also argue the pattern "is hardly unique to Michigan" and cite evidence from several other states.

40. Bryce Covert, "Cities Should Stop Playing the Amazon HQ2 Bidding Game," *New York Times*, November 13, 2018.

41. Yael T. Abouhalkah, "Applebee's Profits from Tax Breaks, Then Says Bye-Bye to Kansas City," *Kansas City Star*, September 4, 2015.

42. Douglas S. Massey and Nancy A. Denton, *American Apartheid: Segregation and the Making of the Underclass* (Cambridge, MA: Harvard University Press, 1993), 217. Racism pervades many sectors besides housing. For a provocative study of how race affects municipal bond decisions and markets, see Destin Jenkins, *The Bonds of Inequality: Debt and the Making of the American City* (Chicago: University of Chicago Press, 2021).

43. Richard Rothstein, *The Color of Law: A Forgotten History of How Our Government Segregated America* (New York: Norton, 2017).

44. Keenaga-Yamahtta Taylor, *Race for Profit: How Banks and the Real Estate Industry Undermined Black Homeownership* (Chapel Hill: University of North Carolina Press, 2019).

45. Leah Platt Boustan, "Was Postwar Suburbanization 'White Flight'?: Evidence from the Black Migration," *Quarterly Journal of Economics* 125, no. 1 (February 2010): 417, 419; Trevon M. Logan and John M. Parman, "The National Rise in Residential Segregation," *Journal of Economic History*, 77 no. 1 (March 2017): 167.

46. Natalia Kolesnikova and Yang Liu, "A Bleak Thirty Years for Black Men: Economic Progress Was Slim in Urban America," *Regional Economist*, Federal Reserve Bank of St. Louis, 2010, 9.

47. Elise Gould and Valerie Wilson, "The Black Unemployment Rate Returns to Historic Low, but Not Really," *Working Economics Blog*, Economic Policy Institute, July 7, 2017; Lincoln Quillian, Devah Pager, Ole Hexel, and Arnfinn H. Midtbøen, "Meta-Analysis of Field Experiments Shows No Change in Racial Discrimination in Hiring over Time," *Proceedings of the National Academy of Sciences* 114, no. 41 (October 2017): 10870–10875; Heather Long and Andrew Van Dam, "The Black-White Economic Divide Is as Wide as It Was in 1968," *Washington Post*, June 4, 2020.

48. Center on Budget and Policy Priorities, "Tracking the COVID-19 Recession's Impact on Food, Housing, and Employment Hardships," December 18, 2020, https://www.cbpp .org/research/poverty-and-inequality/tracking-the-covid-19-recessions-effects-on-food -housing-and.

49. Mike Maciag, "Black and Out of Work: How the Recession Changed Government Employment," *Governing*, December 2015, http://www.governing.com/topics/mgmt/gov -minorities-public-employment-recession.html.

50. Elizabeth Kneebone, "Job Sprawl Revisited: The Changing Geography of Metropolitan Employment, *Metropolitan Opportunity Series*, Brookings Institution, April 2009. The Great Recession slowed "job sprawl" because jobs declined in residential construction and related sectors. See Elizabeth Kneebone, "Job Sprawl Stalls: The Great Recession and Metropolitan Employment Location," *Metropolitan Opportunity Series*, Brookings Institution, April 2013.

51. Richard McGahey, "Back to Office Work, With (or Without) a Covid-19 Vaccine," *Forbes*, November 11, 2020, https://www.forbes.com/sites/richardmcgahey/2020/11/11/back-to -office-work-with-or-without-a-vaccine/?sh=5030c480c455.

52. Milliken v. Bradley, 418 US 717 (1974); C. Kirabo Jackson, Rucker C. Johnson, and Claudia Persico, "The Effects of School Spending on Educational and Economic Outcomes: Evidence from School Finance Reforms," *Quarterly Journal of Economics* 131 no. 1 (February 2016): 157–218; Richard Rothstein, "The Racial Achievement Gap, Segregated Schools, and Segregated Neighborhoods—a Constitutional Insult," *Race and Social Problems* 7, no. 1 (March 2015): 21.

53. Janelle Jones and John Schmitt, *A College Degree Is No Guarantee* (Washington, DC: Center for Economic and Policy Research, 2014), 11, 13.

54. Eric S. Rosengren, "Educational Attainment and Economic Outcomes," April 5, 2013, Early Childhood Summit 2013: Innovation and Opportunity, Federal Reserve Bank of Boston,

transcript and video, https://www.bostonfed.org/news-and-events/speeches/educational
-attainment-and-economic-outcomes.aspx.; Ian Appel and Jordan Nickerson, "Pockets
of Poverty: The Long-Term Effects of Redlining," Working Paper, Boston College, Chestnut Hill, Massachusetts, October 2016, http://dx.doi.org/10.2139/ssrn.2852856.; Darrick
Hamilton, William A. Darity, Jr., Anne E. Price, Vishnu Sridharan, and Rebecca Tippett, *Umbrellas Don't Make It Rain: Why Studying and Working Hard Isn't Enough for
Black Americans* (Oakland, CA: Insight Center for Community Economic Development,
2015), 1–10; William H. Frey, *A 2020 Census Portrait of America's Largest Metro Areas:
Population Growth, Diversity, Segregation, and Youth* (Washington, DC: Metropolitan
Policy Program, Brookings Institution, April 2022), 18.

55. Michael Storper, "Why Do Regions Develop and Change?: The Challenge for Geography
and Economics," *Journal of Economic Geography* 11, no. 2 (2011): 333.

56. Jon Gertner, "Home Economics," *New York Times Magazine*, March 5, 2006, 1.

57. Edward Glaeser, "The Economics Approach to Cities," NBER Working Paper 13696,
National Bureau of Economic Research, Cambridge, MA, December 2007, 26.

58. See Thomas L. Friedman, *The World Is Flat: A Brief History of the Twenty-First Century*
(New York: Farrar Strauss, and Giroux, 2005); Joel Kotkin, "Urban Legends," *Foreign Policy*, August 6, 2010, http://joelkotkin.com/00276-urban-legends-why-suburbs-not-dense
-cities-are-future/.

59. United States Conference of Mayors, "U.S. Metro Economies and GMP Report: 2018–
2020," September 2019, https://www.usmayors.org/wp-content/uploads/2019/09/mer
-2019-09.pdf.

60. Jonathan Miller, "Peak Suburb Has Passed," *Matrix Blog: Interpreting the Real Estate
Economy*, December 28, 2020, https://www.millersamuel.com/peak-suburb-has-passed
/?goal=0_69c077008e-7e05894f5d-120793247; Richard Florida, "This Is Not the End of
Cities," *Bloomberg CityLab*, June 19, 2020, https://www.bloomberg.com/news/features
/2020-06-19/cities-will-survive-pandemics-and-protests?sref=6sywTjmH; David Autor
and Elisabeth Reynolds, *The Nature of Work After the COVID Crisis: Too Few Low-Wage
Jobs*, The Hamilton Project, July 2020.

61. Luke Rogers, "COVID-19, Declining Birth Rates, and International Migration Resulted in
Historically Small Population Gains," U.S. Census Bureau, December 21, 2021; William H.
Frey, "2020 Census: Big Cities Grew and Became More Diverse, Especially Among Their
Youth," Brookings Institution, October 21, 2021, https://www.brookings.edu/research/2020
-census-big-cities-grew-and-became-more-diverse-especially-among-their-youth/.

62. William H. Frey, "New census data shows a huge spike in movement out of big metro areas
during the pandemic," *The Avenue* blog, https://www.brookings.edu/blog/the-avenue
/2022/04/14/new-census-data-shows-a-huge-spike-in-movement-out-of-big-metro-areas
-during-the-pandemic/. For an argument that COVID-19 and working from home are
causing more significant population shifts, see Adam Ozimek, "How Remote Work is
Shifting Population Growth Across the U.S.," Economic Innovation Group, April 13,
2022. https://eig.org/how-remote-work-is-shifting-population-growth-across-the-u-s/.

63. Enrico Moretti, *The New Geography of Jobs* (New York: Houghton Mifflin Harcourt,
2012), 5.

64. Enrico Moretti, "Human Capital Externalities in Cities," in *Handbook of Regional and Urban Economics*, ed. J. Vernon Henderson and Jacques-François Thisse (Amsterdam: Elsevier B.V., 2004), vol. 4, 2243–2291; John V. Winters, "Human Capital Externalities and Employment Differences Across Metropolitan Areas of the U.S.," Discussion Paper 6869, Institute for the Study of Labor, Bonn, Germany, September 2012; Peter Ganong and Daniel Shoag, "Why Has Regional Convergence in the U.S. Stopped?," HKS Faculty Research Working Paper RWP12-028, John F. Kennedy School of Government, Harvard University, June 2012.

65. Moretti, *The New Geography of Jobs*, 230.

66. Glaeser, "The Economics Approach to Cities," 30–31. The classic article is Charles M. Tiebout, "A Pure Theory of Local Expenditures," *Journal of Political Economy* 64, no. 5 (October 1956): 416–424.

67. Rudiger Ahrend, Emily Farchy, Ioannis Kaplanis, and Alexander C. Lembecke, "What Makes Cities More Productive?: Agglomeration Economies and the Role of Urban Governance: Evidence from 5 OECD Countries," Discussion Paper 178, Spatial Economics Research Center (SERC), July 2015; Nestor M. Davidson and Sheila R. Foster, "The Mobility Case for Regionalism," *University of California at Davis Law Review* 47, no. 1 (November 2013): 63–120.

68. Moretti, *The New Geography of Jobs*, on Gates, 75, on Shockley, 186. On state taxes, see Enrico Moretti and Daniel J. Wilson, "The Effect of State Taxes on the Geographical Location of Top Earners: Evidence from Star Scientists," *American Economic Review* 107, no. 7 (2017): 1901.

69. On Silicon Valley's growth, see AnnaLee Saxenian, *Regional Advantage: Culture and Competition in Silicon Valley and Route 128* (Cambridge, MA: Harvard University Press, 1996). On defense spending and the rise of Silicon Valley, see Margaret Pugh O'Mara, *Cities of Knowledge: Cold War Science and the Search for the Next Silicon Valley* (Princeton, NJ: Princeton University Press, 2005). On Seattle, see Sharon Boswell and Lorraine McConaghy, "A Silicon Forest Grows," *Seattle Times*, December 1, 1996.

70. Mariana Mazzucato, *The Entrepreneurial State: Debunking Public vs. Private Sector Myths* (London: Anthem Press, 2013); William H. Janeway, *Doing Capitalism in the Innovation Economy: Markets, Speculation, and the State* (Cambridge: Cambridge University Press, 2012).

71. Alan Berube, Elizabeth Deakin, and Steven Raphael, "Socioeconomic Differences in Household Automobile Ownership Rates: Implications for Evacuation Policy," Working Paper 804, University of California Transportation Center, University of California at Berkeley, December 2007.

72. Daniel Aaronson, Daniel Hartley, and Bhashkar Mazumder, "The Effect of the 1930s HOLC 'Redlining' Maps," Working Paper 2017-12, Federal Reserve Bank of Chicago, Chicago, 2017, 32, 33; Manuel Pastor Jr., Rachel Morello-Frosch, and James L. Sadd, "The Air Is Always Cleaner on the Other Side: Race, Space, and Ambient Air Toxics Exposure in California," *Journal of Urban Affairs* 27, no. 2 (June 2005): 127–148.

73. Moretti, *The New Geography of Jobs*, 246; Rothstein, "The Racial Achievement Gap," 1; William R. Emmons and Lowell R. Ricketts, "College Is Not Enough: Higher Education

Does Not Eliminate Racial and Ethnic Wealth Gaps," *Federal Reserve Bank of St. Louis REVIEW* 99, no. 1 (2017): 7–39.

74. Lisa D. Cook, "Violence and Economic Activity: Evidence from African-American Patents, 1870–1940," *Journal of Economic Growth* 19, no. 2 (May 2014): 221–257.

75. Leah Platt Boustan, *Competition in the Promised Land: Black Migrants in Northern Cities and Labor Markets* (Princeton, NJ: Princeton University Press, 2016); Ellora Derenoncourt and Claire Montialoux, "Minimum Wages and Racial Inequality," Working Paper, Washington Center for Equitable Growth, January 2020; Price B. Fishback, Jessica LaVoice, Allison Shertzer, and Randall Walsh, "Race, Risk, and the Emergence of Federal Redlining," Working Paper 28146, National Bureau of Economic Research, November 2020.

76. This is the Kuznets curve, the basis of 1971 Nobel laureate Simon Kuznets's research and analysis in development economics. Simon Kuznets, "Economic Growth and Income Inequality," *American Economic Review* 45, no. 1 (March 1955): 1–28.

77. Estelle Sommeiller, Mark Price, and Ellis Wazeter, *Income Inequality in the U.S. by State, Metropolitan Area, and County* (Washington, DC: Economic Policy Institute, 2016), 4. Region-specific data can be found at Economic Policy Institute data, http://go.epi.org /unequalstates2016data; Lane Kenworthy, "America's Great Decoupling," in *Inequality and Inclusive Growth in Rich Countries*, ed. Brian Nolan (New York: Oxford University Press), 336; Carter C. Price and Kathryn A. Edwards, "Trends in Income from 1975 to 2018," WR-A516-1, RAND Corporation, September 2020.

78. Economic Policy Institute, "The Productivity-Pay Gap," August 2021, https://www.epi .org/productivity-pay-gap/; Josh Bivens and Lawrence Mishel, "Understanding the Historic Divergence Between Productivity and a Typical Worker's Pay: Why It Matters and Why It's Real," Briefing Paper 406, Economic Policy Institute, Washington, DC, September 2015, 3, 18–19, 23, https://www.epi.org/files/2015/understanding-productivity-pay -divergence-final.pdf.

79. Anna Stansbury and Lawrence Summers, "The Declining Worker Power Hypothesis: An Explanation for the Recent Evolution of the American Economy," *Brookings Papers on Economic Activity* (Spring 2020): 1–77

80. Chris Benner and Manuel Pastor, *Just Growth: Inclusion and Prosperity in America's Metropolitan Regions* (London: Routledge, 2012), 1, 148.

81. Jonathan D. Ostry, Andrew Berg, and Charalambos G. Tsangarides, *Redistribution, Inequality, and Growth* (Washington, DC: International Monetary Fund, 2014); Federico Cinango, "Trends in Income Inequality and Its Impact on Economic Growth," OECD Social, Employment and Migration Working Paper 163, Organization for Economic Co-operation and Development, Paris, 2014.

82. Chris Benner and Manuel Pastor, *Equity, Growth, and Community: What the Nation Can Learn from America's Metro Areas* (Oakland: University of California Press, 2015), 26–27. Among her many important works, see Elinor Ostrom, *Governing the Commons: The Evolution of Institutions for Collective Action* (New York: Cambridge University Press, 1990).

8. ECONOMICS AND POLICY: WHAT CAN CITIES DO?

1. Tim Besley and Peter Hennessy to Queen Elizabeth II, July 22, 2009, British Academy, http://wwwf.imperial.ac.uk/~bin06/M3A22/queen-lse.pdf.

2. Some of that hubris may stem from economists using relatively more sophisticated quantitative methods and large, complex data sets. Economists' empirical strengths were on display during the COVID-19 pandemic, when the National Bureau of Economic Research posted over 520 working papers on pandemic-related research through February 2022. National Bureau of Economic Research, "COVID-19," https://www.nber.org/topics/covid-19?page=1&perPage=50.

3. Edward Glaeser, "The Economics Approach to Cities," NBER Working Paper 13696, National Bureau of Economic Research, Cambridge, MA, December 2007, 28, 29, 31.

4. The many dimensions of inequality include voting and political power, criminal justice, and widespread racial discrimination and gender bias. Scholars recognize these intersect with economic issues, and the analysis is beyond the scope of this chapter. See Marlene Kim, "Intersectionality and Gendered Racism in the United States: A New Theoretical Framework," *Review of Radical Political Economics* 52, no. 4 (2020): 616–625.

5. Michael D. Farren and Matthew D. Mitchell, "Targeted Economic Development Subsidies Don't Work," *Policy Spotlight*, Mercatus Center, George Mason University, August 2020, https://www.mercatus.org/system/files/farren_and_mitchell_-_policy_spotlight_-_targeted_economic_development_subsidies_dont_work_but_an_interstate_compact_could_end_them_-_v1.pdf; Greg LeRoy, *The Great American Jobs Scam: Corporate Tax Dodging and the Myth of Job Creation* (San Francisco: Berrett-Koehler, 2005); Alan Peters and Peter Fisher, "The Failure of Economic Development Incentives," *Journal of the American Planning Association* 70, no. 1 (2004): 32.

6. Even before the headquarters subsidy battle, Amazon was on track to surpass Walmart's record of over $1.2 billion in forty years from a variety of tax preferences, dedicated infrastructure spending, and financial assistance. See Thomas Cafcas and Greg LeRoy, *Will Amazon Fool Us Twice?: Why State and Local Governments Should Stop Subsidizing the Online Giant's Growing Distribution Network* (Washington, DC: Good Jobs First, 2016), 1–25, https://www.goodjobsfirst.org/sites/default/files/docs/pdf/amazon-subsidies.pdf.; Janelle Jones and Ben Zipperer, "Unfilled Promises: Amazon Fulfillment Centers Do Not Create Broad-Based Employment Growth" (Washington, DC: Economic Policy Institute, 2018), 1–27, https://www.epi.org/files/pdf/138921.pdf.

7. Timothy J. Bartik, "Using Place-Based Jobs Policies to Help Distressed Communities," *Journal of Economic Perspectives* 34, no. 3 (Summer 2020): 102; Joseph Kernan quoted in Louis Uchitelle, "States Pay for Jobs, but It Doesn't Always Pay Off," *New York Times*, November 10, 2003.

8. Michael Greenstone, Richard Hornbeck, and Enrico Moretti, "Identifying Agglomeration Spillovers: Evidence from Winners and Losers of Large Plant Openings," *Journal of Political Economy* 118, no. 3 (June 2010): 536–598; Amihai Glazer and Nicholas Kumamoto, "Factors Determining Plant Locations and Plant Survival," Working Paper, Program in Corporate Welfare, University of California at Irvine, January 14, 2020.

9.   David Neumark and Jed Kolko, "Do Enterprise Zones Create Jobs? Evidence from Cal-
     ifornia's Enterprise Zone Program," *Journal of Urban Economics* 68, no. 1 (2010): 1–19;
     Brett Theodos, Eric Hangen, Jorge Gonzalez, and Bradley Meixell, *An Early Assessment
     of Opportunity Zones for Equitable Development* (Washington, DC: Urban Institute, June
     17, 2020.

10. David Neumark and Helen Simpson, "Place-Based Policies," in *Handbook of Regional
     and Urban Economics*, ed. Giles Duranton, J. Vernon Henderson, and William C. Strange
     (Amsterdam: NL, 2015), vol. 5, 1279; David Wessel, "Opportunity Zones: David Wessel's
     Testimony before the Subcommittee on Oversight, House Ways and Means," Brookings
     Institution, November 16, 2021, https://www.brookings.edu/testimonies/opportunity
     -zones-david-wessels-testimony-before-the-subcommittee-on-oversight-house-ways
     -means/.

11. Arthur J. Rolnick and Melvin L. Burstein, "Congress Should End the Economic War
     Among the States," Federal Reserve Bank of Minneapolis, January 1, 1995, https://www
     .minneapolisfed.org/article/1995/congress-should-end-the-economic-war-among-the
     -states. The classic theoretical statement is Charles M. Tiebout, "A Pure Theory of Public
     Expenditures," *Journal of Political Economy* 64, no. 5 (October 1956): 416–424, which has
     been criticized for depending on restrictive assumptions to generate optimally efficient
     outcomes. See Joseph Stiglitz, "The Theory of Local Public Goods Twenty-Five Years
     After Tiebout," in *Local Provision of Public Services: The Tiebout Model After Twenty-Five
     Years*, ed. George R. Zodrow (New York: Academic Press, 1983), 17–53.

12. Glaeser, "The Economics Approach to Cities," 5, 26; Enrico Moretti, *The New Geography
     of Jobs* (New York: Houghton Mifflin Harcourt, 2012), 161.

13. Bartik, "Using Place-Based Jobs Policies"; Benjamin Austin, Edward Glaeser, and Law-
     rence Summers. "Jobs for the Heartland: Place-Based Policies in 21st-Century America,"
     Brookings Papers on Economic Activity (2018): 151–232.

14. David Neumark and Timothy J. Bartik, "Improving the Effectiveness of Place-Based
     Policies to Address Poverty and Joblessness," in "Point/Counterpoint," ed. Paul Decker,
     Journal of Policy Analysis and Management 39, no. 3 (May 2020): 853, 845. Emphasis in
     original.

15. Partnership for Working Families, *Common Challenges in Negotiating Community
     Benefit Agreements—and How to Avoid Them* (Oakland, CA: Partnership for Working
     Families, 2016), 1–21, Vicki Been, "Community Benefits Agreements: A New Local Gov-
     ernment Tool or Another Variation on the Exactions Theme?," *University of Chicago Law
     Review* 77, no. 1 (2010), 5–35; Edward W. De Barbieri, "Do Community Benefits Agree-
     ments Benefit Communities?," *Cardozo Law Review* 37, no. 5 (June 2016): 1773–1825.

16. Jobs to Move America, "US Employment Plan," April 10, 2020, https://jobstomoveamerica
     .org/resource/u-s-employment-plan-2/; Roderick M Hills, Jr., and David Schleicher,
     "Building Coalitions Out of Thin Air: Transferable Development Rights and 'Constitu-
     ency Effects' in Land Use Law," Journal of Legal Analysis 12 (2020): 79–135.

17. Katrina Liu and Robert Danewood, "Local Hiring and First Source Hiring Policies: A
     National Review of Policies and Identification of Best Practices" (Pittsburgh, PA: Regional

Housing Legal Services, 2013), http://rhls.org/wp-content/uploads/First-Source-Hiring-Overview-RHLS.pdf.

18. Richard McGahey, "Regional Economic Development in Theory and Practice," in *Retooling for Growth: Building a 21st-Century Economy in America's Older Industrial Areas*, ed. Richard McGahey and Jennifer S. Vey (Washington DC: Brookings Institution), 3–32.

19. Michael R. Betz, Mark D. Partridge, David S. Kraybill, and Linda Lobao, "Why Do Localities Provide Economic Development Incentives?: Geographic Competition, Political Constituencies, and Government Capacity," *Growth and Change* 43, no. 3 (2012): 361–391; DaimlerChrysler Corp. v. Cuno, 547 U.S. 332 (2006); Walter Hellerstein, "Cuno and Congress: An Analysis of Proposed Federal Legislation Authorizing State Economic Development Incentives," *Georgetown Journal of Law and Public Policy* 4, no. 1 (2006): 73–100.

20. Madeline Janis, "Community Benefits: New Movement for Equitable Urban Development," *Race, Poverty, and the Environment* 15, no. 1 (2008): 73–75; Indivar Dutta-Gupta, Kali Grant, Matthew Eckel, and Peter Edelman, *Lessons Learned from 40 Years of Subsidized Employment Programs: A Framework, Review of Models, and Recommendations for Helping Disadvantaged Workers* (Washington, DC: Georgetown University Center on Poverty and Inequality, 2016), http://www.georgetownpoverty.org/wp-content/uploads/2017/03/GCPI-Subsidized-Employment-Exec-Summary-20160419.pdf.

21. Joan Fitzgerald, *Greenovation: Urban Leadership on Climate Change* (New York: Oxford University Press, 2020).

22. Pavlina R. Tcherneva, *The Case for a Job Guarantee* (Medford, MA: Polity Press, 2020); Alan J. Aja, Darrick Hamilton, and William A. Darity, Jr., "How Cities Can Do Better Than the Fight for $15," *Yes!*, October 6, 2017, https://www.yesmagazine.org/economy/2017/10/06/how-cities-and-towns-can-do-better-than-the-fight-for-15/.

23. Richard McGahey, "The Political Economy of Cities," Schwartz Center for Economic Policy Analysis, New School for Social Research, November 24, 2020, https://www.economicpolicyresearch.org/resource-library/research/inequality-and-austerity-the-political-economy-of-cities.

24. For an overview, see Mike Fishman, Dan Bloom, and Sam Elkin, *Employment and Training Programs Serving Low-Income Populations: Next Steps for Research*, OPRE Report 2020–72, Office of Planning, Research, and Evaluation, Administration for Children and Families, U.S. Department of Health and Human Services, June 2020; on sectoral training, see Sheila McGuire, Joshua Freely, Carol Clymer, Maureen Conway, and Deena Schwartz, *Tuning In to Local Labor Markets: Findings from the Sectoral Employment Impact Study* (Philadelphia, PA: Public/Private Ventures, 2010); on intermediaries and "dual customers," see Anne Roder and Mark Elliott, *Eleven Year Gains: Project QUEST's Investment Continues to Pay Dividends*, Economic Mobility Corporation, September 2021.

25. Paul Osterman, "The Promise, Performance, and Policies of Community Colleges," in *Reinventing Higher Education: The Promise of Innovation*, ed. Ben Wildavsky, Andrew P. Kelly, and Kevin Carey (Cambridge, MA: Harvard Education Press, 2011): 129–158.

26. Annette Bernhardt and Paul Osterman, "Organizing for Good Jobs: Recent Development and New Challenges," *Work and Occupations* 44, no. 1 (February 2017): 89–112; Lawrence Mishel, "Rebuilding Worker Power," *Finance and Development*, International Monetary Fund, December 2020.

27. Milton Friedman, *Capitalism and Freedom* (Chicago: University of Chicago Press, 1962), 148.

28. David Card and Alan B. Krueger, "Minimum Wages and Employment: A Case Study of the Fast-Food Industry in New Jersey and Pennsylvania," *American Economic Review* 84, no. 4 (1994): 772–792. The current debate is largely fought out over methods and data. See, for example, David Neumark, J.M. Ian Salas, and William Wascher, "More on Recent Evidence on Effects of Minimum Wages in the United States," *IZA Journal of Labor Policy* 3, no. 24 (2014): 1–26; John Schmitt, *Why Does the Minimum Wage Have No Discernable Effect on Employment?* (Washington, DC: Center for Economic and Policy Research, 2013).

29. Arindrajit Dube, *Impacts of Minimum Wages: Review of the International Evidence*, HM Treasury, November 2019, https://assets.publishing.service.gov.uk/government/uploads /system/uploads/attachment_data/file/844350/impacts_of_minimum_wages_review_of _the_international_evidence_Arindrajit_Dube_web.pdf, 4; David Neumark and Peter Shirley, "Myth or Measurement: What Does the New Minimum Wage Research Say About Minimum Wages and Job Loss in the United States?," Working Paper 28388, National Bureau of Economic Research, January 2021.

30. "Minimum Wage Tracker," Economic Policy Institute, January 1, 2022, https://www.epi .org/minimum-wage-tracker/.

31. Yuki Noguchi, "As Cities Raise Minimum Wages, Many States Are Rolling Them Back," *National Public Radio*, July 18, 2017, https://www.npr.org/2017/07/18/537901833/as-cities -raise-minimum-wages-many-states-are-rolling-them-back; Arindrajit Dube and Attila S. Lindner, "City Limits: What Do Local-Area Minimum Wages Do?," Working Paper 27928, National Bureau of Economic Research, November 2020, https://www.nber.org /papers/w27928.

32. Economic Policy Institute, "Worker Rights Preemption in the U.S." January 2022, https:// www.epi.org/preemption-map/.

33. Morris M. Kleiner, *Reforming Occupational Licensing Policies*, Working Paper 2005–01, Hamilton Project, Brookings Institute, Washington, DC, March 2015, 6; Morris M. Kleiner and Alan B. Krueger, "Analyzing the Extent and Influence of Occupational Licensing on the Labor Market," *Journal of Labor Economics* 31, no. 2, part 2 (April 2013): S173–S202; Tyler Cowen, "A Radical Solution to the Overuse of Occupational Licensing," *Bloomberg Opinion*, March 5, 2018, https://www.bloomberg.com/view/articles/2018 -03-05/tyler-cowen-s-radical-idea-for-reining-in-occupational-licensing.

34. Beth Avery and Han Lu, "Ban the Box: U.S. Cities, Counties, and States Adopt Fair Hiring Policies," National Employment Law Project, October 1, 2021.

35. Mike Konczal and Marshall Steinbaum, "Declining Entrepreneurialism, Labor Mobility, and Business Dynamism: A Demand-Side Approach," Working Paper, Roosevelt Institute, New York City, July 2016.

36. All-in Cities, *Policy Solutions to Raise the Floor on Low-Wage Work*, PolicyLink, October 30, 2019, https://allincities.org/equity-in-action/webinars/raise-floor-low-wage-work.

37. Abbie Langston, Justin Scoggins, and Matthew Walsh, *Race and the Work of the Future: Advancing Workforce Equity in the United States* (Los Angeles: PolicyLink and the USC Equity Research Institute, 2020), 51.

38. Edward Glaeser, "How Skyscrapers Can Save the City," *The Atlantic*, March 2011.

39. Matson Boyd, "What Does Progressive Urban Planning Look Like?: Why Radicals Should Steer Clear of Homeowner Politics," *Center for Popular Economics* (blog), June 18, 2014, http://www.populareconomics.org/what-does-progressive-urban-planning-look-like-why-radicals-should-steer-clear-of-homeowner-politics/.

40. William H. Frey, "Pandemic Population Change Across Metro America: Accelerated Migration, Less Immigration, Fewer Births and More Deaths," Metropolitan Policy Program, Brookings Institution, May 20, 2021, https://www.brookings.edu/research/pandemic-population-change-across-metro-america-accelerated-migration-less-immigration-fewer-births-and-more-deaths/; Madison Hoff, "Housing in the US Has Not Been Able to Keep Up with Buyer Demand over the Past Decade," *Business Insider*, September 27, 2020.

41. Don Chen, "Linking Transportation Equity and Environmental Justice with Smart Growth," in *Growing Smarter: Achieving Livable Communities, Environmental Justice, and Regional Equity*, ed. Robert D. Bullard (Cambridge MA: MIT Press, 2007), 299–322.

42. Paul Krugman, "Why Can't We Get Cities Right?," *New York Times*, September 4, 2017.

43. Joseph Gyourko and Raven Molloy, "Regulation and Housing Supply," in *Handbook of Regional and Urban Economics*, ed. Giles Duranton, J. Vernon Henderson, and William C. Strange (Amsterdam: NL, 2015), vol. 5, 1291.

44. See the debate between advocate Tom Angiotti and former de Blasio housing commissioner Vicki Been in Tom Angiotti, "Zoned Out in the City: New York City's Tale of Race and Displacement," and Vicki Been, "The Clear and Present Danger of Supply Skepticism," *Poverty & Race* 26, no. 1 (January–March 2017); Noah Smith, "The Left-NIMBY Canon," *Noahpinion*, January 19, 2021, https://noahpinion.substack.com/p/the-left-nimby-canon?; Henry Grabar, "San Francisco's Civil War," *Slate*, June 2017, http://www.slate.com/articles/business/metropolis/2017/06/yimbys_and_the_dsa_can_t_get_along_despite_their_common_enemy_high_rent.html.

45. "Housing Policy in New York City: A Brief History," Working Paper 06–01, Furman Center for Real Estate and Urban Policy, New York University, April 2006.

46. Emma Zehner, "Opening Doors," *Land Lines: Quarterly Magazine of the Lincoln Institute of Land Policy* 32, no. 4 (October 2020): 8–19.

47. Robert Collinson, Ingrid Gould Ellen, and Jens Ludwig, "Low-Income Housing Policy," Working Paper 21071, National Bureau of Economic Research, April 2015, 1.

48. Alexius Marcano, Matthew Festa, and Kyle Shelton, *Developing Houston: Land-Use Regulation in the "Unzoned City" and Its Outcomes* (Houston: Rice University, 2017), 18.

49. Edward Glaeser, *Triumph of the City: How Our Greatest Invention Makes Us Richer, Smarter, Greener, Healthier, and Happier* (New York: Penguin Press, 2011), 210; Chang-Tai Hsieh and Enrico Moretti, "Housing Constraints and Spatial Misallocation," *American Economic Journal: Macroeconomics* 11, no. 2 (April 2019): 1–39,

50. Citizens Budget Commission, *Strategies to Boost Housing Production in the New York City Metropolitan Area*, August 2020, https://cbcny.org/sites/default/files/media/files /CBC_NYC-Housing-Production_08262020_0.pdf; Brian Uhler and Justin Garosi, "Building Permits Update: July 2019," California Legislative Analyst's Office, September 3, 2019, https://lao.ca.gov/LAOEconTax/Article/Detail/397.

51. Noah Kazis, *Ending Exclusionary Zoning in New York City's Suburbs*, Furman Center for Real Estate and Urban Policy, New York University, November 9, 2020.

52. Kriti Ramakrishnan, Mark Treskon, and Solomon Green, "Inclusionary Zoning: What Does the Research Tell Us About the Effectiveness of Local Action?," Research to Action Lab, Urban Institute, January 2019; Terner Center for Housing Innovation, "Affordable Housing Overlay Zones: Oakley," Terner Center Case Studies, University of California at Berkeley, April 2019.

53. Edward Glaeser quoted in Richard Florida, "Two Takes on the Fate of Future Cities," *CityLab*, April 21, 2017, https://www.citylab.com/equity/2017/04/two-takes-on-the-fate -of-future-cities/521907/; Stockton Williams, Ian Carlton, Lorelei Juntunen, Emily Picha, and Mike Wilkerson, *The Economics of Inclusionary Development* (Washington, DC: Urban Land Institute, 2016).

54. Subsidies also can support profit-making development even if market conditions aren't encouraging new construction. See Rachel Weber, *From Boom to Bubble: How Finance Built the New Chicago* (Chicago: University of Chicago Press, 2015).

55. Randy Shaw, *Generation Priced Out: Who Gets to Live in the New Urban America* (Oakland: University of California Press, 2018).

56. Liam Dillon and Taryn Luna, "California Bill to Dramatically Increase Home Building Fails for the Third Year in a Row," *Los Angeles Times*, January 30, 2020; Richard McGahey, "New California Laws Attack the State's Housing Crisis," *Forbes*, September 27, 2021, https://www.forbes.com/sites/richardmcgahey/2021/09/27/new-california-laws-attack -the-states-housing-crisis/?sh=2290b79d3166.

57. Michael Manville, "Liberals and Housing: A Study in Ambivalence," *Housing Policy Debate*, May 15, 2021, https://doi.org/10.1080/10511482.2021.1931933.

58. David Schleicher, "City Unplanning," *Yale Law Journal* 122, no. 7 (May 2013): 1703; Michael Zonta, *Expanding the Supply of Affordable Housing for Low-Wage Workers* (Washington, DC: Center for American Progress, August 10, 2020); Shaw, *Generation Priced Out*.

59. Diana Budde, "AOC Is a YIMBY Now," *Curbed*, January 13, 2022.

60. Quentin Brummet and Davin Reed, "The Effects of Gentrification on the Well-Being and Opportunity of Original Resident Adults and Children," Working Paper 19-30, Federal Reserve Bank of Philadelphia, July 2019; Kacie Dragan, Ingrid Ellen, and Sherry A. Glied, "Does Gentrification Displace Poor Children?: New Evidence from New York City Medicaid Data," Working Paper 25809, National Bureau of Economic Research, May 2019.

61. Glaeser, "The Economics Approach to Cities," "increase choices," 26; "doubts," 28.

62. Paul Krugman, "The New Economic Geography, Now Middle-Aged," *Regional Studies* 45, no. 1 (2011): 4.

63. Michael Storper, "From Retro to Avant-garde: A Commentary on Paul Krugman's 'The New Economic Geography, Now Middle-Aged,'" *Regional Studies* 45, no. 1 (2011): 10.

64. Chris Benner and Manuel Pastor, "Solidarity Economics—for the Coronavirus Crisis and Beyond," *The American Prospect*, March 23, 2020. The framework is amplified in Chris Benner and Manuel Pastor, *Solidarity Economics: Why Mutuality and Movements Matter* (Cambridge: Polity Press, 2021).

65. Emmanuel Saez, "Public Economics and Inequality: Uncovering Our Social Nature," Working Paper 28387, National Bureau of Economic Research, January 2021.

66. William A. Darity, Jr., Darrick Hamilton, and James B. Stewart, "A Tour de Force in Understanding Intergroup Inequality: An Introduction to Stratification Economics," *Review of Black Political Economy* 42 (2015): 3; Stephanie Seguino, "Feminist and Stratification Theories' Lessons from the Crisis and Their Relevance for Post-Keynesian Theory," *European Journal of Economics and Economic Policies* 16, no. 2 (2019): 195; Nancy Folbre, *Greed, Lust, and Gender* (New York: Oxford University Press, 2009).

67. Michael Storper, *Keys to the City: How Economics, Institutions, Social Interaction, and Politics Shape Development* (Princeton, NJ: Princeton University Press, 2013), 5.

68. W. Walker Hanlon and Stephan Heblich, "History and Urban Economics," Working Paper 27850, National Bureau of Economic Research, September 2020.

69. June Sekera, "Why Aren't We Talking About Public Goods?," Demos, September 20, 2013, https://www.demos.org/blog/why-arent-we-talking-about-public-goods.

9. EPILOGUE: CAN CITIES FIGHT INEQUALITY ON THEIR OWN?

1. National League of Cities, "Federal Budget Tracker," October 8, 2020, https://www.nlc.org/resource/federal-budget-tracker/; Aidan Quigley, "Why Trump's Budget Terrifies America's Mayors," *Politico*, April 24, 2017, https://www.politico.com/magazine/story/2017/04/24/donald-trump-budget-mayors-215067; William H. Frey, "A Substantial Majority of Americans live outside Trump counties, Census shows," *The Avenue* blog, Brookings Institution Metropolitan Policy Program, March 23, 2017, https://www.brookings.edu/blog/the-avenue/2017/03/23/a-substantial-majority-of-americans-live-outside-trump-counties-census-shows/.

2. Congressional Research Service, *"Sanctuary" Jurisdictions: Federal, State, and Local Policies and Related Litigation*, Report R44795, updated May 3, 2019.

3. Richard McGahey, "In Debate, Trump Says Biden's Fair Housing Plans Will Destroy the Suburbs," *Forbes*, September 30, 2020, https://www.forbes.com/sites/richardmcgahey/2020/09/30/in-debate-trump-says-bidens-housing-plans-will-destroy-the-suburbs/?sh=1dd86a4b5b4c.

4. Center on Budget and Policy Priorities, *Tracking the Covid-19 Recession's Effects on Food, Housing, and Employment Hardships*, January 2021, https://www.cbpp.org/sites/default/files/atoms/files/8-13-20pov.pdf.

5. Joseph Benitez, Charles Courtemanche, and Aaron Yelowitz, "Racial and Ethnic Disparities in Covid-19: Evidence from Six Large Cities," *Journal of Economics, Race, and Policy* 3 (2020): 243–261.

6. George W. McCarthy and Samuel A. Moody, "Introduction," in *Land and the City*, ed. George W. McCarthy, Gregory K. Ingram, and Samuel A. Moody (Cambridge, MA: Lincoln Institute of Land Policy, 2016), 4.

7. Susan Lund, "What 800 Executives Envision for the Post-Pandemic Workforce," McKinsey Global Institute, September 23, 2020; Future Forum, "Leveling the Playing Field in the Hybrid Workplace," Winter 2021/2022 Future Forum Pulse Survey, January 2022, https://futureforum.com/wp-content/uploads/2022/01/Future-Forum-Pulse-Report -January-2022.pdf.

8. Richard Florida, "This Is Not the End of Cities," *Bloomberg CityLab*, June 19, 2020, https://www.bloomberg.com/news/features/2020-06-19/cities-will-survive-pandemics -and-protests?sref=oEW1j8fJ.

9. William H. Frey, "Despite the Pandemic Narrative, Americans Are Moving at Historically Low Rates," Brookings Institution, November 30, 2021; Arjun Ramani and Nicholas Bloom, "The Donut Effect of COVID-19 on Cities," Working Paper 28876, National Bureau of Economic Research, May 2021.

10. Erika Poethig, Solomon Greene, Christina Stacy, Tanaya Srini, Brady Meixell, Steven Brown, and Diana Elliott, *Inclusive Recovery in US Cities* (Washington, DC: Urban Institute, 2018), 40.

11. Christina McFarland and Michael A. Pagano, *City Fiscal Conditions* (Washington, DC: National League of Cities, 2017), https://www.nlc.org/sites/default/files/2017-09 /NLC%20City%20Fiscal%20Conditions%202017.pdf; OECD, *Making Cities Work for All: Data and Actions for Inclusive Growth* (Paris: OECD Publishing, 2016), http://dx.doi .org/10.1787/9789264263260-en.

12. Richard McGahey, "Biden's Essential Stimulus Won't Solve State and City Budget Problems," *Forbes*, January 15, 2021, https://www.forbes.com/sites/richardmcgahey/2021/01/15 /bidens-essential-stimulus-wont-solve-state-and-city-budget-problems/?sh=57d0e58a3154.

13. Zolan Kanno-Youngs and Madeline Ngo, "Racial Equity in Infrastructure, a U.S. Goal, Is Left to States," *New York Times*, November 16, 2021.

14. William H. Frey, "Even as Metropolitan Areas Diversify, White Americans Still Live in Mostly White Neighborhoods," Metropolitan Policy Program, Brookings Institution, March 23, 2020, https://www.brookings.edu/research/even-as-metropolitan-areas-di versify-white-americans-still-live-in-mostly-white-neighborhoods/.

15. Office of Management and Budget, *Study to Identify Methods to Assess Equity: Report to the President* (Washington, DC: Executive Office of the President, July 20, 2021), 4; Erika Bernabei, *Racial Equity: Getting to Results*, Government Alliance for Race and Equity, July 2017; PolicyLink, *For Love of Country: A Path for the Federal Government to Advance Racial Equity*, July 2021; Jonathan Goldberg, Jeffrey Jiménez-Kurlander, and Silvana Serifimovska, *Measuring Together: A Learning Approach for Inclusive Economies*, The Surdna Foundation, January 2022, https://surdna.org/wp-content/uploads/2022/01 /Measuring-Together_-A-Learning-Approach-For-Inclusive-Economies-1.pdf.

16. National Law Review, "The Sixth Circuit Holds Argument on the Tax Mandate," January 26, 2022, https://www.natlawreview.com/article/sixth-circuit-holds-argument-tax-mandate.

17. Bruce Katz and Jeremy Nowak, *The New Localism* (Washington DC: Brookings Institution, 2017), 243; Economic Development Administration, "$1B Build Back Better Regional Challenge," U.S. Department of Commerce, December 13, 2021, https://eda.gov/arpa/build-back -better/; Richard McGahey, "Can Our Fragmented Metropolitan Regions Work Together?," *Forbes*, March 21, 2022, https://www.forbes.com/sites/richardmcgahey/2022/03/21/can -our-fragmented-metropolitan-regions-work-together/?sh=7386ce8633d6.

18. Yoav Hagler, *America 2050: Defining U.S. Megaregions* (New York: Regional Plan Association, 2009), 1–8.

19. Garrett Dash Nelson and Alasdair Rae, "An Economic Geography of the United States: From Commutes to Megaregions," *PLoS ONE* 11, no. 11 (2016): 20, doi:10.1371/journal .pone.0166083. Some very sparsely populated areas, Alaska and Hawaii, and a few areas with very diverse commuting patterns, were not assigned to any specific region. But the analysis represents 97.4% of all commuter flows in the lower 48 states.

20. Manuel Pastor, *State of Resistance: What California's Dizzying Descent and Remarkable Resurgence Mean for America's Future* (New York: The New Press, 2018).

21. David F. Damore, Robert E. Lang, and Karen A. Danielsen, *Blue Metros, Red States: The Shifting Urban-Rural Divide in America's Swing States* (Washington, DC: Brookings Institution, 2021); Tim Henderson, "Slicing up Liberal Cities Becomes Go-To Redistricting Strategy," Stateline, Pew Memorial Trusts, September 22, 2021, https://www.pewtrusts.org /en/research-and-analysis/blogs/stateline/2021/09/22/slicing-up-liberal-cities-becomes -go-to-redistricting-strategy;nashville gerrymandering times; Michael Wines, "In Nashville, a Gerrymander Goes Beyond Politics to the City's Core," *New York Times*, February 18, 2022, https://www.nytimes.com/2022/02/18/us/nashville-gerrymandering-republican -democrat.html.

22. Raj Chetty, John N. Friedman, Nathaniel Hendren, Maggie R. Jones, and Sonya R. Porter, "The Opportunity Atlas: Mapping the Childhood Roots of Social Mobility." Working Paper 25147, National Bureau of Economic Research, October 2018.

23. David H. Autor, "Work of the Past, Work of the Future," Richard T. Ely Lecture, *AEA Papers and Proceedings 2019*, 109, 22; David R. Howell and Arne L. Kalleberg, "Declining Job Quality in the United States: Explanations and Evidence," *RSF: The Russell Sage Journal of the Social Sciences* 5, no. 4 (September 2019): 43.

24. Edward L. Glaeser, "Urbanization and Its Discontents," *Eastern Economic Journal* 46 (2020): 12.

25. Richard McGahey, "De Blasio Economics: Growth with Equity," *City and State*, September 26, 2014, https://www.cityandstateny.com/articles/policy/de-blasio-economics-growth -with-equity.html.

BIBLIOGRAPHY

Aaronson, Daniel, Daniel Hartley, and Bhashkar Mazumder. "The Effect of the 1930s HOLC 'Redlining' Maps." Working Paper 2017-12, Federal Reserve Bank of Chicago, 2017.

Abouhalkah, Yael T. "Applebee's Profits from Tax Breaks, Then Says Bye-Bye to Kansas City." *Kansas City Star*, September 4, 2015.

Adams, Valerie. "Civil Defense." In *Encyclopedia of the Cold War*, ed. Ruud van Dijk, 164. New York: Routledge, 2008.

Adelman, Robert M., and James Clarke Gocker. "Racial Residential Segregation in Urban America." *Sociological Compass* 1, no. 1 (2007): 404–423.

Advisory Commission on Intergovernmental Relations. *Central City-Suburban Fiscal Disparity and City Distress, 1977*. Washington, DC: U.S. Government Printing Office, 1980.

Aguilar, Louis. "Detroit Sale of $135m in Bonds to Fund Dozens of Projects." *Detroit News*, December 5, 2018.

Ahlfeldt, Gabriel M., and Elisabetta Pietrostefani. "The Economic Effects of Density: A Synthesis." *Journal of Urban Economics* 111 (May 2019): 93–107.

Ahrend, Rudiger, Emily Farchy, Ioannis Kaplanis, and Alexander C. Lembecke. "What Makes Cities More Productive? Agglomeration Economies and the Role of Urban Governance: Evidence from 5 OECD Countries." Discussion Paper 178, Spatial Economics Research Center (SERC), London School of Economics, July 2015.

Airgood-Obrycki, Whitney. "Suburban Status and Neighborhood Change." *Urban Studies* 56, no. 14 (November 2019): 2935–2952.

Aja, Alan J., Darrick Hamilton, and William A. Darity, Jr. "How Cities Can Do Better Than the Fight for $15." *Yes!* (October 6, 2017). http://www.yesmagazine.org/economy/2017/10/06 /how-cities-and-towns-can-do-better-than-the-fight-for-15/.

All-in Cities. *Policy Solutions to Raise the Floor on Low-Wage Work*. PolicyLink, October 30, 2019. https://allincities.org/equity-in-action/webinars/raise-floor-low-wage-work.

Alonso, William. *Location and Land Use: Towards a General Theory of Land Rent.* Cambridge, MA: Harvard University Press, 1964.

Altshuler, Alan, William Morrill, Harold Wolman, and Faith Mitchell. "Central Cities, Suburbs, and Metropolitan-Area Problems." In *Governance and Opportunity in Metropolitan America,* ed. Alan Altshuler, William Morrill, Harold Wolman, and Faith Mitchell, 22–39. Washington, DC: National Academy Press, 1999.

American Trucking Association, Inc. v. the City of Los Angeles, 660 F.3d 384 (9th Cir. 2011).

Angiotti, Tom. "Zoned Out in the City: New York City's Tale of Race and Displacement." *Poverty and Race* 26 no. 1 (January–March 2017): 1, 12–15.

Appel, Ian, and Jordan Nickerson. "Pockets of Poverty: The Long-Term Effects of Redlining." Working Paper, Boston College, Chestnut Hill, MA, October 2016.

Armstrong, Amy, Vicki Been, Caroline H. Bhalla, Ingrid Gould Ellen, Allegra Glashausser, Simon McDonnell, Mary Weselcouch, Benjamin Winter, and Courtney Wolf. *State of New York's Housing and Neighborhoods, 2008.* Furman Center for Real Estate and Urban Policy, New York University, 2008.

Arun, Peter Lobo, and Joseph J. Salvo. *The Newest New Yorkers 2000: Immigrant New York in the New Millennium.* New York City Department of City Planning, 2004.

Ashenfelter, David. "Handshake Deal with State Haunts Detroit." *Bridge Magazine,* March 15, 2013, https://www.bridgemi.com/michigan-government/handshake-deal-state-haunts-detroit.

Atkinson, Robert D., and Stephen J. Ezel. *Innovation Economics: The Race for Global Advantage.* New Haven, CT: Yale University Press, 2012.

Austin, Benjamin, Edward Glaeser, and Lawrence Summers. "Jobs for the Heartland: Place-Based Policies in 21st-Century America." *Brookings Papers on Economic Activity* (Spring 2018): 151–232.

Autor, David H. "Work of the Past, Work of the Future." Richard T. Ely Lecture, *AEA Papers and Proceedings 2019,* 109: 1–32.

Autor, David H., David Dorn, and Gordon H. Hanson. "The China Syndrome: Local Labor Market Effects of Import Competition in the United States." *American Economic Review* 103, no. 6 (October 2013): 2121–2168.

Autor, David, and Elisabeth Reynolds. *The Nature of Work After the COVID Crisis: Too Few Low-Wage Jobs.* Washington, DC: The Hamilton Project, July 2020.

Avery, Beth, and Han Lu. *Ban the Box: U.S. Cities, Counties, and States Adopt Fair Hiring Policies.* Washington, DC: National Employment Law Project, October 1, 2021.

Baker, Bruce D. *School Funding Fairness in New York State: An Update for 2013–14.* Albany, NY: Alliance for Quality Education, 2014.

Baradaran, Mehersa. *The Color of Money: Black Banks and the Racial Wealth Gap.* Cambridge, MA: Harvard University Press, 2017.

Barbanel, Josh. "Control Board Is Re-Emerging as Power Focus." *New York Times,* October 9, 1990.

Barkholz, David. "Casino Foes Set to Play Ace in Hole: Petition Drive Seeks Repeal of Proposal E." *Crain's Detroit Business,* November 17, 1997.

Barrow, Heather B. "'The American Disease of Growth': Henry Ford and the Metropolitanization of Detroit, 1920–1940." In *Manufacturing Suburbs: Building Work and Home on the Metropolitan Fringe,* ed. Robert D. Lewis, 200–220. Philadelphia: Temple University Press.

Bartik, Timothy J. "Using Place-Based Jobs Policies to Help Distressed Communities." *Journal of Economic Perspectives* 34, no. 3 (Summer 2020): 99–127.

Bartlett, Sarah. "Federal Aid Cutback in '80's Hurt New York City." *New York Times*, May 26, 1991.

Batty, Michael, Ella Deeken, and Alice Henriques Volz. "Wealth Inequality and COVID-19: Evidence from the Distributional Financial Accounts." *Feds Notes*, Board of Governors of the Federal Reserve System, August 30, 2021.

Bayer, Patrick, and Kerwin Kofi Charles. "Divergent Paths: Structural Change, Economic Rank, and the Evolution of Black-White Earnings Differences, 1940–2014." Working Paper 22797, National Bureau of Economic Research, November 2016.

Beauregard, Robert A. *When America Became Suburban*. Minneapolis: University of Minnesota Press, 2006.

Becker, Gary. *Human Capital: A Theoretical and Empirical Analysis with Special Reference to Education*. Chicago: University of Chicago Press, 1994.

Been, Vicki. "The Clear and Present Danger of Supply Skeptics." *Poverty & Race* 26, no. 1 (January–March 2017): 2, 15–16.

Been, Vicki. "Community Benefits Agreements: A New Local Government Tool or Another Variation on the Exactions Theme?" *University of Chicago Law Review* 77, no. 1. (2010): 5–35.

Been, Vicki, Mark A. Levine, Ross Moskowitz, Wesley O'Brien, and Ethel Sheffer. *The Role of Community Benefits Agreements in New York City's Land Use Process*. New York City Bar Association, 2010.

Been, Vicki, and Simon McDonnell "How Have Recent Rezonings Affected the City's Ability to Grow?" Policy Brief, Furman Center for Real Estate and Urban Policy, New York University, March 2010.

Belman, Dale, and Matthew M. Bodah. *Building Better: A Look at Best Practices for the Design of Project Labor Agreements*. Briefing Paper No. 274, Economic Policy Institute, August 2010.

Bender, Thomas. *The Unfinished City: New York and the Metropolitan Idea*. New York: New York University Press, 2007.

Benner, Chris, and Manuel Pastor. *Equity, Growth, and Community: What the Nation Can Learn from America's Metro Areas*. Oakland: University of California Press, 2015.

Benner, Chris, and Manuel Pastor. *Just Growth: Inclusion and Prosperity in America's Metropolitan Regions*. London: Routledge, 2012.

Benner, Chris, and Manuel Pastor. "Solidarity Economics—for the Coronavirus Crisis and Beyond." *The American Prospect*, March 23, 2020.

Benner, Chris, and Manuel Pastor. *Solidarity Economics: Why Mutuality and Movements Matter*. Cambridge: Polity Press, 2021.

Bennett, Drake, and Mark Niquette. "Detroit Is Dead. Long Live Oakland County." *Bloomberg Businessweek*, July 25, 2013. https://www.bloomberg.com/news/articles/2013-07-25/detroit-is-dead-dot-long-live-oakland-county.

Bennett, Robert J. "SN 7154—Urban Population Database, 1801–1911." Working Paper, University of Cambridge, 2012. http://doc.ukdataservice.ac.uk/doc/7154/mrdoc/pdf/guide.pdf.

Benzow, August, and Kenan Fikri. *The Expanded Geography of High-Poverty Neighborhoods*. Washington, DC: Economic Innovation Group, May 2020.

Berestein, Leslie. "Coalition Aims to Show the 'Other' Los Angeles." *Los Angeles Times*, September 3, 1995.

Bernabei, Erika. *Racial Equity: Getting to Results*. Government Alliance on Race and Equity, Othering and Belonging Institute, University of California at Berkeley, July 2017.

Bernhardt, Annette, and Paul Osterman. "Organizing for Good Jobs: Recent Development and New Challenges." *Work and Occupations* 44, no. 1 (February 2017): 89–112.

Berube, Alan, Elizabeth Deakin, and Steven Raphael. "Socioeconomic Differences in Household Automobile Ownership Rates: Implications for Evacuation Policy." Working Paper 804, University of California Transportation Center, University of California at Berkeley, December 2007.

Besley, Tim, and Peter Hennessy. "Letter to Her Majesty the Queen." British Academy, London, July 22, 2009. http://wwwf.imperial.ac.uk/~bin06/M3A22/queen-lse.pdf.

Betz, Michael R., Mark D. Partridge, David S. Kraybill, and Linda Lobao. "Why Do Localities Provide Economic Development Incentives? Geographic Competition, Political Constituencies, and Government Capacity." *Growth and Change*, 43, no. 3 (2012): 361–391.

Biles, Roger. *Mayor Harold Washington: Champion of Race and Reform in Chicago*. Urbana: University of Illinois Press, 2018.

Bivens, Josh, and Lawrence Mishel. "Understanding the Historic Divergence Between Productivity and a Typical Worker's Pay: Why It Matters and Why It's Real." Briefing Paper 406, Economic Policy Institute, Washington, DC, September 2015.

Bloomberg, Michael. "State of the City Address Transcript." *Gotham Gazette*, January 23, 2003. http://www.gothamgazette.com/government/1670-mayor-michael-bloombergs-2003-state-of-the-city-address.

Bluestone, Barry. "The Inequality Express." *The American Prospect*, December 10, 2001.

Bluestone, Barry, and Bennett Harrison. *The Great U-Turn: Corporate Restructuring and the Polarizing of America*. New York: Basic Books, 1988.

Bockmeyer, Janice L. "A Culture of Distrust: The Impact of Local Political Culture on Participation in the Detroit EZ." *Urban Studies* 37, no. 13 (December 2000): 2417–2440.

Bomey, Nathan. *Detroit Resurrected: To Bankruptcy and Back*. New York: Norton, 2016.

Boswell, Sharon, and Lorraine McConaghy. "A Silicon Forest Grows." *Seattle Times*, December 1, 1996.

Boushey, Heather. *Unbound: How Inequality Constricts Our Economy and What We Can Do About It*. Cambridge MA: Harvard University Press, 2019.

Boushey, Heather, and Carter C. Price. *How Are Economic Inequality and Growth Connected? A Review of Recent Research*. Washington, DC: Washington Center for Equitable Growth, October 2014.

Boustan, Leah Platt. *Competition in the Promised Land: Black Migrants in Northern Cities and Labor Markets*. Princeton, NJ: Princeton University Press, 2016.

Boustan, Leah Platt. "Race, Migration, and Cities." 2020 Lectures on Urban Economics, Urban Economics Association, June 18, 2020. http://www.urbaneconomics.org/meetings/lectures2020/slides/UEA_Lectures_Boustan.pdf.

Boustan, Leah Platt. "Was Postwar Suburbanization 'White Flight'?: Evidence from the Black Migration." *Quarterly Journal of Economics* 125, no. 1 (February 2010): 417–443.

Boustan, Leah Platt, Devin Bunten, and Owen Hearey, "Urbanization in the United States, 1800–2000." Working Paper 19041, National Bureau of Economic Research, May 2013.

Boyd, Matson. "What Does Progressive Urban Planning Look Like?: Why Radicals Should Steer Clear of Homeowner Politics." *Center for Popular Economics* (blog), June 18, 2014. http://www.populareconomics.org/what-does-progressive-urban-planning-look-like-why-radicals-should-steer-clear-of-homeowner-politics/.

Bradbury, Katherine. "State Government Budgets and the Recovery Act." Public Policy Brief 10–1, Federal Reserve Bank of Boston, February 2010.

Branch, Taylor. *Parting the Waters: America in the King Years, 1954–63.* New York: Simon and Schuster, 1988.

Brash, Julian. *Bloomberg's New York: Class and Governance in the Luxury City.* Athens: University of Georgia Press, 2011.

Brausell, James. "The Media Can't Stop Talking About the End of Cities." *Planetizen* (blog), September 2, 2020. https://www.planetizen.com/blogs/110403-media-cant-stop-talking-about-end-cities.

Brave, Scott A., Ross Cole, and Paul Traub. "Measuring Detroit's Economic Progress with the DEAI." *Chicago Fed Letter* no. 434, Federal Reserve Bank of Chicago, March 2020.

Brecher, Charles, and Jo Brill. *Public Authorities in New York State.* New York: Citizens Budget Commission, 2006.

Brighton-Allston Historical Society. "Annexation Spurned: Brookline's 1873 Rejection of Boston," last modified August 28, 2005, http://www.bahistory.org/HistoryAnnexBrookline.html.

Broder, John M. "Los Angeles Groups Agree to Airport Growth, for a Price." *New York Times,* December 17, 2004.

Brown, Joshua. "Meet the House That Inequality Built: 432 Park Avenue." *Fortune,* November 24, 2014. http://fortune.com/2014/11/24/432-park-avenue-inequality-wealth/.

Brownstein, Ron. "The Prosperity Paradox Is Dividing America in Two." *CNN,* January 23, 2018.

Brueckner, Markus, and Daniel Lederman. "Effect of Income Inequality on Aggregate Output." Policy Research Working Paper 7317, World Bank Group, Washington, DC, June 2015.

Brummet, Quentin, and Davin Reed. "The Effects of Gentrification on the Well-Being and Opportunity of Original Resident Adults and Children." Working Paper WP-19-30, Federal Reserve Bank of Philadelphia, July 2019.

Budde, Diana. "AOC Is a YIMBY Now." *Curbed,* January 13, 2022. https://www.curbed.com/2022/01/aoc-2022-pledge-pro-housing-yimby.html.

Bukowczyk, John J. "The Poletown Case and the Future of Detroit's Neighborhoods." *Michigan Quarterly Review,* 25, no. 2 (1986): 449–458.

Bump, Phillip. "To Avoid Removal, Trump Needs Senators Representing Only 7 Percent of the Country to Support Him." *Washington Post,* December 19, 2019.

Buntin, John. "Does Eric Garcetti Have a Big Enough Vision for L.A.?" *Governing,* August 2014. https://www.governing.com/topics/mgmt/gov-eric-garcetti-los-angeles-mayor.html.

Bureau of Labor Statistics. "Unemployment Rates for the 50 Largest Cities, Annual Averages." US Department of Labor, Washington, DC. https://www.bls.gov/lau/lacilg19.htm.

Bureau of the Census. "American Community Service Demographic and Housing Estimates." US Department of Commerce, Washington, DC. https://factfinder.census.gov/faces/table services/jsf/pages/productview.xhtml?src=.

Bureau of Transportation Statistics. "Top U.S. Foreign Trade Gateways by Value of Shipment." US Department of Transportation, December 20, 2020. https://www.bts.gov/content/top-us -foreign-trade-freight-gateways-value-shipments-current-billions.

Burns, Gus. "Controversial Statue of Racist ex-Dearborn Mayor Orville Hubbard Relocated." *MLive*, September 29, 2015. https://www.mlive.com/news/detroit/2015/09/contoversial_statue _of_racist.html.

Burrows, Edwin G., and Mike Wallace. *Gotham: A History of New York City to 1898*. New York: Oxford University Press, 1999.

Cafcas, Thomas, and Greg LeRoy. *Will Amazon Fool Us Twice? Why State and Local Governments Should Stop Subsidizing the Online Giant's Growing Distribution Network*. Washington, DC: Good Jobs First, 2016.

California Association of Realtors. "Housing Affordability Index—Traditional." December 27, 2020. https://www.car.org/marketdata/data/haitraditional/.

Cannon, Lou. *Official Negligence: How Rodney King and the Riots Changed Los Angeles and the LAPD*. New York: Times Books, 1997.

Card, David, and Alan B. Krueger. "Minimum Wages and Employment: A Case Study of the Fast-Food Industry in New Jersey and Pennsylvania." *American Economic Review* 84, no. 4 (1994): 772–792.

Carp, Benjamin L. *Rebels Rising: Cities and the American Revolution*. New York: Oxford University Press, 2007.

Carpenter, Seth B., and William M. Rodgers III. "The Disparate Labor Market Impacts of Monetary Policy." *Journal of Policy Analysis and Management* 23, no. 4 (September 2004): 813–830.

Celona, Larry. "Former New York City Mayor Ed Koch Dead at Age 88." *New York Post*, February 1, 2013.

Center for New York City Affairs. "The Pandemic Torpedoed New York City's Budget: Now What?" October 28, 2020. http://www.centernyc.org/urban-matters-2/2020/10/28/the-pandemic -torpedoed-new-york-citys-budget-now-what.

Center on Budget and Policy Priorities. *Tracking the Covid-19 Recession's Effects on Food, Housing, and Employment Hardships*. January 2021. https://www.cbpp.org/sites/default/files/atoms/files /8-13-20pov.pdf.

Chang-Tai, Hsieh, and Enrico Moretti. "Housing Constraints and Spatial Misallocation." *American Economic Journal: Macroeconomics* 11, no. 2 (April 2019): 1–39.

Chapin, William S. *We the Americans: Our Homes*. Washington, DC: United States Census Bureau, 1993.

Chen, Don. "Linking Transportation Equity and Environmental Justice with Smart Growth." In *Growing Smarter: Achieving Livable Communities, Environmental Justice, and Regional Equity*, ed. Robert D. Bullard, 299–322. Cambridge MA: MIT Press, 2007.

Chen, Stefanos. "In 2021, New York's Housing Market Made a Stunning Comeback." *New York Times*, December 31, 2021.

Chernick, Howard, David Copeland, and Andrew Reschovsky. "The Fiscal Effects of the COVID-19 Pandemic on Cities." *National Tax Journal* 73, no. 3 (September 2020): 699–732.

Chetty, Raj, John N. Friedman, Nathaniel Hendren, Maggie R. Jones, and Sonya R. Porter. "The Opportunity Atlas: Mapping the Childhood Roots of Social Mobility." Working Paper 25147, National Bureau of Economic Research, October 2018.

Chetty, Raj, John N. Friedman, Nathaniel Hendren, and Michael Stepner. "The Economic Impacts of COVID-19: Evidence from a New Public Database Built Using Private Sector Data." Opportunity Insights, November 2020. https://opportunityinsights.org/wp-content/uploads/2020/05/tracker_paper.pdf.

Chetty, Raj, Nathaniel Hendren, Patrick Kline, and Emmanuel Saez. "Where Is the Land of Opportunity?: The Geography of Intergenerational Mobility in the United States." *Quarterly Journal of Economics* 129, no. 4 (2014): 1553–1623.

Ciccone, Antonio, and Robert E. Hall. "Productivity and the Density of Economic Activity." *American Economic Review* 86, no. 1 (March 1996): 54–70.

Cinango, Federico. "Trends in Income Inequality and Its Impact on Economic Growth." OECD Social, Employment and Migration Working Paper 163, Organization for Economic Co-operation and Development, Paris, 2014.

Citizens Budget Commission. "Less Spending, More Saving: Benchmarks to Assess the NYC Financial Plan." November 13, 2019. https://cbcny.org/research/less-spending-more-saving.

Citizens Budget Commission. "Personal Income Tax Revenues in New York State and City." August 13, 2019. https://cbcny.org/research/personal-income-tax-revenues-new-york-state-and-city.

Citizens Budget Commission. *Strategies to Boost Housing Production in the New York City Metropolitan Area.* New York: Citizens Budget Commission, August 2020.

Citizens Budget Commission. *Where Is the Money Going?: Mayor DeBlasio's Spending Priorities.* City Budget Report, Citizens Budget Commission, June 3, 2016.

City of Clinton v. Cedar Rapids and the Missouri River Railroad, 24 Iowa 455 (1868).

City of Detroit. "Four-Year Financial Plan, FY2021-FY2024." May 29, 2020. https://detroitmi.gov/sites/detroitmi.localhost/files/2020-06/1%20-%20FY%202021-24%20Four-Year%20Financial%20Plan%20-%20Section%20A%20Overview%20-%20Adopted_1.pdf.

City of Detroit. "Proposal for Creditors 2013." http://www.detroitmi.gov/Portals/0/docs/EM/Reports/City%20of%20Detroit%20Proposal%20for%20Creditors1.pdf.

City of Detroit–University Economic Analysis Partnership. "City of Detroit Economic Outlook 2020–2026." September 2021. https://lsa.umich.edu/content/dam/econ-assets/Econdocs/RSQE%20PDFs/RSQE_Detroit_CREC_Slides.pdf.

City of Los Angeles. "Covid-19: Keeping Los Angeles Safe: Data—Health and Wellness." https://corona-virus.la/data.

City of New York. *The de Blasio Years: The Tale of a More Equal City.* December 2021. https://www1.nyc.gov/assets/home/downloads/pdf/press-releases/2021/Wealth-Transfer-Report.pdf.

Clark, Anna. "Racing to Run a City Without a Motor." *The American Prospect*, October 2, 2013.

Clark, Daniel J. *Disruption in Detroit: Autoworkers and the Elusive Postwar Boom.* Chicago: University of Illinois Press, 2018.

Clay, Karen, Joshua Lewis, and Edson Severnini. "What Explains Cross-City Variation in Mortality During the 1918 Influenza Pandemic?: Evidence from 438 U.S. Cities." *Economics and Human Biology*, 35 (December 2019): 42–50.

Clifford, Frank. "Woo, Riordan Differ on Healing L.A.'s Economy." *Los Angeles Times*, November 18, 1992.

Clifton, Jim. "Forget Washington—Cities Will Win or Lose America." *Chairman's Blog, Gallup*, November 14, 2012. http://www.gallup.com/opinion/chairman/169136/forget-washington-cities -win-lose-america.aspx.

Clinton, Hillary Rodham. "Give New York Its Fair Share of Homeland Money." *New York Times*, August 22, 2004.

Collins, William J., and Marianne H. Wanamaker. "African American Intergenerational Mobility Since 1880." Working Paper 23395, National Bureau of Economic Research, May 2017.

Collinson, Robert, Ingrid Gould Ellen, and Jens Ludwig. "Low-Income Housing Policy." Working Paper 21071, National Bureau of Economic Research, April 2015.

Committee for Greater LA. *No Going Back: Together for an Equitable and Inclusive Los Angeles*. Los Angeles, USC Dornsife Equity Research Institute: September 2020.

Community Service Society. "Poverty Declined in New York for Fifth Straight Year." September 18, 2020. https://www.cssny.org/news/entry/statement-poverty-declined-in-new-york-city -for-fifth-straight-year-but-cen.

Congressional Research Service. *Federal Grants to State and Local Governments: A Historical Perspective on Contemporary Issues*. Washington, DC, May 22, 2019.

Conn, Steven. *Americans Against the City: Anti-Urbanism in the Twentieth Century*. New York: Oxford University Press, 2014.

Cook, Lisa D. "Violence and Economic Activity: Evidence from African-American Patents, 1870–1940." *Journal of Economic Growth* 19, no. 2 (May 2014): 221–257.

Cooke, Thomas J. "Residential Mobility of the Poor and the Growth of Poverty in Inner-Ring Suburbs." *Urban Geography* 31, no. 2 (2010): 179–193.

Cornejo, Jackelyn. *Moving L.A. Forward: Promoting Construction Careers at Metro*. Los Angeles: Los Angeles Alliance for a New Economy, 2011.

Cortright, Joe. "Big City Metros Are Driving the National Economy." *City Observatory*, March 23, 2017. http://cityobservatory.org/big-city-metros-driving/.

Cotter, Christopher. "Off the Rails: The Real Effects of Railroad Bond Defaults Following the Panic of 1983." *AEA Papers and Proceedings 2021*, 111 (May 2021): 508–513.

County of Los Angeles. "Death Rates." *LA County Daily Covid-19 Data*, December 27, 2020. http://www.ph.lacounty.gov/media/Coronavirus/data/index.htm#.

Covert, Bryce. "Cities Should Stop Playing the Amazon HQ2 Bidding Game." *New York Times*. November 13, 2018.

Cowen, Tyler. "A Radical Solution to the Overuse of Occupational Licensing." *Bloomberg Opinion*, March 5, 2018. https://www.bloomberg.com/view/articles/2018-03-05/tyler-cowen-s-radical -idea-for-reining-in-occupational-licensing.

Cronon, William. *Nature's Metropolis: Chicago and the Great West*. New York: Norton, 1991.

Crossney, Kristen B., and David W. Bartelt. "The Legacy of the Home Owners' Loan Corporation." *Housing Policy Debate* 16, no. 3–4 (2005): 547–574.

Cutcher-Gershenfeld, Joel, Dan Brooks, and Martin Mulloy. "The Decline and Resurgence of the U.S. Auto Industry." Briefing Paper 399, Economic Policy Institute, May 2015.

Cutler David M., and Grant Miller. "The Role of Public Health Improvements in Health Advances: The Twentieth-Century United States." *Demography* 42, no. 1 (February 2005): 1–22.

DaimlerChrysler Corp. v. Cuno, 547 U.S. 332 (2006).

Daly, Mary, and Fred Furlong. "Profile of a Recession: U.S. and California." *FRBSF Economic Letter* 2002–4, Federal Reserve Bank of San Francisco, February 2002.

Damore, David F., Robert E. Lang, and Karen A. Danielsen. *Blue Metros, Red States: The Shifting Urban-Rural Divide in America's Swing States*. Washington, DC: Brookings Institution, 2021.

Darity, Jr., William A., Darrick Hamilton, and James B. Stewart. "A Tour de Force in Understanding Intergroup Inequality: An Introduction to Stratification Economics." *Review of Black Political Economy* 42, no. 1–2 (2015): 1–6.

Dauenbaugh, Rachel S. "Coleman Young's Detroit: A Vision for a City 1974–1994." Thesis, DePauw University, 2014. https://scholarship.depauw.edu/cgi/viewcontent.cgi?article=1006&context=studentresearch.

Davey, Monica. "For Detroit, a Path to Recovery Under State Oversight." *New York Times*, April 5, 2012.

David, Greg. "NYC Lost a Record 631,000 Jobs to the Pandemic in 2020: So What's Next?" *The City*, March 14, 2021. https://www.thecity.nyc/economy/2021/3/14/22326414/nyc-lost-record-jobs-to-pandemic-unemployment.

Davidson, Nestor M., and Sheila R. Foster. "The Mobility Case for Regionalism." *University of California at Davis Law Review* 47 (2013): 63–120.

Davis, Mike. *Ecology of Fear: Los Angeles and the Imagination of Disaster*. New York: Metropolitan Books, 1998.

De Barbieri, Edward W. "Do Community Benefits Agreement Benefit Communities?" *Cardozo Law Review* 37, no. 5 (June 2016): 1773–1825.

Delmont, Matthew F. *Why Busing Failed: Race, Media, and the National Resistance to School Desegregation*. Oakland: University of California Press, 2016.

DePietro, Andrew. "U.S. Poverty Rate by City In 2021." *Forbes*, November 26, 2021. https://www.forbes.com/sites/andrewdepietro/2021/11/26/us-poverty-rate-by-city-in-2021/?sh=f368e55a544d.

Derenoncourt, Ellora. "Can You Move to Opportunity?: Evidence from the Great Migration." *American Economic Review*, 112 no. 2 (February 2022): 369–408.

Derenoncourt, Ellora, and Claire Montialoux. "Minimum Wages and Racial Inequality." Working Paper, Washington Center for Equitable Growth, January 2020.

Dertouzos, James, and Michael Dardia. *Defense Spending, Aerospace, and the California Economy*. Santa Monica, CA: Rand Corporation, 1993.

Desjardins, Jeff. "MAPPED: The US Cities with the Biggest Economies." *Business Insider*, September 27, 2017. https://www.businessinsider.com/us-cities-with-the-biggest-economies-2017-9.

Deskins, Donald R. "Economic Restructuring, Job Opportunities, and Black Social Dislocation in Detroit." In *Social Polarization in Post-Industrial Metropolises*, ed. John O'Loughlin and Jürgen Friedrichs, 259–282. New York: De Gruyter, 1996.

Detroit Metropolitan Area Planning Commission. *Study of Expansion Trends in the Automobile Industry with Special Reference to the Detroit Region*. Detroit: Metropolitan Area Planning Commission: 1956. https://babel.hathitrust.org/cgi/pt?id=mdp.35128001565876;view=1up;seq=1.

Diamond, Rebecca. "The Determinants and Welfare Implications of US Workers' Diverging Location Choices by Skill." *American Economic Review* 106, no. 3 (March 2016): 479–524.

Digital History. "The Great Migration." http://www.digitalhistory.uh.edu/disp_textbook.cfm?smtID=2&psid=3385.

Dillon, John Forrest. *Treatise on the Law of Municipal Corporations*. Chicago: James Cockroft & Company, 1872. https://babel.hathitrust.org/cgi/pt?id=inu.39000007582039;view=1up;seq=4

Dillon, Liam, and Taryn Lun. "California Bill to Dramatically Increase Home Building Fails for the Third Year in a Row." *Los Angeles Times*, January 30, 2020.

DiNapoli, Thomas P., and Kenneth B. Bleiwas. *The Role of Immigrants in the New York City Economy*. New York: Office of the New York State Comptroller, 2015.

DiSalvo, Daniel. "How to Approach Public Sector Unions." In *A Time for Governing: Policy Solutions from the Pages of National Affairs*, ed Yuval Levin and Meghan Clyne, 308–324. New York: Encounter Books, 2012.

Donaldson, Dave. "Lecture 6: Economic Geography and Path Dependence." 2020 Lectures on Urban Economics, Urban Economics Association, July 16, 2020. http://www.urbaneconomics.org/meetings/lectures2020/slides/UEA_Lectures_Donaldson.pdf.

Donnelly, Frank. "New York's Population and Migration Trends in the 2010s." WCIB Occasional Paper Series 21. Weissman Center for International Business, Baruch College, City University of New York, Fall 2020.

Dragan, Kacie, Ingrid Ellen, and Sherry A. Glied. "Does Gentrification Displace Poor Children?: New Evidence from New York City Medicaid Data." Working Paper 25809, National Bureau of Economic Research, May 2019.

Drayse, Mark, Daniel Flaming, David Rigby, and Michael Beltramo. *The Gateway Cities Economy: Impacts of Aerospace Restructuring*. Los Angeles: Economic Roundtable, 1998.

Dreier, Peter, E. P. Clapp Distinguished Professor of Politics, Politics, Urban and Environmental Policy, Occidental College. Interview by Richard McGahey, July 28, 2014.

Dreier, Peter. "Judging Mister Mayor: Los Angeles Magazine's Rip of Antonio Villaraigosa Put in Perspective." *LA Progressive*, June 22, 2009. http://www.laprogressive.com/judging-mister-mayor-los-angeles-magazines-rip-of-antonio-villaraigosa-put-in-perspective/.

Dreier, Peter. "Reagan's Real Legacy." *The Nation*, February 4, 2011.

Dreier, Peter, John Mollenkopf, and Todd Swanstrom. *Place Matters: Metropolitics for the Twenty-First Century*. Lawrence: University Press of Kansas, 2014.

Drennan, Matthew. "The Economy." In *The Two New Yorks: State-City Relations in the Changing Federal System*, ed. Gerald Benjamin and Charles Brecher, 55–80. New York: Russell Sage Foundation, 1988.

Drennan, Matthew, and Georgia N. Stergiou. "The Local Economy and Local Revenues." In *Setting Municipal Priorities: American Cities and the New York Experience*, ed. Charles Brecher and Raymond D. Horton, 43–68. New York: New York University Press, 1984.

Dube, Arindrajit. *Impacts of Minimum Wages: Review of the International Evidence*. London: HM Treasury, November 2019. https://assets.publishing.service.gov.uk/government/uploads

/system/uploads/attachment_data/file/844350/impacts_of_minimum_wages_review_of
_the_international_evidence_Arindrajit_Dube_web.pdf, 4.

Dube, Arindrajit, and Attila S. Lindner. "City Limits: What Do Local-Area Minimum Wages
Do?" Working Paper 27928, National Bureau of Economic Research, November 2020.

Dudziak, Mary L. *Cold War Civil Rights: Race and the Image of American Democracy*. Princeton,
NJ: Princeton University Press, 2000.

Duffin, Erin. "U.S. Metro Areas—Ranked by Gross Metropolitan Product (GMP) 2020." *Statista*,
October 5, 2020. https://www.statista.com/statistics/183808/gmp-of-the-20-biggest-metro-areas/.

Duranton, Gilles, and Diego Puga. "Diversity and Specialisation in Cities: Why, Where and
When Does It Matter?" *Urban Studies* 37, no. 2 (2000): 533–555.

Duranton, Gilles, and Diego Puga. "Micro-Foundations of Urban Agglomeration Economies."
Working Paper 9931, National Bureau of Economic Research, September 2003.

Duranton, Gilles, and Diego Puga. "Urban Growth and Its Aggregate Implications." Working
Paper 26591, National Bureau of Economic Research, December 2019.

Durrum, Jessica. "Building a Sturdy Blue-Green Coalition at the Ports of Los Angeles and Long
Beach." *Progressive Planning*, no. 197 (2013): 12–16.

Dutta-Gupta, Indivar, Kali Grant, Matthew Eckel, and Peter Edelman. *Lessons Learned from
40 Years of Subsidized Employment Programs: A Framework, Review of Models, and Recommendations for Helping Disadvantaged Workers*. Washington, DC: Georgetown University
Center on Poverty and Inequality, 2016.

Economic Development Administration. "$1B Build Back Better Regional Challenge." US
Department of Commerce, December 13, 2021. https://eda.gov/arpa/build-back-better/.

Economic Policy Institute. "Minimum Wage Tracker." January 1, 2022. https://www.epi.org
/minimum-wage-tracker/.

Economic Policy Institute. "The Productivity-Pay Gap." August 2021. https://www.epi.org
/productivity-pay-gap/

Economic Policy Institute. "Worker Rights Preemption in the U.S." January 2022. https://www
.epi.org/preemption-map/

Ehrenhalt, Samuel M. "Economic and Demographic Change: The Case of New York City."
Monthly Labor Review 116, no. 2 (February 1993): 40–50.

Emmons, William R., and Lowell R. Ricketts. "College Is Not Enough: Higher Education Does
Not Eliminate Racial and Ethnic Wealth Gaps." *Federal Reserve Bank of St. Louis Review* 99,
no. 1 (2017): 7–39.

Employment Development Department. "Employment by Industry Data." State of California.
https://www.labormarketinfo.edd.ca.gov/data/employment-by-industry.html.

Faricy, Christopher. "The Politics of Social Policy in America: The Causes and Effects of Indirect
Versus Direct Social Spending." *Journal of Politics* 73, no. 1 (January 2011): 74–83.

Farley, Reynolds. "The Bankruptcy of Detroit: What Role Did Race Play?" *City & Community*
14, no. 2 (June 2015): 118-137.

Farley, Reynolds, Mick Couper, and Maria Krysan. "Race and Revitalization in the Rust Belt: A
Motor City Story." PSC Research Report 07–620. University of Michigan, April 2007.

Farley, Reynolds, Sheldon Danziger, and Harry J. Holzer. *Detroit Divided*. New York: Russell
Sage Foundation, 2000.

Farren, Michael D., and Matthew D. Mitchell. "Targeted Economic Development Subsidies Don't Work." *Policy Spotlight*. Mercatus Center, George Mason University, August 11, 2020. https://www.mercatus.org/publications/corporate-welfare/policy-spotlight-targeted-economic -development-subsidies-don%E2%80%99t-work

Federal Housing Administration. *Underwriting Manual: Underwriting and Valuation Procedure Under Title II of the National Housing Act*. Washington, DC: U.S. Government Publishing Office, 1936.

Federal Reserve Bank of New York. "The Money and Bond Markets in September 1975." *Monthly Economic Policy Review* 57, no. 10 (October 1975): 240–244.

Financial Crisis Inquiry Commission. *Financial Crisis Inquiry Report: Final Report of the National Commission on the Causes of the Financial and Economic Crisis in the United States*. Washington, DC: U.S. Government Printing Office, 2011.

Fink, Zack. "Revenge Is Coming: How Everything Fell Apart Between Andrew Cuomo and Bill de Blasio." *City & State New York*, January 16, 2017.

Finnegan, Michael. "Labor Money Starts Flowing in for Garcetti." *Los Angeles Times*, April 6, 2013.

Fishback, Price. "How Successful Was the New Deal? The Microeconomic Impact of New Deal Spending and Lending Policies in the 1930s." *Journal of Economic Literature* 55, no. 4 (2017): 1435–1485.

Fishback, Price B., Jessica LaVoice, Allison Shertzer, and Randall Walsh. "Race, Risk, and the Emergence of Federal Redlining." Working Paper 28146, National Bureau of Economic Research, November 2020.

Fishback, Price, Jonathan Rose, and Kenneth Snowden. *Well Worth Saving: How the New Deal Safeguarded Home Ownership*. Chicago: University of Chicago Press, 2013.

Fishback, Price, Jonathan Rose, Ken Snowden, and Thomas Storrs. "New Evidence on Redlining by Federal Housing Programs in the 1930s." Working Paper WP2022-01, Federal Reserve Bank of Chicago, January 3, 2022.

Fisher, Bridget, and Flávia Leite. "The Cost of New York City's Hudson Yards Redevelopment Project." Working Paper 2018–2, Schwartz Center for Economic Policy Analysis, The New School.

Fishman, Mike, Dan Bloom, and Sam Elkin. *Employment and Training Programs Serving Low-Income Populations: Next Steps for Research*. OPRE Report 2020–72, Office of Planning, Research, and Evaluation, Administration for Children and Families, US Department of Health and Human Services, June 2020.

Fitzgerald, Joan. *Greenovation: Urban Leadership on Climate Change*. New York: Oxford University Press, 2020.

Fitzsimmons, Emma G. "Progressives Defeat Brooklyn Project That Promised 20,000 Jobs." *New York Times*, September 23, 2020.

Fitzsimmons, Emma G., and Jefferey C. Mays. "Is New York Still a 'Tale of Two Cities'?" *New York Times*, December 22, 2021.

Flaming, Daniel. *Poverty, Inequality, and Justice: A Vanishing Middle Class in Southern California*. Los Angeles: Economic Roundtable, 2006.

Flaming, Daniel. President, Economic Roundtable. Interview by Richard McGahey, July 23, 2014.

Florida, Richard. "The Creative Class Is Alive and Well." Interview by Jonathan Fowler and Elizabeth Rodd, *BigThink*, March 24, 2013. http://bigthink.com/videos/the-creative-class-is-alive-and-well.

Florida, Richard. *The New Urban Crisis: How Our Cities Are Increasing Inequality, Deepening Segregation, and Failing the Middle Class—And What We Can Do About It*. New York: Basic Books, 2017.

Florida, Richard. *The Rise of the Creative Class, Revisited*. New York: Basic Books, 2012.

Florida, Richard. "This Is Not the End of Cities." *Bloomberg CityLab*, June 19, 2020. https://www.bloomberg.com/news/features/2020-06-19/cities-will-survive-pandemics-and-protests?

Florida, Richard. "Two Takes on the Fate of Future Cities." *CityLab*, April 21, 2017. https://www.citylab.com/equity/2017/04/two-takes-on-the-fate-of-future-cities/521907/.

Florida, Richard. "Where the Good Jobs Are." *Route Fifty*, September 2, 2016. https://www.routefifty.com/2016/09/where-good-jobs-are/131259/.

Florida, Richard, Zara Matheson, Patrick Adler, and Taylor Brydges. *The Divided City and the Shape of the New Metropolis*. Toronto: University of Toronto, 2014.

Fogli, Alessandra, and Veronica Guerrieri. "The End of the American Dream?: Inequality and Segregation in US Cities." Working Paper 26143, National Bureau of Economic Research, August 2019.

Folbre, Nancy. *Greed, Lust, and Gender*. New York: Oxford University Press, 2009.

Ford Foundation. *Community Development Corporations: A Strategy for Depressed Urban and Rural Areas*. New York: Ford Foundation, 1973. http://files.eric.ed.gov/fulltext/ED090328.pdf.

Ford Motor Company. "Ford Reveals Plans for Inclusive, Vibrant, Walkable Mobility Innovation District Around Michigan Central Station." November 17, 2020. https://media.ford.com/content/fordmedia/fna/us/en/news/2020/11/17/ford-plans-mobility-innovation-district.html.

Frank, Annalise. "'Elected by the People Who Stayed': Duggan Targets Equity in State of the City Address." *Crain's Detroit Business*, February 5, 2020.

FRED Economic Data. "All Employees, Manufacturing." Economics Research, Federal Reserve Bank of St. Louis. https://fred.stlouisfed.org/series/MANEMP.

FRED Economic Data. "Personal Consumption Expenditures: Durable Goods." Economics Research, Federal Reserve Bank of St. Louis. https://fred.stlouisfed.org/series/PCDGA.

FRED Economic Data. "Private Residential Fixed Investment (PRFIA)." Economic Research, Federal Reserve Bank of St. Louis. https://fred.stlouisfed.org/series/PRFIA.

FRED Economic Data. "Share of Total Net Worth Held by the Top 1 Percent (99th to 100th Wealth Percentiles)." Economic Research, Federal Reserve Bank of St. Louis. https://fred.stlouisfed.org/series/WFRBST01134.

Freeman, Joshua B. *Working-Class New York: Life and Labor Since World War II*. New York: The New Press, 2000.

Freeman, Lance. *A Haven and a Hell: The Ghetto in Black America*. New York: Columbia University Press, 2019.

Frey, William H. "Despite the Pandemic Narrative, Americans Are Moving at Historically Low Rates." Metropolitan Policy Program, The Brookings Institution, November 30, 2021.

Frey, William H. "Even as Metropolitan Areas Diversify, White Americans Still Live in Mostly White Neighborhoods." Metropolitan Policy Program, The Brookings Institution, March 23, 2020.

Frey, William H. "New Census Data Shows a Huge Spike in Movement out of Big Metro Areas During the Pandemic." *The Avenue* blog, April 14, 2022. https://www.brookings.edu/blog /the-avenue/2022/04/14/new-census-data-shows-a-huge-spike-in-movement-out-of-big -metro-areas-during-the-pandemic/.

Frey, William H. "Pandemic Population Change Across Metro America: Accelerated Migration, Less Immigration, Fewer Births and More Deaths." Metropolitan Policy Program, The Brookings Institution, May 20, 2021.

Frey, William H. "Three Americas: The Rising Significance of Regions." *Journal of the American Planning Association* 68, no. 4 (2002): 349–355.

Frey, William H. "2020 Census: Big cities grew and became more diverse, especially among their youth." The Brookings Institution, October 21, 2021. https://www.brookings.edu/research/2020 -census-big-cities-grew-and-became-more-diverse-especially-among-their-youth/.

Frey, William H. *A 2020 Census Portrait of America's Largest Metro Areas: Population Growth, Diversity, Segregation, and Youth.* Washington DC: Metropolitan Policy Program, Brookings Institution, April 2022.

Friedman, Milton. *Capitalism and Freedom.* Chicago: University of Chicago Press, 1962.

Friedman, Thomas L. *The World Is Flat: A Brief History of the Twenty-First Century.* New York: Farrar Strauss, and Giroux, 2005.

Frum, David. "A Good Way to Wreck a Local Economy: Build Casinos." *The Atlantic,* August 7, 2014.

Frymer, Paul. *Black and Blue: African Americans, the Labor Movement, and the Decline of the Democratic Party.* Princeton, NJ: Princeton University Press, 2008.

Fujita, Masahisa, and Jacques Thisse. *Economics of Agglomeration: Cities, Industrial Location, and Economic Growth,* 2nd ed. New York: Cambridge University Press, 2013.

Furman Center for Real Estate and Urban Policy. "Housing Policy in New York City: A Brief History." Working Paper 06–01, New York University, April 2006.

Future Forum. "Leveling the Playing Field in the Hybrid Workplace." Winter 2021/2022 Future Forum Pulse Survey, January 2022. https://futureforum.com/wp-content/uploads/2022/01 /Future-Forum-Pulse-Report-January-2022.pdf.

Galbraith, James K., Olivier Giovannoni, and Ann J. Russo. "The Fed's *Real* Reaction Function: Monetary Policy, Unemployment, Inequality—and Presidential Politics." Working Paper 511, Levy Economics Institute of Bard College, Bard College, Annandale-on-Hudson, New York, August 2007.

Galbraith, John Kenneth. *The Affluent Society.* Boston: Houghton Mifflin, 1958.

Gallagher, John. "FCA's Jeep Assembly Plant Is Coming to Detroit—but City May Have Paid Too Much." *Detroit Free Press,* May 15, 2019.

Galster, George. *Driving Detroit: The Quest for Respect in Motown.* Philadelphia: University of Pennsylvania Press, 2014.

Ganong, Peter, and Daniel Shoag. "Why Has Regional Income Convergence in the U.S. Declined?" Working Paper 2019-88, Becker-Friedman Institute, Department of Economics, University of Chicago, July 2017.

Gapasin, Fernando E. "The Los Angeles County Federation of Labor: A Model of Transformation or Traditional Unionism?" In *Central Labor Councils and the Revival of American*

Unionism: Organizing for Justice in Our Communities, ed. Immanuel Ness and Stuart Eimer, 79–101. New York: Routledge, 2001.

Garner, Anne. "Cholera Comes to New York City." The New York Academy of Medicine, February 3, 2015. https://nyamcenterforhistory.org/2015/02/03/cholera-comes-to-new-york-city/.

Garreau, Joel. *Edge City: Life on the New Frontier*. New York: Doubleday, 1991.

Garrett, Thomas A. "Economic Effects of the 1918 Influenza Pandemic: Implications for a Modern-day Pandemic." Federal Reserve Bank of St. Louis, November 2007. https://www.stlouisfed .org/~/media/files/pdfs/community-development/research-reports/pandemic_flu_report.pdf.

Gebeloff, Robert, Dana Goldstein, and Winnie Hu. "Cities Lost Population in 2021, Leading to the Slowest Year of Growth in U.S. History." *New York Times*, March 24, 2022.

Gellner, Christopher G. "Occupational Characteristics of Urban Workers." *Monthly Labor Review* 94, no. 10 (October 1971): 21–32.

Georgakas, Dan, and Marvin Surkin. *Detroit, I Do Mind Dying: A Study in Urban Revolution*, Cambridge, MA: South End Press, 1998.

Gertner, Jon. "Home Economics." *New York Times Magazine*, March 5, 2006.

Gibson, Campbell. "Population of the 100 Largest Cities and Other Urban Places in the United States." Working Paper POP-WP027, U.S. Bureau of the Census, Washington, DC, 1998. https://www.census.gov/library/working-papers/1998/demo/POP-twps0027.html.

Gibson, Campbell J., and Emily Lennon. "Historical Census Statistics on the Foreign-Born Population of the United States: 1850–1990." Working Paper POP-WP029, Population Division, U.S. Bureau of the Census, February 1, 1999.

Gilens, Martin, and Benjamin I. Page. "Testing Theories of American Politics: Elites, Interest Groups, and Average Citizens." *Perspectives on Politics* 12, no. 3 (2014): 564–581.

Gillette, Clayton P. "In Partial Praise of Dillon's Rule, or, Can Public Choice Theory Justify Local Government Law?" *Chicago-Kent Law Review* 67, no. 3 (October 1991): 959–1010.

Glaeser, Edward. "How Skyscrapers Can Save the City." *The Atlantic*, March 2011.

Glaeser, Edward L. "The Economics Approach to Cities." NBER Working Paper 13696, National Bureau of Economic Research, Cambridge, MA, December 2007.

Glaeser, Edward L. "Review of *The Rise of the Creative Class* by Richard Florida." *Regional Science and Urban Economics* 35, no. 5 (September 2005): 593–596.

Glaeser, Edward. *Triumph of the City: How Our Greatest Invention Makes Us Richer, Smarter, Greener, Healthier, and Happier*. New York: Penguin Press, 2011, 1.

Glaeser, Edward L. "Urbanization and Its Discontents." *Eastern Economic Journal* 46, no. 2 (2020): 191–218.

Glaeser, Edward L. "Why the Anti-Urban Bias?" *Boston Globe*, March 5, 2010.

Glaeser, Edward, and David Cutler. *Survival of the City: Living and Thriving in an Age of Isolation*. New York: Penguin Press, 2021.

Glaeser, Edward L., and Matthew E. Kahn. "Decentralized Employment and the Transformation of the American City." *Brookings—Wharton Papers on Urban Affairs* (2001): 1–63.

Glaeser, Edward L., Hedi D. Kallal, José A. Scheinkman, and Andrei Shleifer. "Growth in Cities." *Journal of Political Economy* 100, no. 6 (December 1992): 1126–1152.

Glaeser, Edward L., and Matthew G. Resseger. "The Complementarity Between Cities and Skills." *Journal of Regional Science* 50, no. 1 (February 2010): 221–244.

Glaeser, Edward L., José A. Scheinkman, and Andrei Shleifer. "Economic Growth in a Cross-Section of Cities." *Journal of Monetary Economics* 36, no. 1 (August 1995): 117–143.

Glass, Michael R. "Detroit, MI, 1941–1952." In *Cities in American Political History*, ed. Richardson Dilworth, 512–518. Los Angeles: Sage Publications, 2011.

Glazer, Amihai, and Nicholas Kumamoto. "Factors Determining Plant Locations and Plant Survival." Working Paper, Program in Corporate Welfare, University of California at Irvine, January 14, 2020.

Glyn, Andrew, Alan Hughes, Alain Lipietz, and Ajit Singh. "The Rise and Fall of the Golden Age." In *The Golden Age of Capitalism: Reinterpreting the Postwar Experience*, ed. Stephen A. Marglin and Juliet B. Schor, 39–125. New York: Oxford University Press, 1990.

Gold, Howard R. "Never Mind the 1 Percent: Let's Talk About the 0.01 Percent." *Chicago Booth Review*, November 29, 2017.

Gold, Matea. "Labor to Bolster Hahn Endorsement." *Los Angeles Times*, March 11, 2005.

Goldberg, Jonathan, Jeffrey Jiménez-Kurlander, and Silvana Serifimovska. *Measuring Together: A Learning Approach for Inclusive Economies*. New York: Surdna Foundation, January 2022. https://surdna.org/wp-content/uploads/2022/01/Measuring-Together_-A-Learning-Approach -For-Inclusive-Economies-1.pdf.

Goldin, Claudia D. "The Role of World War II in the Rise of Women's Employment." *American Economic Review* 81, no. 4 (September 1991): 741–756.

Goldstein, Alan. "Curmudgeon of Quality: U.S. Industry Listens Now When Once-Ignored International Management Wizard Speaks." *Los Angeles Times*, March 31, 1987.

Goldzwig, Steven R. "LBJ, the Rhetoric of Transcendence, and the Civil Rights Act of 1968." *Rhetoric & Public Affairs* 6, no. 1 (2003): 25–53.

Good Jobs First. "Accountable USA—New York." Washington, DC: Good Jobs First, 2022. http:// www.goodjobsfirst.org/states/new-york.

Gotham, Kevin Fox. "Urban Space, Restrictive Covenants, and the Origins of Racial Residential Segregation in a US City, 1900–1950." *International Journal of Urban and Regional Research* 24, no. 3 (September 2000): 616–633.

Gottlieb, Robert, Mark Vallianatos, Regina M. Freer, and Peter Dreier. *The Next Los Angeles: The Struggle for a Livable City*. Berkeley: University of California Press, 2005.

Gould, Elise, and Valerie Wilson. "The Black Unemployment Rate Returns to Historic Low, but Not Really." *Working Economics Blog*, Economic Policy Institute, July 7, 2017.

Grabar, Henry. "San Francisco's Civil War." *Slate*, June 2017. http://www.slate.com/articles /business/metropolis/2017/06/yimbys_and_the_dsa_can_t_get_along_despite_their_common _enemy_high_rent.html.

Green, Richard K., and Susan M. Wachter. "The American Mortgage in Historical and International Context." *Journal of Economic Perspectives* 19, no. 4 (2005): 93–114.

Greenhouse, Steven. *Beaten Down, Worked Up: The Past, Present, and Future of American Labor*. New York: Alfred A. Knopf, 2019.

Greenstone, Michael, Richard Hornbeck, and Enrico Moretti. "Identifying Agglomeration Spillovers: Evidence from Winners and Losers of Large Plant Openings." *Journal of Political Economy* 118, no. 3 (June 2010): 536–598.

Greenwald, Richard A. *The Triangle Fire, the Protocols of Peace, and Industrial Democracy in Progressive New York*. Philadelphia: Temple University Press, 2005.

Greenwood, Robin, and David Scharfstein. "The Growth of Finance." *Journal of Economic Perspectives* 27, no. 2 (2013): 3–28.

Gregory, James M. "Internal Migration: Twentieth Century and Beyond." In *The Oxford Encyclopedia of American Social History*, ed. Lynn Dumenil, 540–545. New York: Oxford University Press, 2012.

Gregory, James. *The Southern Diaspora: How the Great Migrations of Black and White Southerners Transformed America*. Chapel Hill: University of North Carolina Press, 2005.

Gross, Julian, Greg LeRoy, and Madeline Janis-Aparicio. *Community Benefit Agreements: Making Development Projects Accountable*. Los Angeles: Good Jobs First and the California Partnership for Working Families, 2005.

Grunow, Frances M. "A Brief History of Housing in Detroit." *modelD*, November 17, 2015. http://www.modeldmedia.com/features/detroit-housing-pt1-111715.aspx.

Gyourko, Joseph, and Raven Molloy. "Regulation and Housing Supply." In *Handbook of Regional and Urban Economics, vol. 5*, ed. Giles Duranton, J. Vernon Henderson, and William C. Strange, 1289–1334. Amsterdam: Elsevier B.V., 2015.

Hagler, Yoav. *America 2050: Defining U.S. Megaregions*. New York: Regional Plan Association, 2009.

Hamilton, Darrick, William A. Darity Jr., Anne E. Price, Vishnu Sridharan, and Rebecca Tippett. *Umbrellas Don't Make It Rain: Why Studying and Working Hard Isn't Enough for Black Americans*. Oakland, CA: Insight Center for Community Economic Development, 2015, 1–10.

Hamilton Project, The. "Patenting Is Concentrated in Cities and Near Universities." The Brookings Institution, December 13, 2017. https://www.hamiltonproject.org/charts/patenting_is_concentrated_in_cities_and_near_universities.

Hanlon, W. Walker, and Stephan Heblich. "History and Urban Economics." Working Paper 27850, National Bureau of Economic Research, September 2020.

Harrington, Michael. *The Other America: Poverty in the United States*. New York: Macmillan, 1962.

Harris, Ken. "Blog: New Survey Finds 80 Percent of Detroit's 100 Top Black-Owned Businesses Feel Left Out of Building Boom." *dBusiness*, November 5, 2019. https://www.dbusiness.com/daily-news/blog-new-survey-finds-80-of-detroits-top-100-black-owned-businesses-feel-left-out-of-building-boom/.

Hartigan, John Jr. *Racial Situations: Class Predicaments of Whiteness in Detroit*. Princeton, NJ: Princeton University Press, 1999.

Heller, Walter W. *New Dimensions of Political Economy*. Cambridge, MA: Harvard University Press, 1966.

Hellerstein, Walter. "Cuno and Congress: An Analysis of Proposed Federal Legislation Authorizing State Economic Development Incentives." *Georgetown Journal of Law and Public Policy* 4, no. 1 (2006): 73–100.

Helper, Rose. *Racial Policies and Practices of Real Estate Brokers*. Minneapolis: University of Minnesota Press, 1969.

Henderson, Tim. "Slicing up Liberal Cities Becomes Go-To Redistricting Stragey." *Stateline*, Pew Memorial Trusts, September 22, 2021. https://www.pewtrusts.org/en/research-and-analysis/blogs/stateline/2021/09/22/slicing-up-liberal-cities-becomes-go-to-redistricting-strategy; nashville gerrymandering times

Henderson, Vernon, Ari Kuncoro, and Matt Turner. "Industrial Development in Cities." *Journal of Political Economy* 103, no. 5 (October 1995): 1067–1090.

Herbold, Hilary. "Never a Level Playing Field: Blacks and the GI Bill." *Journal of Blacks in Higher Education*, no. 6 (December 1994):104–108.

Hillier, Amy E. "Who Received Loans?: Home Owners' Loan Corporation Lending and Discrimination in Philadelphia in the 1930s." *Journal of Planning History* 2, no. 1 (2003): 3–24.

Hills, Roderick M., Jr., and David Schleicher. "Building Coalitions Out of Thin Air: Transferable Development Rights and 'Constituency Effects' in Land Use Law." *Journal of Legal Analysis* 12 (2020): 79–135.

Hirschman, Charles, and Elizabeth Mogford. "Immigration and the American Industrial Revolution from 1880 to 1920." *Social Science Research* 38, no. 4 (December 2009): 897–920.

Hobbs, Frank, and Nicole Stoops. *Demographic Trends in the 20th Century: Census 2000 Special Reports*. Washington, DC: U.S. Bureau of the Census, 2002.

Hobsbawm, Eric. *The Age of Extremes: A History of the World, 1914–1991*. New York: Vintage Books, 1994.

Hochschild, Jennifer L., and Michael N. Danielson. "The Demise of a Dinosaur: Analyzing School and Housing Desegregation in Yonkers." In *Race, Poverty, and Domestic Policy*, ed. C. Michael Henry, 221–241. New Haven, CT: Yale University Press, 2004.

Hoff, Madison. "Housing in the US Has Not Been Able to Keep up with Buyer Demand over the Past Decade." *Business Insider*, September 27, 2020.

Hofstadter, Richard. *The Age of Reform: From Bryan to F.D.R.* New York: Vintage, 1955.

Hofstadter, Richard. "The Myth of the Happy Yeoman." *American Heritage* 7, no. 3 (April 1956): 42–47.

Howell, David R., and Arne L. Kalleberg. "Declining Job Quality in the United States: Explanations and Evidence." *RSF: The Russell Sage Journal of the Social Sciences* 5, no. 4 (September 2019): 1–53.

Hoyman, Michele, and Christopher Faricy. "It Takes a Village: A Test of the Creative Class, Social Capital, and Human Capital Theories." *Urban Affairs Review* 44, no. 3 (January 2009): 311–333.

Huddle, Frank P. *Automobiles in the Postwar Economy*. Washington, DC: CQ Press, 1945.

Hurley, Amanda Kolson. "How the Green New Deal Could Retrofit Suburbs." *CityLab*, February 11, 2019. https://www.citylab.com/perspective/2019/02/green-new-deal-greenbelt-suburbs-climate-change/582445/.

Husock, Howard. *The Pension Grand Bargain: A New Reform Model for Cities*. New York: Manhattan Institute, 2016.

International Brotherhood of Teamsters. "California Port Truck Drivers Awarded Over $1.2 Million for Wage Theft." *Teamsters News*, April 17, 2019. https://teamster.org/news/2019/04/california-port-truck-drivers-awarded-over-12-million-wage-theft.

Jackson, C. Kirabo, Rucker C. Johnson, and Claudia Persico. "The Effects of School Spending on Educational and Economic Outcomes: Evidence from School Finance Reforms." *Quarterly Journal of Economics* 131, no. 1 (February 2016): 157–218.

Jackson, Kenneth T. "Federal Subsidy and the Suburban Dream: The First Quarter-Century of Government Intervention in the Housing Market." *Records of the Columbia Historical Society*, 50 (1980): 421–451.

Jackson, Kenneth T. *Crabgrass Frontier: The Suburbanization of the United States.* New York: Oxford University Press, 1985.

Jacobs, Jane. *The Death and Life of Great American Cities.* New York: Random House, 1961.

James, Frank. "Martin Luther King Jr. in Chicago" In *Chicago Days: 150 Defining Moments in the Life of a Great City*, ed. Stevenson Swanson, 202–204. Chicago: Contemporary Books, 1997.

Janeway, William H. *Doing Capitalism in the Innovation Economy: Markets, Speculation, and the State.* New York: Cambridge University Press, 2012.

Janis, Madeline, Co-Founder and National Policy Director, Los Angeles Alliance for a New Economy. Interview by Richard McGahey, July 10, 2014.

Janis, Madeline. "Community Benefits: New Movement for Equitable Urban Development." *Race, Poverty, and the Environment* 15, no. 1 (2008): 73–75.

Jefferson, Thomas. *Notes on the State of Virginia.* Richmond, VA: J.W. Randolph (1853):175–177. https://archive.org/details/notesonstateofvio1jeff.

Jefferson, Thomas. "To Dr. Benjamin Rush Monticello, September 23, 1800." *The Letters of Thomas Jefferson, 1743–1826.* September 23, 1800. http://www.let.rug.nl/usa/presidents/thomas-jefferson /letters-of-thomas-jefferson/jefl134.php.

Jeffries, John W. "Mobilization and Its Impact." In *World War II and the American Home Front*, ed. Marilyn M. Harper. Washington, DC: National Park Service, 2007.

Jenkins, Destin. *The Bonds of Inequality: Debt and the Making of the American City.* Chicago: University of Chicago Press, 2021.

Jenkinson, Clay. "Thomas Jefferson, Epidemics, and His Vision for American Cities." *Governing* April 1, 2020.

Jobs to Move America. "US Employment Plan." April 10, 2020. https://jobstomoveamerica.org /resource/u-s-employment-plan-2/.

Johnson, Robert. "The Climate Crisis and the Global New Deal—Bob Pollin." *Podcast: Economics and Beyond*, Institute for New Economic Thinking, February 25, 2021. https://www .ineteconomics.org/perspectives/podcasts?q=pollin.

Joint Center for Housing Studies. *The State of the Nation's Housing 2019.* Cambridge, MA: Joint Center for Housing Studies of Harvard University, 2019.

Jones, Christopher. "Border Warfare: Can We Do It Differently This Time?" *Regional Plan Association*, January 26, 2010.

Jones, Janelle, and John Schmitt. *A College Degree Is No Guarantee.* Washington, DC: Center for Economic and Policy Research, 2014.

Jones, Janelle, and Ben Zipperer. *Unfilled Promises: Amazon Fulfillment Centers Do Not Create Broad-Based Employment Growth.* Washington, DC: Economic Policy Institute, 2018.

Jones-Correa, Michael. "American Riots: Structures, Institutions and History." Working Paper 148, Russell Sage Foundation, 1999.

Jouppi, Shelby. "Detroit's Community Benefit Ordinance Yields Hours of Dialogue and Almost No Community Benefits." *WDET*, March 19, 2018. https://wdet.org/posts/2018/03/19/86319-detroits-community-benefits-ordinance-yields-hours-of-dialogue-and-almost-no-community-benefits/.

Judd, Dennis R., and Todd Swanstrom. *City Politics: Private Power and Public Policy*. New York: HarperCollins, 1994.

Kaffer, Nancy. "Land Bank Limbo." *Detroit Metro Times*, November 30, 2005.

Kanno-Youngs, Zolan, and Madeline Ngo. "Racial Equity in Infrastructure, a U.S. Goal, Is Left to States." *New York Times*, November 16, 2021.

Kantor, Paul. "The Dependent City: The Changing Political Economy of Urban Economic Development in the United States." *Urban Affairs Review* 22, no. 4 (June 1987): 493–520.

Kantor, Paul, and Stephen David. "The Political Economy of Change in Urban Budgetary Politics: A Framework for Analysis and a Case Study." *British Journal of Political Science* 13, no. 3 (July 1983): 254–274.

Katz, Bruce, and Jeremy Nowak. *The New Localism*. Washington, DC: Brookings Institution, 2017.

Katz, Bruce, and Julie Wagner. *The Rise of Innovation Districts: A New Geography of Innovation in America*. Washington, DC: Brookings Institution, 2014.

Katz, Michael B. *In the Shadow of the Poorhouse: A Social History of Welfare in America*. New York: Basic Books, 1996.

Katznelson, Ira. *When Affirmative Action Was White: An Untold History of Racial Inequality in Twentieth-Century America*. New York: Norton, 2005.

Kazis, Noah. *Ending Exclusionary Zoning in New York City's Suburbs*. NYU Furman Center for Real Estate and Urban Policy, New York University, November 9, 2020.

Kennedy, Randy. "Christie's Reveals Detroit Art Appraisal." *New York Times*, December 4, 2013.

Kenworthy, Lane. "America's Great Decoupling." In *Inequality and Inclusive Growth in Rich Countries*, ed. Brian Nolan. New York: Oxford University Press, 2018.

Kenyon, Daphne A., Adam H. Langley, and Bethany P. Paquin. *Rethinking Property Tax Incentives for Business*. Cambridge, MA: Lincoln Institute of Land Policy, June 2012.

Khanna, Parag. "When Cities Rule the World." *McKinsey and Company*, February 2011, https://www.mckinsey.com/featured-insights/urbanization/when-cities-rule-the-world.

Kim, Marlene. "Intersectionality and Gendered Racism in the United States: A New Theoretical Framework." *Review of Radical Political Economics* 52, no. 4 (2020): 616–625.

Kleiner, Morris M. *Reforming Occupational Licensing Policies*, Working Paper 2005–01, Washington, DC: Hamilton Project, Brookings Institution, March 2015.

Kleiner, Morris M., and Alan B. Krueger. "Analyzing the Extent and Influence of Occupational Licensing on the Labor Market." *Journal of Labor Economics* 31, no. 2, pt. 2 (April 2013): S173–S202.

Klepper, Stephen. "The Evolution of the U.S. Automobile Industry and Detroit as Its Capital." Working Paper, Department of Social & Decision Sciences, Carnegie Mellon University, January 2001. https://www.researchgate.net/scientific-contributions/Steven-Klepper-9626536.

Kling, William. "Wallace Clips Detroit Speech Short as Violence Breaks Out." *Chicago Tribune*, October 30, 1968.

Klowden, Kevin, and Perry Wong. *Los Angeles Economy Project: Executive Summary and Recommendations*. Santa Monica, CA: Milken Institute, 2005.

Kneebone, Elizabeth. "Job Sprawl Revisited: The Changing Geography of Metropolitan Employment." Metropolitan Opportunity Series. Washington, DC: Brookings Institution, April 2009.

Kneebone, Elizabeth. "Job Sprawl Stalls: The Great Recession and Metropolitan Employment Location." Metropolitan Opportunity Series. Washington, DC: Brookings Institution, April 2013.

Kolbert, Elizabeth. "Cuomo's Crime Remedy: 'Produce the Police, Period.'" *New York Times*, September 11, 1990.

Kolesnikova, Natalia, and Yang Liu. "A Bleak Thirty Years for Black Men: Economic Progress Was Slim in Urban America." *The Regional Economist*, Federal Reserve Bank of St. Louis, 2010, 4–9.

Konczal, Mike, and Marshall Steinbaum, "Declining Entrepreneurialism, Labor Mobility, and Business Dynamism: A Demand-Side Approach." Working Paper, Roosevelt Institute, July 2016.

Kotkin, Joel. "Countering Progressives' Assault on Suburbia." *RealClearPolitics*, July 10, 2015. http://www.realclearpolitics.com/articles/2015/07/10/countering_progressives_assault_on _suburbia_127327.html.

Kotkin, Joel. "Urban Legends." *Foreign Policy*, August 6, 2010.

Kotlowski, Dean. "Black Power—Nixon Style: The Nixon Administration and Minority Business Enterprise." *Business History Review* 72, no. 3 (1998): 409–445.

Kravitz, Daniel. *Fighting for Equity in Development: The Story of Detroit's Community Benefits Ordinance*. Detroit People's Platform and Equitable Detroit Coalition, 2017. https://building movement.org/wp-content/uploads/2019/08/Fighting-for-Equity-in-Development-The -Story-of-Detroits-Community-Benefits-Ordinance.pdf.

Krugman, Paul. "Fifty Herbert Hoovers." *New York Times*, December 28, 2008.

Krugman, Paul. "Increasing Returns, Monopolistic Competition, and International Trade." *Journal of Political Economy* 99, no. 3 (1991), 483–499.

Krugman, Paul. "The New Economic Geography, Now Middle-Aged." *Regional Studies* 45, no. 1 (2011): 4.

Krugman, Paul. "Why a Blue City Is Feeling the Blues." *New York Times*, January 17, 2022.

Krugman, Paul. "Why Can't We Get Cities Right?" *New York Times*, September 4, 2017.

Kushner, David. *Levittown: Two Families, One Tycoon, and the Fight for Civil Rights in America's Legendary Suburb*. New York: Walker, 2009.

Kuznets, Simon. "Economic Growth and Income Inequality." *American Economic Review* 45, no. 1 (March 1955): 1–28.

Lander, Brad, Krista Olson, and Andrew McWilliam. "New York by the Numbers: Monthly Economic and Fiscal Outlook." Office of the New York City Comptroller, February 2022, table 1. https://comptroller.nyc.gov/newsroom/new-york-by-the-numbers-monthly-economic-and -fiscal-outlook-no-62-february-7th-2022/.

Lander, Brad, and Laura Wolf-Powers. "Remaking New York: Can Prosperity Be Shared and Sustainable?" Working Paper, Center for Community Development, Pratt Institute, 2004. http://repository.upenn.edu/cplan_papers/43/.

Landis, John D. "The COVID-19 Recession: Which Urban Economies Have Performed Better or Worse and Why." Penn IUR Policy Brief, Penn Institute for Urban Research, University of Pennsylvania, October 2021.

Langston, Abbie, Justin Scoggins, and Matthew Walsh. *Race and the Work of the Future: Advancing Workforce Equity in the United States.* Los Angeles: PolicyLink and the USC Equity Research Institute, 2020.

Larrubia, Evelyn. "Labor, Environmentalists Unusual Allies." *Los Angeles Times*, November 27, 2008.

Lazonick, William R. "Labor in the Twenty-First Century: The Top 0.1 percent and the Disappearing Middle Class." Working Paper 4. Institute for New Economic Thinking, New York, February 2015.

LeBlanc, Beth, Francis X. Donnelly, and Craig Mauger. "Wayne Co. Canvassers Certify Election Results After Initial Deadlock." *Detroit News*, November 18, 2020.

Lemann, Nicholas. "The Myth of Community Development." *New York Times Magazine*, January 9, 1999. https://www.nytimes.com/1994/01/09/magazine/the-myth-of-community-development.html.

Lemann, Nicholas. "The Unfinished War." *Atlantic Monthly* 263, no. 1 (January 1989).

Leonhardt, David. "The Black-White Wage Gap Is as Big as It Was in 1950." *New York Times*, June 25, 2020.

LeRoy, Greg. *The Great American Jobs Scam: Corporate Tax Dodging and the Myth of Job Creation.* San Francisco: Berrett-Koehler, 2005.

LeRoy, Greg, Allison Lack, and Karla Walter, with Philip Mattera. *The Geography of Incentives: Economic Development and Land Use in Michigan* Washington, DC: Good Jobs First, 2006.

Levy, Frank, and Peter Temin. "Inequality and Institutions in 20th Century America." Working Paper 13106, National Bureau of Economic Research, May 2007.

Lincoln Institute of Land Policy. "Fiscally Standardized Cities Data Base." Accessed December 28, 2020. https://www.lincolninst.edu/research-data/data-toolkits/fiscally-standardized-cities.

Liu, Katrina, and Robert Danewood. *Local Hiring and First Source Hiring Policies: A National Review of Policies and Identification of Best Practices.* Pittsburgh, PA: Regional Housing Legal Services, 2013.

Lobo, José, Kevin Stolarick, and Richard Florida. "Growth Without Growth: Population and Productivity Change in U.S. Metropolitan Areas, 1980–2006." Working Paper, Martin Prosperity Institute, University of Toronto, 2011.

Logan, Trevon M., and John M. Parman. "The National Rise in Residential Segregation." *Journal of Economic History* 77, no. 1 (March 2017): 127–170.

Long, Heather, and Andrew Van Dam. "The Black-White Economic Divide Is as Wide as It Was in 1968." *Washington Post*, June 4, 2020.

Los Angeles Alliance for a New Economy. *How We Win, What We Do.* Accessed May 9, 2022. https://web.archive.org/web/20151127012631/http://www.laane.org/what-we-do/how-we-win/.

Los Angeles Bureau of Sanitation. *Request for Proposals: City-Wide Exclusive Franchise System for Municipal Solid Waste Collection and Handling.* Los Angeles: Los Angeles Bureau of Sanitation, 2014.

Los Angeles County Metropolitan Transit Authority. *General Management—Construction Careers Project*. Los Angeles: Los Angeles County Metropolitan Transit Authority, 2012.

Los Angeles County Metropolitan Transit Authority. *Project Labor Agreement*. Los Angeles: Los Angeles County Metropolitan Transit Authority, January 26, 2012. http://media.metro.net /about_us/pla/images/Project_Labor_Agreement.pdf.

Los Angeles 2020 Commission. *A Time for Action*. Los Angeles: Los Angeles 2020 Commission, 2014. https://www.socalgrantmakers.org/sites/default/files/resources/A-Time-For-Action%20 LA%202020%20Report%20April%202014.pdf.

Los Angeles 2020 Commission. *A Time for Truth*. Los Angeles: Los Angeles 2020 Commission, 2013.

Los Angeles 2000 Committee. LA 2000: Final Report of the Los Angeles 2000 Committee. Los Angeles: Los Angeles 2000 Committee, 1988.

Los Angeles World Airports. *Community Benefits Agreement—LAX Master Plan Program*. Los Angeles, Los Angeles World Airports, 2004, 1–35. https://www.lawa.org/-/media/lawa-web /lawa-our-lax/lax_cba_final.ashx.

Lowe, Kate, and Joe Grengs. "Private Donations for Public Transit: The Equity Implications of Detroit's Public–Private Streetcar." *Journal of Planning Education and Research* 40, no. 3 (September 2020): 289–303.

Luce, Henry. "The American Century." *Diplomatic History* 23, no. 2 (1999): 159–171.

Lucking, Liz. "432 Park Avenue Leads Luxury Real Estate in Another Strong Week." *Mansion Global*, April 9, 2018. https://www.mansionglobal.com/articles/93725-432-park-avenue-leads-luxury -real-estate-in-another-strong-week.

Lukas, J. Anthony. *Common Ground: A Turbulent Decade in the Lives of Three American Families*. New York: Vintage, 1986.

Lund, Susan. "What 800 Executives Envision for the Post-Pandemic Workforce." McKinsey Global Institute, September 2020.

Maciag, Mike. "Black and Out of Work: How the Recession Changed Government Employment." *Governing*, December 2015. http://www.governing.com/topics/mgmt/gov-minorities -public-employment-recession.html.

Maciag, Mike, and J. B. Wogan. "With Less State Aid, Localities Look for Ways to Cope." *Governing*, February 2017. http://www.governing.com/topics/finance/gov-state-aid-revenue-sharing -intergovernmental-revenue.html.

Mackinac Center for Public Policy. "Takeover of Detroit Schools Shows Few Intended Results." January 19, 2006. https://www.mackinac.org/7556.

Maguire, Joe. *How Increasing Income Inequality Is Dampening U.S. Economic Growth, and Possible Ways to Change the Tide*. New York: Standard & Poor's, 2014.

Malanga, Stephen. "The Real Reason the Once Great City of Detroit Came to Ruin." *Wall Street Journal*, July 26, 2013.

Mallach, Allan. *The Divided City: Poverty and Prosperity in Urban America*. Washington DC: Island Press, 2018.

Mallach, Stanley. "The Origins of the Decline of Urban Mass Transportation in the United States, 1890–1930." *Urbanism Past and Present* 8 (1979): 1–17.

Manville, Michael. "Liberals and Housing: A Study in Ambivalence." *Housing Policy Debate*, May 15, 2021. https://doi.org/10.1080/10511482.2021.1931933.

Maraniss, David. *Once in a Great City: A Detroit Story*. New York: Simon and Schuster, 2015.

Marcano, Alexius, Matthew Festa, and Kyle Shelton. *Developing Houston: Land-Use Regulation in the "Unzoned City" and Its Outcomes*. Houston, TX: Rice University, 2017.

Markusen, Ann. "Urban Development and the Politics of a Creative Class: Evidence from a Study of Artists." *Environment and Planning A: Economy and Space* 38, no. 10 (October 2006): 1921–1940.

Marshall, Alfred. *Principles of Economics*, 8th ed. London: Macmillan, 1920.

Massey, Douglas S., and Nancy A. Denton. *American Apartheid: Segregation and the Making of the Underclass*. Cambridge, MA: Harvard University Press, 1993.

Mazzucato, Mariana. *The Entrepreneurial State: Debunking Public vs. Private Sector Myths*. London: Anthem Press, 2013.

McCarthy, George W., and Samuel A. Moody. "Introduction." In *Land and the City*, ed. George W. McCarthy, Gregory K. Ingram, and Samuel A. Moody, 1–8. Cambridge, MA: Lincoln Institute of Land Policy, 2016.

McClaughry, John. "Jefferson's Vision." *New York Times*, April 13, 1982.

McClelland, Edward. "Kwame Kilpatrick Exits, with Barack Obama Holding the Door." *Salon*, September 4, 2008. http://www.salon.com/2008/09/04/detroit_2/.

McDonald, John F. *Postwar Urban America: Demography, Politics, and Social Policy*. New York: Routledge, 2015.

McDonald, John F. "What Happened to and in Detroit?" *Urban Studies* 51, no. 16 (December 2014): 3309–3329.

McFarland, Christina, and Michael A. Pagano. *City Fiscal Conditions*. Washington, DC: National League of Cities, 2017.

McGahey, Richard M. "Back to Office Work, with (or Without) a Covid-19 Vaccine." *Forbes*, November 11, 2020. https://www.forbes.com/sites/richardmcgahey/2020/11/11/back-to-office-work-with-or-without-a-vaccine/?sh=5030c480c455.

McGahey, Richard. "Biden's Essential Stimulus Won't Solve State and City Budget Problems." *Forbes*, January 15, 2021. https://www.forbes.com/sites/richardmcgahey/2021/01/15/bidens-essential-stimulus-wont-solve-state-and-city-budget-problems/?sh=57d0e58a3154.

McGahey, Richard. "Covid's Comeback Means Washington Must Help Red and Blue States—Now." *Forbes*, December 8, 2020. https://www.forbes.com/sites/richardmcgahey/2020/12/08/both-red-and-blue-states-need-federal-money-now/?sh=6448d90c7c64.

McGahey, Richard. "De Blasio Economics: Growth with Equity." *City and State*, September 26, 2014. https://www.cityandstateny.com/articles/policy/de-blasio-economics-growth-with-equity.html.

McGahey, Richard. "In Debate, Trump Says Biden's Fair Housing Plans Will Destroy the Suburbs." *Forbes*, September 30, 2020. https://www.forbes.com/sites/richardmcgahey/2020/09/30/in-debate-trump-says-bidens-housing-plans-will-destroy-the-suburbs/?sh=1dd86a4b5b4c.

McGahey, Richard. "Monetary and Fiscal Policy Under Covid-19: The Case of the Fed's Municipal Liquidity Facility." *Forbes*, July 21, 2020. https://www.forbes.com/sites/richardmcgahey/#7734dc4d44a2.

McGahey, Richard. "New California Laws Attack the State's Housing Crisis." *Forbes*, September 27, 2021. https://www.forbes.com/sites/richardmcgahey/2021/09/27/new-california-laws-attack-the-states-housing-crisis/?sh=2290b79d3166.

McGahey, Richard. "The Political Economy of Cities." Schwartz Center for Economic Policy Analysis, New School for Social Research, November 24, 2020. https://www.economicpolicyresearch.org/resource-library/research/inequality-and-austerity-the-political-economy-of-cities.

McGahey, Richard M. "The Political Economy of Growth and Distribution: Economics, Public Policy, and Politics." In *Economics as Worldly Philosophy: Essays in Honour of Robert L. Heilbroner*, ed. Ron Blackwell, Jaspal Chatha, and Edward J. Nell, 161–186. New York: St. Martin's Press, 1993.

McGahey, Richard. "Regional Economic Development in Theory and Practice." In *Retooling for Growth: Building a 21st-Century Economy in America's Older Industrial Areas*, ed. Richard McGahey and Jennifer S. Vey, 3–32. Washington, DC: Brookings Institution Press, 2008.

McGahey, Richard. "Unemployment Benefits, Stimulus Checks, and State and City Aid Needed as Economy Slows." *Forbes*, July 24, 2020. https://www.forbes.com/sites/richardmcgahey/2020/07/24/#30de786e2ba8.

McGahey, Richard. "Why Didn't COVID-19 Wreck State and City Budgets? Federal Spending." *Forbes*, September 1, 2021. https://www.forbes.com/sites/richardmcgahey/?sh=170de00644a2.

McGruder, Kevin. *Race and Real Estate: Conflict and Cooperation in Harlem, 1890–1920*. New York: Columbia University Press, 2015.

McGuckin, Nancy A., and Nanda Srinivasan. *Journey-to-Work Trends in the United States and Its Major Metropolitan Areas, 1960–1990*. Washington, DC: US Department of Transportation, 2003. https://rosap.ntl.bts.gov/view/dot/5543.

McGuire, Sheila, Joshua Freely, Carol Clymer, Maureen Conway, and Deena Schwartz. *Tuning In to Local Labor Markets: Findings from the Sectoral Employment Impact Study*. Philadelphia: Public/Private Ventures, 2010.

McMahon, E. J. "Mario Cuomo, Tax Cutter" *City Journal*, January 2, 2015. https://www.city-journal.org/html/mario-cuomo-tax-cutter-11486.html.

Mears, Hadley. "Cranes Proliferated in L.A. but Don't Call It a Building Boom." *Curbed Los Angeles*, January 2, 2020. https://la.curbed.com/2020/1/2/21034785/los-angeles-development-housing-shortage.

Metzger, Kurt, and Jason Booza. "African Americans in the United States, Michigan, and Metropolitan Detroit." Working Paper 8, Wayne State University, February 2002.

Meyer, David R. "Midwestern Industrialization and the American Manufacturing Belt in the Nineteenth Century." *Journal of Economic History* 49, no. 4 (December 1989): 921–937.

Meyerson, Harold. "L.A. Story." *The American Prospect*, August 6, 2013.

Mian, Atif, and Amir Sufi. *House of Debt: How They (and You) Caused the Great Recession, and How We Can Prevent It from Happening Again*. Chicago: University of Chicago Press, 2014.

Michigan State Police. *2004 Uniform Crime Report*. Lansing: Michigan State Police, 2005, 55–69. http://www.michigan.gov/documents/Cb-AgencyClearance04_140083_7.pdf.

Mielnicki, Lawrence, Farid Heydarpour, and Orlando Vasquez. *New York City's Labor Market: Evidence from the Recent Expansion*. New York: Office of the New York City Comptroller, June 26, 2017.

Mieszkowski, Peter, and Edwin S. Mills. "The Causes of Metropolitan Suburbanization." *Journal of Economic Perspectives* 7, no. 3 (August 1993): 136.

Miller, Jonathan. "Peak Suburb Has Passed." *Matrix Blog: Interpreting the Real Estate Economy*, December 28, 2020. https://www.millersamuel.com/peak-suburb-has-passed/?goal=0_69c077008e-7e05894f5d-120793247.

Milliken v. Bradley, 418 US 717 (1974).

Mills, Edwin S. "An Aggregative Model of Resource Allocation in a Metropolitan Area." *American Economic Review* 57, no. 2 (May 1967): 197–210.

Mishel, Lawrence. *Diversity in the New York City Union and Nonunion Construction Sectors*. Washington, DC: Economic Policy Institute, March 17, 2017.

Mishel, Lawrence. "Rebuilding Worker Power." *Finance and Development*, International Monetary Fund, December 2020.

Mishel, Lawrence, and Jori Kandra. "Wages for the Top 1 Percent Skyrocketed 160 Percent Since 1979 While the Share of Wages for the Bottom 90 Percent Shrunk." Working Economics blog, Economic Policy Institute, December 1, 2020.

Mollenkopf, John. "How 9/11 Reshaped the Political Environment in New York." In *Contentious City: The Politics of Recovery in New York*, ed. John Mollenkopf, 205–222. New York: Russell Sage Foundation, 2005.

Mollenkopf, John H. *A Phoenix in the Ashes: The Rise and Fall of the Koch Coalition in New York City Politics*. Princeton, NJ: Princeton University Press, 1992.

Mollenkopf, John H. "The Post-War Politics of Urban Development." *Politics and Society* 5, no. 3 (1975): 247–295.

Mollenkopf, John H., and Manuel Castells, *Dual City: Restructuring New York*. New York: Russell Sage Foundation, 1992.

Mollenkopf, John, Ana Champeny, Raphael Sonenshein, and Mark Drayse. "Race, Ethnicity, and Immigration in the 2005 Mayoral Elections in Los Angeles and New York." Working Paper 2007-07, Berkeley Institute of Urban and Regional Development, University of California at Berkeley, December 2006.

Mollenkopf, John, and Brad Lander. "Needed: A Progressive Agenda." In *Toward a 21st Century City for All: Progressive Policies for New York City in 2013 and Beyond*, ed. John H. Mollenkopf, 1–15. New York: City University of New York, 2013.

Mollenkopf, John, David Olson, and Timothy Ross. "Immigrant Political Participation in New York and Los Angeles." In *Governing American Cities: Inter-Ethnic Coalitions, Competition, and Conflict*, ed. Michael Jones-Correa, 17–70. New York, Russell Sage Foundation, 2001.

Mollenkopf, John, Joseph Pereira, Steven Romalewski, and Lesley Hirsch. "Shifting Shares: Demographic Change, Differential Mobility, and Electoral Trends in New York City, 2000 to 2011." In *Toward a 21st Century City for All: Progressive Policies for New York City in 2013 and Beyond*, ed. John Mollenkopf, 16–35. New York: City University of New York, 2013.

Molotch, Harvey. "The City as a Growth Machine: Toward a Political Economy of Place." *American Journal of Sociology*, 82 no. 2 (September 1976): 309–332.

Montes, Christian. *American Capitals: A Historical Geography*. Chicago: University of Chicago Press, 2014.

Mordechay, Kfir. *Vast Changes and an Uneasy Future: Racial and Regional Inequality in Southern California*. Los Angeles: Civil Rights Project/Proyecto Derechos Civiles, 2014.

Moretti, Enrico. "The Effect of High-Tech Clusters on the Productivity of Top Inventors." Working Paper 26270, National Bureau of Economic Research, September 2019.

Moretti, Enrico. "Human Capital Externalities in Cities." In *Handbook of Regional and Urban Economics, vol. 4*, ed. J. Vernon Henderson and Jacques-François Thisse, 2243–2291. Amsterdam: Elsevier B.V., 2004.

Moretti, Enrico. *The New Geography of Jobs*. New York: Houghton Mifflin Harcourt, 2012.

Moretti, Enrico, and Daniel J. Wilson. "The Effect of State Taxes on the Geographical Location of Top Earners: Evidence from Star Scientists." *American Economic Review* 107, no. 7 (2017): 1858–1903.

Morris K. Udall, "Reapportionment I: 'One Man, One Vote' . . . That's All She Wrote!" Special Collections at the University of Arizona Libraries, University of Arizona, transcript, October 14, 1964. http://speccoll.library.arizona.edu/online-exhibits/files/original /11ac559f0063813f0a80bed401b4597f.pdf.

Moss, Mitchell. *How New York City Won the Olympics*. New York: New York University Press, 2011.

Moss, Mitchell. "The Redevelopment of Lower Manhattan: The Role of the City." In *Contentious City: The Politics of Recovery in New York*, ed. John Mollenkopf, 95–111. New York: Russell Sage Foundation, 2005.

Moynihan, Daniel Patrick. *Maximum Feasible Misunderstanding: Community Action in the War on Poverty*. New York: Free Press, 1969.

Muro, Mark, Eli Byerly Duke, Yang You, and Robert Maxim. "Biden-Voting Counties Equal 70 Percent of America's Economy: What Does This Mean for the Nation's Political-Economic Divide?" Washington, DC: Brookings Institution, November 10, 2020.

Murphy, Jarrett. "Are Cities on Candidates' Minds? Where They Are on Urban Issues." *City Limits*, May 29, 2007. http://citylimits.org/2007/05/29/are-cities-on-candidates-minds-where -they-are-on-urban-issues/.

Murphy, Patrick, and Jennifer Paluch. *Just the Facts: Financing California's Public Schools*. San Francisco: Public Policy Institute of California, 2018.

Murray, Sheila E., Kim Rueben, and Carol Rosenberg. "State Education Spending: Current Pressures and Future Trends." *National Tax Journal* 60, no. 2 (June 2007): 325–345. https://www .urban.org/sites/default/files/publication/31091/1001132-State-Education-Spending-Current -Pressures-and-Future-Trends.PDF.

Muth, Richard F. *Cities and Housing*. Chicago: University of Chicago Press, 1969.

"N.A.A.C.P. Joins Attack on Detroit Housing Law." *New York Times*, December 22, 1964.

Nathan, Richard. "The Uses of Shared Revenue." *Journal of Finance* 30, no. 2 (May 1975): 557–565.

National Advisory Commission on Civil Disorders. *Report of the National Advisory Commission on Civil Disorders*. Washington, DC: U.S. Government Printing Office, 1968.

National Association of Realtors. "Historic Membership Count." *Historic Report*, National Association of Realtors. https://www.nar.realtor/membership/historic-report.

National Bureau of Economic Research. "COVID-19." Accessed May 9, 2022. https://www.nber
.org/topics/covid-19?page=1&perPage=50.

National Center for Education Statistics. "Concentration of Public School Students Eligible
for Free or Reduced-Price Lunch." Institute for Education Studies, May 2021. https://nces
.ed.gov/programs/coe/indicator_clb.asp.

National Committee Against Discrimination in Housing. *Jobs and Housing: A Study of Employment and Housing Opportunities for Racial Minorities in Suburban Areas of the New York
Metropolitan Area.* New York: National Committee Against Discrimination in Housing,
1970.

National Employment Law Project. *The Low-Wage Recovery: Industry Employment and Wages
Four Years into the Recovery.* New York: National Employment Law Project, 2014.

National Law Review. "The Sixth Circuit Holds Argument on the Tax Mandate." January 26,
2022. https://www.natlawreview.com/article/sixth-circuit-holds-argument-tax-mandate.

National League of Cities. "Federal Budget Tracker." October 8, 2020. https://www.nlc.org/resource
/federal-budget-tracker/.

National League of Cities. *2012 National Municipal Policy and Resolutions.* Washington, DC:
National League of Cities, 2011.

Nelson, Garrett Dash, and Alasdair Rae. "An Economic Geography of the United States: From
Commutes to Megaregions." *PLoS ONE* 11, no. 11 (2016). doi:10.1371/journal.pone.0166083.

Nelson A. Rockefeller Institute of Government. *Giving and Getting: Regional Distribution of Revenue and Spending in the New York State Budget, Fiscal Year 2009–10.* Albany: State University of New York at Albany, 2011.

Neuman, William, and J. David Goodman. "In City Council, Power Shifts Away from Progressives." *New York Times,* February 2, 2018.

Neumark, David, and Timothy J. Bartik. "Improving the Effectiveness of Place-Based Policies to
Address Poverty and Joblessness." *Journal of Policy Analysis and Management* 39, no. 3 (May
2020): 835–857.

Neumark, David, and Jed Kolko. "Do Enterprise Zones Create Jobs? Evidence from California's
Enterprise Zone Program." *Journal of Urban Economics* 68, no. 1 (July 2010): 1–19.

Neumark, David, J.M. Ian Salas, and William Wascher. "More on Recent Evidence on Effects
of Minimum Wages in the United States." *IZA Journal of Labor Policy* 3, no. 24 (2014): 1–26.

Neumark, David, and Peter Shirley. "Myth or Measurement: What Does the New Minimum
Wage Research Say About Minimum Wages and Job Loss in the United States?" Working
Paper 28388, National Bureau of Economic Research, January 2021.

Neumark, David, and Helen Simpson. "Place-Based Policies." In *Handbook of Regional and
Urban Economics, vol. 5,* ed. Giles Duranton, J. Vernon Henderson, and William C. Strange,
1197–1287. Amsterdam: Elsevier B.V., 2015.

Newfield, Jack. "The Full Rudy: The Man, The Mayor, The Myth." *The Nation,* May 30, 2002.

Newfield, Jack, and Paul Du Brul. *The Abuse of Power: The Permanent Government and the Fall
of New York.* New York: Viking, 1997.

New York City Commission on Human Rights. *Building Barriers: Discrimination in New York
City's Construction Trades.* New York: New York City Commission on Human Rights, 1993.
http://www.talkinghistory.org/sisters/images/building_barriers.pdf.

New York City Independent Budget Office. *Recession Ahead: While Concerns Mount, Projections Show Moderate Growth in NYC Tax Revenue for the Upcoming Years.* New York: New York Independent Budget Office, 2019.

Noguchi, Yuki. "As Cities Raise Minimum Wages, Many States Are Rolling Them Back." *National Public Radio*, July 18, 2017. https://www.npr.org/2017/07/18/537901833/as-cities-raise-minimum -wages-many-states-are-rolling-them-back.

Noll, Roger G., and Andrew Zimbalist, eds. *Sports, Jobs, and Taxes: The Economic Impact of Sports Teams and Stadiums.* Washington, DC: Brookings Institution Press, 1997.

Norton, Peter D. *Fighting Traffic: The Dawn of the Motor Age in the American City.* Cambridge, MA: MIT Press, 2008.

Nussbaum, Jeff. "The Night New York Saved Itself from Bankruptcy." *The New Yorker*, October 16, 2015.

Obama, Barack. "Remarks by President Obama and President Hollande of France After Touring Thomas Jefferson's Monticello." The White House, February 10, 2014, transcript. https:// obamawhitehouse.archives.gov/the-press-office/2014/02/10/remarks-president-obama-and -president-hollande-france-after-touring-thom.

Obama for America. "Barack Obama: Supporting Urban Prosperity" January 16, 2008. https:// www.readkong.com/page/barack-obama-supporting-urban-prosperity-714351.

O'Connor, Alice. "Swimming Against the Tide: A Brief History of Federal Policy in Poor Communities." In *Urban Problems and Community Development*, ed. Ronald F. Ferguson and William T. Dickens, 77–109. Washington, DC: Brookings Institution, 1999.

Office of Management and Budget. *Study to Identify Methods to Assess Equity: Report to the President.* Washington, DC: Executive Office of the President, July 20, 2021.

Office of the Mayor. "Mayor de Blasio, Speaker Mark-Viverito, and City Council Reach Early Agreement on FY2018 Budget." June 2, 2017. http://www1.nyc.gov/office-of-the-mayor/news /387-17/mayor-de-blasio-speaker-mark-viverito-city-council-reach-early-agreement-fy2018 -budget-/#/0.

Office of the State Deputy Comptroller. "New York City's Economic Dependence on Wall Street." *Challenge* 42, no. 2 (March/April 1999): 6–22.

O'Loughlin, John, and Dale A. Berg. "The Election of Black Mayors, 1969 and 1973." *Annals of the Association of American Geographers* 67, no. 2 (June 1977): 223–238.

Orfield, Myron. *American Metropolitics: The New Suburban Reality.* Washington, DC: Brookings Institution, 2002.

Organization for Economic Co-operation and Development (OECD). *Does Income Inequality Hurt Economic Growth?* December 2014. http://www.oecd.org/els/soc/Focus-Inequality-and -Growth-2014.pdf.

Organization for Economic Cooperation and Development (OECD). *Making Cities Work for All: Data and Actions for Inclusive Growth.* Paris, OECD Publishing, 2016.

Osterman, Paul. "The Promise, Performance, and Policies of Community Colleges." In *Reinventing Higher Education: The Promise of Innovation*, ed. Ben Wildavsky, Andrew P. Kelly, and Kevin Carey, 129–158. Cambridge, MA: Harvard Education Press, 2011.

Ostrom, Elinor. *Governing the Commons: The Evolution of Institutions for Collective Action.* New York: Cambridge University Press, 1990.

Ostry, Jonathan D., Andrew Berg, and Charalambos G. Tsangarides. *Redistribution, Inequality, and Growth*, Washington, DC: International Monetary Fund, 2014.

Ouazad, Amine. "Blockbusting: Brokers and the Dynamics of Segregation." *Journal of Economic Theory* 157 (2015): 811–841.

Ozimek, Adam. "How Remote Work is Shifting Population Growth Across the U.S." Economic Innovation Group, April 13, 2022. https://eig.org/how-remote-work-is-shifting-population -growth-across-the-u-s/

Panel on Policies and Prospects for Metropolitan and Nonmetropolitan America. *Urban America in the Eighties: Perspectives and Prospects.* Washington, DC: U.S. Government Printing Office, 1980.

Parrott, James. "CityViews: Alarmist Commentary on City Budget Misjudges Responsible Growth." *City Limits.* December 21, 2018. https://citylimits.org/2018/12/21/cityviews-alarmist -commentary-on-city-budget-misjudges-responsible-growth/.

Parrott, James A. *Inequality in New York City: Does Local Policy Matter in the Age of the Covid-19 Pandemic?* New York: Center for New York City Affairs, The New School, June 2020.

Parrott, James. "Neighborhoods and the Fiscal Boom." *Gotham Gazette*, August 7, 2007. http://www .gothamgazette.com/index.php/development/3629-neighborhoods-and-the-fiscal-boom.

Partnership for Working Families. *Common Challenges in Negotiating Community Benefit Agreements—And How to Avoid Them.* Oakland, CA: Partnership for Working Families, 2016.

Pastor, Manuel, Jr. *Racial/Ethnic Inequality in Environmental-Hazard Exposure in Metropolitan Los Angeles.* Berkeley: California Policy Research Center, 2001.

Pastor, Manuel, Jr. *State of Resistance: What California's Dizzying Descent and Remarkable Resurgence Mean for America's Future.* New York: The New Press, 2018.

Pastor, Manuel, Jr., Chris Benner, and Martha Matsuoka, *This Could Be the Start of Something Big: How Social Movements for Regional Equity Are Reshaping Metropolitan America.* Ithaca, NY: Cornell University Press, 2009, 121.

Pastor, Manuel, Jr., Rachel Morello-Frosch, and James L. Sadd, "The Air Is Always Cleaner on the Other Side: Race, Space, and Ambient Air Toxic Exposure in California." *Journal of Urban Affairs* 27, no. 2 (June 2005): 127–148.

Pastor, Manuel, Jr., and Michele Prichard. *LA Rising: The 1992 Civil Unrest, the Arc of Social Justice Organizing, and the Lessons for Today's Movement Building.* Los Angeles: Liberty Hill Foundation and USC Program for Environmental and Regional Equity, 2012.

Peck, Sarah Herman. *"Sanctuary" Jurisdictions: Federal, State, and Local Policies and Related Litigation.* Report R44795. Washington, DC: Congressional Research Service, May 3, 2019.

Perlstein, Rick. *Nixonland: The Rise of a President and the Fracturing of America.* New York: Simon and Schuster, 2008.

Perry, Andre M. *Know Your Price: Valuing Black Lives and Property in America's Black Cities.* Washington DC: Brookings Institution Press, 2020.

Perry, David C., and Alfred J. Watkins. *The Rise of the Sunbelt Cities.* Beverly Hills, CA: Sage Publications, 1977.

Perry, Mark. J. "Understanding America's Enormous $20.6T Economy by Comparing US Metro Area GDPs to Entire Countries." *Carpe Diem* blog, American Enterprise Institute, December 18, 2019. https://www.aei.org/carpe-diem/understanding-americas-enormous-20-6t-economy -by-comparing-us-metro-area-gdps-to-entire-countries/.

Peters, Alan, and Peter Fisher. "The Failure of Economic Development Incentives." *Journal of the American Planning Association* 70, no. 1 (2004): 27–37.

Peterson, Sarah Jo. *Planning the Home Front: Building Bombers and Communities at Willow Run.* Chicago: University of Chicago Press, 2013.

Pew Charitable Trusts. "Federal Share of State Revenue, Fiscal 50: State Trends and Analysis." Updated October 8, 2019. http://www.pewtrusts.org/en/multimedia/data-visualizations/2014 /fiscal-50#ind1.

Phillips-Fein, Kim. *Fear City: New York's Fiscal Crisis and the Rise of Austerity Politics.* New York: Metropolitan Books, 2017.

Pittelko, Brian, Bryan Bommersbach, and George Erickcek. *The Employment Impact of the New Economy Initiative (NEI) on the Detroit Region and the State of Michigan.* Kalamazoo, MI: W. E. Upjohn Institute for Employment Research, 2016.

Plunkert, Lois M. "The 1980's: A Decade of Job Growth and Industry Shifts." *Monthly Labor Review* 113, no. 9 (September 1990): 3–16.

Poethig, Erika, Solomon Greene, Christina Stacy, Tanaya Srini, Brady Meixell, Steven Brown, and Diana Elliott. *Inclusive Recovery in US Cities.* Washington, DC: Urban Institute, 2018.

PolicyLink. *For Love of Country: A Path for the Federal Government to Advance Racial Equity.* Oakland, CA: PolicyLink, July 2021.

PolicyLink and Program for Environmental and Regional Equity. *An Equity Profile of the Los Angeles Region.* Oakland, CA: PolicyLink, 2017.

Porter, Michael E., Christian H. M. Ketels, Anne Habiby, and David Zipper. *New York City: Bloomberg's Strategy for Economic Development.* Cambridge, MA: Harvard Business School, 2009.

Pratt, Chastity. "It's Official: No Vote This Year for Transit Fixes in Southeast Michigan." *Bridge Michigan,* July 19, 2018. https://www.bridgemi.com/detroit-journalism-cooperative /its-official-no-vote-year-transit-fixes-southeast-michigan.

Price, Carter C., and Kathryn A. Edwards. "Trends in Income from 1975 to 2018." WR-A516-1, RAND Corporation, September 2020.

Pryor, Caroline, and Donald Tomaskovic-Devy. "How COVID Exposes Healthcare Deficits for Black Workers." Center for Employment Equity, University of Massachusetts at Amherst, August 2020. https://www.umass.edu/employmentequity/how-covid-exposes-healthcare -deficits-black-workers.

Pugh, Margaret, and O'Mara. *Cities of Knowledge: Cold War Science and the Search for the Next Silicon Valley.* Princeton, NJ: Princeton University Press, 2005.

Quigley, Aidan. "Why Trump's Budget Terrifies America's Mayors." *Politico,* April 24, 2017. https://www.politico.com/magazine/story/2017/04/24/donald-trump-budget-mayors -215067.

Quigley, John M. "Urban Diversity and Economic Growth." *Journal of Economic Perspectives* 12, no. 2 (1998): 127–138.

Quillian, Lincoln, Devah Pager, Ole Hexel, and Arnfinn H. Midtbøen. "Meta-Analysis of Field Experiments Shows No Change in Racial Discrimination in Hiring Over Time." *Proceedings of the National Academy of Sciences* 114, no. 41 (October 2017): 10870–10875.

Radpour, Siavash, and Teresa Ghilarducci. *Gaps in Retirement Savings Based on Race, Ethnicity, and Gender*. Testimony to 2021 Advisory Council on Employee Welfare and Pension Benefit Plans, US Department of Labor, Washington, DC, August 26, 2021.

Ramakrishnan, Kriti, Mark Treskon, and Solomon Green. "Inclusionary Zoning: What Does the Research Tell Us About the Effectiveness of Local Action?" Research to Action Lab, The Urban Institute, January 2019.

Ramani, Arjun, and Nicholas Bloom. "The Donut Effect of COVID-19 on Cities." Working Paper 28876, National Bureau of Economic Research, May 2021.

Rappaport, Jordan. "The Shared Fortunes of Cities and Suburbs." *Economic Review*, Federal Reserve Bank of Kansas City, 90, no. 5 (2005): 33–60.

Raths, David. "Will the Chief Innovation Officer Transform Government?" *Government Technology*, January 21, 2013. http://www.govtech.com/e-government/Will-the-Chief-Innovation-Officer-Transform-Government.html.

Rawson, Michael. *Eden on the Charles: The Making of Boston*. Cambridge, MA: Harvard University Press, 2010.

Reese, Laura A., Jeanette Eckert, Gary Sands, and Igor Vojnovic. " 'It's Safe to Come, We've Got Lattes': Development Disparities in Detroit." *Cities: The International Journal of Urban Policy and Planning* 60 (February 2017): 367–377.

Regional Plan Association. *New York's Next Comeback*. October 2020. https://rpa.org/work/reports/new-yorks-next-comeback.

Reinhold, Robert. "Distinct Choice in Los Angeles Race." *New York Times*, April 22, 1993.

Reynolds v. Sims, 377 U.S. 533 (1964).

Roder, Anne, and Mark Elliott. *Eleven Year Gains: Project QUEST's Investment Continues to Pay Dividends*. New York: Economic Mobility Corporation, September 2021.

Rogers, Luke. "COVID-19, Declining Birth Rates, and International Migration Resulted in Historically Small Population Gains." Washington, DC: U.S. Census Bureau, December 21, 2021.

Romney, Leah Platt. "Community, Developers Agree on Staples Plan." *Los Angeles Times*, May 31, 2001.

Roosevelt, Margot. "As L.A. Ports Automate, Some Workers Are Cheering on the Robots." *Los Angeles Times*, November 7, 2019.

Rosengren, Eric S. "Educational Attainment and Economic Outcomes." Early Childhood Summit 2013: Innovation and Opportunity, Federal Reserve Bank of Boston, April 5, 2013. https://www.bostonfed.org/news-and-events/speeches/educational-attainment-and-economic-outcomes.aspx.

Roser, Max, and Esteban Ortiz-Ospina. "Income Inequality." *Our World in Data*. Last modified October 2016. https://ourworldindata.org/income-inequality/#redistribution-through-tax-and-transfer-policies.

Rothstein, Alan. "The New York State Legislature: How Albany Controls the City." *Gotham Gazette*, January 29, 2001. https://www.gothamgazette.com/government/1586-the-new-york-state-legislature-how-albany-controls-the-city.

Rothstein, Richard. *The Color of Law: A Forgotten History of How Our Government Segregated America*. New York: Norton, 2017.

Rothstein, Richard. "Public Housing: Government-Sponsored Segregation." *The American Prospect*, October 11, 2012.

Rothstein, Richard. "The Racial Achievement Gap, Segregated Schools, and Segregated Neighborhoods—A Constitutional Insult." *Race and Social Problems* 7, no. 1 (March 2015): 21.

Rowthorn, Robert, and Ramana Ramaswamy. *Deindustrialization—Its Causes and Implications*. Washington, DC: International Monetary Fund, 1997. https://www.imf.org/EXTERNAL /PUBS/FT/ISSUES10/INDEX.HTM.

Runyan, Robin, and Aaron Mondry. "Detroit's New Residential Developments, Mapped." *Curbed Detroit*, January 17, 2020. https://detroit.curbed.com/maps/detroit-building-construction-new -residential-map.

Runyan, Robin, and Aaron Mondry. "Mapping the District Detroit." *Curbed Detroit*, December 12, 2019. https://detroit.curbed.com/maps/arena-district-detroit-construction-development-ilitch -olympia.

Saez, Emmanuel. "Public Economics and Inequality: Uncovering Our Social Nature." Working Paper 28387, National Bureau of Economic Research, January 2021.

Saez, Emmanuel, and Gabriel Zucman. "Wealth Inequality in the United States Since 1913: Evidence from Capitalized Income Tax Data." *Quarterly Journal of Economics* 131, no. 2 (2016): 519–578.

Safire, William. "The Cold War's Hot Kitchen." *New York Times*, July 23, 2018.

Santana, Miguel A. *City of Los Angeles: Four-Year Budget Outlook and Update to the Three-Year Plan to Fiscal Sustainability*. Los Angeles: City of Los Angeles, 2012.

Sauter, Michael B. "Ten Years Later, These 28 US Cities Never Recovered from the Great Recession." *USA Today*, October 12, 2018.

Savitch, H. V. "Encourage, Then Cope: Washington and the Sprawl Machine." In *Urban Sprawl: Causes, Consequences, and Policy Responses*, ed. Gregory D. Squires, 141–164. Washington, DC: Urban Institute Press, 2002.

Saxenian, AnnaLee. *Regional Advantage: Culture and Competition in Silicon Valley and Route 128*. Cambridge, MA: Harvard University Press, 1996.

Schaeffer, Robert K. *Understanding Globalization: The Social Consequences of Political, Economic, and Environmental Change*. Lanham, MD: Rowman and Littlefield, 2009.

Schaller, Bruce. "New York City's Congestion Pricing Experience and Implications for Road Pricing Acceptance in the United States." *Transport Policy* 17, no. 1 (August 2010): 266–273.

Schill, Michael H., Ingrid Gould Ellen, Amy Ellen Schwartz, and Ioan Voicu. "Revitalizing Inner-City Neighborhoods: New York City's Ten-Year Plan." *Housing Policy Debate* 13, no. 3 (January 2002): 529–566.

Schleicher, David. "City Unplanning." *The Yale Law Journal* 122, no. 7 (May 2013): 1670–2105.

Schmitt, John. *Why Does the Minimum Wage Have No Discernable Effect on Employment?* Washington, DC: Center for Economic and Policy Research, 2013.

Schultz, Laura, and Michelle Cummings. "Giving or Getting?: New York's Balance of Payments with the Federal Government." SUNY Rockefeller Institute of Government, January 2020. https://rockinst.org/wp-content/uploads/2020/01/1-22-20-Balance-of-Payments.pdf.

Scott, Robert E. *The Manufacturing Footprint and Importance of U.S. Manufacturing Jobs*. Briefing Paper 388. Washington, DC: Economic Policy Institute, January 2015.

Scott, Robert E., and Zane Mokhiber. "Growing China Trade Deficit Cost 3.7 Million American Jobs Between 2001 and 2018." Washington, DC: Economic Policy Institute, January 30, 2020.

Seguino, Stephanie. "Feminist and Stratification Theories' Lessons from the Crisis and Their Relevance for Post-Keynesian Theory." *European Journal of Economics and Economic Policies* 16, no. 2 (2019): 193-207.

Sekera, June. "Why Aren't We Talking About Public Goods? Demos, September 20, 2013. https://www.demos.org/blog/why-arent-we-talking-about-public-goods

Seung, Jin Cho, Jun Yeong Lee, and John V. Winters. "Employment Impacts of the COVID-19 Pandemic Across Metropolitan Status and Size." IZA Discussion Paper 13468, July 2020.

Shaw, Randy. "California Progressives Split Over SB9 and SB10." *LA Progressive*, August 28, 2021. https://www.laprogressive.com/end-exclusionary-zoning/.

Shaw, Randy. *Generation Priced Out: Who Gets to Live in the New Urban America.* Oakland: University of California Press, 2018.

Shaw, Todd C., and Lester K. Spence. "Race and Representation in Detroit's Community Development Coalitions." *Annals of the American Academy of Political and Social Science* 594 (July 2004): 125–142.

Shea, Bill. "How Olympia Financed an Arena in a Bankrupt City." *Crain's Detroit Business*, September 10, 2017.

Shefter, Martin. *Political Crisis, Fiscal Crisis: The Collapse and Revival of New York City.* New York: Columbia University Press, 1992.

Shen, Aviva. "Mayor Bloomberg Sues to Kill New York's Living Wage Law Before He Leaves Office." *ThinkProgress*, December 16, 2013. https://thinkprogress.org/mayor-bloomberg-sues-to-kill-new-yorks-living-wage-law-before-he-leaves-office-57f1126c2ead/.

Sierra Club California. "Letter from Sacramento: A Bill That Works for the Environment and Workers." August 25, 2019. https://www.sierraclub.org/california/letter-sacramento-bill-works-for-environment-and-workers.

Silverstein, Stuart. "L.A. Federation Labor Vote Divides Along Ethnic Lines." *Los Angeles Times*, April 17, 1996. http://articles.latimes.com/1996-04-17/business/fi-59484_1_county-federation.

Sites, William. "The Limits of Urban Regime Theory: New York City Under Koch, Dinkins, and Giuliani." *Urban Affairs Review* 32, no. 4 (March 1997): 536–557.

Skyscraper Museum. "Supertall! New York City." 2022. https://skyscraper.org/supertall/new-york/.

Slater, Robert Bruce. "The First Black Graduates of the Nation's 50 Flagship State Universities." *The Journal of Blacks in Higher Education*, no. 13 (Autumn, 1996): 72–85.

Smith, Adam. *An Inquiry into the Nature and Causes of the Wealth of Nations*, Edwin Cannan, ed. London: Methuen, 1904.

Smith, Noah. "The Left-NIMBY Canon." *Noahpinion*, January 19, 2021. https://noahpinion.substack.com/p/the-left-nimby-canon?.

Smith, Rebecca, Paul Alexander Marvy, and Jon Zerolnick. *The Big Rig Overhaul: Restoring Middle Class Jobs at America's Ports Through Labor Law Enforcement.* New York: National Employment Law Project, 2014.

Soffer, Jonathan. *Ed Koch and the Rebuilding of New York City.* New York: Columbia University Press, 2012.

Sommeiller, Estelle, Mark Price, and Ellis Wazeter. *Income Inequality in the U.S. by State, Metro-politan Area, and County.* Washington, DC: Economic Policy Institute, 2016.

Sonenshein, Raphael J., and Susan H. Pinkus. "The Dynamics of Latino Political Incorporation: The 2001 Los Angeles Mayoral Election as Seen in *Los Angeles Times* Exit Polls." *PS: Political Science & Politics* 35, no. 1 (March 2002): 67–74.

Sonenshein, Raphael J., and Susan H. Pinkus. "Latino Incorporation Reaches the Urban Summit: How Antonio Villaraigosa Won the 2005 Los Angeles Mayor's Race." *PS: Political Science and Politics* 38, no. 4 (October 2005): 713-721.

Stansbury, Anna, and Lawrence Summers. "The Declining Worker Power Hypothesis: An Explanation for the Recent Evolution of the American Economy." *Brookings Papers on Economic Activity* (Spring 2020): 1–77.

State of New York. *The City in Transition: Prospects and Policies for New York: The Final Report of the Temporary Commission on City Finances.* New York: Arno Press, 1978.

Steckler, Beth. Deputy Director, Move LA. Interview by Richard McGahey, July 22, 2014.

Steelman, Aaron. "The Federal Reserve's 'Dual Mandate': The Evolution of an Idea." Economic Brief EB11-12, Federal Reserve Bank of Richmond, December 2011.

Stein, Rona B. "New York City's Economy in 1980." *Federal Reserve Bank of New York Quarterly Review* 6, no. 1 (1981): 1–7.

Stiglitz, Joseph E. "Inequality Is Holding Back the Recovery." *Opinionator* (blog). *New York Times,* January 19, 2013.

Stiglitz, Joseph E. "Moving Beyond Market Fundamentalism to a More Balanced Economy." *Annals of Public and Cooperative Economics* 80, no. 3 (2009): 345–360.

Stiglitz, Joseph E. *The Price of Inequality: How Today's Divided Society Endangers Our Future.* New York: Norton, 2012.

Stiglitz, Joseph E. "The Theory of Local Public Goods Twenty-Five Years After Tiebout: A Perspective." In *Local Provision of Public Services: The Tiebout Model After Twenty-Five Years.,* ed. George R. Zodrow, 17–53. New York, Academic Press, 1983.

Storper, Michael. "From Retro to Avant-Garde: A Commentary on Paul Krugman's 'The New Economic Geography, Now Middle-Aged.'" *Regional Studies* 45, no. 1 (2011): 9–15.

Storper, Michael. *Keys to the City: How Economics, Institutions, Social Interaction, and Politics Shape Development.* Princeton, NJ: Princeton University Press, 2013.

Storper, Michael. "Why Do Regions Develop and Change?: The Challenge for Geography and Economics." *Journal of Economic Geography* 11, no. 2 (2011): 333–358.

Sugrue, Thomas J. *The Origins of the Urban Crisis: Race and Inequality in Postwar Detroit.* Princeton, NJ: Princeton University Press, 2005.

Task Force on Local Government Services and Fiscal Stability. *Final Report to the Governor.* Lansing: Michigan Department of Treasury, 2006. https://www.michigan.gov/documents /FINAL_Task_Force_Report_5_23_164361_7.pdf.

Taylor, Keeanga-Yamahtta. *Race for Profit: How Banks and the Real Estate Industry Undermined Black Homeownership.* Chapel Hill: University of North Carolina Press, 2019.

Tcherneva, Pavlina R. *The Case for a Job Guarantee.* Medford, MA: Polity Press, 2020.

Teaford, Jon C. *City and Suburb: The Political Fragmentation of Metropolitan America, 1850–1970.* Baltimore, MD: Johns Hopkins University Press, 1979.

Temporary Commission on City Finances. *The City in Transition: Prospects and Policies for New York*. New York: Arno Press, 1978.

Terner Center for Housing Innovation. "Affordable Housing Overlay Zones: Oakley." Terner Center Case Studies, University of California at Berkeley, April 2019.

Theodos, Brett, Eric Hangen, Jorge Gonzalez, and Bradley Meixell. *An Early Assessment of Opportunity Zones for Equitable Development*. Washington, DC: Urban Institute, June 17, 2020.

Thiede, Brian, David L. Brown, Jaclyn Butler, and Leif Jensen. "Income Inequality Is Getting Worse in US Urban Areas." *The Conversation*, April 14, 2020. https://theconversation.com/income-inequality-is-getting-worse-in-us-urban-areas-132417.

Thompson, J. Phillip. *Double Trouble: Black Mayors, Black Communities, and the Call for a Deep Democracy*. New York: Oxford University Press, 2006.

Thornton, Daniel L. "The Dual Mandate: Has the Fed Changed Its Objective?" *Review—Federal Reserve Bank of St. Louis* 94, no. 2 (March/April 2012): 117–133.

Tiebout, Charles M. "A Pure Theory of Local Expenditures." *Journal of Political Economy* 64, no. 5 (October 1956): 416–424.

Toll, Ian W. "A Reluctant Enemy." *New York Times*, December 6, 2011.

"Treasury Secretary Hails Fiscal Effort." *New York Times*. April 16, 1981.

Turbeville, Wallace C. *The Detroit Bankruptcy*. Washington, DC: Demos, 2013.

Tynan, Roxana. Executive Director. Los Angeles Alliance for a New Economy. Interview by Richard McGahey, July 16, 2014.

Uchitelle, Louis. "States Pay for Jobs, but It Doesn't Always Pay Off." *New York Times*, November 10, 2003.

Uhler, Brian, and Justin Garosi. "Building Permits Update: July 2019." California Legislative Analyst's Office, September 3, 2019. https://lao.ca.gov/LAOEconTax/Article/Detail/397.

Unionstats.com. "Union Membership and Coverage from the CPS." http://www.unionstats.com/.

United States Bureau of the Census. *Census of Governments, 1972: Volume 5, Local Government in Metropolitan Areas*. Washington, DC: Department of Commerce, 1974, 3, 32–165.

United States Bureau of the Census. "Census Reporter: Detroit." Accessed May 9, 2022. https://censusreporter.org/profiles/16000US2622000-detroit-mi/.

United States Bureau of the Census. *Quick Facts: Los Angeles County, California*. December 2020. https://www.census.gov/quickfacts/fact/table/losangelescountycalifornia/RHI725219.

United States Census Bureau. "Quick Facts. Los Angeles city, California; New York City, New York; Detroit City, Michigan." December 28, 2020. https://www.census.gov/quickfacts/fact/table/losangelescitycalifornia,newyorkcitynewyork,detroitcitymichigan,MI/PST045219.

United States Conference of Mayors. "U.S. Metro Areas Expected to See Real Economic Growth in 2014." January 22, 2014. http://legacy.usmayors.org/pressreleases/uploads/2014/0122-release-metroeconomies.pdf.

United States Conference of Mayors. *U.S. Metro Economies: GDP and Employment, 2018–2020*. Washington, DC, September 2019. https://www.usmayors.org/metro-economies/september-2019/.

United States Department of Commerce, Economic and Statistics Administration, U.S. Census Bureau. *United States Summary: 2010. Population and Housing Unit Counts*, Table 7. September 2012. https://www.census.gov/prod/cen2010/cph-2-1.pdf.

Urahn, Susan K., Michael Ettlinger, Kil Huh, Alyssa Lee, and Matt Separa. *Understanding the Great Recession's Impact on City Bond Issuances.* Washington, DC: Pew Charitable Trusts, 2013.

Urban Institute. *State and Local Finance Initiative.* Washington, DC: Urban Institute, 2019. https://www.urban.org/policy-centers/cross-center-initiatives/state-and-local-finance-initiative/about.

Voith, Richard. "City and Suburban Growth: Substitutes or Complements?" *Federal Reserve Bank of Philadelphia Business Review* (October 1992): 21–33.

Wahid, Raeedah. "Adams Won by Betting on a New York Divided by Race and Income." *Bloomberg Equality,* July 21, 2021. https://www.bloomberg.com/graphics/2021-nyc-mayoral-analysis/.

Waldinger, Roger. "From Ellis Island to LAX: Immigrant Prospects in the American City." *International Migration Review* 30, no. 4 (1996): 1078–1086.

Wang, Vivian. "New Rent Laws Pass in N.Y.: 'The Pendulum Is Swinging' Against Landlords." *New York Times,* June 14, 2019.

Ward, Richard. *New York State Government.* Albany, NY: Rockefeller Institute Press, 2006.

Washington, George. "Letter to Marquis de Lafayette, July 28, 1791." In *The Papers of George Washington,* ed. Mark A. Mastromarino, 238–241. Charlottesville: University Press of Virginia, 1999.

Weber, Rachel. *From Boom to Bubble: How Finance Built the New Chicago.* Chicago: University of Chicago Press, 2015.

Weir, Margaret. "Central Cities' Loss of Power in State Politics." *Cityscape: A Journal of Policy Development and Research* 2, no. 2 (May 1996): 23-40.

Weiss, Marc A. "Urban Land Developers and the Origins of Zoning Law: The Case of Berkeley" *Berkeley Planning Journal* 3, no. 1 (1986): 7–24.

Wessel, David. "Opportunity Zones: David Wessel's Testimony Before the Subcommittee on Oversight, House Ways and Means." Washington, DC: Brookings Institution, November 16, 2021. https://www.brookings.edu/testimonies/opportunity-zones-david-wessels-testimony-before-the-subcommittee-on-oversight-house-ways-means/.

Westcott, Diane N. "Employment and Commuting Patterns: A Residential Analysis." *Monthly Labor Review* 102, no. 7 (July 1979): 3–9.

Wheelock, David C. "The Federal Response to Home Mortgage Distress: Lessons from the Great Depression." *Federal Reserve Bank of St. Louis Review* 90, no. 3, part 1 (May/June 2008): 133–148.

White House. "Memorandum on Reviewing Funding to State and Local Government Recipients That Are Permitting Anarchy, Violence, and Destruction in American Cities." September 2, 2020. https://trumpwhitehouse.archives.gov/presidential-actions/memorandum-reviewing-funding-state-local-government-recipients-permitting-anarchy-violence-destruction-american-cities/.

Wildasin, David E. "Intergovernmental Transfers to Local Governments." In *Municipal Revenues and Land Policies,* ed. Gregory K. Ingram and Yu-Hung Hong, 47-76. Cambridge, MA: Lincoln Institute of Land Policy, 2010.

Wileden, Lydia, and Afton Branche-Wilson. *Detroit's Strategic Neighborhood Fund: A Baseline Report of Resident Perceptions.* Detroit Metro Area Communities Study, University of Michigan, December 2020.

Wilkerson, Isabel. "Primary Will Provide Detroit Mayor a November Opponent." *New York Times*, September 11, 1989.

Wilkerson, Isabel. *The Warmth of Other Suns: The Epic Story of America's Great Migration*. New York: Random House, 2010.

Williams, Joan C. "The Constitutional Vulnerability of American Local Government: The Politics of City Status in American Law." *University of Wisconsin Law Review* 1986, no. 1 (1986): 83–153.

Williams, Paige. "Drop Dead, Detroit!" *New Yorker*, January 19, 2014.

Willis, Carol. *Form Follows Finance: Skyscrapers and Skylines in New York and Chicago*. New York: Princeton Architectural Press, 1995.

Willis, Carol. "The Logic of Luxury: New York's New Super-Slender Towers." Presentation, Shanghai Conference of the Council on Tall Buildings and Urban Habitat, Shanghai, China, September 2014. http://global.ctbuh.org/resources/papers/download/1952-the-logic-of-luxury-new-yorks-new-super-slender-towers.pdf.

Wilson, Valerie. "Inequities Exposed: How COVID-19 Widened Racial Inequities in Education, Health, and the Workforce." Testimony Before the US House of Representatives Committee on Education and Labor, June 22, 2020. https://www.epi.org/publication/covid-19-inequities-wilson-testimony/.

Wines, Michael. "In Nashville, a Gerrymander Goes Beyond Politics to the City's Core." *New York Times*, February 18, 2022.

Winters, John V. "Human Capital Externalities and Employment Differences Across Metropolitan Areas of the U.S." Discussion Paper 6869, Institute for the Study of Labor, Bonn, DE, September 2012.

Witko, Christopher. "The Politics of Financialization in the United States." *British Journal of Political Science* 46 no. 2 (April 2016): 349–370.

Wolla, Scott A. "The Economics of Subsidizing Sports Stadiums." *Page One Economics* (blog), Federal Reserve Bank of St. Louis, May 2017. https://research.stlouisfed.org/publications/page1-econ/2017-05-01/the-economics-of-subsidizing-sports-stadiums/.

Zahniser, David. "L.A. City Employees Receive Last in a Costly Series of Raises." *Los Angeles Times*, January 1, 2014.

Zasloff, Jonathan. "The Secret History of the Fair Housing Act." *Harvard Journal on Legislation* 53, no. 1 (January 2016): 247–278.

Zehner, Emma. "Opening Doors." *Land Lines: Quarterly Magazine of the Lincoln Institute of Land Policy* 32, no. 4 (October 2020): 8–19.

Zerolnick, Jon. *The Road to Shared Prosperity: The Regional Economic Benefits of the San Pedro Bay Ports' Clean Trucks Program*. Los Angeles: Los Angeles Alliance for a New Economy, 2007.

Zonta, Michael. *Expanding the Supply of Affordable Housing for Low-Wage Workers*. Washington, DC: Center for American Progress, 2020.

INDEX

Community Development Block Grant (CDBG), 61
community development corporations (CDCs), 59, 64
community input, 174
concentration, geographic, 13
Conn, Steven, 36–37
consumer goods production, 45
control, lost by cities, 28–31
convergence logic, 19
Cooley, Thomas, 31
COPs. *See* certificates of participation
corporations, subsidies and, 170
costs: housing, 181; labor, 13, 98–99
county governments, 152
COVID-19 pandemic, 17, 18, 145, 189–191; Blacks and, 114, 136; budget and, 190; deaths from, 114, 136; Detroit post, 111–115; economic growth and, 114; employment and, 147; housing and, 88; inequality and, 20–22, 86, 88, 190; LA and, 117, 136–137; in New York City, 81–89; nonwhite workers and, 137; racial gaps and, 156; racial impact of, 21; racial inequalities and, 137, 192; relief for, 22; relocation during, 160, 191
COVID-19 recession, 1–2, 21, 86–88, 114, 146–147
creative capital theory, 10
creative class, 9–10, 76
Creativity Index, 10
creditors, 107
crime, 73
cultural prejudice, 26
culture and art, 9
Cuomo, Andrew, 83
Cuomo, Mario, 73, 75
Cutler, David, 18

data, economic, 168, 186, 241n2
Dearborn, Michigan, 92–93, 224n5
deaths, from COVID-19, 114, 136
DeBlasio Years, The (report), 86

debt: household, 17; New York City, 69–70
decentralization, 37, 92
Declaration of Independence, 25
deindustrialization, 146, 156
DeLeon, Kevin, 136
Democrats, 2–3
demographics: Detroit, 100; LA, 119, 124, 144; New York City, 141–142
density: housing, 27–28, 178; population, 6–7; urban, 13–14
desegregation: school, 59; white opposition to, 96
Detroit, 8–9, 12, 32, 51; automobile industry in, 92–93, 94, 98–99, 113, 223n1; bankruptcy, 105, 107–111, 142; Blacks in, 94; budget, 96, 98, 143; casinos in, 100–101; collapse of, 91; demographics, 100; economic change and, 92–100; economic growth and, 112–113; government, 103; housing in, 93–94, 112–113; inequality in, 111–112; manufacturing in, 140; metropolitan area of, 95; population, 103, 112, 115; post COVID-19 pandemic, 111–115; poverty in, 93, 115; racial conflict and, 92–100; racial segregation in, 53; real estate in, 102; revenues, 103, 105–106; schools in, 106; Treaty of Detroit, 142
Detroit Equity Council, 113
Detroit Institute of Arts (DIA), 109
Detroit Public Schools (DPS), 106
development strategies, 100
DIA. *See* Detroit Institute of Arts
Dillon, John C., 30, 210n23
Dillon's Rule, 30, 31, 151
Dinkins, David, 73–74, 140
discrimination: against Blacks, 142–143; economic, 155; gender, 55; housing, 95; housing anti-, 96; labor market, 56, 163; racial employment, 56
diseases, 34; epidemic, 33
displaced workers, 19–20
diverse population, 8
diversity, 12, 138